# 100
# DRIVES
# 5000
# IDEAS

# 100 DRIVES 5000 IDEAS

WHERE TO GO · WHEN TO GO · WHAT TO SEE · WHAT TO DO

**JOE YOGERST**

**NATIONAL GEOGRAPHIC**

WASHINGTON, D.C.

# Contents

Previous pages: Autumn leaves surround Falling Water Falls in the Ozark National Forest, part of the Razorback Run (page 228) road trip.

Opposite: Along the "World's Longest Yard Sale" (page 108), a mounted moose is for sale in the Kentucky portion of the highway.

# INTRODUCTION

"A prisoner of the white lines," sings Joni Mitchell in a tune she wrote during a road trip through New England in the 1970s. That's how I've felt for most of my life; destined to follow roads to places both familiar and unknown. But a willing prisoner, mind you—there's nothing I relish more than pressing pedal to the metal and cruising down a new road.

That's what this book is all about—100 of the best drives in the United States and Canada and thousands of things you can do along the way, from big cities and small towns to snowcapped peaks, wave-splashed shores, places where the buffalo still roam, and others where history comes alive.

I'm far from the only one stricken by white-line fever. In a recent survey by the American Automobile Association (AAA), 69 percent of respondents named road trips as their favorite kind of vacation. Given their wide-open spaces, Canadians are equally keen on road trips. According to another survey, residents of Alberta and Quebec are the biggest fans of motoring vacations.

It's been in our blood for a long time. The first mass-produced automobile (the 1901 Curved Dash Oldsmobile) had been around for only two years when the first coast-to-coast drive was completed. The road trippers of that epic drive were retired doctor Horatio Nelson Jackson, sidekick Sewall Crocker, and a pit bull named Bud they picked up along their route from San Francisco to New York City.

Since then, long-distance drives have become ingrained in our national consciousness and pop culture. American literature is replete with road trip books like John Steinbeck's *Travels with Charley* and *On the Road* by Jack Kerouac. From *It Happened One Night* and *Easy Rider* through *Thelma and Louise* and *Little Miss Sunshine,* there's an entire genre of cinema devoted to them. And let's not even get into the myriad songs about hitting the road (or getting your kicks on Route 66).

I trace my own addiction to the open road to parents who piled the family into the car each summer for drives that took us to Texas, British Columbia, Yellowstone, and elsewhere across the western half of the continent. As a college student, I undertook an overland journey from Kathmandu to Istanbul. After graduation, I spent a year following roads across Africa from Cape Town to Cairo—including hitchhiking segments in Namibia and Sudan. I've also driven from London to Athens, Hanoi to the Mekong Delta, and all the way from Texas to Argentina along the Pan American Highway.

So when National Geographic asked me to author *100 Drives, 5,000 Ideas*, I felt that I'd spent my entire life thus far laying the groundwork for such a book. Some of the drives are obvious inclusions, like the classic Route 66, the Trans-Canada Highway, and California's Highway One along the Big Sur coast. And at least a dozen derive from bygone family and college road trips or journeys I've undertaken for other writing assignments.

Others are modern motoring versions of trails blazed long ago—not just famous routes like the Oregon Trail, but also lesser known paths like the almost forgotten Gila Trail in New Mexico and Arizona, the poignant Trail of Tears between North Carolina and Oklahoma, and the Wilderness Road through the Appalachians.

Another dozen routes in the book are inspired by Canadian and American history, from a road trip that revolves around the early years of Abraham Lincoln to ones that reflect the American Revolution, the War of 1812, and Manifest Destiny. Others are purely products of my imagination: the Alien Highway, linking extraterrestrial sites in the Southwest, and the Jurassic Drive between western dinosaur digs.

Normally an author can't wait to compose the final words of a book, a mixed sense of accomplishment and that proverbial great weight lifted from your shoulders. But that wasn't the case with *100 Drives, 5,000 Ideas*. Like any great road trip, I was having such a good time writing about these journeys that I didn't want the experience to end. And I want to drive every route again. I hope all of you are similarly inspired to pack your bags and hit the road.

The Yellowhead Highway cuts through picturesque Jasper National Park, a great place to park the car and convene with nature.

# West Coast
## Road Trips

Cathedral Peak glows above the eponymous lake in Yosemite National Park.

# Golden Chain Highway
## California & Nevada

This 300-mile (482.8 km) route through the glorious Gold Country meanders through the oak-studded foothills of the Sierra Nevada range—with its wineries, historic mining sites, and bygone boomtowns—before leaping up and over the great mountains to the high plains of northeastern California.

Recognizing the fact that California's gold rush started in 1849, the state government designated this highway as Route 49 when it opened in 1934. Initially the road connected a string of half-forgotten small towns in the Sierra foothills. But over the past half century, the Golden Chain Highway has attracted an increasing number of visitors seeking fine wines and relics of California's colorful history.

The southern terminus of Highway 49 is **Oakville**, about an hour's drive north of Fresno and the southern gateway to **Yosemite National Park**. Road trippers can easily detour through the park and segue back onto the gold route in **Moccasin**. Oakhurst also boasts the **Children's**

**THE BIG PICTURE**

**Distance:** ca 400 miles (643.7 km) from Fresno, CA, to Reno, NV

**Drive time:** 4-5 days

**Best overnights:** Oakhurst, Mariposa, Jackson-Sonora, Placerville, Nevada City–Grass Valley

**Best seasons:** Anytime

**Highlights:** Mariposa, Columbia, Calaveras Big Trees, Coloma, Nevada City, Tahoe National Forest, Reno

**Museum of the Sierra** and water sports on gorgeous **Bass Lake**.

The first bona-fide mining town along the route is **Mariposa**. Founded by famed explorer John C. Frémont and a handful of other gold seekers, the town quickly evolved into the hub of the southern gold country. It's now home to the **California State Mining and Mineral Museum**—with its 13.8-pound (6.3 kg) gold nugget and simulated mine tunnel—the **Mariposa Museum and History Center**, and an "adventure camp" called **Yosemite Ziplines and Adventure Ranch** with an aerial challenge course and gold panning.

Fifty miles (80.5 km) farther north lies a trio of gold rush relics—**Jamestown**, **Sonora**, and **Columbia**—and their varied attractions. **Railtown 1897 State Historic Park** offers 45-minute excursions on vintage steam trains, and several local outfitters organize **whitewater rafting** on the nearby **Tuolumne River**. The entire town of Columbia is designated a state historic park, with scores of notable buildings.

Right up the road is **Angels Camp**, where Mark Twain penned his celebrated jumping frog story, and the turnoff for the giant sequoias of **Calaveras Big Tree State Park** and

Visitors pan for gold at the Marshall Gold Discovery State Historic Park in Coloma.

Lake Tahoe offers opportunities to stretch your legs along its shoreline or kayak and fish within its waters.

the underground wonders of **Mercer Caverns** and **Moaning Caverns.**

The stretch of Highway 49 between **Jackson** and **Placerville** is the heart of the gold rush **wine country**, with more than 50 vineyards producing varietals that often rival those of Napa and Sonoma.

History engulfs the road again north of Placerville, where **Marshall Gold Discovery State Historic Park** in **Coloma** marks the spot where John Marshall chanced upon gold at Sutter's Mill in January 1848, a discovery that sparked the California gold rush. Today you can float past this site on whitewater rafting trips down the **South Fork of the American River**.

It takes about an hour and a half—via **Auburn** and its downtown historic district—to reach **Nevada City** at the top end of the Gold Country. Once the richest of all the

boomtowns, Nevada City preserves its frontier legacy **Malakoff Diggins State Historic Park** and vintage railbus rides along Gold Run Creek at the **Nevada County Narrow Gauge Railroad Museum**, as well as movies and plays at the 1865 **Nevada Theatre**.

From Nevada City, Highway 49 transitions from foothills to mountains and a long passage through **Tahoe National Forest** with its numerous hiking and biking trails, as well as camping, fishing, and winter sports. Tucked deep in the national forest, **Sierra City** boasts the **Kentucky Mine Museum** and an easily accessible portion of the **Pacific Crest Trail**.

The Golden Chain Highway runs another 50 miles (80.5 km) to **Chilcoot-Vinton** and U.S. Highway 395. From there it's just a half hour into downtown **Reno**. ∎

### SCENIC DETOURS

• **State Route 41** twists and turns 48 miles (77.3 km) between Oakhurst and Yosemite Valley, with Wawona and the turnoff to lovely Glacier Point along the way.

• **State Route 120** runs from Moccasin, California's highest altitude paved road, across the top of Yosemite National Park to 9,945-foot (3,031.2 m) Tioga Pass and Mono Lake.

• **State Route 88:** The Carson Pass Highway offers a secluded, scenic alternative to Lake Tahoe, Carson City, and Reno from Jackson, CA.

• **State Route 89:** Starting on the east side of Tahoe National Forest, this California state scenic highway drops down to Truckee and along the west side of Lake Tahoe.

# A California Classic

## California

Big Sur may be the most celebrated (and spectacular) portion of California's epic Highway One, but it's far from being the only highlight along a road that stretches all the way from the City of Angels to the City by the Bay.

Originally envisioned as a means to connect remote California coastal towns that were otherwise reachable only by foot, horse, or boat, Highway One (also known as the Pacific Coast Highway, or PCH) evolved into one of the world's great vacation drives, a roadway that features on the bucket list of every passionate road tripper.

**Santa Monica Pier** and the funky **Venice Beach Boardwalk** anchor the southern end of this drive. Take a spin on the **West Coaster**, munch some cotton candy, and admire the bodybuilders at **Muscle Beach** before sliding onto the PCH to start the drive.

Just five miles (8 km) up the road is **Getty Villa**, a cliff-top museum suffused with priceless works of ancient Greek, Roman, and Etruscan art that oil tycoon J. Paul Getty opened in 1954 to showcase his personal collection. The Getty marks the start of a tony **Malibu** strip

### THE BIG PICTURE

**Distance:** ca 460 miles (740.3 km) from Los Angeles to San Francisco

**Drive time:** 4-5 days

**Best overnights:** Santa Barbara, Pismo Beach, Morro Bay/Cambria, Carmel/Monterey, Santa Cruz

**Best seasons:** Anytime

**Highlights:** Getty Villa, Santa Barbara, Santa Ynez wine country, Morro Bay, Hearst Castle, Big Sur, Monterey Peninsula, Santa Cruz, Golden Gate Bridge

lined with the beachfront bungalows owned by countless movies stars and music idols.

Malibu offers plenty of places to pull off for a walk on the beach. But the longest (and best) strand is **Zuma Beach** and adjacent **Point Dume**, which form a continuous three-mile (4.8 km) stretch of sand renowned for its great waves and photogenic cliffs.

Highway One takes a northward jog at **Point Mugu** and runs across the lush farm fields to seaside **Ventura**, the jumping-off spot for offshore **Channel Islands National Park**. The park visitor center at **Ventura Harbor** has all the information you need for hiking, camping, and kayaking the park's five islands. Down the waterfront, **Island Packers** offers regular boats to **Santa Cruz, Anacapa**, and **Santa Rosa** islands.

Reaching downtown Ventura, Highway One joins another famous California route (Highway 101) for the coastal cruise into **Santa Barbara**. Founded by Spanish missionaries and soldiers, Santa Barbara looks and feels more Iberian than any other California city. In addition to original structures like the **Queen of the Missions**

A bodybuilder makes use of the equipment at Muscle Beach in Venice, California.

The Bixby Creek Bridge, one of the most photographed bridges in California, offers stunning Big Sur views along Highway One.

(Mission Santa Barbara, opened in 1786) and military **Presidio of Santa Barbara** (1782), the city has superb examples of later California–Spanish Revival architecture like the **Santa Barbara County Courthouse**.

If you didn't get a chance to visit the pier in Santa Monica, stroll the pier at **Stearns Wharf**, rent a bike for a ride along the Santa Barbara shore, watch the sunset from the cliffs at **Shoreline Park**, and browse the eclectic shops along **State Street** before moving on up the coast.

Highway One goes its separate way again just past **Gaviota**, a drive across the Central Coast countryside that's especially pretty in the spring when the golden poppies and other wildflowers bloom. Along the way is a turnoff to supersecluded **Jalama Beach** and a wild horse sanctuary, **Return to Freedom**.

Farther along is **Lompoc**, home to **La Purisima Mission**, the most fully restored of California's Spanish missions and the only one designed in linear fashion rather than as a quadrangle. Although it was founded as a temperance colony, Lompoc is surrounded by **Santa Ynez Valley** vineyards and boasts the urban **Wine Ghetto** with 17 tasting rooms.

Beyond **Vandenberg Air Force Base**, Highway One runs along the

### EN ROUTE EATS

• **Loquita:** An innovative tapas menu and paella dishes bring a taste of Spain to the Southern California shoreline. 202 State St., Santa Barbara. loquitasb.com

• **The Hitching Post:** Legendary barbecue joint (since 1952) off Highway One between Lompoc and Guadalupe. 3325 Point Sal Rd., Casmalia. hitchingpost1.com

• **Nepenthe:** Popular open-air eatery nestled in the cliffs of Big Sur; steaks, fish, salads, and its famous Ambrosiaburger. 48510 Hwy. One, Big Sur. nepenthe.com

• **Passionfish:** This pioneer of sustainable seafood tenders dishes like smoked trout ceviche, striped bass crudo, and sea scallops in tomato-truffle butter. 701 Lighthouse Ave., Pacific Grove. passionfish.net

• **Half Moon Bay Brewing Company:** Surfer dude hangout near Mavericks big wave break, good food, great suds. 390 Capistrano Rd., Half Moon Bay. hmbbrewingco.com

The eclectic interiors of William Randolph Hearst's Hearst Castle are worth stopping for along the PCH.

**Guadalupe-Nipomo Dunes**. The sandy preserve offers hiking trails through the wild coastal terrain and the **Dunes Center** museum with nature exhibits and relics of the giant movie sets erected in the dunes by Cecil B. DeMille for the 1923 version of *The Ten Commandments*.

Pismo Beach and Avila Beach offer additional chances to wiggle your toes in the sand before the highway rolls into **San Luis Obispo (SLO)**. In addition to its own Spanish mission, SLO features a revitalized downtown area packed with shops, restaurants, and bars frequented by students from nearby Cal Poly University.

**Morro Bay** and its giant rock mark the start of a gorgeous stretch of coast that includes the quaint towns of **Cambria** and **San Simeon**—

places where it's easy to linger for days listening to the sound of the seagulls and surf or watching the resident elephant seals.

And then there's that incredible place in the hills above San Simeon—**Hearst Castle**. Another masterpiece of California–Spanish Revival architecture, the sprawling manse reflects the eclectic taste of newspaper magnate William Randolph Hearst, who filled his home with museum-quality furniture, tapestries, statues, and other items spanning ancient Greece through medieval Europe and the Renaissance.

North of San Simeon, Highway One clings to the towering sea cliffs that define the dramatic **Big Sur** coast, a 90-mile (144.8 km) stretch

celebrated as one of the world's most spectacular roadways. There are plenty of places to pull off the road and snap a selfie. For a more in-depth exploration, **Julia Pfeiffer Burns** and **Andrew Molera** State Parks provide access to the redwood-filled canyons and wild beaches of the Big Sur shoreline.

Look for sea otters off **Point Lobos** before cruising into **Carmel**, a cute but crowded seaside village packed with high-end art galleries, boutiques, and restaurants. If that's not your cup of tea, head for the **17-Mile Drive**, a twisting route around the **Monterey Peninsula** past fabulous oceanfront homes, the historic **Pebble Beach Golf Course**, and some of the planet's most photographed trees.

At the other end of the drive are laid-back **Pacific Grove** with its **Monarch Butterfly Sanctuary** and the bayside city of **Monterey**. Steinbeck's **Cannery Row** has morphed from smelly fish factories to kitschy tourist shops. But he would certainly appreciate the spectacular **Monterey Bay Aquarium** and well-preserved frontier-era buildings like the **Custom House** (where the first U.S. flag was raised over California in 1846).

Continue on Highway One around the east side of **Monterey Bay** through the old **Fort Ord Army Base**. Since it was decommissioned in 1994, the huge base has evolved into civilian uses like **Fort Ord Dunes State Park** with its sandy shore and **Fort Ord National Monument**, where 86 miles (138.4 km) of hiking, biking, and horseback trails lead through coastal chaparral and oak woodlands.

Farther north, the highway skirts past artichoke-infused **Castroville**—be sure to snap a selfie with the world's largest (metal) artichoke—and across the wildlife-rich **Elkhorn Slough** salt marsh before rolling into **Santa Cruz**.

Another burg that does double duty as a holiday hangout and college town, Santa Cruz revolves around the bustling **Beach Boardwalk** and an old-fashioned waterfront amusement park renowned for the historic **Giant Dipper** rollercoaster. Among the city's more scholarly attractions are the **Monterey Bay National Marine Sanctuary Exploration Center**, as well as the rare and unique plant species from around the world found at the **U.C. Santa Cruz Arboretum and Botanical Garden**.

Most people bail on the coast route at Santa Cruz and take

## PIT STOPS

• **Lompoc Springfest:** An April extravaganza with carnival rides, arm wrestling contests, Easter egg hunts, and other old-fashioned fun in Ryon Park. lompocvalleyfestivals.com

• **Pismo Vintage Trailer Rally:** From gleaming silver Airstreams and Crown "canned ham" trailers to customized camper shells and cute little Tear Drops, the May rally revolves around things that bring up the rear. classiccalifornia.com

• **Summer Solstice Parade:** Santa Barbara celebrates the year's longest day with a June parade that features giant puppets, whimsical costumes, and more than 1,000 participants. solsticeparade.com

• **Concours d'Elegance:** California car culture reaches fever pitch during the annual August homage to the automobile on the 18th hole of Pebble Beach Golf Club. pebble beachconcours.net

• **Pumpkin Festival:** Half Moon Bay goes gaga over gourds at this annual October event that peaks with a weigh-off to determine the world's heaviest pumpkin. pumpkin fest.miramarevents.com

Highway 17 over the hill to San Jose and Silicon Valley—the fastest way to San Francisco. But there's still 70 miles (112.7 km) of Highway One to cruise and plenty of nature along the way—for example, the massive (10,000-strong) elephant seal colony at **Año Nuevo State Park**, the wetlands trails of **Pescadero Marsh Natural Preserve**, and the legendary "Mavericks" big wave surfing break near **Half Moon Bay**.

At last, Highway One slips through the back door of **San Francisco**, crossing the residential Sunset District to **Golden Gate Park** and the **Presidio**, the former military base that's now part of **Golden Gate National Recreation Area**. End your Highway One odyssey beside the old Civil War bastion at **Fort Point**—the **Golden Gate Bridge** hovering high above and **Alcatraz** floating in the distance. ∎

The Giant Dipper roller-coaster stands out on the Santa Cruz Beach Boardwalk.

# Mojave Montage
## Nevada & California

At first glance, America's hottest, driest region may resemble a wasteland. But for those who dare to drive its back roads, the Mojave Desert offers a fascinating array of natural and human treasures, from its trademark Joshua trees and legendary Badwater to a remote opera house, quirky castle, and rock-star relics.

Stretching north-to-south across the Mojave are a trio of national parks that form the backbone of this backcountry drive: Death Valley, Mojave Preserve, and Joshua Tree. Whether you start the drive from Las Vegas or Palm Springs, be prepared for unrelenting desert and long stretches of lonely highway.

Fleeing the neon canyons of Vegas, U.S. Highway 95 shoots northwest through a part of the Mojave Desert that spills over into Nevada. The town of **Beatty** boasts the turnoff for Death Valley and the **Rhyolite** ghost town. Founded in 1904 as the hub of the Bullfrog mining district, Rhyolite's attractions range from the antique **Bottle House** to the modern **Goldwell**

**THE BIG PICTURE**

**Distance:** 450 miles (724.2 km) from Las Vegas, NV, to Palm Springs, CA

**Drive time:** 5-6 days

**Best overnights:** Furnace Creek, Twentynine Palms

**Best seasons:** Winter, spring, or fall

**Highlights:** Rhyolite ghost town, Death Valley, Mojave Reserve, Joshua Tree National Park

**Open Air Museum** of colossal outdoor art.

From Rhyolite, Highway 374 cruises downhill into **Death Valley, California,** and the first of the three national parks on this drive. The valley's northern end is anchored by **Scotty's Castle,** a 1920s Spanish Revival mansion built by eccentric gold miner Walter Scott. Nearby **Ubehebe Crater** offers trails around the rim and into the belly of the park's paramount volcanic landmark.

Living up to its name, **Furnace Creek** recorded the nation's highest ever temperature in 1913—a scalding 134°F (57°C). Ironically, it's also the valley's human hot spot, home to the main **visitor center** and **Borax Museum,** as well as a campground, golf course, airport, equestrian center, restaurant, gift shop, and the historic **Furnace Creek Inn.** The nearby **Badwater Basin** is another record setter—the lowest point in North America, at 282 feet (86 m) below sea level.

Highway 190 flows out of the park and down to **Death Valley Junction,** where the quirky **Amargosa Opera House** offers dance, comedy, music, and movie shows. From there it's around 80 miles (128.8 km) south to **Baker**—home of the world's tallest thermometer—

The Amargosa Opera House was opened in 1967 in Death Valley Junction.

Stay after the sun sets in Joshua Tree National Park, a flora-heavy desert that is also a mecca for stargazers.

and the entrance to **Mojave National Preserve**.

Founded in 1994, Mojave Preserve is the third largest national park in the lower 48 states, a massive expanse of desert and volcanic wilderness that features the towering **Kelso Dunes, Mitchell Caverns, Cinder Cone Lava Beds**, and a visitor center in the old **Kelso Train Depot**.

Kelbaker Road runs straight across Mojave Preserve to Interstate 40. But rather than hop on the freeway, continue south to Amboy and **Twentynine Palms**, where the national park visitor center provides entrée to **Joshua Tree National Park**.

Named after the tree-like *Yucca brevifolia,* the park has evolved over the past half century from a desolate desert landscape where rock stars like Jim Morrison, Keith

Richards, Donovan, and Gram Parsons found inspiration into one of Southern California's leading outdoor recreation hubs.

**Hiking, biking,** and **rock climbing** are Joshua Tree's big three outdoor pursuits. But the park is also prime for **stargazing, flora photography,** and

**horseback riding**. There are great drives too: the **Park Boulevard loop** through the western region and **Pinto Basin Drive** to Cottonwood Spring in the far east.

From Joshua Tree it's an easy drive to Palm Springs and the Coachella Valley, and onward from there to helter-skelter Los Angeles. ■

## SCENIC DETOURS

• **Red Rock Canyon National Conservation Area:** A Bureau of Land Management park near Las Vegas renowned for its desert hiking trails, historic ranches, and oasis canyons.

• **Mount Charleston:** The highest point in the Mojave Desert region (11,918 feet/3,632.6 m) offers summer hiking and biking trails and winter snow sports.

• **Chiriaco Summit:** This desert

crossroads on the south side of Joshua Tree hosts the General George S. Patton Memorial Museum on the site of a World War II training center for the U.S. Army tank corps.

• **Ash Meadows National Wildlife Refuge:** From bird-watching and boardwalk trails to desert springs and the rare Devils Hole pupfish, there's plenty to do and see year-round at this small refuge near Death Valley.

# Redwood Highways
## California

While the towering coastal redwoods are the main attraction on this 400-mile (643.7 km) drive up the Northern California coast, the region is also renowned for its wilderness hikes and wild beaches, Victorian architecture, and outdoor adventure.

### THE BIG PICTURE

**Distance:** ca 400 miles (643.7 km) from San Francisco to Crescent City

**Drive time:** 7 days

**Best overnights:** Olema/ Point Reyes Station, Bodega Bay, Mendocino, Fort Bragg, Ferndale, Eureka, Trinidad

**Best seasons:** Anytime

**Highlights:** Golden Gate Bridge, Marin Headlands, Point Reyes National Seashore, Fort Ross, Fort Bragg, Humboldt, Redwoods, Ferndale, Eureka, Redwood National and State Parks

Towering as high as 40-story buildings, California's coastal redwoods *(Sequoia sempervirens)* are the world's tallest living things. They once shrouded the entire shore north of San Francisco, but logging greatly reduced their range—and threatened their survival—until 20th-century environmentalists saved them for posterity.

Around 80 percent of the remaining big trees are protected by state and national parks along this route, a region that has also been declared a UNESCO World Heritage site and a California Coast Ranges Biosphere Reserve.

Starting out from **San Francisco**, the road trip moves across the **Golden Gate Bridge** to the emerald green **Marin Headlands** on the north side of the bay. Part of **Golden Gate National Recreation Area**—the single most visited unit in the National Park Service—the Headlands offer stunning panoramas across the bridge and bay.

Ever climbing **Conzelman Road**

offers the best views, as well as access to the park's Rodeo Valley and its eclectic attractions: the **Marine Mammal Center** with its rescued seals and sea lions, the historic **Nike Missile Site**, and untamed **Rodeo Beach**.

Four miles (6.4 km) north of the bridge, exit U.S. Highway 101 onto the **Shoreline Highway**, a lesser known but just as spectacular stretch of California's famous Highway One. Past **Stinson Beach**, the highway runs straight down the middle of the **Olema Valley**, created by a northern extension of the San Andreas Fault.

The funky little towns of **Olema** and **Point Reyes Station** offer art galleries and gourmet eateries, including the delicious locally made cheese, bread, and ice cream at **Cowgirl Creamery** and the shellfish fresh from the bay at **Hog Island Oyster Co.**

Nearby **Bear Valley Visitor Center** is the place to kick off adventures in **Point Reyes National Seashore**. A mosaic of wetlands, woodland, and long, empty beaches, Point Reyes offers a portrait of the California coast before the arrival of humans. The park harbors more than 1,500 species of flora and fauna, from dune grass and

Cross the iconic Golden Gate Bridge from San Francisco to the Marin Headlands.

Add Shasta-Trinity National Forest to your road trip itinerary for easy hikes and stunning cascades.

wildflowers to tule elk and elephant seals. Named after the English sea captain and privateer who allegedly landed there in 1579, **Sir Francis Drake Boulevard** runs 21 miles (33.8 km) to the end of the peninsula and cliff-top **Point Reyes Lighthouse** (built in 1870).

North of Point Reyes, the coast road continues to **Bodega Bay**—where Alfred Hitchcock filmed his famous movie *The Birds*—and **Jenner** at the mouth of the **Russian River**. Wave-splashed **Sonoma Coast State Park** offers a chance to get your feet wet; during the warmer months, there's guided **rafting** and **kayaking** on the river between Guerneville and the sea.

Just north of Jenner, **Fort Ross State Historic Park** preserves the southernmost settlement that

Russian fur traders established in North America. Founded in 1812 by the Russian-American Company,

## SCENIC DETOURS

• **Panoramic Highway:** This side route off the Shoreline Highway in Marin County leads to Muir Woods National Monument and the summit of Mount Tamalpais and its mouth-dropping views across San Francisco Bay.

• **Russian River Route:** State Highway 116 heads inland from Jenner, hugging the north bank of the Russian River to Guerneville and the wine country around Forestville, Graton, and Sebastopol.

• **Trinity Scenic Byway:** Strung between Arcata and Redding, State Route 299 climbs from the coast through Shasta-Trinity National Forest to historic Weaverville and Whiskeytown National Recreation Area.

• **Highway 199:** Originally blazed in 1854, this historic route through the Coastal Range links Crescent City with Jedediah Smith Redwoods State Park, Smith River National Recreation Area, and Oregon Caves National Monument.

the fort endured until 1841. The state park features a reconstructed wooden chapel and stockade, as well as the original commander's house.

Crossing into Mendocino County at **Gualala**, Highway One passes **Point Arena** with its lofty, whitewashed lighthouse before rolling into **Mendocino**. Born as a timber town and fishing village, Mendocino eventually morphed

into an artist colony and popular movie location (*East of Eden, Summer of '42*) owing to the Victorian-era redwood structures of the **Mendocino Historic District**. Surrounded by **Mendocino Headlands, Russian Gulch**, and **Van Damme** State Parks, the town is also an outdoor gateway.

Fifteen minutes farther up the coast is **Fort Bragg**, the western

terminus of the **Skunk Train**, a scenic heritage steam railway that runs 40 miles (64.4 km) through the redwoods from Willets. The three-mile (4.8 km) **Noyo Headlands Trail** renders spectacular sea views along the town's western edge, while **Mendocino Coast Botanical Garden** offers 47 acres (19 ha) of native trees, shrubs, and flowers.

Highway One turns inland near **Rockport** and segues into **Redwood Highway** (U.S. 101) at **Leggett**, the start of a 60-mile (96.6 km) stretch that includes several redwood preserves and the fabled **Avenue of the Giants**. The route's drive-through trees, chainsaw art shops, and other commercial attractions pale in comparison to the living giants that shade **Richardson Grove** and **Humboldt Redwoods** State Parks. With 17,000 acres of old-growth coastal redwoods, Humboldt embraces the world's single largest tall-tree grove.

**Garberville** offers a turnoff to California's aptly named **Lost Coast**, a 25-mile (40.2 km) stretch of shoreline that can only be explored on foot. With trailheads at **Shelter Cove** in the south and **Mattole Point** in the north, the trek is normally done as a three-day hike with overnights on secluded beaches in **King Range National Conservation Area**.

Beyond the Avenue of Giants, Highway 101 descends into the **Eureka-Arcata-Fortuna** metropolitan area, the largest "city" on the west coast between San Francisco and Portland. It's actually a string of towns and cities—with their own distinct personalities—arrayed around Humboldt and Arcata Bays and the mouth of the Eel River.

Founded as a seaport for supplying the gold mines of far northern California (hence the name), **Eureka** boomed as a fishing, shipping, and

Magnificent redwoods border the road along the Avenue of the Giants.

lumber town. The waterfront **Old Town** boasts one of the state's finest assortments of Victorian architecture, in particular, the **Carson Mansion** (built in 1886) and the **Pink Lady** (1889). **Fort Humboldt State Historic Park** and harbor cruises on the **MV** *Madaket*—built in 1910 and now the oldest passenger vessel in continuous service in the United States—offer fascinating overviews of local history.

Other Bay Area towns include funky **Arcata**, home to Humboldt State University and lifestyles that seem to have time-traveled from the psychedelic sixties, and **Ferndale** with its **"Butterfat Palaces"**—Victorian mansions funded by the town's dairy industry.

Looming just 30 miles (48.3 km) north of Arcata are **Redwood National and State Parks**, a patchwork of federal and state lands that protects the world's greatest living giants. **Kuchel Visitor Center** on Highway 101 offers an excellent entrée to all the parks have to offer, from hiking, biking, and horseback riding through the redwoods to tide

A gray seal cruises the waters of the North Coast Marine Mammal Center.

pools, pristine beaches, kayaking the coastal lagoons, and Native American dance demonstrations by the local Tolowa and Yurok tribes.

Trails along **Redwood Creek** lead to some of the tallest trees, although the location of the world-record **Hyperion Tree** (380.3 feet/115.9 m) remains a secret in order to protect it from daredevils and souvenir hunters.

In addition to its big trees, **Prairie Creek Redwoods State Park** is renowned for elk herds, wild **Gold Bluff Beach**, and primordial **Fern Canyon** (where part of the original *Jurassic Park* was filmed). **Klamath River Overlook**, perched 650 feet (198.1 m) above the sea, affords incredible views of the national park coast. The final stretch of the road trip runs through **Del Norte Coast Redwoods State Park** with its remote beaches, cliff-top trails, and cutting-edge projects to restore the logging-devastated redwood forest.

**Crescent City** lies just 10 minutes beyond the state park, its harbor surrounded by seafood eateries and colonized by sea lions and harbor seals. Scattered around town are other maritime attractions like the **Battery Point Lighthouse** museum, **Ocean World** aquarium, the **North Coast Marine Mammal Center**, and a waterfront memorial to the **S.S. Emidio**, an American tanker torpedoed by a Japanese submarine off this coast just two weeks after the attack on Pearl Harbor. ∎

## LAY YOUR HEAD

• **The Inn at the Tides:** Overlooking Bodega Bay, all of the suites and rooms at this modern resort offer bay or ocean views; restaurants, bar, heated pool, spa treatments, sauna, pastry shop; from $199. innatthetides.com

• **Brewery Gulch Inn:** Smugglers Cove provides a dramatic backdrop for this upscale Mendocino bed-and-breakfast; restaurant, enormous great room, beach; from $335. brewerygulchinn.com

• **Gingerbread Mansion:** This extravagant Victorian-era B&B in Ferndale is a treat for all the senses,

but especially the eyes (and camera); restaurant, tea room; from $155. gingerbread-mansion.com

• **Benbow Inn:** Redwood groves are within walking distance of this historic (1926) lodge near the Avenue of the Giants; restaurant, bar, golf course, pool, bikes; from $175. benbowinn.com

• **Lost Whale Inn:** Set on a wooded bluff above Abalone Cove, this cozy B&B offers an awesome base camp for exploring Redwood National and State Parks; beach, tide pools, gardens, afternoon wine; from $199. lostwhaleinn.com

# Pacific Coast Scenic Byway

## Oregon

It may not be as famous as its cliff-hugging cousins to the south, but Highway 101 along the Oregon shore is easily one of the world's most impressive coastal routes, a 340-mile (547.2 km) feast of unspoiled bays and beaches, funky seaports, and fabled lighthouses.

In a similar fashion to Big Sur, the Oregon coast was a string of isolated fishing villages linked by foot and wagon trails until the highway came along. And even then, the first road to connect the scattered coastal communities had an ulterior motive.

Dubbed the Roosevelt Coast Military Highway, the nascent route was a knee-jerk reaction to the American isolationism that followed World War I. It was built to quell the dread that Oregon might be invaded by some foreign power unless an invasion could be quashed by speeding American troops along a new coast road.

By the mid-1920s, motor tourism had surpassed the route's military necessity, and it was designated as part of U.S. Highway 101, the epic new road stretching all the way from Mexico to Canada. Ferries carried vehicles across the coast's many rivers, bays, and estuaries until a flurry of bridge building during the Great Depression. The last watery gap wasn't spanned until 1954 with completion of Bullards Bridge near Bandon.

Tillamook Creamery offers freshly made ice cream and cheeses from its dairy.

## THE BIG PICTURE

**Distance:** ca 340 miles (547.2 km) from Astoria to Brookings

**Drive time:** 3-5 days

**Best overnights:** Seaside, Cannon Beach, Newport, Florence, Coos Bay, Gold Beach, Brookings

**Best seasons:** Anytime

**Highlights:** Fort Clatsop, Cannon Beach, Newport, Cape Perpetua, Oregon Dunes, Cape Arago, Rogue River

...........................................

**Astoria** anchors the northern end of the Oregon coast with the region's most astounding span: the towering **Astoria-Megler Bridge** across the Columbia River. The city's historic riverfront district is spangled with art galleries, antique stores, craft breweries, and offbeat collections like the **Oregon Film Museum** in the old Clatsop Jail. The **Old 300 Riverfront Trolley** trundles visitors past many of Astoria's waterfront landmarks, including passage beneath that huge green monster of a bridge.

After crossing Youngs Bay on a lengthy bridge-causeway, Highway 101 runs through Oregon's Lewis and Clark country, where the famed explorers spent the winter of 1805-06. **Lewis and Clark National Historical Park** offers a replica of **Fort Clatsop**, ranger-guided canoe and kayak trips during the summer months, the **Sacagawea monument**, and walks through the park's woods and wetlands on several trails. On the western side of the highway, **Fort Stevens State Park** offers long beach walks and preserves the remains of the only earthen Civil War bastion on the West Coast, as well as the rusted remnants of a ship that ran aground in 1906.

The highway finally hits the coast at aptly named **Sunset Beach**, where a

Haystack Rock and The Needles rise above the water off the shore of Cannon Beach in Oregon's Ecola State Park.

state recreation area provides easy access to sun, sea, and sand. Nearby **Seaside**, one of the first resort towns along the Oregon shore, is a busy summer holiday hub. **Seaside Aquarium** offers a good overview of coastal wildlife, including a family of harbor seals. Follow in the footsteps of Lewis and Clark on the **Tillamook Head Trail**, which runs eight miles (12.9 km) along the shore of **Ecola State Park**. William Clark called the view from the rocky promontory "the grandest and most pleasing prospects which my eyes ever surveyed."

Sprawling on the park's south side is lovely **Cannon Beach**, where the iconic **Haystack Rock** and **The Needles** rise just offshore. The towering, monolithic sea stacks are probably the most photographed scene along the entire Oregon coast. Tide pools around the base of Haystack are accessible at low tide, but climbing the rock itself is forbidden (for safety reasons). **Cannon Beach History Center and Museum** offers old black-and-white photos of the rugged, early 20th-century coast road.

An hour farther south, the town of **Tillamook** is world renowned for its dairy productions, in particular the cheese produced by the farmer-owned **Tillamook Creamery**. Factory tours offer insight into how they make cheese, ice cream, and other tasty products. West of town, **Three Capes Scenic Loop** leads to **Cape Meares Lighthouse** (opened in 1890) and the nearby oddly shaped 300-year-old **Octopus Tree**. Then it

## PIT STOPS

• **Newport Seafood and Wine Festival:** Discover if salmon pairs better with Merlot or Pinot Gris at this February feast at Newport Marina. seafoodandwine.com

• **Rhododendron Festival:** Florence breaks out the flowers—as well as classic cars and carnival rides—during an annual May bash first staged in 1908. florencechamber.com

• **Scandinavian Festival:** Astoria's Nordic roots are exposed during a June jamboree that features Icelandic ponies, a Swedish meatball–eating

contest, Viking dinner, and Running of the Trolls. astoriascanfest.com

• **Oregon Coast Music Festival:** Classical music performed by renowned musicians from around the United States and Canada highlight this July event in Coos Bay. oregoncoastmusic.org

• **Salt Makers Return:** A living history revival of the Seaside beach camp where the Lewis and Clark expedition made salt for their return journey across the continent; September or October. seasideor.com

is onward to **Cape Lookout** and **Cape Kiwanda** for incredible views up and down the coast.

Beyond the trio of capes, **Nestucca Bay National Wildlife Refuge** offers hiking trails and paddle trips through a coastal wetlands area inhabited by river otters, peregrine falcons, kingfishers, and other creatures.

Next up is **Yaquina Head** with its 19th-century lighthouses and wooden stairs down to a cobblestone beach. If you haven't yet seen sea otters, puffins, and other indigenous species in the wild, go to **Oregon Coast Aquarium** in nearby **Newport**. The town's historic **Bayfront** area harbors seafood eateries, fish markets, docks inhabited by wild sea lions, and the informative **Pacific Maritime Heritage Center**.

Crossing over the lofty **Yaquina Bay Bridge** (opened in 1936), Highway 101 makes a 50-mile (80.5 km) run down to Florence. Much of the route runs through part of **Siuslaw National Forest** that touches the coast. Along the way is **Cape Perpetua**; at more than 800 feet (243.8 m) above sea level it's the highest point that visitors can reach by road along the Oregon coast. **Cape Perpetua Visitor Center** offers ranger-led walks and talks, whale-watching events, and information on hiking the area's coastal and rainforest trails.

Located on the Siuslaw River, **Florence** is another summer vacation hub and active fishing port, as well as the northern gateway to **Oregon Dunes National Recreation Area**. Stretching 40 miles (64.4 km) south along the shore, the shifting sands constitute the largest coastal dunes in North America and are among the highest on Earth; some of the sandy

The Yaquina Head Lighthouse, first lit in 1873, looks out over the Oregon coast.

summits reach more than 500 feet (152.4 m) in height.

Although best known for all-terrain vehicle and dune buggy adventures, the park also offers quiet spots for hiking and paddling. Dunes access starts right across the river from Florence—the South Jetty area at the mouth of the Siuslaw River—and continues down the shore to **Siltcoos Beach**, the towering **Umpqua Dunes**, and **Horsfall Beach** near Coos Bay. **Oregon Dunes Visitor Center** is located in Reedsport, about halfway along the sandy corridor.

Together with neighboring North Bend, **Coos Bay** is the largest urban area along the Oregon coast. Originally founded as Camp Castaway by a band of 1852 shipwreck survivors, the city celebrates its diverse past in several ways, including the **Coos History Museum and Maritime Collection**, movies and live performances at the restored 1925 **Egyptian Theatre**, and a series of murals honoring American running legend and hometown hero **Steve Prefontaine**. On the outskirts of town, you will find tide pools, coastal hikes, and a vintage lighthouse on its own rocky islet at **Cape Arago**.

There's another dramatic stretch of coast around **Bandon Beach**, 25 miles (40.2 km) south of Coos Bay, where the offshore topography includes Face Rock as well as the Cats and Kittens. Bandon's **Washed Ashore Gallery** creates and displays artwork made from plastic ocean pollution in order to publicize that threat to global waterways and marine life.

Poised at the mouth of the **Rogue River**, the town of **Gold Beach** takes its name from an 1850s gold rush. Local outfitters offer guided steelhead fishing trips and whitewater rafting on the Rogue. The final stretch of Oregon's Highway 101 includes the **Samuel H. Boardman State Scenic Corridor**, a dozen miles (19.3 km) of coast with landmarks like **Natural Bridges, Whaleshead rock**, and **Cape Ferrelo**, before reaching the California border at **Crissy Field State Park**.

At **Crescent City**, road trippers can return to where they started by cruising U.S. 199 to Grants Pass and then Interstate 5 to the Portland metropolitan area. Or they can continue down Highway 101 through California's redwood country to San Francisco or Los Angeles. ∎

## LAY YOUR HEAD

• **Cannery Pier Hotel:** Waterfront digs on the site of the old Union Fish Cannery beneath the Astoria-Megler Bridge; spa, sauna, hot tub, bikes; from $239. cannerypierhotel.com

• **Newport Belle:** This floating B&B is a throwback three-deck riverboat on the Newport waterfront; sunroom, bar; from $150. newportbelle.com

• **Sylvia Beach Hotel:** Built in 1912, this literary-themed oceanfront hotel in Newport is named for a famed bookstore owner rather than an

actual beach; restaurant, library, beach access; from $120. sylviabeachhotel.com

• **Heceta Head Lighthouse B&B:** Romantic cliff-top retreat in the 1890s lightkeeper's house; bar, wine and cheese socials; from $239. hecetalighthouse.com

• **Umpqua Lighthouse State Park:** Mongolian-style yurts (with modern amenities) provide a cozy place to sleep beneath the lakeside trees; bathroom, small kitchen; $43-$92. oregonstateparks.org

# America's "Loneliest Road"

## Nevada & Utah

They call it America's "Loneliest Road" for good reason—Highway 50 across central Nevada runs through an area burnished by sagebrush, dry lakebeds, and stark desert mountains with bygone boomtowns that remind drivers of the region's glory days.

**THE BIG PICTURE**

**Distance:** 500 miles (804.7 km) from Carson City, NV, to Holden, UT

**Drive time:** 1-3 days

**Best overnights:** Ely, Eureka, Fallon

**Best seasons:** Spring or fall

**Highlights:** Virginia City, Sand Mountain, Eureka, Great Basin

"It's totally empty," cried *Life* magazine in a 1986 article declaring U.S. Highway 50 through central Nevada as the loneliest road in America. "There are no points of interest. We don't recommend it. We warn all motorists not to drive there unless they're confident of their survival skills."

Hyperbole aside, it's a pretty daunting drive. But there are plenty of interesting things to see along the way. And the only survival skill you really need is to confidently drive dead-straight roads through miles of desert without spacing out.

Leaving **Carson City** behind, there's soon a turnoff for the Silver Rush region of western Nevada, where the Comstock Lode was discovered in 1859. **Virginia City** preserves that heritage in throwback attractions like the **Mark Twain Museum**, steam train rides on the **Virginia and Truckee Railroad**, and live performances at **Piper's Opera House**.

Farther along Highway 50 is **Fallo**, home of the U.S. Navy's "Top Gun" fighter pilot school (not open to the public), and the **Churchill County Museum** with its copious Native American artifacts.

Half an hour east of town is **Sand Mountain Recreation Area**, where 600-foot (182.9 m) dunes tower over the highway and the ruins of a **Pony Express station**. If you're feeling hungry, **Middlegate Station** roadhouse is just up the road. Founded in the 1850s, the remote restaurant is renowned for its legendary Monster Burger.

The middle section of the loneliest road is spangled with backwater burgs that would probably be ghost towns today if not for the uptick in tourism along Highway 50 since that *Life* article.

The silver lode that sparked the funky little town of **Austin** was

Wheeler Peak soars above the road into Great Basin National Park in Nevada.

Nevada preserves its Old West heritage through the Mark Twain Museum and the Piper's Opera House in Virginia City.

allegedly discovered in 1862 when a Pony Express kicked an ore-laden stone. Three-story **Stokes Castle** on the edge of town is a remnant of those days. There's even older stuff nearby: the marine dinosaur fossils of **Berlin-Ichthyosaur State Park** and the ancient Native American art of **Hickison Petroglyph Recreation Area**.

Seventy miles (112.7 km) farther east, **Eureka** also preserves a good deal of its 19th-century boom days, including the **Jackson House Hotel** (1877), **Eureka Opera House** (1880), and **Eureka Sentinel Museum** (1879) with its eclectic artifacts—Victorian-era hair combs, an 1880s printing press, and a solid oak barber chair.

**Ely**, around 80 minutes west, is the largest and last of the old mining towns along this stretch of Highway 50. It didn't boom until the early 20th century, and the mineral that sparked its rush was copper rather than gold or silver. Among the town's curiosities are the beehive-shaped **Ward Charcoal Ovens**, the 12,000-year-old cave bear skeletons at the **White Pine Public Museum**, and rides on the old **Nevada Northern Railway**.

Before it slips into Utah, Highway 50 wraps around the north end of **Great Basin National Park**. With landscapes that range from desert flats to pine forest and 13,000-foot (3,962.4 m) peaks, the park is a microcosm of the Intermontane region that covers so much of the American West. Among its many activities are **hiking, biking, camping, climbing, tours of Lehman Caves, astronomy programs, snowshoeing,** and **cross-country skiing**.

Reaching **Holden** and I-15 in central Utah, drivers have a choice of cruising north to **Provo** and **Salt Lake City**, or south to **Bryce** and **Zion** National Parks and **Las Vegas**. Either way it's quite an attitude adjustment—negotiating a busy interstate after 500 miles (804.7 km) on the loneliest road. ∎

# El Camino Real

## California

California's 21 Spanish missions were once linked by a foot, horse, and cart path called El Camino Real (King's Highway), a route that's easily traced today by driving the coast between San Diego and Sonoma.

**THE BIG PICTURE**

**Distance:** ca 780 miles (1,255.9 km) from San Diego to Sonoma

**Drive time:** 7 days

**Best overnights:** Dana Point, Los Angeles, Santa Barbara, San Luis Obispo, Monterey-Carmel, San Francisco

**Best seasons:** Anytime

**Highlights:** San Diego, San Juan Capistrano, Santa Barbara, La Purisima, Carmel, Dolores, and Sonoma missions

Between 1769, when Father Serra established the first of the Alta California missions in San Diego, and 1823, when the last of the Franciscan compounds opened in Sonoma, Franciscan friars shaped the Golden State in ways that continue to reverberate today.

In addition to Christian and European cultures, the friars launched a distinctive architectural style, introduced grapes and wine, named most of the state's future cities, and had a profoundly negative effect on the Native American populations. Whether for historic or spiritual reasons, visiting all 21 of California's missions has been a popular road trip pilgrimage for more than a century.

A combination of state and federal roadways shadows the route of the old Camino Real, starting with **Mission San Diego de Alcalá**, a whitewashed relic where the state's first vineyards were planted. Interstate 5 leads north along the coast to Oceanside's **Mission San Luis Rey**, still an active place of worship, and **Mission San Juan Capistrano**, where swallows famously come home to roost each summer.

The hardest part of the journey lies ahead: the drive across traffic-clogged Orange County and Los Angeles on I-5. But along the way are two oases of tranquility—**San Gabriel Mission** and **San Fernando Mission**—both with gardens that mute the urban hustle and bustle.

Highway 101 provides the means to reach little **Mission San Buenaventura** in downtown Ventura and **Mission Santa Barbara** on a hilltop above the coastal city. Nicknamed the "Queen of the Missions," Santa Barbara is the only one of the chapels that looks and feels like a European cathedral, a sizable structure that endures as a cultural and religious hub.

Road trippers can take Highway 101 along the coast or State Route 154 through the mountains to reach **Old Mission Santa Inés** in Danish-inspired Solvang, which is surrounded by some of California's premier wineries. Farther down the valley (via State Route 246) is Lompoc's **La Purisima Mission**, a state historic park with a modern visitor center museum and living history demonstrations.

Cruising inland along Highway

Mission San Juan Bautista, founded in 1797, is the largest of the mission churches.

Mission San Diego de Alcalá was moved to its current location in 1774, then rebuilt after an 1812 earthquake.

101, the Camino Real visits **Mission San Luis Obispo, Mission San Miguel, Mission San Antonio**, and **Soledad Mission** before reaching Monterey Bay. Snug beside the sea, **Carmel Mission** holds the remains of Father Serra, who was buried there in 1784. **Mission San Juan Bautista** featured famously in the Alfred Hitchcock film *Vertigo*.

Highway 17 connects Mission Santa Cruz with two Bay Area chapels: **Mission Santa Clara** and **Mission San Jose** (which is actually in Fremont). It's about a 60-mile (97 km) drive, via the Dumbarton Bridge, from Fremont to **Mission Dolores**, the oldest surviving building in San Francisco, also with Hitchcock credentials (*Vertigo* again).

In days gone by, the friars would have taken a boat across San Francisco Bay. Today the Camino Real uses the Golden Gate Bridge to reach Marin County and **Mission San Rafael**.

It takes another hour to reach the youngest (and northernmost) of the Franciscan compounds: **Mission San Francisco Solano**, overlooking the town square in hip Sonoma. The **California Missions Museum** at Cline Cellars on Sonoma's south side offers scale models of all 21 missions, made for the 1939 World's Fair in San Francisco. ■

## LAY YOUR HEAD

• **La Valencia:** Opened in 1926, La Jolla's elegant "Pink Lady" overlooks the sea on San Diego's north side; restaurants, bar, pool, spa, fitness center; from $318. lavalencia.com

• **Beverly Hills Hotel:** The Golden Age of Hollywood lives on at this legendary retreat, which also inspired the Eagles' haunting "Hotel California"; restaurants, bars, spa, pool; from $595. dorchester collection.com

• **Biltmore Santa Barbara:** This posh beachfront resort and its sub-tropical garden debuted in 1927; restaurants, bars, pool, beach club, spa; from $545. fourseasons.com/ santabarbara

• **Sonoma Mission Inn and Spa:** Built around an ancient thermal spring, the historic resort first opened in the 1840s; restaurants, bar, spa, pool, golf course; from $199. fairmont.com/Sonoma

# Cascades to Whitecaps

## Oregon

One of Oregon's most intriguing drives is State Route 126 between Redmond and Florence, an eclectic road trip that includes four of the Beaver State's iconic landscapes: high desert, snowcapped peaks, lush valleys, and wild coast.

### THE BIG PICTURE

**Distance:** ca 190 miles (305.8 km) from Redmond to Florence

**Drive time:** 2-4 days

**Best overnights:** Sisters, McKenzie Bridge, Eugene, Florence

**Best seasons:** Anytime

**Highlights:** Cascades Range, Hoodoo, McKenzie River Valley, Eugene, Florence, Oregon Dunes

Located right up the road from Bend, the high desert town of **Redmond** anchors the eastern end of **McKenzie Highway** (Route 126). It doesn't take long on the road to find the photo ops—right on the edge of town is **Cline Falls Scenic Viewpoint**, where the **Deschutes River** rumbles through boulder-strewn narrows. Take a quick dip or test your skill at angling in one of the state's best fly-fishing rivers before getting back in the car.

Dead ahead are **Willamette National Forest** and the town **Sisters**, named after a trio of snowy peaks that count among Oregon's five highest mountains. Winter or summer, Sisters offers a variety of outdoor recreation options, from summertime golfing, mountain biking, and horseback riding to winter downhill and cross-country skiing, as well as snow-tubing at nearby **Hoodoo Ski Area**.

There's also great hiking here, including the 3.9-mile (6.3 km) trail to the top of **Black Butte** with its vintage copula-style fire lookout and a panorama that sweeps from high desert to high mountains. The **Pacific Crest Trail** cuts across the highway near Hoodoo, an awesome segment that ambles through thick forest between **Mount Washington** and **Three Fingered Jack**.

Just past Hoodoo, Route 126 curves to the south and **Upper McKenzie Valley**, which features hiking and biking trails, as well as campgrounds and picnic areas around **Clear Lake, Sahalie-Koosah Falls**, and the **Tamolitch Blue Hole**. **McKenzie River National Recreation Trail**—best done as a two- or three-day backpacking trip—runs 26 miles (42 km) down the gorge, but numerous sections of the path are ripe for much shorter hikes.

At **Belknap Springs,** the river and highway turn west for a downhill run into the **Willamette Valley**. This stretch of water is one of Oregon's top fly-fishing spots, with salmon, steelhead, and trout as the main catch on drift trips in traditional McKenzie wooden boats. Local outfitters offer guided whitewater rafting and tubing experiences down the river. Or you can soothe your sore hiking muscles at the **Terwilliger (Cougar) Hot**

Pack your sand board for hitting the Oregon Dunes National Recreation Area.

Stop for a picnic in the resting area at Sahalie-Koosah Falls in the Upper McKenzie Valley, a great spot to hike.

**Springs** found in the Willamette National Forest.

Entering the **Eugene-Springfield** metropolitan area, Route 126 morphs into a hard-core urban highway. You can bypass the bright lights or linger at big city hot spots like the **Jordan Schnitzer Museum of Art** on the University of Oregon campus, the "living tree museum" at **Mount Pisgah Arboretum**, or the feather-centric **Cascades Raptor Center**. Eugene also offers live events, from performing arts at the **Hult Center** to world-class track and field competitions at **Hayward Field**.

West of Eugene, Route 126 rises again in a gentle climb into the **Coastal Range** mountains between the Willamette Valley and the ocean. About an hour out from Eugene, the highway reaches **Mapleton** and a turnoff to the **Sweet Creek Falls Trail**, a path that features 11 cascades over just three miles (4.8 km).

The remainder of the road trip glides down the scenic **Siuslaw River Valley** to **Florence**, a fishing port and the northern gateway to **Oregon Dunes National Recreation Area**. The city's waterfront tenders tasty seafood restaurants and the open-air **Siuslaw Interpretive Center** with its views of the vintage **Siuslaw River Bridge** (erected 1936). ■

## PIT STOPS

• **Rhododendron Festival:** Florence has greeted spring since 1908 with the flower-filled "Rhody Fest" in mid-May, which features parades, street fairs, carnival rides, car shows, food, and music. florencechamber.com

• **Sisters Rodeo:** Staged every summer since 1941, the June event brings bull riders and broncobusters to the Oregon Cascades. sistersrodeo.com

• **Eugene Beer Week:** Oregon's ongoing obsession with craft brews is the focus of this June jamboree that includes microbrewery tours, tastings, trivia contests, and wonderful things on tap. eugenebeerweek.org

• **Sisters Folk Festival:** The mountain town comes alive again during a September bash that features American roots music from blues to bluegrass. sistersfolkfestival.org

• **Mount Pisgah Mushroom Festival:** The woodsy arboretum hosts an October fest with foods, drinks, crafts, music, and most anything to do with shrooms. mountpisgaharboretum.com

# Olympic Peninsula Loop
## Washington

Wrapped around Olympic National Park, this 450-mile (724.2 km) circular route around the Olympic Peninsula offers a montage of wild seashores and snowcapped peaks, Native American homelands, and vintage Victorian towns at the extreme northwest corner of the lower 48 states.

A giant thumb of land that separates the Puget Sound and Salish Sea from the open Pacific, the Olympic Peninsula is a wonderland of woods and water. Although it's most renowned as one of the great wilderness areas of the Pacific Northwest, the peninsula also preserves Native American ways of life and the region's pioneer-era heritage.

**Olympia**, the mild-mannered capital of Washington State, offers a

**THE BIG PICTURE**

**Distance:** ca 450 miles (724.2 km) round-trip from Olympia

**Drive time**: 7-8 days

**Best overnights:** Ocean Shores, Forks, Port Angeles, Port Townsend

**Best seasons:** Anytime

**Highlights:** Olympia, Quinault Lake, Kalaloch Coast, Olympic Wilderness Coast, Neah Bay, Sol Duc, Port Angeles, Port Townsend

beginning to your journey. The **Olympia Lacey Tumwater Visitor Center** on Syd Snyder Avenue is a great place to start, first and foremost because of the maps, brochures, and other information you can collect for your trip. Then there is what lies outside—the towering **Washington State Capitol** building. Free guided tours are offered daily. Visitors can also tour the nearby **Governor's Mansion**, completed in 1909.

More architectural wonders await in Olympia's **Downtown Historic District**, which harbors more than 50 buildings, including the **Old State Capitol** and restored **Capitol Theatre** (which screens vintage, indie, and offbeat films), as well as the small but interesting **Puget Sound Estuarium** aquarium.

Exit the capital via State Highway 8 and cruise across the bottom of the Olympic Peninsula to **Aberdeen** and your first contact with the Pacific Ocean. The city prides itself as the hometown of celebrated grunge rocker Kurt Cobain (born there in 1967). But a century ago, during its heyday as a major salmon fishing port, it was dubbed the "Hellhole of the Pacific" owing to plentiful vice and violence.

Thankfully, little remains of those

A mountain goat grazes along the Bailey Range in Olympic National Park.

The Cape Flattery Trail, inside the Makah Indian Reservation, leads to the northwesternmost point of the contiguous U.S.

days other than Aberdeen's **Grays Harbor Historical Seaport**, where the tall ships *Lady Washington* and *Hawaiian Chieftain* are home-ported. Learn more about their past at the **Aberdeen Museum of History** and check out the vodka, gin, and other locally made spirits at **Wishkah River Distillery** before continuing on State Highway 109 to the shore.

With its waterfront condos, golf course, and gift shops, **Ocean Shores** is the only thing approaching a traditional beach resort along the Olympic coast. But there's also the **Coastal Interpretive Center** and **Damon Point Natural Area** with a four-mile (6.4 km) round-trip trail through a restored coastal bird habitat.

Highway 109 continues north along the shore to other state parks at **Copalis Beach** and **Pacific Beach**, as well as the fascinating **Museum of the North Beach** in Moclips.

Turning inland, the Moclips Highway (S-26) runs 20 miles (32.2 km) northeast to U.S. Highway 101, the main route around the Olympic Peninsula. Just before reaching the junction, **Quinault National Fish Hatchery** on the Quinault Indian Reservation offers a visitor center

## SCENIC DETOURS

• **Mystic Journeys:** Board the 42-foot (12.8 m) *Traveler* for a sail on the Puget Sound and Salish Sea from Olympia. mjnyoly.com

• *Lady Washington:* The replica 19th-century brig makes day sails from Aberdeen, Port Angeles, Port Townsend, Olympia, Tacoma and other Washington State ports. historicalseaport.org/ships/lady-washington.

• **Black Ball Ferry:** This 90-minute, year-round passenger and vehicle service on the MV *Coho* connects Port Angeles and Victoria, British Columbia, on Vancouver Island. cohoferry.com

• **Neah Bay Fishing:** Several outfitters, including Excel Fishing Charters, offer angling in the Strait of Juan de Fuca or open Pacific. excelfishingcharters.com

• **Hood Canal Adventures:** Kayaks, paddleboards, and crab pots are available for rent, and biologist-guided ecotours are offered along the eastern edge of the Olympic Peninsula. kayakbrinnon.com

• **Puget Sound Express:** Single- and multiday birding and wildlife cruises are offered from Port Townsend to Puffin, Protection Island, and San Juan Island. pugetsoundexpress.com

and guided tours of a facility that nurtures as many as three million salmon and trout at any given time.

Nearby **Quinault Lake** anchors the southwest corner of massive **Olympic National Park**. Arrayed around the lakeshore are a park information station, campgrounds, picnic areas, boat ramps, and short nature trails. There's also access to much longer, tougher trails in the rainforest-covered **Quinault River Valley** to the east. Highway 101 curves back around to the coast, with a side road that provides access to the national park's remote **Queets Valley**, home to some of the region's largest Douglas fir and Sitka spruce, trees that tower more than 200 feet (61 m) tall.

Up ahead is the **Kalaloch Coast**, what many people consider the most striking spot on the peninsula. Rocky headlands and long sandy beaches strewn with driftwood make this a photographer's paradise. Seals, sea otters, whales, and other marine creatures frolic in the **Olympic Coast National Marine Sanctuary**, which extends 35 to 50 miles (56.3-80.5 km) offshore. Trails lead along the beach and through the adjacent forest.

Heading up the picturesque **Hoh River Valley**, Highway 101 runs beside a turnoff to **Hoh Rain Forest Visitor Center** in a lush grove of old-growth forest. It's also the main trailhead for **Blue Glacier**—a 2.6-mile-long (4.2 km) glacier—and 7,980-foot (2,432.3 m) **Mount Olympus**, the peninsula's highest point. Rated moderate to difficult (depending on the time of year), the climb requires a Park Service wilder-

ness permit, as well as technical climbing skills and equipment.

Bending around the park's northwest corner, Highway 101 runs through the town of **Forks**, a former logging town now much better known as the setting for the *Twilight* book and film series. Fictional vampires aside, the small town offers the **Forks Timber Museum** and the quirky **John's Beachcombing Museum**. State Highway 110 heads west from Forks to the national park's spectacular **Olympic Wilderness Coast** and **Rialto Beach**, another stretch of sea stacks and driftwood— and memorials to those who died in long-ago shipwrecks.

A dozen miles (19.3 km) north of Forks is a turnoff on the left to **Neah Bay** and the Northwest Coast via State Highway 113 and the shoreline-hugging **Juan de Fuca Highway**. Perched at the end of the road, the Makah Indian Reservation offers the **Cape Flattery Trail** to the northwesternmost point of the contiguous United States and the **Makah Museum** featuring wooden canoes,

Sample rotating local wines at Hoodsport Winery's tasting room.

A bridge from the Sol Duc Hot Springs Resort leads to wilderness trails through ancient tree growth.

whale skeletons, totem poles, and other Native American artifacts.

Highway 101 soon reaches long, languid **Lake Crescent**, the best place in the national park for boating, fishing, and swimming at sandy **East Beach**. The **Spruce Railroad Trail** (10.5 miles/16.9 km) runs along the entire north shore. And there's a turnoff for the park's **Sol Duc Hot Springs**, where visitors can soak in outdoor pools that reach a toasty 104°F (40°C). Sol Duc Valley is renowned for ancient trees and trails leading to **Sol Duc Falls, Mink Lake**, and the remote **Seven Lakes Basin**.

Crowning the top of the peninsula, **Port Angeles** is home to the main **Olympic National Park Visitor Center**. It also boasts a hustle-bustle harbor area that features

waterfront restaurants, **Feiro Marine Life Center** aquarium, the **NOAA Olympic Coast Discovery Center**, and ferries to Victoria, British Columbia. From the visitor center, a 17-mile (27.4 km) drive leads up to the national park's **Hurricane Ridge** area and a summer-only road to lofty **Obstruction Point**.

From Port Angeles, the highway continues its eastward tack to the hiking, paddling, and wildlife-watching of **Dungeness National Wildlife Refuge** and the birds of the **Dungeness River Audubon Center**.

Reaching Discovery Bay, you can detour along State Highway 20 to **Port Townsend**. The one-time queen of the Olympic Peninsula harbors some of the nation's best Victorian architecture, with more than 40 structures on the National Register

of Historic Places. Among its many landmarks are the **Kelly Art Deco Light Museum**, the **Northwest Maritime Center**, old **Fort Worden**, and the flamboyant **Starrett House**.

South of Port Townsend, road trippers have a choice of jumping over **Port Gamble** and returning to Olympia via **Bremerton** and **Tacoma** or continuing on U.S. 101 down the east side of the peninsula. The latter route runs along the **Hood Canal**, the longest arm of Puget Sound. Along the way are turnoffs for **Rocky Brook Falls**, several waterfront state parks, and the **Buckhorn, Brothers**, and **Mount Skokomish** wilderness areas.

Tasting rooms in **Hoodsport** offer a final chance to sample Olympic Peninsula wine before the 40-minute drive back to Olympia. ■

# Steinbeck's Roadway
## California

Like a chapter from *East of Eden,* John Steinbeck's California is still alive along the little-used rural roads of the Coast Range and San Joaquin Valley. Spangled with ranches, roadside diners, and rugged wilderness, the route offers a bucolic back-road alternative to driving between Los Angeles and the San Francisco Bay Area.

**THE BIG PICTURE**

**Distance:** 450 miles (724.2 km) from Los Angeles to San Francisco

**Drive time:** 1-3 days

**Best overnights:** Ojai, Pinnacles National Park, Salinas

**Best seasons:** Spring or fall

**Highlights:** Ojai, Carrizo Plain, Pinnacles, Mission San Juan Bautista, National Steinbeck Center

With that classic 1970s song playing in your head, cruise the Ventura Highway (101) west from Los Angeles through the ever-expanding suburbs until it reaches the Pacific Ocean at Ventura. But don't linger by the coast: hang a right onto Highway 33 and head inland to **Ojai**, renowned for its organic farms, New Age shops, boutique hotels, and the annual June Ojai Music Festival, which draws top classical performers from around the globe.

From Ojai, the Mariposa Highway (33) climbs into the rugged **Los Padres National Forest**, one of the primary spots where the California condor, North America's largest bird, has been reintroduced into the wild after near-extinction.

**Maricopa** is the southern gateway to **Carrizo Plain National Monument**, a Bureau of Land Management reserve that protects California's largest remaining tract of native grasslands, as well as tule elk, pronghorn antelope, giant kangaroo rats, the San Joaquin kit fox, and many other endemic species. Carrizo also features a huge slice of the San Andreas Fault.

Route 33 continues through the old oil country at the south end of the San Joaquin Valley, an area that inspired the Upton Sinclair novel *Oil!* and the Oscar-winning film *There Will Be Blood.* Learn more about the region's petroleum past at the **West Kern Oil Museum** in Taft.

Reaching a lonesome crossroads called Blackwells Corner, hang a left onto the Paso Robles Highway (46) and motor back into the Coast Ranges mountains and another dusty junction, **Cholame**, where a monument and other tributes mark the spot where actor James Dean died in 1955 while piloting his silver Porsche along this highway.

Starting on Cholame Valley Road, zigzag through the oak-studded backcountry to Parkfield, Highway 198, and Peach Tree Road (Route 25) to **Pinnacles National Park**. Established in 1908 by Teddy Roosevelt, the park revolves around spectacular

Wildflowers paint the slopes of the Carrizo Plain National Monument.

There are more than 32 miles (51.5 km) of trails within Monterey County's Pinnacles National Park.

volcanic pillars. Thirty-two miles (51.5 km) of trails lead to caves, slot canyons, forested areas, and those namesake pinnacles. The park's **Bear Gulch** area renders a shady campground, as well as ranger-led hikes and other interpretive programs.

Airline Highway (25) connects Pinnacles to **Hollister**, a downtown area packed with historic buildings like the 1906 **Carnegie Library** (now the city hall), red-brick United Methodist Church (1868), and numerous Victorian mansions. Nearby **San Juan Bautista** boasts one of the original California missions, built in 1797 and renowned as the spot where Alfred Hitchcock filmed the edge-of-your-seat finale to *Vertigo* in 1958.

Reaching Highway 101, road trippers have two choices: turn north and cruise through aromatic **Gilroy** ("Garlic Capital of the World") to San Jose and the Bay Area, or turn south and head into **Salinas**. Birthplace of John Steinbeck, Salinas is home to the **National Steinbeck Center** with its tributes to the legendary California author. The center offers an ongoing slate of readings, workshops, concerts, and films for visitors. The town also hosts the bull-riding and bronco-busting **California Salinas Rodeo** each July.

From Salinas, you can make a U-turn and travel Highway 101 to San Francisco. Or hop over the coast for a cruise up Highway One or Highway 17 through the **Santa Cruz Mountains** and the **Big Basin Redwoods** to the City by the Bay. ∎

## EN ROUTE EATS

• **Osteria Monte Grappa:** With a menu that revolves around Ojai's super-fresh organic produce and olive oil, "OMG" offers homemade pasta, pizza, soups, and salads. 242 East Ojai Ave., Ojai, CA. omgojai.com

• **Tina's Diner:** Classic roadside eatery with yummy comfort food and old-time ambience. 346 California St. (Hwy. 33), Maricopa, CA. 661-769-9495

• **Jack Ranch Cafe:** Burgers, chicken, cheesecake, and locally produced Hearst Ranch wines flavor the menu at this rural restaurant that doubles as a tribute to the late James Dean. 19215 East Hwy. 46, Cholame, CA. 805-238-5652

• **Jardines de San Juan:** The Santana family's alfresco eatery features fresh takes on Mexican dishes like tacos, quesadillas, burritos, and enchiladas, as well as regional specialties from Mexico. 115 Third St., San Juan Bautista, CA. jardinesrestaurant.com

# Via de la Vulcan

## Washington, Oregon & California

Volcanoes and the incredible landscapes they form are the focus of this drive through the Cascade Range of Washington, Oregon, and Northern California. From behind the wheel, take in lava fields, cinder cones, slumbering snowcapped giants, and the very special Crater Lake.

As part of the Ring of Fire around the Pacific Basin, the Pacific Northwest is rife with volcanoes—some active and others dormant, but all breathtaking to behold.

The **Seattle-Tacoma** metropolitan area rests beneath the most famous of them all—mighty **Mount Rainier**—which soars 14,411 feet (4,392.5 m) above the Puget Sound and western Washington State. Although John Muir and other conservationists campaigned for decades to have Rainier designated as a national park in order to protect the area from mining and timber extraction, that didn't happen until

**THE BIG PICTURE**

**Distance:** ca 1,150 miles (1,850.7 km) from Seattle, WA, to Sacramento, CA

**Drive time:** 12-14 days

**Best overnights:** Mount Rainier, Portland, Bend, Crater Lake, Klamath Falls, Lassen

**Best seasons:** Spring, summer, or fall

**Highlights:** Mount Rainier, Mount Saint Helens, Portland, Mount Hood, Newberry, Crater Lake, Lava Beds, Lassen

1899, shortly after Rainier's last eruption.

From Seattle, it's about a two-hour journey on the **Chinook Scenic Byway** (Highway 410) to **Sunrise Visitor Center**, the highest point (6,400 feet/1,950.7 m) that you can drive a motor vehicle inside the park. It's also the entry point for half a dozen great hikes—including the 93-mile (149.7 km) Wonderland Trail that encircles perpetually snowcapped Rainier.

Around the south side of the park are two additional visitor centers and the **Longmire Museum**, housed in a national historic landmark district that preserves some of the nation's oldest national park buildings and an 1880s pioneer settlement. Exiting the park via the Stevens Canyon Entrance gives you a chance to stand among 1,000-year-old trees in the **Grove of the Patriarchs** or hike a short loop to **Silver Falls**.

U.S. Highway 12 leads south through the scenic **Cowlitz River Valley** to a turnoff in the town of Randall for **Mount Saint Helens National Volcanic Monument**. From there it's about an hour's drive (via State Highway 99) to **Windy Ridge**, the highest point

Find charming coffee shops and tasty restaurants in Portland's Pearl District.

Wildflowers bloom in the meadows beneath Mount Saint Helens, just 50 miles (80.5 km) northeast of Portland.

you can reach by road on the most destructive volcano in modern American history.

No one, other than volcanologists, thought much about Mount Saint Helens until it erupted with unprecedented fury in 1980, an explosion that sheared 1,300 feet (396.2 m) off the summit, devastated 230 square miles (595.7 sq km) of wilderness, and killed 57 people who couldn't escape the toxic gases, lava bombs, and massive pyroclastic flow. Although the last volcanic activity was in 2008, Saint Helens is still very much an active volcano and should be approached with caution.

## SCENIC DETOURS

• **Kenmore Air** offers 90-minute scenic flights over Mount Rainier and Mount Saint Helens from Seattle's Boeing Field. kenmoreair.com

• **RMI Expeditions** has been leading climbers to the top of Mount Rainier since 1969; overnights at 10,000-foot (3,048 m) Camp Muir. rmiguides.com

• **Mount Saint Helens Institute** organizes guided summit and crater hikes, field seminars, and winter group activities in the national volcanic monument. mshinstitute.org

• **Timberline Mountain Guides** leads guided ascents, glacier skiing, and ski mountaineering excursions on Mount Hood, including programs for entry-level climbers. timberlinemt guides.com

• **Crater Lake Boat Tours** operates two-hour scenic cruises, Wizard Island tours, and the Wizard Island shuttle for access to hiking, swimming, and fishing in the lake. travelcraterlake.com

• **Manzanita Lake Camper Store** rents kayaks, canoes, paddleboards, and catarafts for use in Lassen Volcanic National Park. lassenlodging .com/manzanita-lake-activities

Phantom Ship rock island adds to the many wonders of Crater Lake.

there entails a 136-mile (218.9 km), three-hour journey off the main road trip route. Still, for those who make the effort, the north side offers the **Forest Learning Center**—with a virtual reality Eruption Chamber that simulates the 1980 disaster—exhibits and ranger talks at **Johnson Ridge Observatory**, and the short **Eruption Trail** through the lava-strewn blast zone.

From Windy Ridge, it's about a three-hour drive on State Highway 503 and Interstate 5 to **Portland**, Oregon. With its rose gardens and craft breweries, Oregon's largest city makes a nice break from the volcanology that dominates this drive.

Portland is a city of neighborhoods, ranging from the hip breweries and art galleries of the resurrected **Pearl District** to the authentic eateries of **Old Town Chinatown** and the historic structures and cultural institutions along the **South Park Blocks**. Many of the city's top attractions cluster in 410-acre (166 ha) **Washington Park**, including the **Oregon Zoo, Japanese Garden, International Test Rose Garden**, and **Hoyt Arboretum**, with its 10,000 trees from around the world.

**Mount Hood National Forest**—and its dormant volcanic namesake—lies around 70 miles (112.7 km) east of Portland via U.S. Highway 26. More people climb the 11,244-foot (3,427.2 m) peak each year than any other glaciated mountain in the world after Mount Fuji in Japan. The ascent normally takes four to five hours. For those who don't climb, the national forest offers plenty of scope for summer hiking and biking or winter snow sports.

Descending from Mount Hood, Highway 12 eventually merges with U.S. 97, which runs all the way down the eastern side of the Oregon

On the way up to Windy Ridge are viewpoints for **Spirit Lake** and the ghostly **Blown-Down Forest**, as well as trailheads for the five-mile (8 km) **Monitor Ridge Trail** to the summit and the 28-mile (45.1 km) **Loowit Loop** around the entire volcano.

More twisted volcanic landscapes await around the north side of Saint Helens. By foot it's less than nine miles (14.5 km), but driving

Cascades with several interesting stops along the way. **Erickson Aircraft Collection** in Madras features an amazing array of historic planes and scenic flights in vintage warbirds. Bend's **High Desert Museum** offers an excellent introduction to the region's natural and human history, including live bird of prey and otter encounters.

Another five miles (8 km) down the highway, **Lava Lands Visitor Center** is the gateway to the eruptive wonders of **Newberry National Volcanic Monument**. Among the parks many geological landmarks are Big Obsidian Flow lava field, Lava Butte cinder cone, the 4,200-foot-long (1,280.2 m) Lava River Cave, and the massive Newberry Caldera.

Sixty-six miles (106.2 km) south of Lava Lands, U.S. 97 reaches Diamond Lake Junction and a turnoff to **Crater Lake National Park**, one of the nation's most visually stunning natural attractions. North America's deepest lake (nearly 2,000 feet/609.6 m) is also one of its bluest, a color derived from the almost total absence of human and natural pollutants. The crater was created by the eruption of Mount Mazama in the sixth century B.C.,

an explosion estimated to be 42 times bigger than the 1980 event at Mount Saint Helens.

Viewpoints and short trails line the 33-mile (53.1 km) **Rim Drive** around the crater. **Rim Village** offers some of the most spectacular panoramas, as well as ranger walks and talks, trolley tours, and the historic **Crater Lake Lodge** (opened in 1915). During the summer, boat service is available from Cleetwood Cove to **Wizard Island.**

From Crater Lake, the Volcanic Legacy Scenic Byway leads to **Klamath Falls**, an old logging town that's making the transition into tourism with attractions like the **Favell Museum** (which specializes in contemporary western art and Native American artifacts) and **Badger Run Wildlife Rehab** center.

The scenic byway continues across the California border to **Lava Beds National Monument**, a small but incredibly diverse park that boasts more than 700 lava caves (many of them home to bats) and a vast lava field created by the **Medicine Lake shield volcano**—the largest volcano by volume in the entire Cascade Range. The park also offers dramatic views of snowcapped **Mount Shasta** volcano, as well as

Native American rock art and Modoc War battlefields.

A combination of state highways (139, 299, and 89) meanders through the Northern California highlands to the last of the eruptive landmarks on this road trip: **Lassen Volcanic National Park**. What it lacks in beauty, the 10,457-foot (3,187.3 m) peak more than compensates with thermal fury—the only volcano other than Mount Saint Helens to erupt during the 20th century in the lower 48 states.

The park's 30-mile (48.3 km) **Scenic Drive** meanders past whimsically named landmarks like **Chaos Jumble**, **Sulphur Works**, and **Bumpass Hell**. Along the way are several lakes (paddle sports, picnics, swimming) and two visitor centers with maps, information, and museum exhibits. Some of the park's most dramatic scenery occupies the secluded northeast corner, a **Butte Lake** area that offers trails leading to the **Fantastic Lava Beds, Painted Dunes**, and 690-foot-high (210.3 m) **Cinder Cone**.

Exiting Lassen Park, Scenic Drive morphs back into State Highway 89, the start of a three-hour drive to Sacramento via Red Bluff and Interstate 5. ■

## LAY YOUR HEAD

- **Paradise Inn:** Opened in 1916, this historic lodge renders rustic comfort on the south side of Mount Rainier; restaurant, post office, gift shop; open May to October; from $138. mtrainierguestservices.com

- **Timberline Lodge:** As soon as the snow melts off Oregon's Timberline Mountain, this vintage 1930s ski lodge morphs into a hiking, biking, and mountain climbing base; restaurants,

bars, outdoor pool, gym, sauna; from $180. timberlinelodge.com/lodge

- **McMenamins Old St. Francis School:** 1930s Catholic school converted into funky digs in downtown Bend, Oregon; restaurant, bars, brewery, cinema, indoor soaking pool; from $145. mcmenamins.com/old-st-francis-school

- **Crater Lake Lodge:** Located right on the crater rim, this masterpiece of

American "parkitecture" features rooms with stunning lake views; restaurant, bar, grand fireplace; open May to October; from $202. travelcraterlake.com

- **Drakesbad Guest Ranch:** Horseback trips, hot springs, and hiking trails highlight this historic dude ranch in Lassen Volcanic National Park; restaurant, bar, outdoor pool; from $220. lassenlodging.com/drakesbad

# Rain Shadow Route
## California & Nevada

There are definitely faster ways to drive between San Diego and Reno, but none of those other routes is anywhere near as scenic as U.S. Highway 395 and this laid-back road trip along the arid eastern side of the Sierra Nevada.

**THE BIG PICTURE**

**Distance:** ca 560 miles (901.2 km) from San Diego, CA, to Reno, NV

**Drive time:** 7-8 days

**Best overnights:** Riverside, Lone Pine, Bishop, Mammoth Lakes, Bridgeport, Carson City

**Best seasons:** Anytime

**Highlights:** Balboa Park, Temecula wineries, Mojave Desert, Manzanar, Mammoth Lakes, Tioga Road, Mono Lake, Bodie ghost town, Virginia City

Tracing the original path of Highway 395, this road trip kicks off in downtown **San Diego, California,** with a leafy leg along CA 163 through **Balboa Park** and its world-famous zoo and multiple museums. Interstate 15 carries the route to **Escondido**, where the **San Diego Safari Park** and 1846 **San Pasqual Battlefield** are the main attractions worth stopping for, before moving on to **Temecula** and its increasingly tasty collection of **wineries**.

North of Temecula, Interstate 215 overlays the old highway through **Riverside** and **San Bernardino**. Possible stops along this part of the trip include the **March Field Air Museum**, which features 70 historic aircraft including a B-52 Stratofortress, and the historic **Mission Inn** in downtown Riverside.

Crawling up the **Cajon Pass**, drivers pass through **San Bernardino National Forest** before reaching the Joshua tree–studded **Mojave Desert** and a junction where 395 finally splits from the interstate to start its own journey northward.

It's pretty much unrelenting desert for the next 100 miles (160.9 km) as the highway cuts through the heart of the Mojave. If you're looking for something to see, there's a huge roadside solar farm near **Kramer Junction**, and dusty **Randsburg** offers antique shops and a few gold mining relics.

But there's really nothing of substance until you reach **Ridgecrest**, a town that evolved on the edge of China Lakes U.S. Navy Base. In addition to the natural and human history of the Mojave, the **Maturango Museum** offers guided tours of the nearby **Coso Rock Art District** and its 20,000 images, the largest petroglyph concentration in the Western Hemisphere.

Just beyond Ridgecrest, U.S. 395 links up with State Route 14 for a scenic run up the eastern side of the mountains that was called the **Sierra Highway** or **El Camino Sierra** in the days before American highways started to be numbered. The route

Have close encounters of the animal kind at the San Diego Safari Park.

The historic Mission Inn began as a boardinghouse in 1876. In 1903 Frank Miller expanded the inn to include 200 guest rooms.

runs right up the middle of the **Owens Valley**, where the California water wars of the early 20th century pitted local ranchers and farmers against the thirsty city dwellers of Los Angeles.

**Lone Pine** is the gateway to climbing 14,505-foot (4,421.1 m) **Mount Whitney**, the highest point in the lower 48 states. The **Museum of Western Film History** reflects how many Hollywood movies have been shot in and around Lone Pine over the past century—including classics like *High Sierra, Bad Day at Black Rock, Tremors,* and *Gunga Din.* The **Eastern Sierra Visitor Center** is the place to pick up brochures, maps, and information about the northward journey.

The next stretch of 395 runs past **Manzanar National Historic Site**— where more than 110,000 Japanese Americans were interned during World War II—and the **Eastern California Museum** in Independence before breezing into the town of **Bishop**. Flush with hotels and restaurants, Bishop is a popular overnight stop along the Rain Shadow Route, as well as a staging area for hiking, camping, and fishing in nearby **Inyo National Forest**.

Finally climbing out of the desert, Highway 395 makes its way to the **Mammoth Lakes** region, where the extensive offerings of summer and winter activities feature downhill and cross-country skiing, hiking and mountain biking, hot springs, copious nightlife, **Devil's Postpile National Monument**—with its odd volcanic formations—and gorgeous **Rainbow Falls**.

One of a string of four large lakes along a loop road, **June Lake** offers summertime swimming, trout fishing, sailing, paddle sports—a marina

### SCENIC DETOURS

• **Highway 190:** Death Valley is the destination of this lonely desert road that calves off 395 at Olancha.

• **Tioga Road:** Starting from Lee Vining, the "back way" into Yosemite National Park is normally closed from October to May due to snowfall.

• **Highway 108:** Sonora Junction marks the beginning of this route over the Sierra to California's Gold Country.

• **Mount Rose Highway:** Highway 431 connects Reno and Lake Tahoe, with Galena Creek and Mount Rose Ski Area along the way.

• **Highway 395:** Runs beyond Reno for another 760 miles (1,223.1 km) through the wilds of northeastern California and central Oregon to Spokane, Washington.

## LAY YOUR HEAD

• **Mission Inn:** Renowned for its architecture and holiday light displays, this landmark hotel looms above downtown Riverside; restaurants, bars, spa, pool, guided tours; from $209. missioninn.com

• **Creekside Inn:** Guest rooms are perched beside outdoor fire pits and sitting areas along the creek in downtown Bishop; restaurant, swimming pool, hot tub, laundry; from $140. bishopcreeksideinn.com

• **Tamarack Lodge:** A lakeside retreat by summer, cross-country ski hub by winter on the edge of Mammoth Lakes; restaurant, bar, ski center, boat and bike rental, fish-cleaning station; cabins from $127. tamaracklodge.com

• **Virginia Creek Settlement:** Rustic roadside lodging between Mono Lake and Bridgeport, opened in 1927; restaurant, picnic areas, horseshoes, fishing in the creek; cabins from $85. virginiacrksettlement.com

• **Gold Hill Hotel:** Nevada's oldest hotel (est. 1861) flaunts period furnishings, a vintage saloon, and balcony rooms overlooking Virginia City; restaurant, bar; from $140. goldhill hotel.net

rents watercraft—and a small ski area for winter recreation.

Another 15 minutes up the road is **Lee Vining** and its turnoff to **Tioga Road** (Highway 120)—the superscenic back way into **Yosemite National Park**. That big blue thing on the other side of Lee Vining is **Mono Lake**, one of California's oddest natural attractions. The shallow, saline lake is renowned for its tufa (calcium carbonate) towers and the millions of migratory birds that feed off its brine shrimp.

**Mono Basin Scenic Area Visitor Center** offers a great orientation to the lake, while the **South Tufa Area** affords the best chance of seeing the melted-wax-like towers up close. **Naturalist-led walks** are offered throughout the year, plus **guided paddle trips** in summer.

Just north of the lake, **Bodie State Historic Park** preserves the considerable remains of a 19th-century gold mining community that once boasted more than 10,000 residents. One of the West's most impressive ghost towns, Bodie offers dozens of structures in a state of "arrested decay"—as if the owners vacated them just yesterday.

Ten minutes north of the Bodie turnoff, **Bridgeport** is another picture-perfect eastern Sierra town renowned for its trout fishing in local lakes and streams,

Mono Lake, a 695-square-mile (1,800 sq km) inland sea, is dotted with unique tufa towers.

hot springs, and backcountry winter adventure. The northward meander continues through **Humboldt-Toiyabe National Forest** and down through the **Walker River Valley** to **Topaz Lake** on the California-Nevada border.

If you can resist the lure of the little state line casino, carry on along Highway 395 to **Gardnerville, Nevada,** in the broad **Carson Valley.** Road trippers have two choices at this point: cruise over the mountains to **Lake Tahoe** (one hour) or keep heading north to the Nevada state capital.

Founded in 1858, **Carson City** is flush with history, taken in through the vintage structures arrayed along the self-guided **Kit Carson Trail** in the old town. Many of the city's landmarks overlook Highway 395, including the **Nevada State History Museum** in the Old Mint, **Nevada State Capitol** (built in 1871), and the **Nevada State Railroad Museum** with its scenic train rides.

Carson City's other vintage rail service is the **Virginia and Truckee Railway**, which offers 90-minute rides between the state capital and Virginia City during the summer (and several daily services between Virginia City and Gold Hill between May and October).

Focal point for the Comstock Lode—the largest silver strike in U.S.

Frank Sinatra's 1961 Dual Ghia Hardtop at the National Automobile Museum

history—**Virginia City** preserves its boomtown heritage through silver rush relics like the **Washoe Club, Piper's Opera House,** the **Mark Twain Museum,** the **Bucket of Blood Saloon**, and the **Mackay Mansion** of the Hearst family, which made its fortune in Comstock silver.

**Reno** lies a mere 30 minutes north of Carson City, and you can get there via Highway 395, which makes its way through the middle of the "Biggest Little City" beneath the famous **Reno Arch** neon sign. While not quite as over the top as Las

Vegas, Reno definitely boasts its fair share of nightclubs, lounges, and gambling establishments. But the city also offers plenty of other activities.

Among the stars of the **National Automobile Museum** are cars once owned by Elvis, Sinatra, JFK, and John Wayne. Wrapped inside a striking postmodern structure, the **Nevada Museum of Art** focuses on contemporary painting, sculpture, and photography, while nature's creativity is the essence of the city's **Animal Ark** zoo and desert-centric **Reno Arboretum**. ■

## EN ROUTE EATS

• **Outpost Cafe:** Breakfast is the bomb at this desert diner—huevos rancheros, pork chops and eggs, Frank's Gunslinger Hash, and Road Kill Omelet are just a few of the choices; 8685 U.S. Hwy. 395, Oak Hills, CA. outpostcafe.net

• **Tom's Place:** This Crowley Lake lodestar has been serving dishes like

country fried steak, prime rib, and turkey with mashed potatoes since 1917; 8180 Crowley Lake Dr., Mammoth Lakes, CA. tomsplace resort.com

• **Whoa Nellie Deli:** Nobody drives Tioga Road without fueling up on fish tacos, buffalo meatloaf, or angus burgers at this gourmet gas

station café near Mono Lake; 22 Vista Point Road, Lee Vining, CA. whoanelliedeli.com

• **Villa Basque Cafe:** The menu at this savory mash-up of Mexican and Iberian foods runs all the way from chorizo omelets and lamb stew to chile verde burritos; 730 Basque Way, Carson City, NV. villabasquecafe.com

# Alaska Route One

## Alaska

A combination of the Seward Highway and the Sterling Highway, Alaska Route One spans nearly the entire length of the scenic Kenai Peninsula between Anchorage and Homer, a route peppered with spectacular fjords and funky tourist towns, incredible wildlife reserves, and quirky historical attractions.

The fastest way to escape into the wilderness of Alaska isn't heading north toward Denali National Park and Preserve, but driving in the opposite direction, down Route One to the Kenai Peninsula. Within 20 minutes, you're cruising down the Seward Highway along the **Turnagain Arm** of Cook Inlet in **Chugash State Park**.

At 13,000 acres (5,260.9 hectares) and with snowcapped peaks rising to 13,000 feet (3,962.4 m), Chugash is one of the nation's largest state parks—and one of its most spectacular. In any other state, it would likely be a *national* park. Chugash is home to some of the greatest treasures of Alaskan wildlife: bears, moose, mountain goats, wolves, Dall sheep,

### THE BIG PICTURE

**Distance:** ca 300 miles (482.8 km) from Anchorage to Seward and Homer

**Drive time:** 6-10 days

**Best overnights:** Girdwood, Seward, Homer

**Best season:** Summer

**Highlights:** Chugash State Park, Seward, Kenai Fjords National Park, Kenai Wildlife Refuge, Homer, Kachemak

and around 200 bird species, as well as the marine mammals that live on its coastal portions.

**Potter Section House**, a restored 1920s railroad building, is the park's visitor center, a great place to snag maps and information on park adventures and activities. There's certainly plenty to do: summertime hiking, biking, camping, and fishing, and wintertime snow sports like cross-country skiing.

Farther down the coast are the 1901 **Indian Valley Mine** (guided tours and gold panning) and **Bird Point**, where road trippers can experience America's largest tides (as much as 40 feet/12.2 m) and contemplate the fact that Captain Bligh of *Mutiny on the Bounty* fame sailed these waters in 1778.

Right around the bend is the town of **Girdwood** and **Alyeska Resort**, Alaska's biggest and best winter sports hub. During the summer, Girdwood is a springboard for two of the state's best hikes: the 23-mile (37 km) **Crow Pass Trail** (the southernmost segment of the Iditarod Trail) and the 38-mile (61.2 km) **Eklutna Traverse**, which crosses four glaciers.

Perched at the east end of Turnagain Arm is the **Alaska Wildlife Conservation Center**, a sanctuary for many endemic critters, from bald

It's not uncommon to spot a moose wandering through the Alaska wilderness.

Tree-topped shale spires were formed in the bay of Kenai Fjords National Park after centuries of erosion.

eagles and brown bears to caribou, musk oxen, wood bison, and lynx. Up ahead at **Tern Lake**, the road splits. Route One continues west with a new name (Sterling Highway), while the Seward Highway veers off to the south with a new number (9).

**Seward** town lies about 45 minutes south along the eponymous highway. As the gateway to **Kenai Fjords National Park**, there's plenty to see and do around Seward, including stopping at the park visitor center and the **Alaska SeaLife Center** zoo and aquarium; driving to **Exit Glacier** and the 8.2-mile (13.2 km) **Harding Icefield Trail**; seeing World War II relics at **Caine Head**; and options for **boat and flightseeing tours**.

Continuing west from Tern Lake, Sterling Highway traverses the thick boreal forest of the **Russian River** region before gliding back to the coast near **Soldatna**, homesteaded

after World War II and now the major stopover between Anchorage and Homer. Just outside the town is the massive **Kenai National Wildlife Refuge** with its myriad hiking, paddling, camping, fishing, and wildlife viewing possibilities.

Route One hugs the shoreline of **Cook Inlet** down to **Anchor Point** (where Captain Cook lost an anchor in 1778) and **Homer**. In

addition to art galleries, seafood eateries, and dive bars, the "cosmic hamlet by the sea" is renowned for sports fishing (salmon and halibut) and boat tours to nearby **Kachemak Bay State Park**. The **Center for Alaskan Coastal Studies** and the **Alaska Islands and Ocean Visitor Center** provide insight into the local human and natural history. ■

## OFF ROAD

• **Major Marine** (Seward) offers narrated half-day and full-day boat trips of the Kenai Fjords. majormarine.com

• **Liquid Adventures** (Seward) specializes in guided multiday kayak camping journeys through the Kenai Fjords. liquid-adventures.com

• **Alaska Ultimate Safaris** (Homer) offers helicopter "bear safaris" to see and photograph grizzlies in Katmai

and Lake Clark National Parks. alaskaultimatesafaris.com

• **Beryl Air** (Homer) uses float planes for scenic flights over Kachemak Bay State Park, Harding Icefield, and Kenai Fjords. berylair.com

• **Rainbow Tours** (Homer) floats full-day guided wildlife boat tours to Kachemak Bay and Seldovia. rainbowtours.net

# Heartland Highways
## Alaska

This epic drive around central Alaska follows some of the most famous highways in the Last Frontier, a route that runs past legendary peaks and glaciers, down wild river valleys, and through towns that epitomize the Alaskan lifestyle.

### THE BIG PICTURE

**Distance:** 1,300 miles (2,092.1 km) round-trip from Anchorage

**Drive time:** 10-14 days

**Best overnights:** Denali, Fairbanks, Tok, Glennallen, McCarthy, Valdez

**Best seasons:** Summer or early fall

**Highlights:** Denali National Park, Tanana River Valley, Wrangell–St. Elias National Park, Worthington and Columbia glaciers, Chugash Range

Alaska's wide-open spaces and almost always empty highways make the 49th state an almost ideal place for a long-distance road trip, a journey that's even more enticing when you figure in the national parks, historic towns, and dramatic landscapes along the route.

Before hitting the road, orient yourself with a trio of stops in **Anchorage**. First up is the **Log Cabin Visitor Information Center** on Fourth Avenue. Then visit the **Anchorage Museum at Rasmuson Center**, which functions as the de facto state museum of art, history, and science, followed by the **Alaska Native Heritage Center** (ANHC) with its indigenous story-telling, dance, and crafts.

The ANHC lies just off **Glenn Highway** (AK-1) on the northern outskirts of town, which makes it a convenient last stop as you leave Anchorage. Those thirsting for a quick fix of Alaskan nature can find it just half an hour from downtown; exits off the Glenn Highway lead to **Eagle River Nature Center, Thun-** **derbird Falls**, and **Lake Eklutna** in massive **Chugash State Park**.

After passing over the Matanuska River, veer left onto the **George Parks Highway** (AK-3) to Wasilla and Fairbanks. Named after a local Dena'ina chief, **Wasilla** is *the* spot for global sled dog racing—it's home to the **Iditarod Trail Museum** and the **Mushers Hall of Fame**.

From Wasilla, it's an easy 90-mile (144.8 km) drive to the **Denali region**, a larger-than-life landscape protected within the confines of huge state and national parks. The Parks Highway runs straight up the middle of **Denali State Park**, renowned for rafting on the **Chulitna River**, great wildlife viewing, spectacular mountains, and hiking along the 22-mile (35.4 km) **K'esugi Ridge Trail**.

Centered on the highest point in North America, **Denali National Park and Preserve** lies farther north. The nation's third largest national park sprawls across an area equal to Connecticut, Delaware, and Rhode Island combined. At 20,310 feet (6,190.5 m), **Denali Peak** is only for the most experienced climbers. But there are plenty of places around the park to get a glimpse of the snowcapped giant.

Wildflowers line the bank of the Tanana Valley State Forest.

Hike atop glaciers and grasslands in Wrangell–St. Elias National Park and Preserve, one of the world's largest protected areas.

**Denali Park Road** heads due west into the heart of the park. But only the first 15 miles (24.1 km) are open to private vehicles. Visitors can then hike or bike the remainder of the gravel road, or hop aboard one of three narrated bus tours that ply the route from the **Wilderness Access Center** near the park's main entrance. Wildlife is plentiful along the route: Spot and photograph brown bears, moose, and caribou.

Adventure outfitters in towns along the Parks Highway—**Talkeetna, Cantwell, McKinley Park,** and **Healy**—offer a variety of ways to discover the region, from guided backpack camping, mountain climbing, and off-road safaris, to whitewater rafting, fly-fishing, and aurora borealis viewing.

It's about a two-hour drive from Healy to Fairbanks via the Nenana and Tanana river valleys. You can break the journey in **Nenana** town, located at the confluence of the two rivers, with a visit to the **State of Alaska Railroad Museum** or the **Alfred Starr Cultural Center** with its eclectic displays on the Athabaskan people, sled dogs, riverboat racing, and other aspects of local life.

Alaska's second largest city, **Fairbanks**, was founded more or less by accident in the early 20th century by a riverboat captain whose boat ran aground on the site. It didn't flourish until World War II, when Fairbanks became the state's major military hub and stopover on the recently completed Alaska Highway.

Located in an old cinema, **Fairbanks Ice Museum** features ice sculptures, an ice bar, and ice carving demonstrations. The University of Alaska's futuristic **Museum of the North** safeguards more than 2.2 million cultural artifacts and natural

### ART AVENUES

- **Best Books:** *Into the Wild* by Jon Krakauer; *The Call of the Wild* by Jack London; *Ice Palace* by Edna Ferber; *Winterdance: The Fine Madness of Running the Iditarod* by Gary Paulsen

- **Best Movies:** *White Fang* (1991); *Mystery, Alaska* (1999); *Grizzly Man* (2005); *Into the Wild* (2007); *Big Miracle* (2012); *Bears* (2014)

- **Best Music:** *Entertain the Entertainers* by Artis the Spoonman; *Where Legends Are Born* by Hobo Jim; *The Song of the Month Project* by Marian Call; *Alaska Gwich'in Fiddler* by Bill Stevens

- **Best TV Shows:** *The Alaskans* (1959-60); *Northern Exposure* (1990-95); *Deadliest Catch* (2005-present); *Alaskan Bush People* (2014-present)

history specimens from around the state. Or view living wildlife (like musk oxen and reindeer) at the university's **Large Animal Research Station** or **Creamer's Field Migratory Waterfowl Refuge**.

Fairbanks is also Alaska's best festival city, staging a number of special events each summer, including the **Midnight Sun Festival** in June, **Golden Days** and the **World Eskimo-Indian Olympics** (WEIO) in July, and the **Tanana Valley State Fair** and **Sandhill Crane Festival** in August.

Leaving Fairbanks, the Richardson Highway (AK-2) runs east along the **Tanana River** into an increasingly remote and wild region that was once the realm of prospectors and fur trappers. **Big Delta State Historic Park** preserves an old roadhouse, sod-roofed cabin, telegraph station, and other mementos of those days. Reaching Delta Junction, the road trip segues onto the Alaska Highway (also AK-2) for a 107-mile (172.2 km) drive southeast to Tok.

Although it's primarily known as the junction of the Alaska and Glenn highways, **Tok** also boasts a quirky little theme park called **Mukluk Land**, a blast from the past that features old Skee-Ball machines, miniature golf, antique vehicles, a candy store, and Santa's Rocket Ship.

This northeastern end of the Glenn Highway (AK-1) drops down to **Wrangell–St. Elias National Park and Preserve**, the nation's largest national park, and together with nature reserves across the border in Canada, part of a UNESCO World Heritage site that's among the globe's largest protected areas of any kind.

Take a side trip into the park's super-remote north end on the

A Yup'ik girl wears a traditional headdress at the Alaska Native Heritage Center.

unpaved **Nabesna Road**. Or continue along the highway to the **Copper Center Visitor Center** and **Ahtna Cultural Center** for a great introduction to the region's natural history and native Alaskan heritage. An hour south of the visitor center (via Richardson and Edgerton highways), the tiny riverside hamlet of **Chitina** is the gateway to the park's heartland along 60-mile (96.6 km), gravel-surfaced **McCarthy Road**, one of the state's most intriguing drives given its washboards, copious curves, and jaywalking mammals.

The road ends near a pedestrian bridge that crosses the Kennicott River to shuttle buses that take visitors into **McCarthy**. Once a rowdy boomtown for the nearby copper mines, McCarthy is now the jumping-off spot for just about everything that happens in the park, including wilderness guide services, air taxis, and outfitters for backpack camping, river trips, and mountain biking.

Five miles (8 km) up the road, **Kennecott Mines National Historic Landmark** harbors the remarkably well-preserved remains of the old

copper complex. Ranger-led tours of the rust-red buildings start from **Kennecott Visitor Center,** which is also the entry point for walks along the edge of **Root Glacier** and into much more ambitious hikes to the glacier-flanked **Donoho Basin**.

Backtracking to the Richardson Highway, the road trip continues south, running past **Worthington Glacier** and through waterfall-laden **Keystone Canyon** to the coast. The road dead-ends in Valdez, the town on the **Prince William Sound** that doubles as a fishing port and southern terminus of the Trans-Alaska Pipeline. Local companies expedite scenic cruises to **Columbia Glacier**, rock climbing, glacier trekking, and kayaking on the sound.

The return to Anchorage entails a 300-mile (482.8 km) drive along the Richardson Highway to **Glennallen** and along the northern edge of the **Chugash Range** on the Glenn Highway. The final leg of the road trip passes through Palmer, the site of the **Alaska State Fair,** a great way to punctuate the drive if you're passing through in late summer. ■

## LAY YOUR HEAD

• **Kantishna Roadhouse:** Deluxe wilderness lodge at the end of the road deep inside Denali National Park; interpretive programs, guided hiking, fishing equipment, mountain bikes, evening excursions; open June to September; from $460 per person all-inclusive. kantishnaroadhouse.com

• **River's Edge Resort:** Riverside cottages with private patios highlight this popular Fairbanks lodge; restaurant, bar, airport/train shuttle; open May to September; from $103. riversedge.net

• **Caribou Cabins:** Rustic log cabins on 30 acres (12 ha) of woods near Tok and the Alaska-Glenn highways

junction; breakfast included, potbelly stoves, satellite TV; from $129. cariboucabins.info

• **Ma Johnson's Hotel:** This "living museum" in McCarthy features authentic copper rush–era decor inside a 1923 clapboard building; restaurant, bar, library/lounge, shared bathrooms; open May to September; from $249. mccarthylodge.com

• **Prince William Sound Lodge:** Cozy waterfront wilderness retreat 25 miles (40.2 km) from Valdez; guided hikes, fishing, and boat trips; from $325 per person all-inclusive. princewilliamsound.us

# Puget Sound Island Hopping
## Washington

An awesome network of roads, bridges, and Washington State Ferries enables this island-hopping adventure between Seattle and the San Juan Islands, a road trip that features old-growth forests, secluded beaches, incredible wildlife, and America's most peculiar war history.

**S**eattle is the starting point for this offshore journey across the **Puget Sound**, a warren of waterways and islands created by glacial retreat at the end of the last Ice Age. At the **Seattle Ferry Terminal** (Pier 52), hop a vehicle vessel to **Bremerton**, an hour's sail across the sound.

Strolling the refurbished **Bremerton Boardwalk**, quaff a gourmet coffee or craft brew, board the

U.S.S. *Turner Joy* floating museum, or visit the **Puget Sound Navy Museum** before heading north on State Route 3.

Poised on Liberty Bay, **Poulsbo** honors its Norwegian founders with Scandinavian-themed attractions like the **Norseman Statue**, an 1886 **Lutheran church**, and **Sluys Bakery** with its delicious treats like kransekake (a traditional confec-

tion), Viking cups, Danish pastries, and handcrafted breads.

After crossing the **Hood Canal Floating Bridge**, follow State Routes 104 and 19 to **Port Townsend**. The "City of Dreams" is renowned for its well-preserved Victorian buildings, many now home to **cafés, art galleries**, and quirky collections like the **Kelly Art Deco Light Museum**.

Time for another vehicle ferry: from Port Townsend across the main entrance to Puget Sound to **Coupeville** on Whidbey Island (30 minutes). Beside the ferry dock, **Fort Casey State Park** features gun batteries, underground bunkers, and a giant cannon that once protected the sound from foreign invasion.

State Route 20 meanders across **Whidbey Island**, a gorgeous drive that features **Ebey's Landing National Historical Reserve** with its vintage farms, trails through forest and prairie, and **Island County Historical Museum**.

Crowning the island's north end is **Deception Pass,** the most popular state park in Washington, with around three million visitors per year. That's because there's a lot to do: hiking, biking, and horseback riding; beaches and lakes; two museums; and one very famous span—the

Deception Pass is Washington's most visited state park, for good reason.

A mural depicting sailing Norsemen proudly showcases Poulsbo's Norwegian heritage.

1,487-foot-long (453.2 m), doubled-arched **Deception Pass Bridge**, which you can walk or drive across.

On the north side of the bridge, Route 20 crawls across **Fidalgo Island** to **Anacortes** with its waterfront trails, lofty views from the summit of **Mount Erie**, and **Predators of the Heart** wolf and wildlife sanctuary. Anacortes is also the southern terminus for the **San Juan Islands ferry**—a service that calls on Lopez, Shaw, Orcas, and Friday Harbor in the archipelago above the Puget Sound.

**Orcas** is the largest of the San Juans, an island celebrated for its fresh shellfish, historic **Rosario Resort** (built in 1905), and the leafy trails of **Moran State Park**, where the stone tower atop 2,399-foot (731.2 m) **Mount Constitution** offers a panoramic view stretching from Vancouver Island to Mount Rainier.

Flanking the western side of the archipelago, **San Juan Island** is where America's third conflict with Britain played out in summer 1859—the notorious Pig War. Sparked by the "murder" of a British hog by an American squatter, the boundary dispute ended peacefully and without human injury. **San Juan Islands National Historic Park** features both the American Camp and British Camp from that oddball conflict.

But the island's main attraction is **Lime Kiln Point State Park**, one of the best places in the world to watch whales from the shore—orcas, humpbacks, and several other species that live in the San Juans year-round or migrate through during the warmer months. ◼

## SCENIC DETOURS

- **Crystal Seas Kayaking** in Friday Harbor offers full- and half-day kayak tours, as well as multiday bike camping and kayak camping adventures. crystalseas.com

- **Outer Island Expeditions** on Orcas Island undertakes whale-watching and fishing charters in small, fast boats. outerislandx.com

- **Schooners North** uses a classic wooden windjammer, the *Spike Africa,* for guided sailing trips around the San Juan Islands from Friday Harbor. sanjuansailcharter.com

- **Westwind Aviation** in Friday Harbor takes to the air on 45-minute scenic flights over the San Juan archipelago. westwindav.com

- **Exotic Aquatics Scuba** on Bainbridge Island organizes guided dives in Puget Sound in search of the giant Pacific octopus, wolf eels, and other denizens of the deep. exoticaquaticsscuba.com

# Rocky Mountain
## Road Trips

Canoes are docked on Lake McDonald in Glacier National Park.

# International Selkirk Loop

## Washington, Idaho & British Columbia

North America's only multinational scenic byway circles the rugged Selkirk Range in the northern Rockies, a journey along roads less traveled in Washington State, British Columbia, and the Idaho Panhandle.

Conceived in the 1990s as a means to market a part of the Pacific Northwest that wasn't getting its fair share of visitors, the Selkirk Route offers a montage of snow-capped mountains, wild rivers and lakes, national forests, and provincial parks along roads with clusters of down-to-earth country towns.

The range is named for Scottish nobleman Thomas Douglas, the Fifth Earl of Selkirk, who encouraged and sponsored European settlement on Canada's western frontier. Long past its gold mining and fur trapping days, the Selkirks are now a haven for hiking, biking, water sports, and winter adventure.

Although there are a number of places where road trippers can join the Selkirk Loop, the official starting point on the American side is

A snowboarder makes fresh tracks in extreme terrain at Whitewater Resort.

**THE BIG PICTURE**

**Distance:** ca 280 miles (450.6 km) round-trip from Newport, WA

**Drive time:** 3-5 days

**Best overnights:** Newport, Nelson, Creston, Sandpoint

**Best seasons:** Anytime

**Highlights:** Pend Oreille River Valley, Colville National Forest, Nelson, Kootenay Lake, Lake Pend Oreille

**Newport**, which straddles the Washington-Idaho state line. Visit **Pend Oreille County Historical Museum** in the old train depot for a good overview of the region before hopping aboard the **Scenic Pend Oreille River Train** (summer and fall) for a 22-mile (35.4 km) return trip to Dalkena.

The loop kicks off with a drive down the Pend Oreille River Valley to **Tiger**. Named after its founder rather than a big cat, the town once thrived as a river port. Now all that's left is the 1913 **Tiger Store**, a combined museum, information center, and artisan gallery.

North of Tiger, State Route 20 doubles as the **North Pend Orielle Scenic Byway** through **Colville National Forest**. Along the way are turnoffs to **Sullivan Lake** and hiking trails that lead into the remote **Salmo-Priest Wilderness**, where bears, bighorn sheep, moose, and the last caribou herd in the lower 48 states roam eastern Washington's last old-growth forest.

After border formalities at **Nelway**, the Selkirk route traverses a remote region of British Columbia to **Nelson**, the largest town along the loop. Located on the western arm of vast **Kootenay Lake**, Nelson has morphed from a frontier mining

Lake Pend Oreille is Idaho's largest and deepest lake, with stunning forested surrounds and plenty to see and do along its shores.

and railroad town into a modern outdoor adventure hub with activities like lake fishing, paddling, and sailing and winter sports at nearby **Whitewater Resort**.

Leaping the lake on the Nelson Bridge, the loop continues along the north shore to Balfour and the **Kootenay Lake Ferry**—a half-hour crossing billed as North America's longest free ferry ride. Reaching **Kootenay Bay** on the far side, the road trip runs down the lake's main arm to **Lockhart Beach Provincial Park** (where you can take a dip in the chilly water) and the bizarre **Glass House**, made from 500,000 embalming fluid bottles.

After crossing the border at **Porthill**, the Selkirk follows the Kootenay River to **Bonners Ferry**, where the **Boundary County Museum** provides a glimpse of pioneer life and **Kootenai National Wildlife**

**Refuge** another chance to see moose, elk, bear, and other creatures.

U.S. Highway 2 carries the loop down the panhandle to the gorgeous north shore of **Lake Pend Oreille** and the town of **Sandpoint**, with beaches for swimming, paddling, and other water activities. Nearby

**Schweitzer Mountain** segues from snow sports in winter to hiking, biking, horseback riding, and huckleberry picking during the warmer spring and summer months.

Completing the loop, Highway 2 cruises along the north bank of the Pend Oreille River back to Newport. ■

## SCENIC DETOURS

• **Crowsnest Highway (BC 3):** The highway shoots west from Salmo to the Okanogan Valley and its copious wineries and gourmet eateries.

• **US/BC 95:** Starting from Copeland, Idaho, this transborder route traverses British Columbia's Kootenay River Valley to Radium Hot Springs and Kootenay National Park in the Canadian Rockies.

• **Balfour-Kaslo-Galena Bay Highway (BC 31):** This partially paved route through the Selkirk Range

connects Kootenay, Trout, Duncan, and Arrows lakes north of Balfour.

• **US Highway 2:** From Bonners Ferry, the highway cuts across Kootenai National Forest to Montana's Flathead Valley and Glacier National Park.

• **Spokane-Coeur d'Alene Loop:** Make the trip a figure-eight with a second loop that includes U.S. 2 from Newport to Spokane, I-90 to Coeur d'Alene, and U.S. 95 to Sandpoint.

# Rocky Mountain High(way)

## Montana & Wyoming

This classic national park road trip links Glacier in northern Montana with Yellowstone and Grand Teton in western Wyoming, a 600-mile (965.6 km) drive that includes some of the most spectacular scenery—and geological phenomena—on Earth.

Three of America's foremost national parks are linked along this route through the northern Rocky Mountains, a drive that includes glaciers and snowy peaks, large beasts roaming their natural habitats, geysers and hot springs, and hip little mountain towns.

There may not be a more breath-taking start to any drive in this book than cruising along the shore of **St. Mary Lake** in **Glacier National Park** at the break of dawn and watching the sunrise glimmer off the water, peaks, and ice fields that spread out before you. Along the lakeshore is **Two Dog Flats**, a patch of prairie where grizzly bears and

elk are often seen, especially in the early morning.

You can stick around and catch one of the **90-minute boat tours** that ply St. Mary Lake, take a short hike along the waterfront (including a 3.2-mile/5.2-km trail that takes in three waterfalls), or start the drive into the highlands. Constructed by the Civilian Conservation Corps (CCC) during the Great Depression, 50-mile (80.5 km) **Going-to-the-Sun Road** zigzags up and over the **Continental Divide**. At the top, 6,646-foot-high (2,025.7m) **Logan Pass** offers a visitor center, trails through the alpine landscape, and a chance to spot bighorn sheep or mountain goats.

Plunging down the western side of the divide, the route runs past long, lovely **Lake McDonald** and into the broad Flathead Valley, one of Montana's main agricultural areas and adventure playgrounds. With its trendy eateries, hip watering holes, and boutique hotels, **Whitefish** anchors the valley's north end. The former railroad town is a huge hub for outdoor sports, from skiing and snowboarding to trout fishing.

U.S. Highway 93 drops due south to **Kalispell** (take the bypass) and enormous **Flathead Lake**—its shore-line dotted with campgrounds and

Peek inside the J. K. Wells Hotel in the Garnet Ghost Town . . . if you dare.

Yellowstone's Grand Prismatic Spring, located in the Midway Geyser Basin, is the third largest hot spring in the world.

boat ramps. Beyond is **Flathead Indian Reservation** and the **National Bison Range**, where hundreds of buffalo roam the undulating landscape.

Rolling into **Missoula**, take a spin on the riverfront **carousel** and at the **Smokejumper Visitor Center**, find out how the Forest Service fights wildfires. Jumping onto Interstate 90, head 40 miles (64.4 km) east to Bearmouth and the turnoff for **Garnet Ghost Town**, a 19th-century gold mining settlement tucked into Last Chance Gulch.

Farther down the interstate is **Deer Lodge**, where the **Old Montana Prison** (opened in 1871) now houses five museums. At the north end of town, **Grant-Kohrs Ranch National Historic Site** honors the legacy of western cowboys and cattle ranchers at the headquarters of a spread that once embraced 10 million acres (4.05 million ha).

Just up the road is **Butte**, once the world's richest copper town. From the notorious **Dumas Brothel** (1890) and **Rookwood Speakeasy** (1912) to the lavish **Copper King Mansion** (1888), the historic district preserves more than 6,000 original structures. Visitors can join a guided tour of the **Orphan Girl Mine** at the **World Museum of Mining** or gaze into the mile-wide (1.6 km) **Berke-**

**ley Open Pit Mine** from a viewing stand along the rim. Out near the airport, **Mountain View Cemetery** is the last resting place of daredevil Evel Knievel, born and raised in Butte.

Continue along I-90 to **Three Forks**, where the Missouri River starts its long journey across the American heartland. The **Headwaters Heritage Museum**, **Missouri Headwaters State Park**, and **Lewis and**

## ART AVENUES

• **Best Movies:** *Shane* (1957); *The River Runs Through It* (1992); *Legends of the Fall* (1994)

• **Best TV Shows:** *Yellowstone* (2018) and *Longmire* (2012-17)

• **Best Books:** *The Horse Whisperer* (1995) by Nicholas Evans; the short story "Brokeback Mountain" by E. Annie Proulx; and the Glacier

National Park murder mystery *Blood Lure* (2001) by Nevada Barr

• **Best Music:** "Livingston Saturday Night" by Jimmy Buffett and John Mayer's *Paradise Valley* album

• **Best Art:** The Yellowstone paintings of Thomas Moran and Roland W. Reed's early 20th-century photos of Glacier National Park

**Clark Caverns** pay tribute to nature and the intrepid duo who crossed this point in 1805.

Exit the interstate at **Belgrade** and head south on U.S. Highway 191 through majestic **Gallatin River Canyon**. The river is world renowned for its gnarly whitewater, especially a stretch called the **Mad Mile** with Class IV rapids that challenge even veteran paddlers. Calmer stretches are celebrated for outstanding fly-fishing. During the winter, bighorn sheep are often seen crossing the highway. And just south of the canyon is **Big Sky Resort**, which morphs from mountain biking and zip lines in summer to radical downhill skiing and snowboarding come winter.

Another hour on Highway 191, and you're in **West Yellowstone**, one of the major gateways to the world's first and most famous national park. The town isn't everyone's cup of tea (it borders on being a tourist trap), but during the winter, it offers the best chance for exploring the park by **snowmobile and snow coach tours** offered by half a dozen outfitters. Learn more about two of the park's iconic species (and see them up close) at the nonprofit **Grizzly and Wolf Discovery Center**.

Crossing the state line into Wyoming, our Glacier-to-Grand Teton route follows Highway 191 through **Yellowstone National Park** with stops at iconic spots like the **Grand Prismatic Spring, Old Faithful Geyser**, and the western shore of **Yellowstone Lake**. But there are tons of other driving options inside the park—including the **Grand Loop Road**, a 142-mile (228.5 km) figure-eight route through the heart of the

The 308-foot-tall (93.9 m) Lower Falls can be seen from numerous spots within Yellowstone.

park that takes in **Yellowstone Falls** and the **Grand Canyon of the Yellowstone**, as well as the wildlife-rich **Hayden Valley** and **Lamar Valley, Mammoth Hot Springs**, and **Norris Geyser Field**.

Exiting Yellowstone at the park's south entrance, Highway 191/89 casually rolls into the **John D. Rockefeller Memorial Parkway**, a 24,000-acre (9,712.5 ha) federal reserve that connects Yellowstone and Grand Teton National Parks. The road runs beside the upper reach of the **Snake River**, through a habitat favored by both bear and moose.

By the time you reach **Jackson Lake**, you've crossed the line into **Grand Teton National Park** with its trademark granite peaks. Just past Jackson Lake Lodge, hang a left onto Teton Park Road, which takes you even deeper into the woods.

Rising almost straight up 7,000 feet (2,133.6 m) from the Snake River Valley, the granite **Tetons** are one of the nation's most impressive mountain ranges and a bucket-list summit for every serious climber. Mere mortals

can enjoy the views along the shore from Jackson Lake and nearby **Jenny Lake**. Take to the water on scenic cruises or guided fishing trips from **Coulter Bay Marina** or the little shuttle that chugs across Jenny Lake to trailheads on the west shore.

Dozens of outfitters offer gentle **float trips and guided fishing** on the Snake River through the park. Those who want to learn more about the Tetons' human heritage should browse the Vernon Collection of Native American artifacts at the **Craig Thomas Discovery and Visitor Center** and visit the **Menors Ferry Historic District**.

Highway 191/89 continues south into **Jackson Hole**, the toniest little town in the West, a one-time fur trapping center that now draws a steady stream of movie idols and rock stars. In addition to art galleries, gourmet restaurants, and recreational ski areas, Jackson Hole is home to the **National Museum of Wildlife Art**, an awesome exclamation point on a road trip that features so many wild things. ■

---

## EN ROUTE EATS

• **Tupelo Grille:** The wilds of northern Montana may seem like a strange place for Cajun food, but locally sourced fresh fish, meat, and produce make the gumbo taste awful good; 17 Central Ave. tupelogrille.com

• **Buffalo Cafe:** Down-to-earth dining in a no-frills place that Montana locals seem to dig just as much as the tourists; soup, salads, burgers, wraps, and bison meatloaf; 514 Third St. East. buffalocafewhitefish.com

• **Loula's:** Munch Montana's favorite dessert—huckleberry pie—straight up or mixed with peach, raspberry, or cherry; two dozen kinds of pie; 300 Second St. East. loulaswhitefish.com

• **Montana Coffee Traders:** Another Whitefish-local hangout, MCT is the place to grab your caffeine fix and morning munchies. 110 Central Ave. coffeetraders.com

• **Great Northern Brewing Co.:** Going to the Sun IPA, Good Med Montana Red Ale, and Wild Huckleberry Lager are just a few of the beers on tap at this popular Whitefish craft brewery; 2 Central Ave. greatnorthern brewing.com

• **Spotted Bear Spirits:** Locally distilled vodka, gin, and coffee liqueur fortify the cocktails at this hip boutique bar in Montana; 503 Railway St. spottedbearspirits.com

# Red Rock Route

## Arizona & Utah

Acclaimed as one of the world's most scenic drives, U.S. Highway 89 snakes its way through the red-rock wonderland of northern Arizona and southern Utah—with national parks, distinctive towns, historic sites, and jaw-dropping views along the way.

**THE BIG PICTURE**

**Distance:** 309 miles (497.3 km) from Sedona, AZ, to Bryce Canyon, UT

**Drive time:** 7-10 days

**Best overnights:** Flagstaff, Page, Kanab, Springdale

**Best seasons:** Anytime

**Highlights:** Flagstaff, Grand Canyon, Navajo Nation, Lake Powell, Zion, Bryce Canyon

Hundreds of millions of years ago, much of the Southwest was a vast inland sea. The sedimentary deposits formed during that ancient maritime era were eventually shaped by tectonic forces, volcanic events, and erosion into the red-rock fantasyland we have today.

Perched at the southern end of this drive, **Sedona, Arizona,** is world renowned for its scenery, arts scene, and New Age activities like yoga, meditation, and vortex hikes. Heading north from town, Highway 89 climbs through gorgeous **Oak Creek Canyon** and **Slide Rock State Park** to high-altitude **Flagstaff** (elevation 6,910 feet/ 2,106.2 m), a lively college town that also boasts the **Museum of Northern Arizona** and stargazing programs at **Lowell Observatory**.

Flagstaff makes a great base for exploring the area's natural and human wonders: the ancient ruins at **Wupatki** and **Walnut Canyon** National Monuments, the remarkable lava landscapes of **Sunset Crater**, and the gaping hole at **Meteor Crater**, as well as the denizens of **Bearizona Wildlife Park** in Williams. If you make the drive in the winter, there's skiing and snowboarding at **Arizona Snowbowl** at the base of 12,633-foot (3,850.5 m) **Humphreys Peak**.

Back on the road, Highway 89 crosses the aptly named **Painted Desert**, baptized by Spanish explorer Francisco Vásquez de Coronado and his men while searching for the legendary Seven Cities of Gold. By the time you reach **Cameron**—turnoff for the **South Rim** of the Grand Canyon—you have entered the **Navajo Nation**.

**Navajo shops and galleries** arrayed around the Cameron traffic circle feature a range of Native American artwork, jewelry, books, rugs, and ceramics, as well as interpretive exhibits on the Navajo people. The tiny visitor center at the crossroads offers information on Navajo Tribal Parks arrayed along Highway 89, including **Dinosaur Tracks, Coal Mine Canyon, Little Colorado River**, and **Antelope Canyon**.

Relaxing is easy with the red rocks of Sedona, Arizona, as your view.

Raft the Colorado River to see the dramatic, rocky landscapes it has carved over millennia.

Farther along, the highway splits at **Bitter Springs**. The left fork (89A) veers off in a westerly direction, bound for **Marble Canyon, Vermilion Cliffs National Monument**, and the **North Rim** of the Grand Canyon. Along the way is vertiginous Navajo Bridge (now pedestrian only), which dangles 467 feet (142.3 m) above the **Colorado River**. Far below is **Lees Ferry**, the main staging point for **float trips** through the Grand Canyon.

The main branch of Highway 89 continues north to **Lake Powell**, the shimmering centerpiece of **Glen Canyon National Recreation Area** along the flooded **Colorado River**. The park takes its name from Glen Canyon Dam, a massive concrete arch structure that towers 726 feet (221.3 m) above the river. **Hayden**

**Visitor Center** offers exhibits, maps, and ranger programs, while nearby **Wahweap Marina** is the place to rent watercraft or hop boat tours to **Rainbow Bridge National Monument.**

Crossing into Utah, Highway 89 curves to the west and eventually meets up with 89A again in **Kanab**, a hub for guided 4x4, all-terrain vehicle, and hiking tours to local landmarks like **Peek-A-Boo Slot Canyon**, **White Pocket**, the **Wave**, and the spectacular **Coral Pink Sand Dunes**.

Just north of Kanab, **Mount Carmel Junction** is the place to turn off for **Zion National Park**, a 40-minute drive via the Zion–Mount Carmel Tunnel, once the nation's longest road tunnel. Highway 89 continues into the bucolic

**Sevier River Valley** and turnoffs to **Cedar Breaks National Monument/ Brian Head Ski Resort** (Route 14) to **Bryce Canyon National Park** (Route 12). ∎

## OFF ROAD

• **Lake Powell:** In addition to boats, Wahweap Marina rents personal watercraft, paddleboards, kayaks, water skis, and wakeboards. lakepowell.com

• **Colorado River:** Float trips through the Grand Canyon on rubber rafts or wooden dories range anywhere from three days to nearly three weeks. Most trips depart from Lees Ferry. The National Park Service allows 16 outfitters to make this trip of a lifetime. nps.gov/grca/planyour visit/river-concessioners.htm

# Gila Trail
## Arizona & New Mexico

One of the routes less traveled through the American Southwest, this desert road trip traces the path of the old Gila Trail from New Mexico's Rio Grande Valley to the Colorado River in western Arizona.

### THE BIG PICTURE

**Distance:** ca 542 miles (872.3 km) from Truth or Consequences, NM, to Yuma, AZ

**Drive time:** 4-5 days

**Best overnights:** Silver City, Globe, Phoenix, Chandler

**Best seasons:** Winter, spring, or fall

**Highlights:** Truth or Consequences, Silver City, salsa trail, Globe, Phoenix, Yuma

The first thing everyone should learn about the Gila Trail is how to pronounce the name. The correct way is *Hee-la*—like the venomous lizard, the intermittent river, and that wind-blown town in the Arizona desert with so many gas stations (Gila Bend).

General Stephen Kearny and famed guide Kit Carson pioneered the trail in 1846 when they marched the Army of the West straight across the wilderness to expedite their invasion of California during the Mexican War.

Their starting point was the old Spanish town of Alamocitos on the Rio Grande—modern-day **Truth or Consequences** in New Mexico. The city's historic **Hot Springs Bathhouse District** and the Native American–oriented **Geronimo Springs Museum** are worth a look before heading west on State Highway 152.

The highway climbs from the **Chihuahuan Desert** into the wooded heights of **Gila National Forest** and **Emory Pass** with its lofty views back across the Rio Grande. Winding down from the mountains, the drive continues through the **Mimbres Valley** to **Silver City**. Apache raids and boomtown days are recalled at the **Silver City Museum**, while the **Western New Mexico University Museum** and nearby **Gila Cliff Dwellings National Monument** revolve around Native American cultures.

Traverse the headwaters of the Gila River on U.S. 180 and take a left onto State Route 78, which crosses into Arizona near the spot where Kearny and Carson did the same in 1846. Today the Upper Gila Valley is a hotbed of Arizona-Mexican cuisine, a **"salsa trail"** that includes the annual **September Salsa Fest** in Safford and the old **La Casita Café** in Globe. When you're not eating, hike the lush oasis trails of **Gila Box Riparian National Conservation Area** or wander the **Globe Historic District** with its architectural relics of the town's 19th-century copper boom.

West of Globe, Highway 60 cuts across a corner of **Tonto National Forest** that includes the **World's Smallest Museum** and **Boyce Thompson Arboretum** before skirting around the legendary **Superstition Mountains** into the **Phoenix** metropolitan area.

With attractions that range from the renowned **Heard Museum**, din-

New Mexico's Geronimo Springs Museum displays sculptures and murals.

The Gila Cliff Dwellings National Monument preserves the homes Mogollon people built into the cliffs in the 1200s.

ing at **Heritage Square,** and the **Roosevelt Row** arts district, to **South Mountain Park** hiking trails and futuristic **Taliesin West**, road trippers could easily linger for a week in Phoenix.

Or you can skip the urban experience, detouring around the city's south side via suburban Chandler and Maricopa and the Bureau of Land Management's **Sonoran Desert National Monument**. The cactus-studded route (State Highway 238) merges onto Interstate 8 at **Gila Bend**.

From there, it's 116 miles (186.7 km) of freeway driving down the **Gila River Valley** to the Colorado River and the crossing into California. Along the way is **Dateland Farm and Nursery**, where Medjool palms imported from Morocco in

the 1920s produce fruit for delicious shakes, butter, barbecue sauce, and other culinary treats.

Despite its repute at the epitome of a remote desert town, **Yuma** is

actually a lively little burg with an annual **Tunes and Tacos Festival** in April, tubing and boating on the **Colorado River**, and historical sights like **Yuma Territorial Prison**. ■

## SCENIC DETOURS

• **Coronado Trail:** This national scenic byway through the White Mountains of eastern Arizona runs past Aker Lake and 10,955-foot (3,339.1 m) Escudilla Mountain on a 164-mile (263.9 km) run between Safford and Springerville that also features 400 switchbacks.

• **Salt River Canyon Scenic Drive:** This 87-mile (140 km) stretch of U.S. 60 between Globe and Show Low in Arizona features a classic art deco bridge across the Salt River and the Fort Apache Reservation.

• **Apache Trail:** State Route 188 from Globe, Arizona, runs through Tonto National Forest to the cliff dwellings of Tonto National Monument, Teddy Roosevelt Lake, and Hellsgate Wilderness on the edge of the Mogollon Rim.

• **Arizona 85:** The route on Arizona 85 shoots south from Gila Bend into the heart of the Sonoran Desert and Organ Pipe Cactus National Monument with its namesake succulent and many other species of cacti.

# El Camino Real de Tierra Adentro

## Texas & New Mexico

New Mexico's Spanish colonial legacy and Native American heritage are the focus of this overland journey between El Paso, Texas, and Taos, New Mexico, following an ancient route along the upper Rio Grande Valley.

In the 1590s, conquistadors discovered an ancient trade route along the northern Rio Grande that Pueblo Indians had used for centuries to trade with Mesoamerican civilizations. The Spanish immediately recognized the path as an ideal way to colonize yet another part of the New World and christened it El Camino Real de Tierra Adentro—the Royal Road of the Interior Land. Then they set about sending soldiers, settlers, and clergy north to new settlements like Santa Fe. By the end of the 17th century, Spanish-style missions, military presidios, and haciendas serviced by *conducta* (loosely meaning "community in miniature") caravans from

**THE BIG PICTURE**

**Distance:** ca 472 miles (759.6 km) from El Paso, TX, to Taos, NM

**Drive time:** 7 days

**Best overnights:** Las Cruces, Albuquerque, Santa Fe, Taos

**Best seasons:** Anytime

**Highlights:** Las Cruces, Salinas Pueblo Missions, Albuquerque, Santa Fe, High Road, Taos

Mexico City had been built along the route.

As a western extension of the Santa Fe Trail, 19th-century American pioneers used the route to reach Arizona and California. By the 1920s, the road was paved and designated U.S. Highway 85, a status that endured until the 1960s when the interstates arrived.

And that's how this drive kicks off: a 90-mile (144.8-km) segment of Interstate 10 between El Paso, Texas, and **Las Cruces**, New Mexico. Despite its Spanish name, the city wasn't founded until 1849 and grew into a Mexican-American hybrid that today embraces both cultures. **Old Mesilla Village** preserves this heritage in the bars and restaurants set around a central plaza, the handsome **Basilica San Albino**, movies at the vintage **Fountain Theatre** (opened 1905), and the **Gadsden Museum** of local history, which includes a section dedicated to local antihero Billy the Kid.

Las Cruces pays further tribute to its Wild West days through the **New Mexico Farm and Ranch Heritage Museum**, with its living history and livestock program, cultural series, family activities, and historic collections. Part of that farming legacy is the **chile pepper**, introduced by Spanish settlers more than 400 years

A large flock of snow geese gather at Bosque del Apache National Wildlife Refuge.

Santa Fe's Cathedral Basilica of St. Francis of Assisi houses the oldest representation of the Virgin Mary in the United States.

ago. Since then, New Mexico has evolved a number of its own cultivars, including the famous Hatch chile of the Las Cruces region. No one should pass through Las Cruces without sampling the local specialty, either in restaurants or at the twice-weekly **Farmers and Crafts Market of Las Cruces**.

El Camino Real continues north along the Rio Grande to **Fort Selden** (established in 1865 to protect settlers from Apache raids) and oddly named **Truth or Consequences**. Originally called Alamocitos and Hot Springs, the town changed its name in 1950 to the title of a popular radio game show. Hot springs are still the main attraction at **modern mineral spas** arrayed along the Rio Grande or in the downtown **Hot Springs Bathhouse District**.

About an hour beyond Truth or Consequences lie the ruins of **Fort Craig**, a Union stronghold during the Civil War. The visitor center exhibits spin tales of Geronimo, Kit Carson, Buffalo Soldiers, and the nearby Battle of Valverde, an 1862 clash between Yankee troops and a Rebel army bent on bringing New Mexico into the Confederacy.

Nature is the main attraction along the Camino Real on either side of Socorro. **Bosque del Apache National Wildlife Refuge** features both Rio Grande wetlands and Chihuahuan Desert that's especially lively in the fall when sandhill cranes, Arctic geese, and thousands of other birds pay a visit.

## PIT STOPS

• **Santa Fe Summer Art Markets:** Hispanic, Native American, folk, and contemporary art are on display during 10 different festivals staged between May and August. santafe.org

• **Taos Pueblo Powwow:** Indian dance groups from around the nation compete in this July festival of Native American culture, crafts, and cuisine. taos.org/events/taos pueblo-pow-wow

• **Hatch Valley Chile Festival:** Food booths, cooking contests, mariachi music, and crowning of the Chile Queen flavor this September fiesta near Las Cruces dedicated to the region's famous pepper. hatchchilefest.com

• **Albuquerque International Balloon Fiesta:** More than 500 balloons transform this week-long October event into the world's largest assemblage of hot air. balloonfiesta.com

Amble through art galleries and historic buildings in Albuquerque's colorful Old Town Plaza.

On the western side of the river, **Sevilleta National Wildlife Refuge** protects a broad expanse of desert, grasslands, and woodlands inhabited by pronghorn antelope, prairie dogs, deer, coyotes, and many bird species.

Just north of Sevilleta, the road trip takes a temporary detour away from Rio Grande Valley. U.S. Highway 60 leads to **Mountainair** and the visitor center for **Salinas Pueblo Missions National Monument**. Constructed between 1622 and 1625, the ruined **Abó**, **Gran Quivira**, and **Quarai** missions are among the state's oldest European structures— although truth be told, the architecture is far more reminiscent of pueblo design than anything Iberian.

Back along the Rio Grande, the interstate speeds north to **Albuquerque**, a bygone Spanish settlement (founded in 1706) that has grown

---

**SCENIC DETOURS**

• **U.S. Highway 70** from Las Cruces to Alamogordo expedites visits to the White Sands Missile Test Range Museum, White Sands National Monument, and the New Mexico Museum of Space History.

• **State Road 502** heads west from Pojoaque to the Los Alamos atomic bomb sites, Bandelier National Monument, and Valles Caldera National Preserve.

• **Turquoise Trail** is a national scenic byway that links the old gold mining towns of Golden, Madrid, and Cerrillos along a 50-mile (80.5 km) "back way" between Albuquerque and Santa Fe.

• **State Road 522** runs north from Taos to the D. H. Lawrence Ranch, Wild Rivers Recreation Area on the Rio Grande, and historic San Luis, Colorado.

---

into the state's largest city. **Old Town Plaza** is the hub of a historic district strewn with restaurants, art galleries, curio shops, and heritage buildings, as well as the **Albuquerque Museum** and the **New Mexico Museum of Natural History**.

Road trippers can stretch their legs by hiking the **Paseo del Bosque Trail** along the Rio Grande; a path also meanders past the **Albuquerque Botanic Gardens** and **ABQ BioPark Aquarium and Zoo**. On the eastern outskirts, a **tramway** rises to the crest of 10,378-foot (3,163.2 m) **Sandia Peak** for a bird's-eye view of the Rio Grande Valley and the rugged hiking trails of **Cibola National Forest**.

**Santa Fe** is just an hour up the interstate from Albuquerque. The city's heady blend of Hispanic, Native American, and American influence fuels a cultural scene that reverberates far beyond New Mexico in everything from art and architecture to clothing and cuisine.

Founded in 1610, a full decade before the Pilgrims landed at Plymouth Rock, Santa Fe is by far the nation's oldest state capital. But ironically, the **State Capitol** building is one of the newest, dedicated in 1966 and based on the design of the Zia sun symbol. The Old Santa Fe Trail links the capitol with **Museum Hill** and its eclectic cultural offerings: the **Museum of Spanish Colonial Art**, the **Museum of International Folk Art**, and two **American Indian museums**, as well as the **Santa Fe Botanical Garden**.

North of the **Santa Fe River parkway** is the old town, a mix of Spanish colonial and American frontier-era buildings arrayed around **Santa Fe Plaza**. The 17th-century **Palace of the Governors** houses the **New Mexico History Museum** and several thousand years of local artifacts. **St. Francis Cathedral** (dedicated in 1886) safeguards the nation's oldest Madonna

while the neo-Gothic **Loretto Chapel** (1878) features a celebrated helix-shaped staircase.

Santa Fe also has its modern side, personified by trendy **Canyon Road** with its upscale art galleries and gourmet eateries, as well as the **Meow Wolf** interactive art attraction and **Santa Fe Opera** with its futuristic **Cosby Theatre**

overlooking the desert on the northern edge of town.

Exiting the capital on U.S. Highway 285, the El Camino route continues to **Española** (founded in 1598 as the first Spanish settlement in New Mexico) and the **High Road** to Taos. Meandering 57 miles (91.7 km) through the **Sangre de Cristo** mountains, the scenic byway passes through pueblo villages and Spanish colonial settlements like **Chimayo, Truchas, Trampas,** and **Peñasco**.

High-altitude **Taos** is renowned for one of the most famous structures in the Southwest. Constructed between A.D. 1000 and 1450 and continuously occupied since then, **Taos Pueblo** is living history. Around 150 Taos Indians live in the towering adobe structure, a UNESCO World Heritage site.

The adjacent Spanish American town revolves around **Taos Plaza**, flanked by art galleries and throwbacks like the **Kit Carson House** and **Governor Bent Museum**. The homes of Taos-based artists like **Ernest Blumenschein, Burt Harwood**, and **Nicolai Fechin** are now museums. ■

Sandia Peak Tramway whisks you to an overlook of the Rio Grande Valley.

# Heart of Texas Highway

## Texas

A journey through many of the landscapes and legends that make Texas special, U.S. Highway 90—between Houston and El Paso—follows a pioneer-era path through the Hill Country and Big Bend to the banks of the Rio Grande.

Anxious to reach the California gold rush, in the 1840s Texans blazed a westward trail to link Houston, San Antonio, and other South Texas cities with the Gila Trail (page 64) and other west coast routes. For more than 30 years, the Lower Emigration Road, or Military Road, as it was called, was the main means of travel from one end of the Lone Star State to the other. Scores of wagon trains, stagecoaches, military patrols, and desperadoes trekked the dusty route before railroads eventually sidelined the famous trail.

Today, U.S. Highway 90 more or less traces the historic road. Although superseded by I-10 in recent times, the older highway offers a glimpse of Texas past that you can't get from the modern interstate.

Gleaming high-rise-filled **Houston** preserves little of its pioneer roots. But here and there, the past seeps through in places like the **Bayou Bend Collection and**

**Gardens**, which is set around a plantation-style mansion with 28 showrooms displaying American decorative arts from 1620 through 1876. Its must-see **Texas Room and Alcove** features objects made by 1850s German immigrants, African-American stoneware pottery, and ceramics honoring Texas independence.

Those who are interested in Texas history should also pay a visit to the **San Jacinto Museum and Monument** on the outskirts of Houston, where the final battle to achieve Texas independence from Mexico played out in 1836. The **battleship U.S.S. Texas**, which saw action in both world wars, is docked along nearby Buffalo Bayou. Another worthwhile historic stop is the **George Ranch Historical Park**, a combination living history museum and working ranch that covers 100 years of Texas history in four home sites including an 1830s pioneer farm.

Rather than taking main U.S. 90 (which hugs the interstate), exit Houston on U.S. 90 Alternate through Sugar Land and Rosenberg. Two hours of driving past farmland and ranchland takes you to **Gonzales.** Founded in 1825 as one of the first Anglo-American settlements in a Mexican territory, the city was famously burned to the ground by

A cowboy rounds up his cattle in George Ranch Historical Park.

## THE BIG PICTURE

**Distance:** ca 970 miles (1,561.1 km) from Houston to El Paso

**Drive time:** 8-10 days

**Best overnights:** Gonzales, San Antonio, Del Rio, Big Bend, Alpine, Marfa

**Best seasons:** Anytime

**Highlights:** Gonzales, San Antonio, Lake Amistad, Big Bend, Alpine, Marfa

The 15-mile (24.1 km) San Antonio Riverwalk connects the Alamo to other sites like the Museum Reach at historic Pearl.

revolutionary army commander in chief Sam Houston to keep it from falling to General Santa Anna during the war for independence.

Eventually rebuilt into a fine Victorian town, Gonzalez's rich history is evident through sights like **Texas Heroes Square**, the **Old Jail Museum**, **Pioneer Village Living History Center**, a number of historic houses, and the **Gonzales Memorial Museum**, where the Texas War of Independence collection includes the celebrated "Come and Take It" cannon that fired the first shot of the revolution.

San Antonio is another hour up the road. While the **Alamo** is the undisputed champ of the city's historic sites, there are plenty of other relics. Right across the street from the celebrated mission-fort is the historic **Menger Hotel**, which has hosted a dozen U.S. presidents since opening in 1857. Dark and brooding, the **Menger Bar** is where

Teddy Roosevelt recruited (and entertained) many of his Rough Riders before the Spanish-American War.

You can now hike, bike, or even kayak from downtown to historic sites along the San Antonio River thanks to a new 8-mile (12.9 km) extension of the popular **San Antonio Riverwalk** called the Mission Reach. Meandering through riparian woodland, the route leads to **Villa Finale Museum and Gardens**, the **Steves Homestead Museum**, the new **Blue Star** arts and eating complex in old riverside industrial buildings, and finally **San Antonio Missions National Historic Park**, a UNESCO World Heritage site that preserves five 18th-century Spanish missions.

From San Antonio, Highway 90 runs due west through the southern **Hill Country** and its mesquite wilds to **Uvalde**. The town started life as Fort Inge, a U.S. Army outpost that

functioned as the jumping-off spot for the Lower Emigrant Road and the dangers (like Comanche raids and Mexican bandits) that lay beyond. The fort is long gone, but Uvalde's blasts from the past include the 1890s **Grand Opera House** (which still hosts plays and concerts) and the **Briscoe-Garner Museum**, dedicated to former Texas governor Dolph Briscoe and U.S. vice president "Texas" Jack Garner.

Beyond Uvalde, U.S. 90 makes a beeline for **Del Rio** and road trippers' first contact with the Rio Grande River. **Whitehead Memorial Museum** is actually a small pioneer village in the middle of town, which features nine historic buildings and the grave of Judge Roy Bean and his lawman son. Truth be told, Del Rio doesn't do much with its riverfront, although you can cross the bridge into Ciudad Acuña, Mexico. However, just north of town is **Amistad National Recreation Area**. Created in the 1960s when the Rio Grande was dammed, **Lake Amistad** sprawls along 83 miles (133.6 km) of the river valley and the U.S.-Mexico border. It's myriad recreational options range from boating, swimming, and scuba diving to camping, hiking, and excellent birding.

The highway crosses Lake Amistad on the **Governor's Landing Bridge** and continues up the Rio Grande Valley to **Langtry**. Larger-than-life Judge Roy Bean dispensed "Law West of the Pecos" for nearly 20 years from the front porch of his **Jersey Lilly Saloon**. The ramshackle saloon and nearby "opera house" built by Bean constitute the town's **Judge Roy Bean Visitor Center**.

It's a long, lonely, two-hour drive

Ancient limestone canyons provide a stunning vista in Big Bend National Park.

across the arid Edwards Plateau to **Marathon** and a left turn onto Highway 385 for **Big Bend National Park**. One of the nation's largest and most rugged national parks, Big Bend offers an enticing blend of river, mountains, and desert that's changed little since Wild West days. Rafting and kayaking float trips on the **Rio Grande** take anywhere from half a day to three weeks. Hiking can range from short jaunts like the **Hot Springs Historic Trail** (1.1 miles/1.8 km) to month-long wanders through the Big Bend wilderness.

Exit the park via the Maverick Junction entrance station and cruise Highway 118 to **Alpine**. There's nothing faintly "alpine" about this

---

### SCENIC DETOURS

• **U.S. Highway 183** heads south from Gonzales to historic Goliad, with its historic Spanish mission and presidio and famous Hanging Tree.

• **U.S. Highway 87** runs north from San Antonio through the heart of the Texas Hill Country to Fredericksburg and the LBJ Ranch, National Historical Park, and State Park and Historic Site.

• **U.S. Highway 277** shoots north from Del Rio onto the Edwards Plateau and Devil's River State Natural Area, where paddlers challenge the wild and scenic river.

• **The River Road (FM-170)** connects Big Bend National Park with Lajitas and Presidio, most of the route along the Rio Grande through Big Bend Ranch State Park.

• **U.S. Highway 62** leads east from El Paso to Guadalupe Mountain and Carlsbad Caverns National Parks.

---

high desert town. But there are plenty of antique shops and art galleries, the excellent **Museum of the Big Bend**, and minor league baseball at Kokernot Field, courtesy of the **Alpine Cowboys** of the Pecos League.

Back on Highway 90, it's just a 30-minute drive to another funky West Texas town. **Marfa** is renowned for its mysterious nighttime lights (allegedly caused by aliens) and a lively cultural scene that includes the sprawling **Chinati Foundation** museum and the **Block**, the home and studio of minimalist artist Donald Judd.

A 20-minute side trip from Marfa or Alpine, **Fort Davis National Historic Site** is the best surviving example of the outposts that once lined the Lower Emigrant Road. Nearby are the **Chihuahuan Desert Nature Center and Botanical Gardens** and **McDonald Observatory** with its star parties and other astronomy activities.

Reaching Van Horn, Highway 90 segues into Interstate 10 for the rest of the drive into **El Paso**, three hours from Marfa if you cruise straight through. Although it was founded in 1680 as a small Spanish settlement, virtually nothing remains from colonial days other than **Ysleta del Sur Pueblo**, the oldest continuously active church in Texas.

El Paso's renown as the "Six Shooter Capital" of the Wild West is reflected in the **San Elizario Jail Museum** (which Billy the Kid broke *into* while liberating a gang member), the **General Pershing House** at Fort Bliss, and the 1875 **Magoffin Home State Historic Site**. **Concordia Cemetery**—El Paso's version of Boot Hill—is also a state historic site. Among the outlaws buried there is John Wesley Hardin. ■

# Trail of the Ancients

## CO, AZ, UT & NM

Spangled with archaeological sites and stunning red-rock scenery, this loop through the fabled Four Corners region of the American Southwest offers a fascinating insight into the ancient people who once occupied one of the country's most astonishing landscapes.

**THE BIG PICTURE**

**Distance:** ca 350 miles (563.3 km) round-trip from Cortez, CO

**Drive time:** 4-5 days

**Best overnights:** Cortez, Monument Valley, Bluff, Mesa Verde

**Best seasons:** Spring, fall, or winter

**Highlights:** Monument Valley, Bears Ears, Hovenweep, Canyons of the Ancients, Mesa Verde

When asked about archaeology, most folks think of Egypt or the Andes. But the United States boasts its own rich and wondrous archaeological heartland: the Four Corners region that various Native American peoples have called home for at least 10,000 years.

The Trail of the Ancients Scenic Byway links a number of the region's most significant archaeological sites, a mosaic of cliff dwellings, pueblos, and petroglyphs along a looping journey across the Colorado Plateau.

The **Cortez Cultural Center** in the Colorado city of the same name offers an excellent entrée to the road trip. Lodged inside a 1909 pueblo-style building, the center features exhibits on the region's ancient Puebloans (Anasazi) and current Native American nations, as well as

American Indian dances and story-telling in the summer, and indoor lectures and musical programs between September and May.

Road trippers can start the drive along three different routes from Cortez, including a 40-mile (64.4 km) run down to **Four Corners Monument**—the only place in the United States where four states meet at one point and a favorite selfie spot. On the way down, detour into the **Ute Mountain Tribal Park**, where guided tours lead to previously inaccessible cliff dwellings and rock art galleries.

Cruising into the **Navajo Nation** in northeastern Arizona, the route leads to the celebrated red-rock buttes of **Monument Valley**—Tsé' Bii' Ndzisgaii, in the language of its Navajo caretakers. Immortalized in the movies of John Ford and John Wayne, the valley offers a quintessential Southwest landscape, which visitors explore via a **17-mile (27.4 km) scenic loop road** or guided **4x4 tours**.

U.S. Highway 163 crosses the border into Utah and another huge selfie spot—**Forrest Gump Point**—where a popular scene from the beloved 1994 movie was filmed. The town of **Mexican Hat** (named for a rock formation) offers access to geological landmarks like the **Goose-**

Take a selfie standing in four states at once at the Four Corners Monument.

Along the 17-mile (27.4 km) Valley Drive, see the magnificent sandstone buttes that make up Arizona's Monument Valley.

necks of the **San Juan River** and **Valley of the Gods**.

Farther along, Highway 163 crosses **Bears Ears National Monument**, a new federal reserve that sparked controversy when it was created in 2016 by President Barack Obama and then reduced in size a year later by President Donald Trump. The park's southernmost portion includes the impressive **River House** cliff dwelling and portions of the historic **Hole-in-the-Wall Trail**, as well as the nearby **Sand Island Petroglyph Panel**.

The scenic byway continues to **Hovenweep National Monument**, which harbors six ancient Puebloan sites, including the three-story **Square Tower**. Leaping back into Colorado, the route passes through **Canyons of the Ancients**, a Bureau of Land Management national monument that protects more than 6,300 ruins—the highest density of

archaeological sites anywhere in North America. The **Anasazi Heritage Center** in Dolores (the park's visitor center and museum) offers interpretive displays, curator tours, and stargazing programs.

The final stop on the road trip is probably the most spectacular: **Mesa Verde National Park** in the pine-shaded heights above Cortez. Among the mesa's 600 cliff dwellings are iconic structures like the extenuated **Long House**, the vertigo-inducing **Balcony House**, and a masterpiece of ancient Puebloan architecture, the **Cliff Palace**. ∎

## SCENIC DETOURS

• **Moki Dugway:** It's only three miles (4.8 km) long, but this series of unpaved switchbacks carved into the western edge of Utah's Cedar Mesa near Mexican Hat offers one of America's most adrenaline-packed driving experiences.

• **Utah Route 95:** Between Blanding and Natural Bridges National Monument, the highway traverses the middle of Bears Ears National Monument and sights like the Butler Wash Ruins, Mule Canyon, and Salvation Knoll.

• **U.S. Highway 191:** Starting from Utah's Sand Island on the San Juan River, this remote route crosses the Navajo Nation in Utah and Arizona to the ancient cliff dwellings and gorgeous red-rock landscapes of Canyon de Chelly National Monument.

• **Colorado Highway 145:** The 76-mile (122.3 km) drive from Cortez to Telluride offers a never-ending panorama of Colorado's snow-capped peaks and deep forest that's especially attractive in the fall.

# Southern Arizona Circle

## Arizona

Tucson provides the jumping-off spot for this 450-mile (724.2 km) wander across the desert basins and mountain ranges of southern Arizona, an odyssey that ranges between Spanish missions and old silver towns, Native American riches, and Mother Nature's treasures.

The saguaro cactus–studded landscape of southern Arizona came into the Union in 1854 via the Gadsden Purchase. By then, it had been the homeland of indigenous people for several thousand years and under the Spanish and Mexican flags for a full century.

Americans didn't waste any time putting their own stamp on the land, building copper and silver mining boomtowns that were more renowned for gunslingers, outlaws, and cattle rustlers than any riches dug from the ground.

While people tend to think of the entire region as desert, the landscape is just as mottled as the region's history, a blend of desert, grasslands, riparian habitats, and mountain woodlands where the weather can range from triple-digit temperatures to winter snowstorms.

**Tucson** provides the perfect launching point for this expedition into Arizona's deep south. Start with

### THE BIG PICTURE

**Distance:** ca 390 miles (627.6 km) round-trip from Tucson

**Drive time:** 5-6 days

**Best overnights:** Willcox, Bisbee, Tombstone, Sierra Vista, Tubac

**Best seasons:** Anytime

**Highlights:** Fort Bowie, Chiricahua National Monument, Bisbee, Tombstone, Arizona wine country, Tumacácori, Tubac, San Xavier del Bac

the awesome **Arizona-Sonora Desert Museum**. Mirroring local diversity, the museum is a combination zoo, aquarium, botanical garden, art institute, and natural history collection that interprets the area's natural history to near perfection.

Two great parks flank the desert museum. To the north, the Tucson Mountain District of **Saguaro National Park** renders hiking trails through the vast cactus garden to Native American petroglyphs and incredible places to watch sunsets over the Sonoran Desert. To the south, **Tucson Mountain Park** protects similar habitats and offers even more outdoor adventures, plus the added attraction of **Old Tucson Studios**, a frontier film set where a number of celebrated western movies and TV shows have been shot since the 1930s.

After exploring Tucson's west side parks, head east on Interstate 10 to Willcox. The drive takes a little more than an hour. There are places to stop along the way like the **Pima Air and Space Museum** with its 300 historic aircraft and tours of the U.S. Air Force **"boneyard"** of mothballed military planes.

When you reach **Benson**, detour down to the beautiful limestone

Find a historic Grumman F-14A Tomcat at the Pima Air and Space Museum.

Chiricahua National Monument offers a paved eight-mile (12.9 km) drive and 17 miles (27.4 km) of hiking trails.

show cave at **Kartchner Caverns State Park**. Farther up the interstate, the **Amerind Museum** in Dragoon revolves around the art, ethnology, and archaeology of Native American peoples.

Slide off the freeway in Willcox onto State Route 186. If you don't mind driving on dirt surfaces, there's another great detour along this stretch: an eight-mile (12.9 km) drive along Apache Pass Road to **Fort Bowie National Historic Site**. Constructed in the 1860s, the adobe bastion was on the frontline of the U.S. Army's conflict with the Chiricahua Apache under their great leaders Cochise and Geronimo. A 1.5-mile (2.4 km) walking trail leads to a visitor center, fort ruins, and **Butterfield Stage Station**.

Back on Route 186, it's only 11 miles (17.7 km) to the turnoff for **Chiricahua National Monument**, an extraordinary "wonderland of

rocks" best explored by foot or road. An eight-mile (12.9 km) scenic drive and 17 miles (27.4 km) of hiking trails weave between hoodoos, oddly balanced boulders, and stands of cypress and pine along the western edge of the Chiricahua Mountains. One of the nation's oldest national monuments (established 1924) also includes the **Faraway Ranch Historic District**. Chiricahua is the only unit of the National Park System that lists the jaguar as one of its native species, although you're not likely to spot one.

Back on the highway, follow 186 to Sunizona and hang a left onto U.S. Highway 191 along the eastern side of **Whitewater Draw** where the remains of prehistoric mammoths and Archaic human culture were discovered at the **Double Adobe** archaeological district. Opposite Bisbee Douglas Airport, turn right on Double Adobe Road and follow it

23 miles (37 km) due west to **Bisbee**.

Founded in 1880, Bisbee flourished on copper, silver, gold, and

### SCENIC DETOURS

• **Tucson-Ajo Highway** (State Route 86) runs across the Tohono O'odham Nation to Kitt Peak National Observatory and Organ Pipe Cactus National Monument.

• **State Route 80** from Bisbee heads east to Douglas, the place where Geronimo surrendered, and the Chiricahua Desert Museum in New Mexico.

• **Sky Island Parkway** (Catalina Highway) links Tucson and the summit of 9,159-foot (2,791.7 m) Mount Lemmon in Coronado National Forest.

• **State Route 77** shoots due north from Tucson to Catalina State Park and Biosphere 2.

turquoise. The boom days are recalled at the 900-foot-deep (274.3 m) **Lavender Pit**, the **Bisbee Mining and Historical Museum**, and during underground tours of the **Copper Queen Mine**. Among the town's architectural gems are the art deco **Cochise County Courthouse, Copper Queen Hotel**,

and the bygone buildings along **Erie Street**.

State Route 80 leads half an hour north to an even more famous Arizona boomtown. **Tombstone** also flourished in the 1880s on the back of mines that produced more than $40 to $85 million in silver. But the town is best known for its

gunslingers—in particular, Wyatt Earp and his brothers—and their legendary 1881 shootout at the O.K. Corral.

Today Tombstone makes a living from tourism, including stagecoach rides, mine tours, and reenactments of the famous gunfight, as well as saloons and shopping along Wild West–style **Allen Street**. Among the town's many landmarks are **Boothill Graveyard**, the **Bird Cage Theatre**, and the *Tombstone Epitaph* newspaper office. Yeah, it's touristy, but in a charming, laid-back manner that revolves around history rather than kitsch.

For a complete change of pace, head west on State Route 82 to the **Arizona wine country** around the towns of **Sonoita** and **Elgin**. Although grapes were introduced by Spanish friars 400 years ago, the currently trendy wine region didn't

Gearing up for a gunfight, reenactors re-create a shootout at the O.K. Corral in Tombstone, Arizona.

The museum at Tucson's Mission San Xavier del Bac showcases its unique history.

come along until the 1980s, when the Sonoita American Viticulture Area was established. Many of the best tasting rooms are right along 82, including hilltop **Rune Wines**, family-run **Arizona Hops and Vines**, and **Dos Cabezas Wine-Works** with its innovative carbonated pink canned wine.

Route 82 threads the mountains to **Patagonia**, where the Tucson Audubon Society's **Paton Center for Hummingbirds** and **Sonoita Creek State Natural Area** offer excellent opportunities to study the desert flora and fauna.

You can continue on 82 into border-town **Nogales** or take a short-cut on River Road (opposite the 1920s **Little Red Schoolhouse**) and Ruby Road to Interstate 19. From there, it's a straight shot back to Tucson through the **Santa Cruz River Valley** along the route of the 17th-century Spanish El Camino Real.

There is plenty of history and culture along the way, starting with **Tumacácori National Historical Park**. Established by Jesuits in 1691,

Tumacácori and its three missions were a melting pot of Spanish and Native American cultures for more than 150 years. The ruined chapels are now the centerpiece of a small but very active park that features guided tours, cultural demonstrations, night sky programs, fiestas, and hikes along the **Juan Bautista de Anza National Historic Trail**.

The trail (and freeway frontage road) leads 3.5 miles (5.6 km) north to **Tubac Presidio State Historic Park**, which preserves the remains of an 18th-century Spanish military compound and three pioneer-era buildings. Arizona's oldest state park also offers eight **themed gardens** and the **Tubac Presidio Museum** that traces 2,000 years of local history.

Along the final leg of I-19 into Tucson, the **Titan Missile Museum** offers underground Cold War tours of the nation's only Titan II missile silo open to the public. Farther along is **Asarco Mineral Discovery Center**, which offers tours of an active open-pit copper mine.

The final stop on this loop around Arizona's southern desert is one of the best: **Mission San Xavier del Bac** on the southern fringe of Tucson. Built between 1783 and 1797, the parish church of the San Xavier Indian Reservation is a masterpiece of Spanish colonial art and architecture that features a gorgeous whitewashed facade, a baroque altar, and 17th-century frescoes. ∎

## PIT STOPS

• **Cochise County Cowboy Poetry and Music Gathering:** In February, Sierra Vista hosts this annual tribute to cowpoke words and songs; includes a barn dance and treasure hunt. cowboypoets.com

• **Tucson Festival of Books:** More than 150,000 people gather at the University of Arizona campus for one of the nation's largest literary gatherings every February. tucson festivalofbooks.org

• **Wa:k Pow Wow:** This March celebration of Native American song, dance, food, art, and crafts, hosted by the Tohono O'odham Nation,

takes place at the San Xavier del Bac Mission. visittucson.org

• **Rose Festival:** Tombstone celebrates the April blooming of a rose tree planted in 1886 with western-style music, food, and a grand parade down Allen Street. tomb stonerosetree.com

• **Bisbee 1000 The Great Stair Climb:** Competitors take on nine staircases—more than 1,000 steps—on a 4.5-mile (7.2 km) course that winds through the old mining town every September; includes an ice-block carrying competition. bisbee1000.org

# Around the Grand Canyon
## Nevada, Arizona & Utah

One of the nation's best national park road trips is an 800-mile (1,287.5 km) loop around the Grand Canyon that includes both the North and South Rims, the only place you can drive to the bottom of the canyon, and six national parks, monuments, and recreation areas along the way.

In Wild West days, the only way to circumnavigate the Grand Canyon (by foot, horse, or wagon) was by hopping aboard a small wooden boat at Lees Ferry above the canyon or Pearce Ferry beyond its lower extreme—and hoping the Colorado River was calm enough to survive the crossing. But with the completion of Navajo Bridge in the late 1920s and the Hoover Dam in 1936, it became possible to drive around the entire Grand Canyon for the first time in cars, without navigating dangerous waters.

This journey has various starting points, but the most convenient (in terms of air connections and rental car options) is **Las Vegas, Nevada**. You may or may not want to linger in Sin City, but if you do, the Nevada metropolis offers a lot more than gambling. It's actually one of the nation's best places for museum hopping, with no fewer than 75 collections of one sort or another,

including the **National Atomic Testing Museum** and the **Nevada State Museum, Las Vegas**, which covers very different aspects of the region's natural and human heritage.

Several roads (including Interstate 515) lead south from Vegas into the Nevada desert and **Hoover Dam**. Called Boulder Dam when it was originally opened, the giant concrete arch-gravity dam is still considered a wonder of modern engineering as well as a masterpiece of art deco design. You can browse exhibits at the **Hoover Dam Visitor Center,** descend into the bowels of the massive structure on a **power plant tour**, or walk across the new **Mike O'Callaghan–Pat Tillman Memorial Bridge**, which hovers 900 feet (274.3 m) above Black Canyon and the Colorado River just downstream from the dam.

From the dam's south side, U.S. Highway 93 runs arrow-straight across the Arizona desert to **Kingman** and a confluence with Interstate 40. From there, it's another 114 miles (183.5 km) to **Williams** and the turnoff to **Grand Canyon Village**.

Road trippers can cruise all the way through to the South Rim in around four hours. Or make an entire day of this leg by visiting the **Grand Canyon Skywalk** on the Hualapai tribal lands near Kingman.

For those who don't want to hike, mule rides are offered along the South Rim.

**THE BIG PICTURE**

**Distance:** ca 780 miles (1,255.3 km) round-trip from Las Vegas

**Drive time:** 7-14 days

**Best overnights:** Williams, South Rim, North Rim, Page, Springdale, St. George

**Best seasons:** Anytime (other than the North Rim)

**Highlights:** Hoover Dam, Grand Canyon, Navajo Bridge, Vermilion Cliffs, Zion

Tour the Hoover Dam, a magnificent feat of engineering dedicated by President Franklin D. Roosevelt in 1935.

In addition to a glass pedestrian bridge that hangs 4,000 feet (1,219.2 m) above the canyon, the Hualapai offer **helicopter and pontoon boat trips** through the gorge.

Another worthwhile detour is the **Bearizona**, a drive-through wildlife park near Williams that offers close encounters of the critter kind with bears, wolves, bison, bighorn sheep, and other western wildlife. Just off State Route 64 between Williams and the canyon, the **National Geographic Visitor Center Grand Canyon** offers an IMAX theater with large-screen movies and exhibits on the canyon, as well as airplane, helicopter, four-wheel-drive, and river tours.

**Grand Canyon Village** anchors the South Rim with a variety of indoor and outdoor attractions, including the national park's main **Visitor Center**, a national historic landmark district that harbors architectural gems like the **El Tovar Hotel** and **Hopi House**, and legendary viewpoints like **Mather Point** and **Hermits Rest**.

One of the best things about the South Rim is that you don't have to drive everywhere. You can park your car in the visitor center lot and hop shuttle buses to most of the main sights along the South Rim, walk all or part of the 13-mile (20.9 km) **Rim Trail**, or rent a bike and cycle the **Tusayan Greenway** or **Hermit Road**. The village is also the jumping-off point for hikes or guided mule treks into the canyon along the **Bright Angel Trail** and **South Kaibab Trail**.

Once you've had your fill of the village, take a slow cruise along 22-mile (35.4 km) **Desert View Drive** to other fabulous canyon panoramas at spots like **Yaki Point,**

## ART AVENUES

- **Best Books:** *Down the Great Unknown* by Edward Dolnick and *The Man Who Walked Through Time* by Colin Fletcher

- **Best Art:** The 1880s landscapes of William Henry Holmes and the black-and-white photos of Edward Weston and Ansel Adams

- **Best Poetry:** *Grand Canyon Search Ceremony* by Philip Wofford

- **Best Architecture:** Mary Colter's early 20th-century Grand Canyon creations like Hopi House, Hermit's Rest, and Desert View Watchtower

- **Best Music:** *Grand Canyon Suite* by Ferde Grofé, especially the third movement, "On the Trail"

- **Best Movie:** Disney's *Grand Canyon*, which won a 1959 Oscar for Best Short Subject

**Grandview Point**, and **Lipan Point**. Tucked among the pines, the **Tusayan Ruin and Museum** revolves around the remains of a 12th-century ancestral Puebloan village. Looming above the road's eastern end is the **Desert View Watchtower**, which features an observation deck with an even higher view of the canyon, as well as murals by renowned Hopi artist Fred Kabotie.

As it exits the national park, Desert View Drive segues into State Highway 64 and a run across the **Navajo Nation** and the **Painted Desert**. Reaching **Cameron**, a great place to browse for Navajo art and handicrafts, road trippers need to take a left onto U.S. Highway 89. At Bitter Springs, the highway splits into two separate routes. The right fork (89) leads north to **Glen Canyon National Recreation Area** and **Lake Powell**; the left fork (89A) leaps across **Marble Canyon** on the new **Navajo Bridge**.

On either side of the modern span are places where you can park and stroll across the historic old bridge for vertigo-inducing views into the multicolored gorge. Just beyond the bridge is the turnoff to **Lees Ferry**, the only place along a 700-mile (1,126.5 km) stretch of canyons in southern Utah and northern Arizona where you can actually drive down to the **Colorado River**. The ferry landing functions as the put-in spot for most river-running trips through the canyon. But there's history too: the ruins of pioneer-era **Lees Ferry Fort** and **Lonely Dell Ranch**.

From Navajo Bridge, Highway 89A blazes a trail along the **Vermilion Cliffs**, a Bureau of Land Management national monument with

The Virgin River rushes through the Narrows hiking path.

primitive roads and hiking trails that lead to celebrated rock formations like **The Wave** and **Paw Hole**. Not far off the highway is a **condor viewing area**, where drivers can learn about the release program and search the cliffs for North America's largest bird.

Climbing into **Kaibab National Forest**, Highway 89A reaches the small mountain town of **Jacob Lake** and the turnoff for the Grand Canyon's **North Rim**. With only a fraction of the visitors of its southern counterpart, the north side offers a quieter, calmer, and much more solitary take on the canyon. At around 8,000 feet (2,438.4 m), it's also higher than the South Rim, which means cooler temperatures and winter snow that closes the rim between December 1 and mid-May.

The North Rim village revolves around the **Visitor Center** and historic **Grand Canyon Lodge**, which perches on the verge of **Bright Angel Point**. There are a number of hiking options around the village, from the two-mile (3.2 km) **Transept Trail** (which leads past an ancient pueblo ruin), to the 9.8-mile (15.8 km) **Ken Patrick Trail** through the woods to **Point Imperial** with its view into the

Grand Canyon's eastern depths. Driving options range from the scenic **Cape Royal Road** and its dramatic viewpoints to the rugged, unpaved track along the rim to **Point Sublime**, recommended only for vehicles with 4x4 and high clearance.

Retracing your route to Jacob Lake, Highway 89A continues into southern Utah and a turnoff at Mount Carmel Junction to **Zion National Park**. Along the way are easy side trips to the frontier fort at **Pipe Springs National Monument** (State Route 389) and the spectacular **Coral Pink Sand Dunes** (Hancock Road).

The road into Zion runs through the **Mount Carmel Tunnel** and past **Checkerboard Mesa** with its natural crisscross fissures before descending into the heart of the park. Like the South Rim of the Grand Canyon, you can park your car at the **Zion Canyon Visitor Center** or **Zion Human History Museum** and take a shuttle up the canyon to various trails and viewpoints, including a path along the Virgin River through the **Narrows** where you're bound to get wet. From Zion, it's about a three-hour drive (via **St. George**) back to Las Vegas. ∎

---

## LAY YOUR HEAD

• **Grand Canyon Railway Hotel:** Opened in 1908, this historic hotel lies within walking distance of downtown Williams, Arizona, and the train depot; restaurant, bar, fitness center, indoor pool, golf; from $80. thetrain.com

• **El Tovar:** Landmark national park lodge and architectural icon with Grand Canyon views; restaurant, bar; from $194. grandcanyonlodges.com

• **Hyatt Place Page:** Newly opened,

near Glen Canyon Dam and Lake Powell; restaurant, bar, pool, fitness center; from $104. hyatt.com

• **Grand Canyon Lodge:** Cozy cabins on the North Rim; restaurants, bar; open mid-May to mid-October; from $141. grandcanyonforever.com

• **Zion Lodge:** The only hotel inside the Utah national park features a modern main lodge and vintage 1920s cabins; restaurants, gift shop; from $216. zionlodge.com

# Colorado's Golden Circle

## Colorado

From big-city Denver to far-flung ghost towns, this journey across Colorado follows a trail of bygone gold and silver boomtowns through the heart of the Rocky Mountains, a road trip that blends Wild West history and incredible western landscapes.

### THE BIG PICTURE

**Distance:** ca 894 miles (1,438.8 km) round-trip from Denver

**Drive time:** 7-9 days

**Best overnights:** Manitou Springs, Cañon City, Durango, Aspen

**Best seasons:** Spring, summer, or fall

**Highlights:** Pike's Peak, Cripple Creek, Cañon City, Durango, Silverton, Aspen, Leadville, Mesa Verde

Colorado's first gold was discovered in 1850 in Clear Creek, what's now suburban **Denver**. Gold fever spread like wildfire across the Colorado Rockies, sparking a boom that yielded more than a million ounces of the gold each year until 1916.

That heritage comes alive at the **History Colorado Center** in downtown Denver, just blocks away from the **Colorado State Capitol** with its golden dome and the **U.S. Mint**

**Denver**, where much of the state's gold was molded into coinage and commemorative medals.

Interstate 25 provides a smooth ride south to **Colorado Springs** and a short drive along U.S. 24 to **Manitou Springs**. The funky little town offers an artsy historic district and the famous **Pike's Peak Toll Road**, which snakes its way to the 14,115-foot (4,302.3 m) summit for an astonishing view across the Rockies.

Over on the peak's western flank

is **Cripple Creek**, where the last of the great Colorado gold rushes kicked off in 1890. Visitors can descend 1,000 vertical feet (304.8 m) into the **Mollie Kathleen Gold Mine** or chug through the old gold fields on the narrow-gauge **Cripple Creek and Victor Narrow Gauge Railroad**.

**Cañon City** is another hour south on State Highway 9. Founded in 1858 during the Pike's Peak gold rush, the town is now the gateway to the **Royal Gorge**, spanned by a pedestrian suspension bridge, gondola ride, and zip line that hovers 1,200 feet (365.8 m) above the gorge floor.

The longest leg of the Golden Circle is a 250-mile (402.3 km) cruise from Cañon City to Durango along U.S. Highways 50, 285, and 160, a drive with possible side trips to **Great Sand Dunes National Park** and the bubbling hot pools of **Pagosa Springs**.

**Durango** sprang to life in the 1880s as a railroad terminus and service center for the San Juan Mining District. The train endures as the **Durango and Silverton Narrow Gauge Railroad**, which offers steam-powered tours between the two towns. Durango's historic downtown is flush with restaurants, bars, and shops. Meanwhile, the city makes a great base for rafting the **Animas**

The Durango-Silverton steam engine takes visitors between the two towns.

A good pit stop: Crystal Creek Reservoir offers fishing, kayaking, and stunning views of snowcapped Pikes Peak.

**River**, clambering through cliff dwellings at **Mesa Verde**, or winter snow sports at **Purgatory Resort**.

The scenic **Million Dollar Highway** (U.S. 550) climbs to **Silverton** in the gorgeous San Juan Mountains. **Mayflower Gold Mill** preserves relics of the boom days, and visitors can ride a vintage electric mine train into the **Old Hundred Gold Mine**. Among other old-time attractions in the area are the **Ouray Alchemist Museum**, **Animas Forks** ghost town, and tours of **Bachelor Syracuse Mine**.

With its outdoor sports and upscale lifestyle, **Aspen** makes a good stop on the return trip, a five-hour drive from Silverton via the towns of **Delta** and **Carbondale**.

You can hop I-70 for a quick return to Denver or detour to one more boomtown. Perched at 10,000 feet (3,048 m) in the Rockies, **Lead-ville** is the nation's highest city. The one-time silver trove offers the **National Mining Hall of Fame and Museum**, rides on the old **Leadville, Colorado and Southern Railroad**, and several mine tours. From Leadville, it's about a two-hour drive to Denver. ◼

## PIT STOPS

• **Ouray Ice Festival:** This annual January ice-climbing jamboree includes professional and amateur events, clinics, equipment stalls, music, and food. ourayicepark.com/ouray-ice-festival

• **Snowdown:** Durango's February winter blowout features more than 100 offbeat events, from a paintball biathlon and Polish doughnut Frisbee competition to a barista latte art show and pantyhose bowling. snowdown.org

• **Pike's Peak International Hill Climb:** First staged in 1916, this annual "Race to the Clouds" has cars, trucks, and motorcycles racing 12 miles (19.3 km) to the summit every June. ppihc.org

• **Aspen Music Festival and School:** The hills are alive with classical music during this eight-week summer fest (July-August) with more than 400 events. aspenmusicfestival.com

• **Gold Camp Christmas:** Cripple Creek's ode to the yuletide season features decorated mine head-frames, a craft fair, Christmas parade, and hot hooch from Thanksgiving to New Year's Day. visitcripplecreek.com

# Great Coastal Wildlife Trail

## Texas

Half a dozen national wildlife refuges and one of the oldest national seashores highlight this slow mosey down the Lone Star shore between Port Arthur and Beaumont.

Although Texas is the second most populous American state (29 million), its Gulf of Mexico coast remains refreshingly underdeveloped, a mosaic of wetlands, bays, and barrier islands along 367 miles (590.6 km) of shoreline.

**Port Arthur** anchors the eastern end of the Texas coast with three contiguous parks: **McFadden** and **Texas Point** national wildlife refuges and **Sea Rim State Park**. Together they offer opportunities for birding, beachcombing, fishing, paddle sports, and hiking. Nearby **Sabine Pass Battleground** saw an 1863 Confederate victory over Union naval forces.

A string of state highways (73, 124, and 87) connects Port Arthur and the sandy **Bolivar Peninsula**, where a vehicle and passenger ferry crosses the channel to **Galveston**.

Once called the "Free State of Galveston" because of its wicked ways, the seaside city boasts **six historic districts** and seafaring sights like the *Ocean Star* **Offshore Drilling Rig and Museum**, **Galveston Naval Museum**, and the **tall ship** *Elissa*. However, its star attractions are the flora and fauna inside the giant glass pyramids of **Moody Gardens**.

Pick up State Highway 35 outside Galveston and make your way to **Aransas National Wildlife Refuge** near Port Lavaca. The park shelters more than 400 avian species (including the rare whooping crane), as well as alligators, manatees, sea turtles, dolphins, peccaries, coyotes, bobcats, and deer. Visitors can explore the various habitats on several hiking trails and an auto tour loop.

Highway 35 continues into **Corpus Christi**, home of the **Texas State Aquarium**, the **Texas Surf Museum**, and the **U.S.S.** *Lexington* aircraft carrier museum. It's also the gateway to nearby **Padre Island National Seashore**.

Traditional beach activities are available around the **Malaquite Visitor Center**. But the park's real treat is a **primitive gulf beach** stretching 60 miles (96.6 km) down the Gulf Coast, open to 4x4 vehicles and with primitive camping sites along the way. Padre Island is renowned for sea turtles, but the park also welcomes 380 bird species and a variety of

A whooping crane skims the water at Aransas National Wildlife Refuge.

There are 60 miles (96.6 km) of coastline, dunes, and tidal flats, plus more than 380 bird species on Padre Island.

terrestrial animals, from coyotes and white-tailed deer to the Padre Island kangaroo rat.

Backtracking into Corpus Christi, catch southbound U.S. Highway 77 to Kingsville and the legendary **King Ranch**. The largest ranch in Texas sprawls across 1,289 square miles (3,338.5 sq km), an area four times larger than all of New York City. The ranch offers daily 90-minute guided tours, as well as four-hour nature and birding (363 species) tours through the coastal mesquite woodland.

Highway 77 drops another 96 miles (154.5 km) south to **Harlingen** in the Lower Rio Grande Valley. If it suddenly feels tropical, that's because it basically is: both the temperature and humidity levels are in the 90s during the summer months. Cool off inside the **Harlingen Arts and Heritage Museum** (which includes three historic homes) before heading out into the wilds again. To the east of town, **Arroyo Colorado World Bird-**

**ing Center** provides nature trails through thicket and ebony woodland inhabited by many neotropical birds.

The final leg of the road trip follows Interstate 69E down to Brownsville, where the **Sabal Palm Sanctuary** preserves an old-growth sabal palmetto forest and 19th-century riverside plantation. Farther

downstream, **Lower Rio Grande Valley National Wildlife Refuge** provides a habitat for rare or endangered animals like ocelot and jaguarundi wildcats, southern yellow bats, and Kemp's Ridley sea turtles. At the end of the road is **Boca Chica**, the southernmost beach in the lower 48 states. ∎

## PIT STOPS

• **Galveston Mardi Gras:** The nation's third largest pre-Lenten carnival features concerts, balcony parties, elegant balls, and 23 parades. mardigrasgalveston.com

• **International Migratory Bird Day:** Educational programs and bird-watching excursions highlight this May event at Aransas National Wildlife Refuge. fws.gov/refuge/Aransas

• **Hatchling Releases:** Padre Island National Seashore releases baby sea turtles into the wild at Malaquite

Beach from mid-June through August. nps.gov/pais

• **Rio Reforestation:** Every October volunteers help Valley Proud and the U.S. Fish and Wildlife Service plant thousands of trees and shrubs to restore the natural habitat of Lower Rio Grand Valley National Wildlife Refuge. valleyproud.org/rio-reforestation.php

• **Rio Grande Valley Bird Festival:** Harlingen's annual ode to feathered friends spans a whole week in November. rgvbf.org

# Alien Highways

## TX, NM, AZ & NV

The truth is out there—or maybe not—on this ramble between West Texas and southern Nevada that touches down at some of the nation's most celebrated extraterrestrial landmarks, from strange lights and crash sites to vast arrays and mysterious caches.

The American Southwest has witnessed more alleged alien activity than just about anywhere else on Earth. Spread across hundreds of miles, the sites associated with these strange events have no apparent connection other than the fact that you can close-encounter all of them on this extraterrestrial road trip.

The journey launches from **Marfa**, the rustic West Texas town renowned for two films shot on location there (*Giant* and *No Country for Old Men*) and a recurring paranormal phenomenon. First spotted by cowboys in the 1880s, the mysterious "**Marfa lights**"—unexplained glowing orbs appearing in the desert—have been attributed to visitors from outer space and are best viewed from the elevated **Marfa Lights Viewing Area** beside U.S. Highway 90.

A five-hour drive to the north (via Texas Highway 17 and U.S. 285) is

Arizona's Meteor Crater is about 3,900 feet (1,200 m) in diameter.

**Roswell**, New Mexico, where a flying saucer supposedly crashed in 1947. The so-called Roswell incident sparked myriad conspiracy theories and a tourism scene that includes the **International UFO Museum and Research Center** and various alien-oriented souvenir shops. Roswell's **Goddard Planetarium** at the **Roswell Museum and Art Center** offers science-based exhibits, films, and sky shows.

Turning west, the alien trail continues along U.S. Highways 380 and 60 to **Socorro**, New Mexico, and the **Very Large Array**. Made famous by the 1997 movie *Contact,* the array consists of 27 huge radio telescopes attached to railroad tracks arranged in a Y-shape on the remote Plains of San Agustin set up to investigate black holes, supernovas, quasars, pulsars, and distant galaxies—where there just might be intelligent life-forms. The **National Radio Astronomy Observatory Visitor Center** offers a self-guided tour along trails beneath the metal behemoths.

Highway 60 leaps the border into Arizona and **Apache-Sitgreaves National Forest**, where lumberman Travis Walton was allegedly abducted by aliens in 1975 and held for five days in their spaceship. Immortalized by the movie *Fire in the Sky,* the inci-

Twenty-seven radio antennas in a Y-shaped configuration make up New Mexico's observatory dubbed Very Large Array.

dent was said to take place at a remote location near **Snowflake**. Unlike other self-styled arrival sites, Snowflake has yet to commercialize its otherworldly fame. But it does offer the **Stinson Pioneer Museum** and several nicely restored **Victorian homes**.

The only bona fide extraterrestrial on this entire drive comes next: **Meteor Crater** in northern Arizona. Located about 90 miles (144.8 km) from Snowflake via State Highway 77 and Interstate 40, the Earth's best preserved meteorite impact site was created around 50,000 years ago. The **Visitor Center** showcases chunks of that space rock; a widescreen movie, ***Impact;*** an Apollo program test capsule; the **Astronaut Wall of Fame**; a rock shop; and guided **rim tours**.

Just up the interstate is **Lowell Observatory** in Flagstaff. One of the nation's premier astronomy centers offers guided tours, astronomer talks, multimedia shows, night sky programs, and a chance to look through the **giant telescopes** at the facility where Clyde Tombaugh discovered Pluto in 1930.

The longest leg of this road trip stretches from Flagstaff to a celebrated spot in southern Nevada: 400 miles (643.7 km) of desert driving along I-40, U.S. 93, and State Route 375 (aka the **"Extraterrestrial Highway"**), which run alongside **Area 51**—the government's super-secret test facility and allegedly where any alien beings or spacecraft captured are held.

UFO enthusiasts gather in **Rachel**, Nevada, where attractions like the **Little A'Le'Inn** and **Alien Research Center** feed off the many conspiracy theories. Round off the road trip by backtracking to that forbidden planet they call **Las Vegas**. ■

## ART AVENUES

- **Best Movies:** *Contact* (1997); *Independence Day* (1996); *Fire in the Sky* (1993); the comedy *Alien Autopsy* (2006)

- **Best TV:** *Roswell* (1999-2002); *Seven Days* (1998-2001); and two *X-Files* episodes: "Dreamland" (1998) and "Nisei" (1995)

- **Best Books:** *The Roswell Incident* by Charles Berlitz and William Moore; *Area 51: An Uncensored History of America's Top Secret Military Base* by Annie Jacobsen; *The Walton Experience* by Travis Walton; *The Shimmer* by David Morrell

- **Best Event:** Marfa Lights Festival (August)

# Pan-Regional
## Road Trips

Gettysburg National Military Park is a worthwhile venture for any history buff.

# The National Road

## Maryland to Missouri

Twenty-six years in the making, the National Road was the first major federal highway project—a route established between the Atlantic seaboard and the recently acquired Louisiana Purchase to expedite American trade and settlement of the West.

Thomas Jefferson is celebrated as an author of the Declaration of Independence, as well as the president who bought Louisiana from Napoleon and dispatched Lewis and Clark to the Pacific. But he's also the spiritual father of the interstate highway system, the man who hatched an ambitious plan to build the first road across the entire nation.

Constructed between 1811 and the mid-1830s, the National Road stretches 620 miles (997.8 km) across six states, from Cumberland, Maryland, to Vandalia, Illinois. Starting in Baltimore or St. Louis, drivers can cruise Interstate 70 (the modern successor to the National Road) or old U.S. 40 along the original alignment. This route traces the latter.

From **Baltimore** it's a quick two-hour drive along I-70 to

A replica sits at the C&O National Historical Park Visitors Center.

## THE BIG PICTURE

**Distance:** ca 820 miles (1,319.7 km) from Baltimore, MD, to St. Louis, MO

**Drive time:** 5-6 days

**Best overnights:** Cumberland, Wheeling, Columbus, Indianapolis, Vandalia

**Best seasons:** Spring, summer, or fall

**Highlights:** Cumberland museums, Fort Necessity, Wheeling Suspension Bridge, Indianapolis Motor Speedway, Vandalia

**Cumberland**, where the **C&O Canal Visitor Center** and **Allegheny Museum** provide an entrée to early 19th-century transportation. The National Road (Alt U.S. 40) heads north through the **Cumberland Narrows** on the first leg of its long journey.

The stretch through Maryland's panhandle includes the **LaVale Toll Gate House** (1833)—where it once cost six cents to transport a score of sheep or hogs—and **Casselman River Bridge** (1813), the world's longest single-span stone arch bridge when it opened.

U.S. 40 heads into Pennsylvania and a rendezvous with **Fort Necessity**, where George Washington saw his first combat during the French and Indian War. The road swings around the southern fringe of the **Pittsburgh** metropolitan area and into that sliver of West Virginia that pokes up between Pennsylvania and Ohio.

Six of the original National Road **mile markers** highlight the West Virginia stretch of U.S. 40 between the state line and **Wheeling**. Established as a British frontier settlement in 1769, the city's **National Road Corridor Historic District**

Wheeling Suspension Bridge—the longest suspension bridge in the world from 1849 to 1851—crosses the Ohio River.

embraces a number of historic buildings and the **Madonna of the Trail monument**. The route leaps the Ohio River on the towering **Wheeling Suspension Bridge**, the world's longest suspension span when it opened in 1849.

Continuing across central Ohio on U.S. 40, drivers will pass through a number of towns that once featured prominently in America's westward expansion. Among the road related are an original section of the National Road called **Peacock Road** near Cambridge, the **National Road and Zane Grey Museum** in Norwich, and **Wagner-Hagans Auto Museum** in Columbus.

The **Old National Road Welcome Center** in Richmond, Indiana, offers the first of 15 interpretive panels scattered along U.S. 40 in the Hoosier State. Washington Street carries the road across Indianapolis, past the **Indiana State House,**

**Monument Square**, and **White River State Park**, with the possibility of a detour to the **Indianapolis Motor Speedway Museum.**

Crossing into Illinois near **Terra Haute**, U.S. 40 makes a beeline across the prairie to **Vandalia**. The state capital when the National Road was completed in 1837, Vandalia boasts the **National Road Interpretive Center** and its fine museum about the highway, as well as another **Madonna of the Trail monument** in front of the **old state capitol**. **St. Louis** lies another 70 miles (112.7 km) to the west. ∎

## EN ROUTE EATS

- **The Filling Station:** Meatloaf, chipped beef, frog in a log, and peanut butter pie are some of the tasty throwback dishes at this classic roadside diner in western Maryland. 927 National Hwy., La Vale, MD. 301-876-4725

- **Avenue Eats:** The National Road Corridor History District is home to this West Virginia café in a restored Victorian home; soups, salads, sandwiches, and amazing burgers. 1201 Valley View Ave., Wheeling, WV. avenueeats.com

- **Red Brick Tavern:** Ohio's second oldest stagecoach stop has been serving National Road trippers since 1837; steaks, fish, pasta, and hot sandwiches. 1700 Cumberland St. (U.S. 40), Lafayette, OH. historicred bricktavern.com

- **Willy's Drive-In:** Fried pickles, funnel cake fries, toasted raviolis, and cheesy tots are just a few of the sides you can get with your burgers, dogs, or steak sandwiches at this classic Illinois diner. 710 West Orchard St., Vandalia, IL. 618-283-1300

# Route 66
## Illinois to California

One of the world's iconic road trips, U.S. Highway 66 spans roughly 2,400 miles (3,862.4 km) between Chicago and Los Angeles, a drive through eight states that reflects not just motoring history but American architecture, pop culture, and social evolution since Route 66 was established in the 1920s.

### THE BIG PICTURE

**Distance:** ca 2,300 miles (3,701.5 km) from Chicago to Los Angeles

**Drive time:** 7-10 days

**Best overnights:** Springfield, IL; St. Louis; Springfield, MO; Oklahoma City; Amarillo; Albuquerque; Flagstaff

**Best seasons:** Spring, summer, or fall

**Highlights:** Lincoln's Springfield, Tulsa's art deco, Oklahoma City museums, Texas Panhandle, Santa Fe, Petrified Forest NP, Flagstaff, Mojave Desert

John Steinbeck dubbed it the "Mother Road," a path that nearly 200,000 Americans traveled to escape the Dust Bowl and the Great Depression of the 1930s and that hundreds of thousands more drove after World War II in search of their California dream.

There's a strong argument that Route 66 gave birth to the modern road trip when it was built as one of the first transcontinental highways in 1926. It was also the cradle of road trip accoutrements: gas stations, fast-food eateries, motor hotels (motels), and all variety of tourist traps.

The route officially starts in downtown Chicago with a sign at the intersection of Michigan Avenue and Adams Street opposite the **Art Institute of Chicago**. And just eight blocks west along Adams, **Willis Tower** (aka the Sears Tower) offers a Skydeck atop what for many years was the tallest building on Earth.

Exiting Chicago, purists will want to follow **Ogden Avenue** and

Interstate 55 along the original path of Route 66. On the outer edge of the metropolitan area, the **Joliet Area Historical Museum** doubles as a Route 66 welcome center, as well as the place to schedule tours of the **Old Joliet Prison**. Half an hour farther south stands the **Gemini Giant**, a famed fiberglass sculpture beside the highway in Wilmington. Interstate 55 continues to the **Route 66 Hall of Fame** in Pontiac and many **Abraham Lincoln** sights in Springfield before reaching the Mississippi River and **Cahokia Mounds State Historic Park,** which preserves a Native American city that was larger than medieval London.

On the other side of the Big Muddy, **St. Louis** offers a chance to ride to the top the **Gateway Arch** or catch a ball game at nearby **Busch Stadium** before tracing the historic path of Route 66 (now State Route 366) through south St. Louis. The **Ulysses S. Grant National Historic Site** begs a final stop before the old highway segues into I-44 for the drive across Missouri.

**Route 66 State Park** in Eureka features a visitor center museum (with exhibits on the highway)

Opened in 1949, the 66 Drive-In Theatre still operates in Carthage, Missouri.

Bob Waldmire's 1972 VW Microbus is one of many pieces of memorabilia at the Route 66 Association Hall of Fame and Museum.

lodged inside an original 1935 roadhouse. I-44 crosses the northern edge of the **Ozarks** before cruising through Springfield and nearby **Carthage**, where the vintage **66 Drive-In Theatre** (opened in 1949) screens movies four nights a week from April through mid-September.

The original route cuts across the southeast corner of Kansas to **Galena**, where a rusty old tow truck at the **Cars on the Route** diner inspired the "Tow Mater" character in the animated movie *Cars*. Just up the road is another roadside relic, the **Old Riverton Store**, opened in 1925.

Much of historic Route 66 lives on in Oklahoma, stretches of the original road that parallel the modern turnpike down to Tulsa and Oklahoma City, then Interstate 40 across the western half of the Sooner State. The Oklahoma stretch also boasts more original roadside kitsch than any other state, including

structures like the **Blue Whale of Catoosa**, the 76-foot-high (23.2 m) **Golden Driller** of Tulsa, and **Pops 66 Soda Ranch** in Arcadia.

There's also legit stuff: the **Woody Guthrie Center** and all that fabulous art deco architecture in Tulsa and the incredible **National Cowboy and Western Heritage Museum**, revamped **Bricktown**, and the **Oklahoma City National Memorial** in Oklahoma City. Way out west, the highway offers an eclectic array of stops, including the **Stafford Air and Space Museum** in Weatherford and the awesome **Oklahoma Route 66 Museum** in Clinton before sliding across the border.

Truth be told, the 190-mile (305.8 km) drive across the Texas Panhandle is pretty bleak. But here and there are splashes of roadside color, starting with the quirky **Tower Station and U Drop Inn**, an old-time gas station turned visitor center

in Shamrock. **Amarillo** offers a neon-spangled **Route 66–Sixth Street Historic District** and the amusing **Cadillac Ranch** public art installation. An hour west of Amarillo, **Midpoint Café** in Adrian sits exactly 1,139 miles (1,833 km) from either end of Route 66.

**Tucumcari**, New Mexico, flaunts its position astride the famous highway with the **New Mexico Route 66 Museum** and classic kitsch like the **Tee Pee Curios** shop and **Blue Swallow Motel** sign. Beyond Santa Rosa, the original highway jogged to the northwest, tracing the Old Pecos Trail into the Sangre de Cristo Mountains and Santa Fe. Along the way is **Pecos National Historical Park**, which harbors the 900-year-old Pecos Pueblo, historic Forked Lightning Ranch, and Glorieta Pass Battlefield, where an 1862 Civil War clash took place.

**Santa Fe** was just coming into its own as an art haven when Route 66 was being built in the 1920s. Nearly a century later, the New Mexico capital continues to stoke its creative fires with a wide range of museums, art galleries, and performance spaces. Its artistic splendors range from the **Georgia O'Keeffe Museum** and **Wheelwright Museum of the American Indian** to the futuristic **Santa Fe Opera House** and the edgy **Meow Wolf** installation.

The road trip flows through the lush Rio Grande Valley to **Albuquerque**, which boasts more vintage 66 architecture than any other city. Arrayed along Central Avenue are classic structures like the **Jones Motor Company** (now **Kellys Brew Pub**), the streamlined **66 Diner**, and **KiMo Theatre** with its docent-led tours.

The Blue Swallow Motel in Tucumcari, New Mexico, is a must-park stop for a classic snapshot along the route.

## LAY YOUR HEAD

• **Wagon Wheel:** Opened in 1938, this Cuba, Missouri, roadside motel features original stone cottages; gift shop, original neon sign; from $60. wagonwheel66cuba.com

• **La Fonda on the Plaza:** Pueblo Revival architecture and Southwest interiors highlight this luxurious Santa Fe hotel; restaurant, bars, spa, swimming pool, fitness center; from $149. lafondasantafe.com

• **El Rancho Hotel:** John Wayne, Spencer Tracy, Katharine Hepburn, and Kirk Douglas are a few of the Hollywood greats who've bunked here while shooting movies around Gallup, New Mexico; restaurant, bar, Native American jewelry shop; from $56. elranchohotelgallup.com

• **Wigwam Motel:** Erected in the 1930s, this Native American–themed lodging on the edge of the Petrified Forest National Park features 15 concrete teepees with television, air-conditioning, and full bathrooms; from $69. galerie-kokopelli.com/wigwam

• **Stagecoach 66 Motel:** Norwegian woods, John Wayne, and Harley-Davidson motorcycles are a couple of the theme rooms at this classic 1960s motor court in Seligman, Arizona; restaurant, bar; from $51. stagecoach66motel.com

In western New Mexico, much of historic Route 66 survives as the Frontage Road along I-40 through towns like **Grants** and **Gallup** before crossing the border into Arizona. Running along the southern edge of the **Painted Desert**, the stretch between the state line and Flagstaff features geological wonders like **Petrified Forest National Park** and **Meteor Crater**, and new pop culture landmarks like the Eagles **Standin' on a Corner** tribute in Winslow.

High-altitude **Flagstaff** (6,900 feet/2,103 m) offers a brief respite from the Arizona summer heat before the long drive across the desert. I-40 breezes through historic **Williams** and its turnoff to the **Grand Canyon** before gliding downhill into **Ash Fork**, the eastern terminus of the longest remaining section of the original road. Stretching roughly 160 miles (257.5 km) from stem to stern, the old road moseys through **Seligman** with its fifties-style **Snow Cap Drive-In** and **Oatman** with its free-range donkeys before a confluence with I-40 at the **Colorado River**.

Threading the California desert between **Mojave National Preserve** and **Joshua Tree National Park**, the route makes a beeline for **Barstow** and the **Route 66 Mother Road Museum**. Turning south, the drive dives down Cajon Pass to the Inland Empire east of Los Angeles.

From San Bernardino, the historic route follows Foothill Boulevard through a maze of suburbs that were farm towns when Route 66 was born. It eventually reaches **Pasadena**—where you can pop into the **Huntington Library and Gardens** or tour superstars of the science world like the **California Institute of Technology** (Caltech) and the **Jet Propulsion Lab** (JPL)—before continuing along Arroyo Seco Parkway into downtown **Los Angeles**.

Finally, it's on to the sea. The home stretch of Route 66 cruises Santa Monica Boulevard through **Hollywood** and **Beverly Hills** before arriving at **Santa Monica Pier** and the Pacific Ocean. ∎

# Oregon Trail
## Missouri to Oregon

This legendary pioneer path to the West Coast spans six states and more than 2,100 miles (3,379.6 km) of American geography, from the Great Plains and Rocky Mountains to the arid Snake River Valley and lush Columbia River Gorge.

## THE BIG PICTURE

**Distance:** ca 2,100 miles (3,379.6 km) from Kansas City, MO, to Portland, OR

**Drive time**: 6-10 days

**Best overnights:** Kearney, Casper, Rock Springs, Pocatello, Twin Falls, Boise, Pendleton

**Best seasons:** Spring, summer, or fall

**Highlights:** National Frontier Trails Museum, Fort Kearny, Chimney Rock, Scotts Bluff, Fort Laramie, Three Islands Crossing, Columbia Gorge

Blazed by fur trappers and traders in the early 19th century, the Oregon Trail presented the easiest and safest way to travel from back east to the Pacific coast. The first wagon train rumbled across the route in 1836. In the years that followed, more than 400,000 migrants made their way along the Oregon Trail and its offshoots to new homes in the West.

Today a string of state and federal roadways traces the route, starting from **Upper Independence Landing** (aka Wayne City Landing) near **Kansas City, Missouri**. As a primary steamboat port on the Missouri River, the landing is where hundreds of wagon trains started down the Oregon Trail nearly 200 years ago.

The **National Frontier Trails Museum** in Independence offers a great orientation to the Oregon Trail, as well as a comprehensive look at the exploration and settlement of the American West.

From Kansas City, Interstate 70 heads west across the Kansas prairie to exit 346 (NW Carlson Road) and the start of **"Oregon Trail National Historic Trail"** signs that mark the route all the way to Oregon. **Alcove Springs** near Marysville was a popular Oregon Trail encampment. Look out for wagon ruts and a Donner Party monument.

The zigzag route continues to **Hollenberg Pony Express Station** and its exhibits on the intrepid horsemen who road the Oregon Trail from 1860 to 1861. Cross the state line into Nebraska, where historic **Fort Kearny** offers reconstructed buildings, an interpretive center, living history events, and sandhill crane viewing.

Beyond Fort Kearny, the road trip follows Interstate 80 and U.S. Highway 26 along the **North Platte River** and some of the key landmarks along the Oregon Trail, including **Chimney Rock** and **Scotts Bluff**.

Dead ahead is **Fort Laramie** in southeastern Wyoming. Founded in 1834 as a trading post, the bastion evolved into an Army base and major resupply station. Nearby **Register Cliff** preserves the memory of thousands of migrants who carved their names in the sandstone.

The **National Historic Trails Interpretive Center** in Casper offers

This dormitory housed Army soldiers at Fort Laramie, Wyoming, in the mid-1800s.

Beautiful views of the Columbia River Gorge await outside the Vista House museum in Oregon.

an 18-minute multimedia show that revolves around the pioneers, explorers, and Native Americans of the 19th-century American frontier.

Tracing the Oregon Trail through central Wyoming—one of the least populated parts of the lower 48 states—entails carefully following the National Historic Trail signs. Along the way are relics like **Independence Rock, South Pass** (across the Continental Divide), and **Fort Bridger.**

The route meanders into Idaho and the **National Oregon/California Trail Center** in Montpelier, with its simulated wagon train experience. Highway 30 follows much of the trail route across southern Idaho. **Three Islands Crossing State Park** near Glenns Ferry offers an **Oregon Trail History and Education Center** at a spot where migrants had to choose between north and south routes along the **Snake River** into Oregon.

Eastern Oregon harbors several noteworthy stops, including the **National Historic Oregon Trail Interpretive Center** at Flagstaff Hill and **Blue Mountain Crossing Interpretive Park** near La Grande.

Reaching the mighty **Columbia River**, the Oregon Trail and Interstate 84 turn to the west and a passage down the gorgeous **Columbia Gorge** to the outskirts of **Portland**, where the **End of the Oregon Trail Interpretive Center** punctuates the trip. ∎

## PIT STOPS

• **Old Fashioned Fourth of July:** Fort Laramie, Wyoming, celebrates Independence Day with living history military drills, equestrian events, a fiddle concert, old-time games, and a Native American warrior program. nps.gov/fola

• **Oregon Trail Days:** First staged in 1921, Nebraska's oldest festival features parades, a quilt show, chili cook-off, street dance, horseshoe tournament, and mud volleyball in Gering every July. oregontrail days.com

• **Oregon Trail Brewfest:** Oregon City presents two days in August of cider and craft beer made in breweries along the trail between Kansas City, MO, and Portland, OR. oregon cityguide.com

• **Labor Day Weekend Wagon Encampment:** Costumed volunteers reenact wagon train life along the trail during this late-summer event at the National Historic Oregon Trail Interpretive Center in eastern Oregon. blm.gov

# Lewis & Clark Trail

## Missouri to Washington

One of America's longest and most alluring road trips traces the route Lewis and Clark followed from the Mississippi River to the Pacific Coast across the golden plains and prairies, lofty mountains, and lush valleys that are just as much a discovery today as in the early 1800s.

**THE BIG PICTURE**

**Distance:** ca 2,700 miles (4,345.2 km) from St. Louis, MO, to Cape Disappointment, WA

**Drive time:** 8-14 days

**Best overnights:** Kansas City, Omaha, Pierre, Bismarck, Great Falls, Missoula, Lewiston, Portland, Astoria

**Best seasons:** Late spring to early fall

**Highlights:** St. Louis, Kansas City, Omaha, Missouri National Recreational River, Upper Missouri River Breaks National Monument, Great Falls, Bitterroot Range, Columbia River Gorge and mouth

Other than going to the moon, the most ambitious journey in American history has been the Corps of Discovery expedition, an odyssey that began in 1804 when President Thomas Jefferson dispatched Meriwether Lewis and William Clark to explore the newly acquired Louisiana Purchase and the country beyond.

Their journals and maps, as well as the scientific specimens that Lewis and Clark collected during their 28 months on the trail, provided some of the world's first insights into the Native Americans, flora and fauna, and landscapes of the American West. A road trip along their route is bound to enlighten modern travelers in much the same way.

Administered by the National Park Service, the **Lewis and Clark National Historic Trail** traces their route across 10 states from Missouri to the mouth of the Columbia River in Oregon and Washington. Most of the trail is along rural highways close to the river, but road trippers can also use interstates to travel between many of the sites and cities along the way.

Those with a deep and abiding sense of history will want to start their journey in Missouri at **Gateway Arch National Park** on the **St. Louis** waterfront. Located beneath the 630-foot (192 m) stainless steel arch, the park's **visitor center museum** documents the Lewis and Clark expedition and other ways the West was won. Interstate 70 leads a short way to **Bellefontaine Cemetery**, where the grave of William Clark (who died in 1838) lies beneath a bust and white obelisk.

**Lewis and Clark Boat House and Nature Center** in St. Charles offers a last stop in the St. Louis metropolitan area before the trail heads along the north bank of the **Missouri River** on State Route 94. This region was heavily settled by German immigrants, a heritage that is clear by the many wineries around **Hermann**. The bluff-top **Lewis and Clark Monument** in **Jefferson City**, beside the towering **Missouri State Capitol**, is one of the more impressive along the trail's entire length.

During the winter of 1805-06, Lewis and Clark camped at Fort Clatsop, Oregon.

The Lewis and Clark Monument, dedicated to the iconic duo, sits outside the state capitol building in Jefferson City, Missouri.

State Route 179 leads to the eastern edge of **Kansas City**. Clark aided the 1808 construction of **Fort Osage**, a national historic landmark near Sibley. Farther along, Independence harbors the **National Frontier Trails Museum** and the **Harry S. Truman Presidential Library**.

North of Kansas City, the trail leaps across the Missouri River into Kansas and Nebraska, a stretch that includes the *Captain Meriwether Lewis* riverboat museum in Brownville's Riverside Park, and the **Missouri River Basin Lewis and Clark Visitor Center** in Nebraska City.

An hour farther north is **Omaha**, where the **Durham Museum** and Western collections at the **Joslyn Art Museum** offer a sweeping panorama of frontier history and culture. The "Big O" also houses the official **Lewis and Clark National Historic Trail Visitor Center** with a store that

specializes in books on the explorers. Leaping over to the Iowa side, **Council Bluffs** offers more frontier tales at the **Western Historic Trails Center** and the quirky **Squirrel Cage Jail** (built in 1885).

Bending to the northwest, the trail runs beside the **Missouri National Recreational River**, a 100-mile (160.9 km) stretch that seems little changed from two centuries ago when Lewis and Clark passed this way. South Dakota looms ahead, with possible stops at the **Akta Lakota Museum** in Chamberlain and the **Cultural Heritage Center** in Pierre, a unique underground collection that showcases the region's Native American and pioneer heritage.

Two hundred miles (321.9 km) farther north—on the other side of the **Cheyenne River** and **Standing Rock** reservations—North Dakota's frontier past comes alive at **Fort Abraham Lincoln State Park** in

## ART AVENUES

• **Historical Accounts:** *Undaunted Courage* by Stephen Ambrose; *The Journals of Lewis and Clark* edited by Bernard DeVoto; *Thomas Jefferson and the Stony Mountains* by Donald Jackson; *Bird Woman (Sacajawea): The Guide of Lewis and Clark* by James Schultz; *Lewis and Clark on the Trail of Discovery* by Rod Gragg

• **Guidebooks:** *National Geographic Guide to the Lewis and Clark Trail* by Thomas Schmidt; *Traveling the Lewis and Clark Trail* by Julie Fanselow; *Lewis and Clark Trail Guide* by Bruce W. Smalley

• **Movies and TV Shows:** *Lewis and Clark: The Journey of the Corps of Discovery* by Ken Burns (1997); *National Geographic's Lewis and Clark: Great Journey West* (2003); *Sacagawea: Heroine of the Lewis and Clark Journey* (2003); *The Far Horizons* (1955)

Mandan, which includes a reproduction of a Native American village and the base where Custer and the Seventh Cavalry were posted before their legendary last stand.

An hour north of Bismarck, the **Washburn** area offers three related sights: the **Lewis and Clark Interpretive Center**, a riverside replica of **Fort Mandan** (where the explorers spent the winter of 1804-1805), and **Knife River Indian Villages National Historic Site**, where the expedition engaged the services of Sacagawea that same winter.

The trail passes into Montana near the confluence of the Missouri and Yellowstone Rivers, a bustling crossroads in frontier days, as illustrated at the **Fort Union Trading Post National Historic Site** and **Fort Buford State Historic Site** with their living history programs. The nearby **Missouri-Yellowstone Confluence Interpretive Center** features large murals with quotes from the diaries of Lewis and Clark.

Owing to the presence of massive **Fort Peck Reservoir**, it's nearly impossible to follow in the expedition's footsteps along the Missouri River through eastern Montana unless you abandon your vehicle in favor of walking, pedaling, or paddling. Otherwise, reaching Great Falls entails a 400-mile (643.7 km) cruise along U.S. Highway 2 (north) or State Highway 200 (south). Either way you can take a side trip into remote **Upper Missouri River Breaks National Monument**, a Bureau of Land Management–managed park with several Lewis and Clark sites and more scenery largely unchanged since their time.

The Upper Missouri River Breaks National Monument is known for steep bluffs and grassy plains.

The explorers spent nearly a month portaging their boats and supplies around the cascades that give **Great Falls** its name. Learn more about their adventures at the city's **Lewis and Clark Interpretive Center** or hike the riverside trails around **Giant Springs**. The explorers continued up the Missouri River through the **Gates of the Mountains Wilderness area** near present-day **Helena** and crossed the Continental Divide at 7,373-foot (2,247.3 m) **Lemhi Pass** in the Bitterroot Range.

Downhill from the pass, the **Sacajawea Center** in Salmon, Idaho, tells the story of the expedition's most celebrated guide and her native people. Around 130 miles (209.2 km) due north, **Travelers' Rest State Park** marks the spot where the party camped before their agonizing traverse of **Lolo Pass**, during which they ate horses and candles to keep from starving. This once-harrowing route is now easy via the **Northwest Passage Scenic Byway** (U.S. 12), which tumbles downhill to **Nez Perce National Historical Park** and Lewiston, where **Hells Gate State Park** offers another **Lewis and Clark Discovery Center**.

With help from the Nez Perce, the expedition team built new boats and began a float trip down the **Snake River** to its confluence with the **Columbia River** near Pasco, Washington. Highway 12 is the easiest way to traverse the same ground, with stops at **Fort Walla Walla** (established 1856) and **Whitman Mission** (founded 1937).

It's pretty much a straight shot down the gorgeous **Columbia River Gorge** through the **Coast Range** mountains to the ocean. Among the many landmarks along this stretch of the trail are 620-foot (189 m) **Multnomah Falls** and the old Hudson Bay Company trading post at **Fort Vancouver**, as well as the bright lights and breweries of **Portland, Oregon**.

Set around the mouth of the Columbia River, **Lewis and Clark National Historical Park** on the Oregon side includes a visitor center and reproduction of **Fort Clatsop** (where the expedition spent the winter of 1805-1806) and the **Lewis and Clark Interpretive Center** at **Cape Disappointment State Park** on the Washington State side. "O! the joy," wrote Clark in his journal upon seeing the Pacific for the first time from the bluffs near the park's **North Head Lighthouse**. And that just might be your reaction on reaching the spectacular climax of the Lewis and Clark drive. ■

## SCENIC DETOURS

- **Interstate 90** points west from Pierre, South Dakota, to Badlands National Park, the Black Hills of South Dakota, Devils Tower, and Little Bighorn Battlefield.

- **Interstate 94** shoots across the prairie to Teddy Roosevelt National Park, the Yellowstone River Valley, and the Billings gateway to Yellowstone National Park.

- **U.S. Highway 89** links Great Falls along the Upper Missouri River and the eastern side of Glacier National Park, 150 miles (241.4 km) to the northwest.

- **U.S. Highway 95** heads north from Lewiston to Coeur d'Alene and Lake Pend Oreille, with onward connections to Canada's Okanagan Valley.

- **U.S. Highway 97** dives south from Biggs Junction, Oregon, to Bend, Crater Lake, and the Mount Shasta region of Northern California.

# Great Lakes Odyssey
## New York to Michigan

The American shores of the five Great Lakes are the focus of this ramble between upstate New York and Michigan's Upper Peninsula, which blends big cities and small towns, wilderness shores, and waterfront parks.

Harboring more than one-fifth of the world's surface freshwater, the Great Lakes are both a phenomenal resource and a natural wonder. After booming during the industrial revolution, much of the region literally rusted away before the Clean Water Act began to reverse the rot and spark the revival of lakeside cities.

Poised at the confluence of the Erie Canal and Lake Ontario, **Rochester, New York**, exploded into the first great American city west of the Appalachians. Among its many accomplishments were giant leaps in the development of cameras and photographic film, a legacy reflected in the **George Eastman Museum** in the 50-room mansion of the man who founded Kodak. The 13-mile (20.9 km) **Genesee Riverway** provides a hiking, biking, and paddling route to **Ontario Beach Park** with its boardwalk, band shell, and early 18th-century lighthouse.

Detroit's Guardian Building has art deco interiors.

## THE BIG PICTURE

**Distance:** ca 1,250 miles (2,011.7 km) from Rochester, NY, to Copper Harbor, MI

**Drive time:** 10-14 days

**Best overnights:** Niagara Falls, Buffalo, Cleveland, Sandusky, Detroit, Bay City, Mackinaw City, Marquette

**Best seasons:** Spring, summer, or fall

**Highlights:** Niagara Falls, Buffalo waterfront, Rock and Roll Hall of Fame, Cedar Point, Lake Erie islands, Henry Ford Museum, Mackinac Island

Lake Ontario State Parkway runs 80 miles (128.8 km) along the lakeshore to **Fort Niagara** and nearby **Niagara Falls**. Nobody (legally) goes over the falls in a barrel these days. But there are other ways to explore the thundering cascades, like the famous *Maid of the Mist* tour boat and the bright-red stairs that descend into the spray zone from **Goat Island**.

Farther up the Niagara River, **Buffalo** parlayed its lakefront/canal location into a 19th-century industrial powerhouse. In the midst of an urban revival, New York's second largest city embraces its Lake Erie shoreline with attractions like the historic warships of the **Buffalo Naval Park**, the trendy **Canalside** district (winter ice skating and summertime concerts), and kayaking or paddleboarding **Elevator Alley** on the lake.

Highway 5 hugs the shoreline in far western New York and that sliver of Pennsylvania that reaches Lake Erie. **Presque Isle State Park** in the Keystone State lures hikers, bikers, and beachgoers, as well as history buffs seeking the place where Commodore Matthew C. Perry launched his leg-

Niagara Falls is America's oldest state park, with awe-inspiring views of the magnificent cascade.

endary lakes fleet to defeat a British armada during the War of 1812.

Cruise busy I-90 or U.S. 20 down to Cleveland, Ohio, another former Rust Belt city undergoing a long-overdue renaissance that includes waterfront attractions like the **Rock and Roll Hall of Fame**, the **Great Lakes Science Center**, and the **Steamship** *William G. Mather* floating museum.

An hour west of Cleveland, **Cedar Point** amusement park and its 17 roller-coasters is a "must stop" for anyone with kids in the car. Ferries from nearby **Marblehead** and **Catawba** serve Ohio's **Lake Erie Archipelago**, where lakeshore parks offer camping, boating, fishing, and War of 1812 memorials.

Browse the **National Museum of the Great Lakes** in **Toledo** before heading up I-75 to Detroit, Michigan, which rises along the river connecting Lakes Erie and Huron. American ideas and innovation— and Detroit's pivotal role in the development of motorized transport—headline the **Henry Ford Museum**, while the city's musical heritage is celebrated at the **Motown Museum**. Detroit's art deco legacy includes the **Guardian Building, Fisher Building,** and Diego Rivera's "Detroit Industry Murals" in the **Detroit Institute of Arts**.

From Detroit, you can speed across Michigan's Lower Peninsula on I-75, or take the scenic route, a journey along State Highway 25 and U.S. Highway 23 that runs all the way up the western side of Lake Huron via **Bay City**. Either way, you end up on the **Straits of Mackinac**, a narrow waterway that connects Lakes Michigan and Huron. Floating in the middle of the straits, **Mackinac Island** offers a Revolutionary War fort and Victorian-era vacation town.

The stupendous **Mackinac Bridge** carries the route across the water to the **Upper Peninsula**, a land of deep woods and wild waters that retains much of its frontier feel. Beyond the span, drive Highway 2 along Lake Michigan's northern coast and then Highway 41 across the peninsula to Lake Superior. U.S. 41 dead-ends in **Copper Harbor**, where you can hop summertime ferries to remote **Isle Royale National Park**. ■

# Travel Across Hallowed Ground

## Pennsylvania to Virginia

From Gettysburg in the North to Monticello in the South, this journey across four states unfolds through 400 years of American history, with a special emphasis on the Founding Fathers and the Civil War.

**THE BIG PICTURE**

**Distance:** 180 miles (289.7 km) from Gettysburg, PA, to Charlottesville, VA

**Drive time:** 5 days

**Best overnights:** Frederick, Leesburg, Warrenton, Culpeper, Orange

**Best seasons:** Spring, summer, or fall

**Highlights:** Gettysburg, Frederick, Leesburg, Manassas, Montpelier, Virginia wine country, Monticello

"Where America Happened" is the motto of this national scenic byway, a 180-mile (289.7 km) road trip through Pennsylvania, Maryland, West Virginia, and Virginia that features presidential homes and legendary battlefields.

The drive's northern end is anchored by **Gettysburg National Military Park** in Pennsylvania. The **Museum and Visitor Center** provides an outstanding overview of both the war and its bloodiest battle, as well as the famous "**Cyclorama" painting** rendered in the 1880s, and information on ranger programs and guided tours.

Adjacent to Gettysburg, **Eisenhower National Historic Site** is where the 34th president spent weekends away from the White House in the 1950s.

Catoctin Mountain Highway (U.S. 15) takes the route into Maryland and **Catoctin Mountain Park**, where 25 miles (40.2 km) of trail arrayed around historic Camp David cater to hikers, horseback riders, and cross-country skiers.

Just down the pike is **Frederick**, a major crossroads of the Civil War. The well-preserved downtown harbors myriad restaurants, bars, shops, and the **National Museum of Civil War Medicine. Monocacy National Battlefield** lies on the outskirts of town, and both **Harpers Ferry** and **Antietam National Battlefield** are a short drive to the west.

U.S. 15 reaches the **Potomac River** at Point of Rocks, where road trippers can abandon their vehicles (temporarily) for a walk along the historic **Chesapeake and Ohio Canal**, which started as George Washington's project to improve transportation in the new nation.

The first stop in northern Virginia is **Leesburg**, where the assemblage of historic architecture includes **Morven Park** (1780), **Oatlands Historic House and Gardens** (1804), and the **Marshall House**

Take a break in Charlottesville, Virginia, to explore Thomas Jefferson's Monticello.

A statue of Andrew Jackson overlooks the Manassas Civil War battlefield where the infamous Battle of Bull Run was fought.

(1820s). Just for a lark, you can cross the river again, this time on **Historic White's Ferry**, the last of 100 ferries that once plied the Potomac.

Another 30 miles (48.3 km) down U.S. 15 is a turnoff for **Manassas National Battlefield Park**, where the Confederates earned two great victories over Union forces. South of Manassas, **Warrenton** is a historic old town flush with **wineries, craft breweries**, and the **Fauquier History Museum at the Old Jail** (built in 1808).

The stretch of U.S. 15 between Warrenton and Orange includes **Brandy Station Battlefield**, where the largest ever cavalry engagement on American soil played out in 1863, and **Cedar Mountain Battlefield**, where Stonewall Jackson notched another victory in 1862.

Upon reaching Orange, the trip segues onto the **Constitution High-**way (Route 20) for the rest of its length. **James Madison's Montpelier** residence (built circa 1764) is just five miles (8 km) beyond Orange.

Farther along, **Barboursville** lies at the heart of the **Virginia wine country** and its various tasting rooms. The ruins of **Barboursville Mansion**, designed by Thomas Jefferson, provide a unique vineyard experience.

The road trip ends in **Charlottesville**, where Thomas Jefferson's striking **Monticello** estate and the **University of Virginia** campus that he helped found provide a fitting end to this heritage drive. ∎

## LAY YOUR HEAD

• **Inn at Stone Manor:** Eighteenth-century lodging located on a grand 135-acre (54.6 ha) estate near Frederick, MD; gardens, afternoon tea, fishing, wine and beer tastings; from $200. innatstonemanor.com

• **Lansdowne Resort and Spa:** Modern luxury beside the Potomac on the outskirts of Leesburg, VA; restaurants, bars, golf, tennis, pools, spa, river adventures, winery tours, hiking and biking trails; from $167. lansdowneresort.com

• **Chilton House:** Ten generations of the Chilton family have lived in this early 19th-century Warrenton, VA, manse, now an upscale B&B; library, garden, evening drinks; from $95. thechiltonhouse.com

• **The Inn at Willow Grove:** Boutique hotel tucked inside a restored 1770 plantation house on a 40-acre estate near Orange, VA; restaurant, bar, spa, fitness center, heated outdoor pool; from $199. innatwillowgrove.com

# The Longest Yard Sale

## Alabama to Michigan

Tens of thousands of motorists take to U.S. Highway 127 between Michigan and Alabama every August to hunt for bargains along the World's Longest Yard Sale — a 690-mile (1,110.5 km) rural route through six states that could easily double as the world's longest barbecue and block party.

Starting on the first Thursday of August, more than 2,200 vendors set up their stalls along rural Highway 127 in Alabama, Georgia, Tennessee, Kentucky, Ohio, and Michigan, beginning a rambling, four-day feast of art and antiques, knickknacks, apparel, housewares, and homemade foods.

The 127 Corridor Sale kicked off in 1987 as a way to attract motorists away from the interstates and onto local roads. For those who can't make the trip in August, there are plenty of year-round adventures and attractions along the way. Because the route initially follows highways other than U.S. 127, it's advisable to plot your drive ahead of time using the official yard sale website: 127sale.com.

Located about an hour north of Birmingham on the banks of the Coosa River, **Gadsden**, Alabama, is the southern terminus of this elongated emporium. Once upon a time a thriving steamboat port, the town

### THE BIG PICTURE

**Distance:** 690 miles (1,110.5 km) from Gadsden, AL, to Addison, MI

**Drive time:** 3-5 days

**Best overnights:** Chattanooga, Frankfort, Cincinnati

**Best season:** Summer

**Highlights:** Lookout Mountain, Sequatchie Valley, Kentucky bourbon country

is best known these days for **Noccalula Falls**, which tumbles over a precipice near mile one of the yard sale.

From there, the route follows the Lookout Mountain Parkway north through the Alabama backcountry, across a tiny portion of northwestern Georgia and into Tennessee. Among possible stops along the way are **DeSoto State Park** (Alabama's largest nature reserve) and the rugged topography of **Little River Canyon National Preserve** with its waterfalls, swimming holes, and scenic overlooks.

The parkway eventually runs right across **Lookout Mountain** and its Civil War shrines before dropping down into **Chattanooga** and the start of Highway 127. Snaking its way up the picturesque **Sequatchie Valley** of central Tennessee, the route takes in more American wartime history: the **Military Memorial Museum** in Crossville, the boyhood home of World War I hero Sgt. Alvin York in **Pall Mall**, and a motor trail that traces Confederate **General Hood's 1864 Campaign**.

Crossing into Kentucky, Highway 127 meanders along the western shore of 101-mile-long (162.5 km) **Lake Cumberland**, where bargain hunters can take a brief respite on boats, speedboats, and other watercraft. Next comes a string of

Tour and taste at the Maker's Mark distillery in Kentucky.

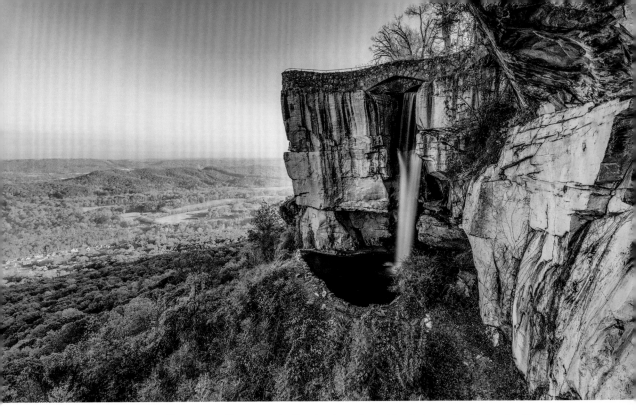

Hike Lookout Mountain near Chattanooga, Tennessee, for the stunning natural vistas that sprawl out below the ridge.

towns—**Russell Springs, Danville,** and **Harrodsburg**—where antiques are a big deal year-round. And then good old Kentucky bourbon country: **Wild Turkey** and **Four Roses** distilleries near Lawrenceburg and **Buffalo Trace** in Frankfort.

Dead ahead is **Kentucky Speedway** in Sparta, which hosts an annual NASCAR race and the **Richard Petty Driving Experience**, where motorists can leave their street-legal vehicle in the parking lot for a chance to pilot a genuine stock car around the 1.5-mile (2.4 km) oval at speeds up to 165 miles per hour (265.5 km/h).

Crossing the **Ohio River** on the Clay Wade Bailey Bridge, U.S. 127 bisects downtown **Cincinnati** before rolling into the countryside again. The long stretch across western Ohio is mostly farmland and a few scattered towns. But the heartland is

not without its roadside amusements: **Pyramid Hill Sculpture Park and Museum** in Hamilton with its 60 pieces of enormous outdoor artwork, the short hiking trails of **Shawnee Prairie Reserve** in Greenville, and the vintage **Starliter**

**Drive-In Theater** in Maria Stein, which has been screening movies since 1949.

The World's Longest Yard Sale finally peters out in **Addison**, MI, about 90 minutes west of **Detroit** via U.S. 127 and Interstate 94. ∎

---

### SCENIC DETOURS

• **Appalachian Highlands Scenic Byway:** Parallel to the yard sale route in northern Alabama, this 80-mile (128.8 km) drive meanders through the southernmost reach of the Appalachians.

• **Ocoee Scenic Byway:** Just east of Chattanooga, this 26-mile (41.8 km) wilderness route winds through Cherokee National Forest and the remote Ocoee River Gorge with its world-class whitewater paddling.

• **Shakertown Road:** Short but sweet, this 2.6-mile (4.2 km) drive in

central Kentucky includes a meticulously restored Shaker village and hand-built stone fences.

• **Kentucky Bourbon Trail:** Fourteen signature bourbon distilleries are located along a rambling route between Louisville and Lexington that intersects with Highway 127 in Lawrenceburg.

• **Maumee Valley Scenic Byway:** The War of 1812 is the focus of this 60-mile (96.6 km) route through northwestern Ohio between Defiance and Toledo.

# Dixie Highway
## Illinois to Florida

One of America's first long-distance motor roads, this nearly 1,500-mile (2,414 km) route from the Midwest to Florida helped pioneer the road trip vacation to somewhere far away and exciting, and planted a seed that would grow into the interstate highway system.

**THE BIG PICTURE**

**Distance:** ca 1,460 miles (2,349.6 km) from Chicago to Miami

**Drive time:** 10-14 days

**Best overnights:** Indianapolis, Louisville, Nashville, Atlanta, Gainesville, Orlando

**Best seasons:** Spring or fall

**Highlights:** Indy Speedway, Columbus architecture, Louisville, Mammoth Cave, Nashville music scene, Chattanooga battlefields, Atlanta, Gainesville wildlife, Orlando theme parks

Part of the National Auto Trail network, the Dixie Highway was constructed between 1915 and 1929, largely with private funding. Although it originated as a single route between Chicago and Miami, it expanded into several ways to drive between the Midwest and South.

Our modern road trip follows the original route, a journey through at least six major cities and small towns that were later bypassed by the interstate highways.

Starting out from Chicago, the first leg follows Illinois Route One to **Danville** and U.S. Highway 136 into Indiana. The first stop is **Crawfordsville**, where the historic city center preserves the place where **General Lew Wallace** wrote *Ben-Hur* and the **Montgomery County Rotary Jail Museum**, where the cells rotate like a carousel.

**Indianapolis** is dead ahead, the old highway ambling right by the **Indianapolis Motor Speedway** into downtown Indy and exiting out the other side as U.S. Highway 30. Forty miles (64.4 km) down the road is **Columbus**, **Indiana**, the architectural oasis of the Midwest, where guided tours take in structures designed by I. M. Pei, Eero Saarinen, Richard Meier, Robert Venturi, and other "starchitects."

U.S. 31 leaps the Ohio River to **Louisville** with its slugger bats, boxing heritage, and thoroughbred horses before heading into the Kentucky countryside. Pop into **Swope's Cars of Yesteryear** in **Elizabethtown** to see what people drove down the Dixie Highway 100 years ago, and then **Mammoth Cave** in central Kentucky, one of the highlights along the original touring route.

**Nashville, Tennessee**, beckons, with visits to Andrew Jackson's **Hermitage** and the **Country Music Hall of Fame and Museum** on the bucket list, as well as tunes at **Ryman Auditorium** or the **Grand Ole Opry**.

"Music City" also marks the transition from Highway 31 to Highway 41 for the drive down to Georgia. With **Murfreesboro**, the **Chattanooga battlefields**, and **Kennesaw Mountain** along the way, there's plenty to see and do on this stretch for Civil War aficionados.

Reaching **Atlanta**, Highway 41

The Country Music Hall of Fame and Museum displays gold and platinum records.

The Indianapolis 500-Mile Race (Indy 500) is the world's oldest car race, first held in 1911 at the Indianapolis Motor Speedway.

skirts around the western edge of the central city—close to major sights like the **Georgia Aquarium, Centennial Olympic Park**, and the **Center for Civil and Human Rights** before slipping south of town via the Metropolitan Parkway.

Forty-one rambles down to **Macon**, where the **Allman Brothers Museum at the Big House** pays tribute to one of the best road-song bands of all time, and **Ocmulgee Mounds National Historical Park** recalls 17,000 years of Native American culture in the Southeast.

The vintage Dixie Highway split into two branches at Macon, but our road trip blazes a middle course along Highway 41 to Florida. Gainesville offers an array of animal attractions like the **Butterfly Rainforest, Lubee Bat Conservancy**, and **Carson Springs** wildlife rescue center.

Highway 441 meanders through Central Florida's lake district to **Orlando** and all those theme parks, and then southward to Okeechobee, where **airboat adventures** and **bass fishing** are all the rage on Florida's largest lake.

From Okeechobee's southern shore, it's pretty much a straight shot across the **Everglades** tropical wetlands on U.S. 27 to the **Miami** metropolitan area and a rendezvous with a street that's still called the Dixie Highway. ∎

## LAY YOUR HEAD

• **Severin Hotel:** Marble staircases and crystal chandeliers decorate this historic landmark hotel, opened in 1913 opposite Indy's Union Station; restaurant, bars, fitness center, indoor heated pool; from $169. omnihotels.com

• **Brown Hotel:** Louisville's grand dame since 1923 has hosted celebrities including Liz Taylor, President Truman, and the Duke of Windsor; restaurants, bar, fitness center, shops; from $152. brownhotel.com

• **Hermitage Hotel:** Opened in 1910 to much acclaim, this luxurious downtown landmark still boasts Nashville's most impressive lobby; restaurant, library, bar, spa, fitness center, boutique; from $290. thehermitagehotel.com

• **Park Plaza:** This vintage Florida boutique (opened in 1922) is the only hotel along Winter Park's historic Park Avenue; breakfast, wrought-iron balconies; from $179. parkplazahotel.com

# Jurassic Drive
## Alberta to Colorado

The ultimate prehistoric road trip is a 1,760-mile (2,832.5 km) meander between Calgary and Denver that takes in some of the globe's paramount dinosaur digs, fossil finds, primordial landscapes, and top-notch museums where the colossal, terrifying, and totally magnificent beasts from the past are reconstructed.

**THE BIG PICTURE**

**Distance:** ca 1,760 miles (2,832.5 km) from Calgary, AB, to Denver, CO

**Drive time:** 7-10 days

**Best overnights:** Lethbridge, Helena, Butte, Idaho Falls, Pocatello, Provo, Vernal, Vail

**Best seasons:** Late spring, summer, or early fall

**Highlights:** Royal Tyrell, Dinosaur Provincial Park, Two Medicine, Fossil Butte, Cleveland-Lloyd Quarry, Dinosaur National Monument, Dinosaur Ridge

Much of North America was once covered in shallow seas surrounded by lush vegetation nurtured by a climate that was decidedly tropical compared to today. A multitude of primordial creatures roamed that landscape, including dinosaurs both large and small.

The seas drained and great mountains arose, but the bones of those dinosaurs remained hidden for millions of years—until their discovery in modern times in the Rocky Mountain areas of both the United States and Canada.

Ninety minutes east of **Calgary**, amid the rolling prairies of the province of Alberta, lies one of the world's best dinosaur fossil depositories: the **Royal Tyrell Museum** (RTM) in Drumheller. Among its collection of prized fossils are a complete *Triceratops* skeleton, a ferocious *Albertosaurus,* a giant *Camarasaurus,* and a *T. rex* nicknamed "Black Beauty" because of its dark-colored bones. RTM offers numerous **guided programs** (many of them kid friendly), including dig experiences, fossil casting, and raptor

assembly, as well as a 25-minute film, *Passion for the Past.*

Many of the bones on display at RTM were discovered in the remote badlands of southeastern Alberta, a rich fossil bed along the Red Deer River now protected within the confines of **Dinosaur Provincial Park**. The numbers are astounding: More than 500 separate dinosaurs have been unearthed there over the years, including 150 complete skeletons and every known group of Cretaceous dinosaurs.

The park's **Dinosaur Visitor Centre** features reconstructed skeletons, dinosaur-related films, and interpretive activities, including a two-hour **bus tour**, **fossil casting, guided hikes, paleontologist-for-a-day experience**, and a family-oriented **Fossil Safari**. The park also offers five short **interpretive trails, canoeing or kayaking** in the Red Deer River, and driving along the **Scenic Loop Road** through the deeply eroded badlands.

After crossing the international border at **Coutts-Sweet Grass**, the next stop on this wide-ranging dinosaur drive is **Two Medicine Dino-**

Get up close to our prehistoric roots at the Royal Tyrell Museum.

Dinosaur National Monument's "Wall of Bones" contains nearly 1,500 dinosaur fossils in its cliff face.

saur Center in Bynum, Montana. Dedicated to paleontological research and education, this non-profit institute offers intriguing public programs that take visitors out into the real world of fossil hunting, recovery, and inspection.

Among the highlights of the small **museum** at Two Medicine are the still-embedded remains of *Maiasaura* and a *T. rex* skull (both found nearby), as well as actual size models of the first baby dinosaurs discovered in North America and a 137-foot-long (41.8 m) *Seismosaurus*. But the real focus is field programs, from family-friendly half-day and full-day digs to serious week-long workshops like **World of Dinosaurs** and **Beginner Field Techniques**.

Interstate 15 snakes its way through western Montana and eastern Idaho to McCammon and a turnoff for U.S. Highway 30 and **Fossil Butte National Monument**

in a remote corner of Wyoming. Alternatively, you can make the drive via **Yellowstone** and **Grand Teton** National Parks. The distance is about the same (around 600 road miles/965.6 km), but detouring through the parks will add at least two hours to the drive—not includ-

ing time spent watching geysers, grizzly bears, and granite peaks.

"America's Aquarium in Stone" is **Fossil Butte**'s well-earned nickname, a fantastic assemblage of fossilized fish, mammals, birds, reptiles, insects, and plants from the Eocene epoch (34-56 million years ago)

113

Head toward the peaks on the road to Grand Teton National Park.

when the area was covered by a subtropical lake and its shoreline.

The national monument **Visitor Center** has more than 800 fossils on display, with entire walls dedicated to ancient fish, birds, turtles, and plants, as well as a prehistoric crocodile and alligator, miniature horse, early bats, and a lemur-like mammal that once called North America home. Dioramas show what the shoreline and forest habitats must have looked like in those days.

Among Fossil Butte's interpretive programs are a **quarry visit, fossil preparation demonstration**, and

**ranger talks** on the area's flora and fauna, past and present. The national monument maintains four miles (6.4 km) of **hiking trails** through the surrounding sagebrush desert, as well as the unique **Journey Through Time** outdoor exhibit along the road leading to the visitor center.

From Fossil Butte, it's a pretty quick run down into central Utah and across the **Wasatch Range** to the **Provo-Orem** metropolitan area. From there, cruise U.S. Highway 6 into central Utah's deeply eroded "Castle Country" and the

**Utah State University Eastern Prehistoric Museum** in Price.

Unlike the other collections along this drive, the university museum covers the region's original human inhabitants as well as ancient flora, fauna, and geology. The museum's 700,000 **archaeological artifacts** include relics from the Paleo-Indian, Desert Archaic, Ancestral Puebloan, Fremont, and Ute cultures that have occupied central Utah.

But make no mistake: There are ancient creatures too. Among them are the Huntington Mammoth, the fearsome *Utahraptor,* a carnivorous *Allosaurus,* an armorplated *Gastonia burgei,* and a duckbilled *Prosaurolophus.*

Many of the bones on display came from the legendary **Cleveland-Lloyd Dinosaur Quarry**, located about 30 miles (48.3 km) south of Price near the tiny town of Elmo. The internationally famed dinosaur dig has yielded more than 12,000 bones from at least 74 dinosaur species since its discovery in 1929. The Bureau of Land Management paleontological park features short trails to **dig sites, geological strata, scenic vistas**, and Native American **rock art galleries**.

It's 130 miles (209.2 km) from Price to America's biggest and best-known prehistoric creature feature:

## EN ROUTE EATS

- **Sublime Food & Wine:** Fresh, modern, locally sourced Canadian cuisine is the specialty at this eatery near the Royal Tyrell. 109 Centre St., Drumheller, AB. sublimefoodandwine.com

- **Log Cabin Café:** Soups, salads, sandwiches, burgers, and marvelous pies are the essence of this country café near Two Medicine. 102 Main

Ave. South, Choteau, MT. 406-466-2888

- **Jody's Diner:** An hour south of Fossil Butte, this classic roadside diner makes a great stop on the drive down to Provo, Utah; steaks, burgers, Navajo tacos. 260 Bear River Dr., Evanston, WY. jodysdiner.com

- **Sherald's Drive-In:** Time-trip back

to the 1950s at this bygone burger joint two blocks east of the Prehistoric Museum; hot dogs, burritos, gyros, shakes, frosties. 434 East Main St., Price, UT. 435-637-1447

- **Vernal Brewing Company:** Allosaurus Amber Ale is just one of the craft beers on tap at this gastropub near Dinosaur, NM. 55 South 500 East, Vernal, UT. vernalbrewing.com

**Dinosaur National Monument.** Straddling a remote section of the Utah-Colorado border, the park harbors more than 800 paleontological sites including the incomparable **"Wall of Bones."** Housed within the futuristic steel-and-glass **Quarry Exhibit Hall**, the 150-foot-long (45.7 m) rock slab is embedded with the bones of numerous dinosaurs, including *Allosaurus, Apatosaurus, Camarasaurus, Diplodocus,* and *Stegosaurus.*

**Fossil Discovery Trail** leads from the Wall of Bones to the **Dinosaur Quarry Visitor Center**, with three of the monument's early 20th-century digs along the way. More sites await along **Cub Creek Road**, including the ancient petroglyphs and pictographs at **Swelter Shelter**.

The rest of the massive park (210,844 acres/85,325.5 ha) is all about raw nature, a rugged semidesert landscape best explored by foot, four-wheel-drive, or whitewater rafting trips down the swift-flowing **Yampa** and **Green Rivers**. The only other all-vehicle access is 32-mile (51.5 km) **Harpers Corner Road**, which heads north from the park's **Canyon Visitor Center** to an overlook several thousand feet above the confluence of the two rivers.

Road trippers can cross Colorado and the Rockies via Interstate 70 or U.S. Highway 40. Either way, you end up on the west side of the Denver metropolitan area and another well-known dig. Wedged between Red Rocks Amphitheater and Green Mountain, **Dinosaur Ridge** is where the world's first *Stegosaurus* skeleton was discovered in 1877. In subsequent years, the site surrendered many other ancient treasures, including a "Dinosaur Freeway" of footprints uncovered in the 1930s.

Dinosaur Ridge offers many ways to learn about the prehistoric giants, such as the **Trek Through Time** exhibit hall, **short trails** to excavation sites around the park (including those world-famous dinosaur tracks), family-friendly **guided tours**, and **adult field trips**.

If you still haven't had your fill of bygone bones by the time you reach Denver, check out the **Morrison Natural History Museum**, just five minutes down Hog Back Road from Dinosaur Ridge. On display are a variety of Jurassic, Cretaceous, and Cenozoic flora and fauna, from a *T. rex* skull and baby dinosaur tracks to mammoth and saber-tooth cat bones. Compare the ancient beasts to the museum's live reptiles and amphibians. ■

For an adrenaline rush beyond the steering wheel, paddle the Class III and IV rapids of the Yampa and Green Rivers.

# Sports Hall of Fame Track

## Ohio to Rhode Island

Two hundred years of athletic achievement unfold on this pilgrimage from Ohio to Rhode Island through the heartland of American sports. Along the way, stop at five shrines that honor legendary athletes and coaches, as well as history's greatest wins.

Let the games begin at the **Pro Football Hall of Fame** in Canton, Ohio, where the lineup features more than 300 gridiron stars, including bygone marvels like Jim Thorpe, Bronko Nagurski, George Halas, Curly Lambeau, and Red Grange.

With a pigskin-shaped dome, the structure itself is a tribute to the popular sport. Canton was chosen as the hall's location because it's where the National Football League (NFL) was born in 1920. Just 14 teams played the first season, including long-forgotten squads like the Muncie Flyers, Dayton Triangles, and Canton Bulldogs.

From Canton, the journey heads

**THE BIG PICTURE**

**Distance:** ca 740 miles (1,190.9 km) from Canton, OH, to Newport, RI

**Drive time:** 5 days

**Best overnights:** Cleveland, Syracuse, Cooperstown, Albany, Springfield

**Best seasons:** Anytime

**Highlights:** Football, boxing, baseball, basketball, and tennis halls of fame

north through Akron and Cleveland—where road trippers can visit the **Rock and Roll Hall of Fame**—before cruising up Interstate 90 into upstate New York.

Just past Syracuse is the **International Boxing Hall of Fame** in Canastota, New York. The museum features a wide range of memorabilia, including the gloves, shoes, robes, and championship belts of all-time greats like Joe Louis, Sugar Ray Leonard, and Marvin Hagler, as well as the entire Madison Square Garden ring used in the 1971 heavyweight title fight between Muhammad Ali and Joe Frazier.

A right hook from I-90 onto State Route 28 takes you to the **National Baseball Hall of Fame and Museum** in Cooperstown, New York. The hall was founded in 1939 on the 100th anniversary of General Abner Doubleday inventing baseball in Cooperstown in 1839, a claim that's now disputed by baseball historians. Nevertheless, the museum endures as the holy grail of American baseball.

From Babe Ruth and Ted Williams to Sandy Koufax and Hank Aaron, all the greats are here—more than 300 total inductees, including Negro Leagues (1885-1951) players, managers, umpires, administrators, and one woman (sports executive

Henry "Hammering Hank" Aaron's memorabilia is on display in Cooperstown, New York.

Appropriately designed in the shape of a basketball, the Naismith Memorial Basketball Hall of Fame is worth visiting.

Effa Manley). A Viva Baseball exhibit revolves around Caribbean and Latin American hall of famers, and just for laughs there's a continuous loop of Abbott and Costello's legendary "Who's on First" comedy routine.

State Route 80 leads north from Cooperstown to another rendezvous with I-90 and a drive through the Albany metropolitan area and western Massachusetts. Dead ahead is Springfield and the **Naismith Memorial Basketball Hall of Fame**. The museum is named after James Naismith, who invented basketball in 1891 as a "distraction" for rowdy kids at the Springfield YMCA.

Although the hall of fame was started in 1959, its distinctive basketball-shaped sphere didn't come along until 2002, when the museum expanded. Unlike the other halls of fame on this trip, the Naismith honors professionals and amateurs, as well as male and female players and coaches. More than 400 hoops legends are featured.

Continue east on I-90 to Worchester and then head south via a combination of state highways and interstates to Newport, Rhode Island, and the oldest of the halls on this journey. Founded in 1954, the

**International Tennis Hall of Fame** is located inside historic Newport Casino. In addition to exhibits on more than 250 tennis stars, both men and women, the museum also offers the public a chance to play the game on an indoor hard court and outdoor grass courts. ■

## EN ROUTE EATS

• **Benders Tavern:** Opened in 1902, many gridiron stars have dined on surf and turf at this legendary Canton, Ohio, restaurant. 137 Court Ave. SW, Canton, OH. bendersrestaurant.com

• **Doubleday Cafe:** Located between the Baseball Hall of Fame and the Heroes of Baseball Wax Museum, this low-key eatery in New York is the ideal place for a seventh-inning stretch. 93 Main St., Cooperstown, NY. facebook.com/DoubledayCafé

• **Samuel's Tap and Table:** Craft beers, cocktails, and pub grub inside the Basketball Hall of Fame. Heartier meals are available at Max's Tavern on the museum's other side. 1000 West Columbus Ave., Springfield, MA. samuelstapandtable.com

• **La Forge Casino Restaurant:** This oldie but goodie (opened 1880) offers a raw bar with fresh New England seafood and an outdoor terrace beside the Tennis Hall of Fame grass courts. 186 Bellevue Ave., Newport, RI. laforgenewport.com

# Pan-American Highway
## Texas to Minnesota

Spanning nearly 1,700 miles (2,735.9 km) between Laredo, Texas, and Grand Portage, Minnesota, the U.S. portion of the Pan-American Highway meanders through small towns and big cities, corn fields and cattle ranches—a classic journey across the American heartland.

### THE BIG PICTURE

**Distance:** ca 1,700 miles (2,735.9 km) from Laredo, TX, to Grand Portage, MN

**Drive time:** 14-21 days

**Best overnights:** San Antonio, Fort Worth, Oklahoma City, Wichita, Kansas City, Des Moines, Minneapolis–St. Paul, Duluth

**Best seasons:** Spring, summer, or fall

**Highlights:** The Alamo, Fort Worth Stockyards, Dallas JFK sights, Oklahoma City National Memorial, Kansas City Union Station, Mississippi River, Lake Superior

Born of the same era as other engineering wonders like the Hoover Dam and the Empire State Building, the Pan American Highway is the greatest single roadway project ever attempted.

Initially running from Mexico to Argentina, the highway was later expanded to encompass routes from Alaska to Patagonia, including a U.S. portion that traces Interstate 35 across six states.

Anchoring the southern end of the road, **Laredo, Texas,** is no longer the dusty "cowboy's lament" of the *Streets of Laredo* but a modern city that has prospered as one of the world's busiest border crossings. The **Republic of the Rio Grande Museum** illuminates Laredo's role as the capital of a small, independent nation that existed between January and November 1840. The historical district along **Zaragoza Street** also harbors **San Agustín Cathedral** (opened in 1871) and the **Border Heritage Museum** in the restored Villa Antigua.

I-35 shoots due north through the mesquite woodland of South Texas to **San Antonio**. Although most renowned for the 1836 battle that sparked Texas independence, the "Mission City" was founded in 1718 by Spanish padres who established a fortified mission compound that came to be called the **Alamo**.

Now the nation's seventh largest city (1.5 million people), San Antonio offers an enticing blend of past and present, from the **San Antonio Missions National Historical Park** and Victorian-era painted ladies of the **King William Historic District**, to the 750-foot (228.6 m) tall **Tower of the Americas** and **Six Flags Siesta Texas** theme park.

Many of the city's landmarks and attractions are spread along the **River Walk**, a restaurant- and museum-lined waterfront path that connects lively **Alamo Square** and the new **Pearl District**, a brewery complex filled with food, drink, art, and entertainment outlets.

Eighty miles (128.8 km) up the

You'll always remember your drive to the Alamo in San Antonio, Texas.

The Fort Worth Herd Longhorn Cattle Drive makes its way through the Fort Worth Stockyards Historic District.

interstate, **Austin** does triple duty as a state capital, college town, and hipster boomtown renowned for its dynamic arts and music scene. "Keep Austin Weird" is the battle cry of those who want to maintain its offbeat reputation, typified by the bars, cafés, and music joints along **South Congress Avenue**.

One of the nation's most distinguished statehouses, the **Texas Capitol Building** offers exhibits and guided tours, while the nearby **University of Texas** campus features the **LBJ Presidential Library**, the **Texas Memorial Museum** of natural history, and a chance to "hook 'em horns" at the huge **Darrell K Royal–Texas Memorial Stadium** during college football season.

**Fort Worth** lies three hours to the north—and 150 years in the past. It's a city that recalls its Wild West days with the **Stockyard National Historic District**, where Texas longhorn cattle are herded down the cobblestone streets twice each day, the **National Cowgirl Museum and Hall of Fame**, and a rodeo at the **Cowboy Coliseum**. Alternatively, you can follow I-35 East to Dallas and the John F. Kennedy landmarks around **Dealey Plaza**, the graves of notorious outlaws **Bonnie and Clyde**, or world-class museums like the **Nasher Sculpture Center**.

Crossing the Red River into Oklahoma, I-35 makes a beeline for **Oklahoma City**. Although best known for the **National Cowboy and Western Heritage Museum** and the **National Memorial and Museum** on the site of the Murrah Federal Building tragedy, Oklahoma City also has its offbeat side, including the skeleton-filled **Museum of Osteology** and the bars, cafés, and galleries of the funky **Paseo Arts District**. Another place to eat and imbibe, **Bricktown** also boasts minor league baseball at **Chickasaw Ballpark** and the imposing **Centennial Land Run Monument**.

## PIT STOPS

• **Washington's Birthday Celebration:** Laredo's month-long fiesta of food, fun, and fireworks is the nation's largest event dedicated to the first president; February. wbcalaredo.org

• **Wichita Riverfest:** Kansas's largest annual June event features A-list musical acts, water activities, athletic contests, and lots of food. wichitariverfest.com

• **Iowa State Fair:** Nothing says American Heartland like this annual August gathering full of carnival rides, freaky and fried foods, and farm animals staged in Des Moines since 1878. iowastatefair.org

• **Red Steagall Cowboy Gathering and Western Swing Fest:** Fort Worth Stockyards hosts an annual October event that mixes rodeo, fiddling, dancing, and chuck wagon cook-offs. redsteagallcowboygathering.com

The modern interstate sticks close to the route of the old cattle-drive Chisholm Trail on its way to **Wichita** in central Kansas. Although it started life as "Cowtown," the prairie city gradually rose into the "World's Air Capital" on the wings of companies like Cessna, Learjet, and Boeing that set up shop there. Discover those diverse sides of Wichita heritage at **Old Town** living history center and **Kansas Aviation Museum**. Among the city's other top attractions are the excellent **Great Plains Nature Center** and the eclectic **Museum of World Treasures**.

Jogging to the northeast, I-35 cruises into **Kansas City, Missouri**. Another heartland city that's undergone a renaissance in recent years, "K.C." has resurrected the once-dilapidated **River Market** and **Crown Center** neighborhoods and historic **Union Station** into modern arts, eating, and entertainment areas with attractions ranging from the *Arabia Steamboat Museum* to the family-friendly **Science City** and **Sea Life Aquarium**. Kansas City also boasts two world-class collections: the **Nelson-Atkins Museum of Art** and the **National World War I Museum**.

Cutting across the corn and soybean fields of northwestern Missouri and into central Iowa, the road-trip route runs through **Des Moines**, the third of four state capitals along this drive. Tucked between the golden-domed **State Capitol** and the Des Moines River, the historic **East Village** offers restaurants, bars, and shops, as well as the **State Historical Museum of Iowa** and at the nearby **Greater Des Moines Botanical Garden**.

Although the countryside north of Des Moines may seem like nothing but endless farms, here and there are reasons to stop—for instance, the **Frank Lloyd Wright homes** and Prairie School architecture of Mason City, the **Buddy Holly crash site** near Clear Lake, and the woods and wetlands trails of **Myre–Big Island State Park** in southern Minnesota.

Reaching the **Minneapolis–St. Paul** metropolitan area, I-35 splits into west and east legs through the Twin Cities. The region's bygone days are on full display in old neighborhoods like the **Mill District** and **Northeast River** in Minneapolis, as well as historic structures like **Fort Snelling, Cathedral of St. Paul**, and the enormous Victorian-era **Hill House**. With water, water everywhere, there's plenty of nature too: **Minnehaha Falls** of "Song of Hiawatha" fame or hiking, biking, and boating the 72-mile-long (115.9 km) **Mississippi National River and Recreation Area**.

Finally leaving the grasslands behind, the route makes its way through the forest of northern Minnesota, a journey past countless small lakes to the biggest one of them all— **Lake Superior**. Interstate 35 segues into an ordinary surface street along the lakeshore in **Duluth**. Many "Zenith City" landmarks are found along the waterfront, including the **Great Lakes Aquarium**, the **S.S. *William A. Irvin* Ore Boat Museum**, and the **Aerial Lift Bridge**.

But there's something that keeps pulling you northward—that final stretch of the Pan-American Highway along State Highway 62. Also called the **North Shore Scenic Drive**, the route hugs Lake Superior for 154 ultrascenic miles (247.8 km), with stops along the way at historic lighthouses, the lakeside hiking trails of **Superior National Forest** and a dozen state parks, and lofty overlooks like **Palisades Head**. Near the end of the road, the **Grand Portage National Monument** offers hikes along a route pioneered centuries ago by Native Americans and French voyageurs, while **Grand Portage State Park**'s 120-foot-high (36.6 m) cascade, High Falls, divides the U.S. and Canada. ∎

Split Rock Lighthouse sits on the shore of Lake Superior, Michigan.

---

## EN ROUTE EATS

• **The Frutería:** Celebrity chef Johnny Hernandez's modern take on Mexican street food, plus fresh fruit smoothies and creative tequila cocktails. 1401 S. Flores St., San Antonio, TX. chefjohnnyhernandez.com

• **Güero's Taco Bar:** Hipster hangout with awesome Mexican grub and sidewalk tables in south Austin. 1412 S. Congress Ave., Austin, TX. gueros.com

• **The Pump Bar:** Vintage gas station transformed into a trendy bar and grill in the Paseo Arts District. 2425 N. Walker Ave., Oklahoma City, OK. www.pumpbar.net

• **Arthur Bryant's:** Classic Kansas City barbecue at the restaurant's original location; the burnt ends and pulled pork are to die for. 1727 Brooklyn Ave., Kansas City, MO. arthurbryantsbbq.com

• **B&B Grocery, Meats and Deli:** It's hard to choose between the Killer Breaded Pork Tenderloin sandwich and the four-patty Quadzilla Cheeseburger at this sandwich shop. 2001 SE Sixth St., Des Moines, IA. bbgrocerymeatdeli.com

• **The Bachelor Farmer:** Housemade cow's milk cheese, wild rice porridge with oyster mushrooms, and charred golden beets with cashew butter are among the delightful dishes at this farm-to-table eatery. 50 N. Second Ave., Minneapolis, MN. thebachelorfarmer.com

# Northwest Wine & Dine

## British Columbia to Washington

One of the globe's gourmet hot spots, the Pacific Northwest harbors foodie havens Vancouver and Seattle, as well as the wine regions of British Columbia and Washington State, destinations featured on this delicious 800-mile (1,287.5 km) drive.

### THE BIG PICTURE

**Distance:** ca 825 miles (1,327 km) from Vancouver, BC, to Seattle, WA

**Drive time:** 5-7 days

**Best overnights:** Kelowna, Penticton, Osoyoos, Chelan, Tri-Cities, Yakima

**Best seasons:** Summer, fall, or winter

**Highlights:** Vancouver, Similkameen, Okanagan, Lake Chelan, Grand Coulee, Tri-Cities, Yakima, Cascades range, Seattle

Fresh seafood, farm-to-table ingredients, and increasingly fine wines have transformed the Pacific Northwest into a major food destination. The forte of **Vancouver, British Columbia,** is Asia-Pacific fusion food; eateries like **Kissa Tanto** (Japanese-Italian) and **Vij's** (contemporary Indian) count among Canada's top 30 restaurants.

The first vineyards you'll come to are less than an hour west of Vancouver along the **Trans-Canada Highway**, a **Fraser Valley** terroir around **Langley** and **Abbotsford** known for wines made with Siegerrebe grapes.

Reaching Hope in the upper Fraser Valley, the wine route veers onto the **Crowsnest Highway** (Route 3) and into the Cascades. **Manning Provincial Park** provides a great chance to stretch your legs on summer hiking trails or winter ski runs.

The park is actually the northern anchor of the **Pacific Crest Trail**.

The Crowsnest continues into the arid **Similkameen Valley**, renowned for its organic grapes. Local wineries produce eight different varietals, from Merlot and Pinot Noir to Chardonnay and Pinot Gris. Most of the vineyards are around **Keremeos**, also known for its fresh fruit stands and craft ciders.

From Keremeos, it's just a half-hour drive on Highway 3A to the famed **Okanagan Valley**. Stretching 125 miles (201.2 km) from north to south, the massive glacial trough is filled by **Okanagan Lake** and scores of vineyards, wineries, and tasting rooms. The area boasts seven grape-growing subregions and more than 80 percent of British Columbia's total vineyard acreage.

In addition to all that sipping, the lake region offers **hiking and biking trails, golf courses, luxury spas**, and a wide variety of water activities including **fishing, swimming, and boating**. With around 900 restaurants, the Okanagan also offers one of Canada's most diverse dining scenes.

The **Okanagan Highway** (Route 97) drops down to **Lake Osoyoos** and the Canada-U.S. border. After

Seattle's Pike Place Market is a historic district with a farmers and artisans market.

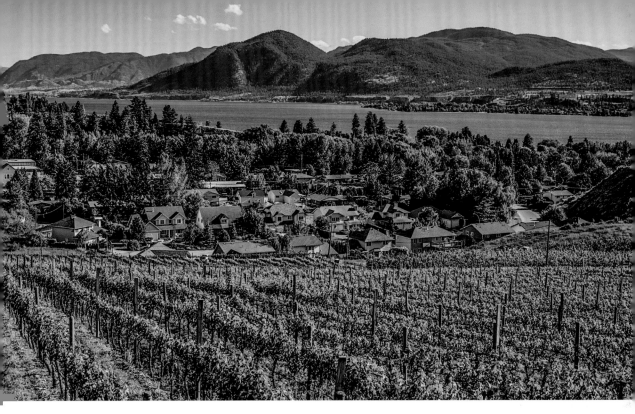

In British Columbia's Okanagan Valley, Hillside Winery's vines ripen with Okanagan Lake in the distance.

clearing customs and immigration, the wine and dine route continues on U.S. Highway 97 through the valley's American portion (spelled "Okanogan") to **Brewster, Washington,** where the Okanogan River flows into the mighty **Columbia River.**

From Brewster, road trippers have two options: continue on U.S. 97 to **Chelan** and a drive along gorgeous **Lake Chelan,** or cruise State Route 17 to **Grand Coulee** for a peek at the historic **Coulee Dam** and a chance to explore **Lake Roosevelt** by boat. Either way, you should make your way to **Coulee City** and rejoin Highway 17 for a rural drive down to Washington's **Tri-Cities wine country.**

Spread around the cities **of Pasco, Kennewick,** and **Richland,** the Tri-Cities region, like Bordeaux in southwestern France, has more than 300 days of sunshine every year. The area supports nearly 200 wineries, with the greatest concentration around **Red Mountain** and **Prosser.**

Beyond wine, the Tri-Cities area offers plenty, including **Sacajawea State Park** at the confluence of the Snake and Columbia Rivers and the **Reach Museum** of regional nature, science, and atomic history.

Changing direction, Interstates 82 and 90 run northwest through the **Yakima wine region** and **Snoqualmie Pass** before coasting into **Seattle, Washington.** Don't leave town before tasting the fresh-off-the-farm **Canlis, Bateau,** or **Spinasse** restaurants. ∎

### OFF ROAD

• **Lake Okanagan sightseeing tours:** Go With The Wind offers sailing by the hour in a 26-footer (7.9 m) MacGregor sailboat based at Kelowna Yacht Club from May to October. gowiththewind.com

• **Lake Chelan:** The *Lady of the Lake* has been plying Washington's most picturesque lake since 1900, a journey of 60 to 90 minutes across the 50 miles (80.5 km) of water between Chelan and Stehekin. Private charters available. ladyofthelake.com

• **Lake Roosevelt:** The 130-mile-long (209.2 km) lake created by the Grand Coulee Dam in 1942 can be explored by houseboat, pontoon, or speedboat rented from Lake Roosevelt Adventures at two marinas on the lake's south shore. lakeroosevelt adventures.com

• **Columbia River:** Water2Wine offers sightseeing, dinner or lunch, comedy, and even murder-mystery cruises on the big river from Richland, WA. water2winecruises.com

# Underground Road Trip
## New Mexico to Kentucky

The middle of America is riddled with underground wonders, a subterranean wilderness scattered between southern New Mexico and central Kentucky. In addition to stalactites and stalagmites, these caves offer strange nocturnal creatures and plenty of adventure.

Linking some of the nation's most famous caves, this 1,500-mile (2,414 km) meander across the American heartland offers below-the-surface encounters for both new and veteran spelunkers. Adventures range from easy strolls through illuminated show caves to crawling on your hands and knees—and sometimes your belly—to reach the darkest corners of wild caverns.

Discovered in 1898 by a teenage ranch hand—who called it "a whale of a big cave"—**Carlsbad Caverns** is the world's premier show cave. Formed around 250 million years ago during the Permian Period and declared a national park in 1930, the New Mexico cave complex boasts geological marvels like the Big Room and Devil's Den. Wild cave tours plunge even deeper to remote grottoes like the House of the White Giant and Spider Cave,

**THE BIG PICTURE**

**Distance:** 1,500 miles (2,414 km) from Carlsbad Caverns, NM, to Mammoth Cave, KY

**Drive time:** 1 week

**Best overnights:** Amarillo, Kansas City, St. Louis

**Best seasons:** Anytime

**Highlights:** Carlsbad Caverns, Underground Kansas City, Mammoth Cave

which require half a day of scrambling through tight spaces and across slick surfaces.

If that's not enough to make your palms sweat and heart pound, perch yourself outside Carlsbad's main entrance at sunset (between May and October) when thousands of Brazilian free-tailed bats exit the cave en masse as a swirling, screeching black cloud.

It's 500 miles (804.7 km) from Carlsbad Caverns (via Amarillo) to the next subterranean attraction—**Alabaster Caverns** in western Oklahoma. The stark prairie on the surface belies an underworld that features the planet's largest natural gypsum cave and four wild caves reserved for experienced spelunkers (permits required).

Another five hours to the east (via Wichita) is **Kansas City, Missouri**, much of the urban area underpinned by a limestone formation with 55 million square feet (5.1 million sq m) of man-made caves. This underground city (dubbed **SubTropolis**) features bars, restaurants, distilleries, a paintball course, and even a subterranean orchid nursery.

With more than 6,400 known caverns, Missouri likes to call itself the "Cave State." Some of the best are clustered around **Leasburg**, on Interstate 44 just west of St. Louis. Tours of **Onondaga Cave** and

Visitors walk the winding paved trail into New Mexico's Carlsbad Caverns.

On the Historic Tour through Mammoth Cave, learn how the ancient cave system played a role in the War of 1812.

**Cathedral Cave** in Onondaga Cave State Park, and **Fisher Cave** in Meramec State Park, are offered between April and October. The rest of the year, these caves are closed to protect the resident bat populations.

**St. Louis** is said to have more caves beneath its surface than any other major world city. Once used for everything from Civil War arsenals and the Underground Railroad to breweries and Prohibition speakeasies, most of the caves are now off-limits. An exception is the one beneath the old **Lemp Brewery** in Marine Villa, which transforms into an underground haunted house for the month leading up to Halloween.

Crossing the Mississippi River, a combination of Interstates 64 and 65 leads to the last stop on this journey through underground America—**Mammoth Cave** in central Kentucky, the Earth's largest known cave system, with more than 400 miles (643.7 km) of passages and more yet to be discovered.

Occupied by Native Americans at least 6,000 years ago, Mammoth was the focus of the "Kentucky Cave Wars" between competing tourist barkers until it was made a national park in 1941. Frozen Niagara, Grand Avenue, and the underground River Styx are among its landmark formations. Among the many ranger-led activities are an Introduction to Caving workshop for those who want to learn more about exploring the netherworld and a Wild Cave tour into the cool, muddy, guano-strewn belly of the beast. ∎

## PIT STOPS

• **Groundhog Run:** SubTropolis in Kansas City hosts an underground 5K/10K event in January that benefits local charity. abilitykc.org

• **Midwest Bat Fest:** Close encounters of the furry, flying mammal kind are the focus of this totally batty April event held every year at Missouri's Onondaga Cave State Park. onondagafriends.org

• **Mammothon:** With a walking portion staged inside the famous cave, this is the nation's only triathlon with an underground segment. The biking and hiking legs of this September event ramble through the park's lush forest. nps.gov/maca

• **Night Sky Programs:** From stargazing to ranger-guided moon hikes, Carlsbad Caverns National Park in New Mexico hosts regular after-dark programs between June and October. nps.gov/cave

# Black & Yellow Trail

## Illinois to Wyoming

Named after its two superstar attractions, this vintage motor route across the Northern Plains links the outskirts of Chicago with the Black Hills of South Dakota and Yellowstone National Park in Wyoming.

### THE BIG PICTURE

**Distance:** ca 1,370 miles (2,204.8 km) from Chicago, IL, to Yellowstone, WY

**Drive time:** 10-14 days

**Best overnights:** Madison, La Crosse/Winona, Rochester, Pierre, Rapid City, Sheridan, Cody

**Best seasons:** Summer or early fall

**Highlights:** Madison, Rochester, Badlands, Black Hills, Devils Tower, Cody, Yellowstone

One of the first federal numbered highways—designated in 1926—U.S. 14 was considered a road trip route from its very birth. Dubbed the Yellow and Black Trail to highlight its main destinations, the highway runs around 1,400 miles (2,253.1 km) from downtown Chicago to northern Wyoming.

Starting from Arlington Heights outside Chicago, catch U.S. 14 as it glides into the Illinois countryside.

Linger a spell at gorgeous **Geneva Lake** in southern Wisconsin and walk a stretch of the **Historic Indian Trail** (26 miles/41.8 km) before heading up the pike to **Madison**. In addition to the **Wisconsin State Capitol**, the university town offers lively student bars and restaurants along **State Street**, nine **Frank Lloyd Wright** buildings, and **Olbrich Botanical Gardens**.

Highway 14 dips into the leafy **Wisconsin River Valley** before meeting the Mississippi River at **La Crosse**. Cruise the river on the *La Crosse Queen* and then cross the Big Muddy to Minnesota and visit the **Minnesota Marine Art Museum** in Winona before motoring through the dairy country to **Rochester**. The tour of the **Mayowood Mansion** and the **Mayo Clinic Historical Suite** in the art deco **Plummer Building** are just what the doctor ordered.

Beyond Rochester, U.S. 14 becomes the **Laura Ingalls Wilder Historic Highway,** with sights along the way associated with the celebrated author of *Little House on the Prairie,* including the **Sod House on the Prairie** in Sanborn and the **Wilder Museum** in Walnut Grove (where the popular TV series was set).

It's a long haul across the short grass prairie to **Pierre**, the South Dakota state capital. But it's worth the drive just to visit the cutting-edge **Cultural Heritage Center**, its underground building chockablock with exhibits on the Northern Plains Indians and pioneer days.

Highway 14 zigzags its way down to **Badlands National Park** and then joins I-90 for the run into **Rapid City**, gateway to the **Black Hills** of South Dakota and celebrated sights

Frank Lloyd Wright built Madison's First Unitarian Society's Meeting House.

Striated sandstone rock formations border a road running through South Dakota's Badlands National Park.

like **Mount Rushmore**, the **Crazy Horse Monument**, the bison herds of **Custer State Park**, and **Deadwood** of Wild West fame.

Descending from the hills through scenic **Spearfish Canyon**, U.S. 14 mingles with I-90 (off and on) for the journey across eastern Wyoming—including a close encounter of the geological kind at **Devils Tower National Monument**.

**Sheridan** provides a brief urban interlude before U.S. 14 crawls up and over the mountains of **Big Horn National Forest** and across the arid badlands of central Wyoming to **Cody**.

Named for Buffalo Bill (real name William Frederick Cody), who helped found the town in 1896, Cody offers a variety of Western-themed attractions, including a razzle-dazzle **Night Rodeo** (June to August) and **Old Trail Town** with 25 authentic frontier buildings. But the town's main allure is the incredible **Buffalo Bill Center of the West**, which includes the **Whitney Western Art Museum, Draper Natural History Museum, Plains Indian Museum, Cody Firearms Museum**, and of course a collection of William F. Cody memorabilia.

Snaking up the canyon that holds old **Buffalo Bill Dam** and reservoir, Highway 14 enters **Yellowstone National Park** through the East Gate and the northern shore of **Yellowstone Lake**, a spectacular end to an epic drive across the Northern Plains. ■

## LAY YOUR HEAD

• **The Edgewater:** Lavishly restored historic lakeshore hotel in downtown Madison, WI; restaurants, bar, spa, indoor pool, ice rink; from $144. theedgewater.com

• **Alexander Mansion:** Expansive 1880s Victorian B&B near the Mississippi River in Winona, MN, with five guest rooms and a five-course breakfast; from $97. alexandermansionbb.com

• **Hotel Alex Johnson:** Native America motifs and "Germanic Tudor" architecture blend easily at this landmark 1928 hotel in Rapid City; restaurant, roof bar, fitness room; from $83. alexjohnson.com

• **Irma Hotel:** Buffalo Bill opened his downtown Cody, WY, lodging in 1902 and named it after his youngest daughter; restaurant, bar, cowboy music; from $80. irmahotel.com

• **Pahaska Tepee:** Located just outside Yellowstone's East Gate, this rustic log cabin lodge was also founded by Buffalo Bill (1904); restaurant, bar, trail rides, fishing; from $109. pahaska.com

# French & Indian War Path

## Nova Scotia to Pennsylvania

The bloody colonial brawl between Britain and France for control of North America is the focus of this meander across eastern Canada and the northern Appalachians, a road trip that features impressive forts and forgotten battlefields, romantic shorelines and handsome highland scenery.

### THE BIG PICTURE

**Distance:** 1,784 miles (2,871.1 km) from Louisbourg, NS, to Fort Necessity, PA

**Drive time:** 10-14 days

**Best overnights:** Quebec City, Lake George, Niagara Falls, Pittsburgh

**Best seasons:** Summer or fall

**Highlights:** Fort Necessity, Niagara region, Quebec City, Fort Ticonderoga, Louisbourg

Waged along the frontier between New France and British America between 1754 and 1763, the French and Indian War was a colonial sideshow to the Seven Years' War (1756-1763) in Europe and a prelude to the American Revolution (1765-1783). By the end of the war, Britain had gained complete control of Canada, but nearly doubled its national debt in the process, leading to the harsh taxation that sparked revolt in the 13 colonies.

**Fort Necessity National Battlefield** in southwestern Pennsylvania witnessed the first battle of the French and Indian War and George Washington's debut as an army commander. The 1754 clash ended in humiliating surrender for the young Virginian, but thankfully not the end of his military career. In addition to the reconstructed stockade, the park features living history programs, weapons demonstrations, and five miles (8 km) of hiking and cross-country ski trails.

Sixty miles (96.6 km) north—at the confluence the Allegheny and Monongahela Rivers in downtown Pittsburgh—**Point State Park** preserves the memory of French **Fort Duquesne** (1754) and British **Fort Pitt** (1764). An excellent **history museum** details the Steel City's 18th-century wartime birth.

A combination of Interstates 79 and 90 leads from Pittsburgh to the **Buffalo/Niagara Falls** region, another strategic crossroads of the French and Indian War. Built by the French, **Old Fort Niagara** didn't fall until 1759 after a 19-day siege. Today the stout stone bastion presents lakeside encampments, 18th-century cooking demonstrations, and eerie "lantern and lore" tours.

Leaving the western front behind, cruise Interstates 90 and 87 to the **Lake Champlain** region in upstate New York, where three major battles

At the Fortress of Louisbourg reenactors dress in French soldier uniforms.

Opened as a historic site and museum in 1934, Old Fort Niagara is the oldest continuously occupied military site in North America.

played out during the war. A faithfully restored reconstruction of **Fort William Henry** overlooks Lake George, a British-built bastion that hosts living history tours and 18th-century lifestyle demonstrations.

An hour farther north is **Fort Ticonderoga**, where 3,600 French troops bested 18,000 British regulars and their Native American allies during the 1758 Battle of Carillon, the bloodiest clash in North America before the Civil War. The rebuilt fort now offers guided tours by uniform-clad docents, musket and cannon volleys, a corn maze, an English garden, and 90-minute cruises on Lake Champlain.

Crossing the international border, take the Trans-Canada Highway to **Quebec City**, site of the war's most famous clash—a 1759 battle on the **Plains of Abraham** that sealed France's fate in North America. Now the city's best and biggest park, the grassy plateau offers hiking, snowshoe and cross-country ski trails, the

**Plains of Abraham Museum**, and the adjacent **Fortifications of Québec National Historic Site**.

Back on the Trans-Canada Highway, make the long drive across New Brunswick to Nova Scotia—with a stop along the way at **Fort Beauséjour** in Aulac and its outstanding new museum.

Lying at the end of this drive is the queen of all French and Indian

War strongholds—the massive **Fortress of Louisbourg** on the Atlantic coast, which famously fell to British forces in 1758. The largest historical reconstruction project in North American history brought the French citadel back to life in the 1960s as a living history showcase that includes skilled artisans producing chocolate, rum, and other goodies inside the fort. ∎

## PIT STOPS

- **Montcalm's Cross:** This annual reenactment of the epic 1758 Battle of Carillon between French and British forces at Fort Ticonderoga wages across a weekend in mid-July. fortticonderoga.org

- **Escape Louisbourg:** Monday and Tuesday evenings in July and August, several ancient spaces inside the historic citadel transform into puzzling escape rooms for the general public. pc.gc.ca/en/lhn-nhs/ns/louisbourg

- **Plains of Abraham Concerts:** Edwin-Bélanger Bandstand offers free live music on select evenings between June and August, including pop, folk, jazz, country, and world music. theplainsofabraham.ca/en

- **Fort Necessity Encampment:** The Pennsylvania battlefield park transforms into French and British military camps during this annual living history weekend in May with reenactments and living history demos. nps.gov/fone

# Cannonball Run Revival

## New York to California

One of America's classic road trips is the drive between New York City and Los Angeles, a 2,800-mile (4,506.2 km) feat first done by Erwin "Cannon Ball" Baker piloting a Stutz Bearcat in 1915, and later immortalized by the eponymous mega-hit Burt Reynolds movie.

The original Cannonball Run was an unsanctioned cross-country motor race between New York and Los Angeles that took place five times between 1971 and 1979. Among those who participated were auto-racing legends Dan Gurney and Jacques Villeneuve.

The race was created by the ambitious editors of *Car and Driver* magazine as an homage to legendary car and motorcycle racer Erwin "Cannon Ball" Baker and, secondarily, in protest against the 55-mile-per-hour (88.5 km/h) speed limit imposed throughout the nation at the time. The 1980 movie *The Cannonball Run* propelled the race into pop culture immortality.

The record time for finishing the Cannonball Run was set in 1979 at 32 hours 51 minutes. But this road trip isn't about breaking records (or snagging speeding tickets).

Keeping to the speed limit, anyone can make the drive from New York City to Los Angeles in 42 to 44 hours. That's nonstop—just long enough to fill the tank, empty the bladder, and grab some snacks. But why rush? Our route—2,800 miles (4,506.2 km) through 13 states—makes a nice week-long journey with stops at spots that honor the internal combustion engine.

Start your engine outside the **Red Ball Garage** on East 31st Street in Manhattan, where the historic Cannonball Run originally kicked off. Pass through the **Holland Tunnel** and along Interstate 78 to **America on Wheels** and the **Mack Trucks Historical Museum** in Allentown, Pennsylvania.

Continue along Interstates 76 and 70 to **Columbus**, Ohio, and the **Wagner-Hagans Auto Museum** with its exquisite collection of old cars, license plates, road signs, gas pumps, and other auto paraphernalia. Waving goodbye to Columbus, I-70 zips across the heartland to Dayton (home of **America's Packard Museum**) and **Indianapolis**.

**THE BIG PICTURE**

**Distance:** ca 2,800 miles (4,506.2 km) from New York City to Los Angeles

**Drive time:** 7-10 days

**Best overnights:** Pittsburgh, Columbus, Indianapolis, St. Louis, Kansas City, Denver, Las Vegas

**Best seasons:** Spring, summer, or fall

**Highlights:** America on Wheels, Wagner-Hagans, Indy Motor Speedway, Forney Museum, Shelby Factory, Petersen Automotive

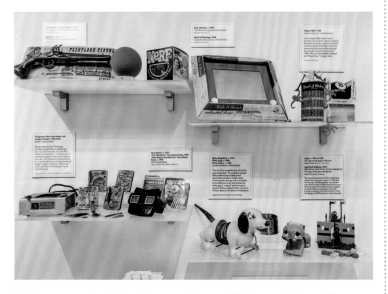

Find retro toys at the National Museum of Toys and Miniatures in Kansas City.

Take a trip down racing car history at the Indianapolis Motor Speedway Museum; then visit the famous track.

If you make no other pit stop in Indy, be sure to visit the **Indianapolis Motor Speedway Museum** for a chance to kneel down and kiss those famous bricks and tee off at **Brickyard Crossing Golf Course**.

Interstate 70 takes the Cannonball Run through southern Illinois—tracing the route of the old National Road—and across the **Mississippi River** to downtown **St. Louis**. Take a spin around the **Gateway Arch** and visit the **National Museum of Transportation**. Next stop is **Kansas City** and the **National Museum of Toys and Miniatures**, worth a gander just for the baby Oscar Meyer Wienermobile, as well as the vintage Barbie dolls and Matchbox vehicles.

And across the prairie we go on a 600-mile (965.6 km) run on Interstate 70 between Kansas City and Denver, with stunning snowcapped peaks eventually looming in the distance. Among the gems at the Mile High City's **Forney Museum** are the Indian Motorcycle collection, 1923 Hispano-Suiza limousine, and Amelia Earhart's 1923 Kissel "Gold Bug" convertible.

Our old friend I-70 plows across the Rockies and the red-rock country of central Utah before merging into Interstate 15 for the run down to Las Vegas. Besides the obligatory cruise down the **Strip**, road trippers should tour **Count's Kustoms**, the **Shelby Factory**, and **Nostalgia Street Rods**.

Snaking across the **Mojave Desert**, I-15 descends into the City of Angels and a homestretch that runs near the **Auto Club Speedway** in Fontana, **NHRA Motorsports Museum** in Pomona, and the **Petersen Automotive Museum** on the Miracle Mile before the Cannonball Run gets the checkered flag at the oceanfront **Portofino Inn** in **Redondo Beach**. ■

## ART AVENUES

- **Best Road Trip Flicks:** *It Happened One Night* (1934); *Easy Rider* (1969); *Vanishing Point* (1971); *The Cannonball Run* (1980); *Thelma and Louise* (1991); *Little Miss Sunshine* (2006)

- **Best Motor Sport Movies:** *Grand Prix* (1966); *LeMans* (1971); *Death Race 2000* (1975); *Days of Thunder* (1990); *The World's Fastest Indian* (2005); *Rush* (2013); and both the silent (1929) and Elvis (1968) versions of *Speedway*

- **Best Motor Racing Documentaries:** *On Any Sunday* (1971); *Senna* (2010); *Steve McQueen: The Man and Le Mans* (2015)

# Northeast
## Road Trips

Sweeping views of the Allegheny Plateau await atop Bear Rocks.

# A Dash of Downeast

## Massachusetts, New Hampshire & Maine

The New England coast from Boston to the Canadian border provides the backdrop for this 400-mile journey through cities, towns, and seascapes that have shaped the region's essence for nearly 400 years.

*D*owneast is a vintage nautical term that describes the direction—downwind and in an easterly direction—that sailing ships from Boston and New York traveled to reach the Maine coast. And that fairly well describes this road trip along the Cape Ann Peninsula, the short New Hampshire coast, and the entire length of Maine.

Much of this route follows U.S.

Highway 1, starting with a short stretch through **Boston's** historic **Charlestown** neighborhood. If you're not in any rush, climb **Bunker Hill** and board the **U.S.S. Constitution** before leaving Boston.

Otherwise, it's about 25 miles (40.2 km) to **Salem**. Legendary witch trials played out here in 1692 and 1693. From the **House of the Seven Gables** and the **Salem Witch**

Dig into the freshest shellfish at the Maine Lobster Festival.

### THE BIG PICTURE

**Distance:** ca 400 miles (643.7 km) from Boston, MA, to Lubec, ME

**Drive time:** 8-10 days

**Best overnights:** Salem, Gloucester, Portsmouth, Portland, Rockport/Camden, Bar Harbor, Lubec/Eastport

**Best seasons:** Anytime

**Highlights:** Salem, Gloucester, Portsmouth, Portland, Penobscot Bay, Acadia National Park, Campobello

**Trials Memorial** to after-dark **ghost tours**, there are plenty of ways to experience Salem's supernatural side.

**Salem Maritime National Historic Site** safeguards much of the city's secular history, including the old **U.S. Custom House** (where Nathaniel Hawthorne set the start of *The Scarlet Letter*), a row of historic waterfront mansions from the golden age of sail, and a replica of the 18th-century sailing ship *Friendship of Salem*.

Yankee Division Highway spirits the road trip to the Cape Ann Peninsula and **Gloucester**, a seafaring town that's even older than Boston or Salem. Founded in 1623, just three years after the Pilgrims landed at Plymouth, Gloucester developed into a huge shipbuilding center and fishing port. The 1.2-mile (1.9 km) **Gloucester HarborWalk** features 42 information panels, and the restored wharfs at **Maritime Gloucester** offer museum exhibits, the **Sea Pocket Lab Aquarium**, and summer day sails on the **Schooner** *Ardelle*.

State Route 133 cuts across the base of the peninsula to **Essex** with its old **Burial Ground, Hearse House**, and the riverfront **Shipbuilding Museum** that spins the

Built in 1928, the 59-room Stuart-style Castle Hill Mansion sits on the 2,100-acre (849.8 ha) Crane Estate in Ipswich, Massachusetts.

story of a town where 4,000 wooden vessels were constructed in the 19th century. Nearby **Castle Hill on the Crane Estate** offers tours of an expansive, early 20th-century country mansion with coastline that can be hiked or biked.

The northern Massachusetts coast ends in spectacular fashion with **Plum Island**, one of the largest stretches of true coastal wilderness along the New England shore. The **Mass Audubon Joppa Flats Education Center** in Newburyport offers an excellent introduction to the island's **Parker River National Wildlife Refuge**, home to more than 300 bird species.

After crossing the Merrimack River, Highway 1 cruises into New Hampshire. Seaside **Hampton** offers a chance to take a dip in the sea or a short walk along the **Little Boar's Head Seaside Trail**. But the undisputed gem of the Granite State's 18.57-mile (29.9 km) coastline (shortest of any state) is **Portsmouth**.

While much of the focus is on the city's maritime heritage—sights like the **John Paul Jones House** and **U.S.S. *Albacore*** submarine museum—Portsmouth is also strong on landlubber sights. **Strawbery Banke** is a sprawling outdoor museum with historic houses, gardens, and living history demonstrations. The **Wentworth Lear Historic Houses** offer seasonal guided tours of several 18th-century waterfront mansions. Portsmouth also dabbles in modern culture, as exemplified by the eclectic menu of concerts, lectures, films, and comedy at the **Music Hall** (opened in 1878).

Maine looms on the north bank of the Piscataqua River, a short drive up the coast to **Kennebunkport**. The **First Families Museum** and **Bush Compound** at Walker's Point reflect the town's contribution to American politics. By contrast, the **Rachel Carson National Wildlife Refuge**—named for one of the guid-

ing lights of the environmental movement—protects 50 miles (80.5 km) of estuaries, salt marshes, and

## SCENIC DETOURS

- **State Route 101:** Wanders inland from Hampton to Manchester and Keene in New Hampshire's largely unexplored southwest corner.

- **Old Canada Road (U.S. 201):** An epic drive from Brunswick, ME, to the Canadian border and onward to Quebec City; total distance 252 miles (405.5 km).

- **Roosevelt Trail (U.S. 302):** A meandering route from downtown Portland, ME, into the heart of New Hampshire's mighty White Mountains.

- **State Route 187:** This coastal loop takes in Jonesport, ME, and the Great Wass Island Preserve.

- **U.S. Highway 1:** Go from Eastport, ME, to the Canadian border through the Acadian-American country around Presque Isle.

other coastal geography on either side of Kennebunkport.

Thirty miles (48.3 km) farther up Highway 1 lies **Portland**, the funkiest town on the Maine coast and New England's largest urban center north of Boston. Renowned for its liberal lifestyles, lively nightlife, vibrant arts scene, and cutting-edge food culture, Portland is often ranked among the nation's "most livable" cities.

Although the city boasts its fair share of historic homes and museums—in particular **Victoria Mansion** and the **Portland Museum of Art**—its foremost treasure is its neighborhoods. Areas like the **Old Port, East End**, and **Arts District** harbor many of the best bars, shops, and restaurants. Portland is also a great city for pedestrians, with the **Eastern Promenade, Harborwalk Trail**, and **Back Cove Trail** among the best paths.

North of Portland, **Bowdoin College** in Brunswick begs a brief stop to browse the **Peary-MacMillan Arctic Museum**, dedicated to a couple of alumni who pioneered exploration of the frozen north. The **Harriet Beecher Stowe House** preserves the memory of the famed 19th-century author and abolitionist.

From Brunswick, Highway 1 takes on a new tag—the Atlantic Highway—as it meanders back to the coast. Along the way are the **Maine Maritime Museum** in Bath, as well as turnoffs to **Boothbay Harbor** with its aquarium and botanical gardens, the **Colonial Pemaquid State Historic Site**, and reconstructed **Fort William Henry**, where 17th-century English colonists braved Native American and French attacks.

Anchored sailboats pepper the harbor in Camden, Maine.

---

## LAY YOUR HEAD

- **The Inn at Castle Hill:** Historic 1899 B&B on the 2,100-acre (849.8 ha) Crane Estate in northern Massachusetts; bikes, lawn games, massage; from $195. thetrustees .org/the-inn-at-castle-hill

- **The Press Hotel:** Art deco home of the *Portland Press Herald* newspaper converted into Old Port boutique hotel; restaurant, bar, art gallery, fitness center, bikes; from $179. thepresshotel.com

- **Riggs Cove Houseboats:** Super-cute "floating cottage" rentals on the Sasanoa River near Brunswick, ME; from $235. robin hoodmarinecenter.com

- **Norumbega Castle:** Erected in 1886 by eccentric inventor Joseph Stearns, this stone manse near Camden, ME, is now a cozy B&B; from $289. norumbegainn.com

- **West Quoddy Station:** Historic lighthouse digs at the easternmost point of the U.S. mainland; from $90. quoddyvacation.com

---

The highway hits the coast again at **Rockland**, where the **Farnsworth Art Museum** displays its prize collection of Andrew Wyeth paintings and Louise Nevelson sculptures. The quintessential Maine coastal town, Rockland hosts the **Maine Lobster Festival** in August and the **Maine Lighthouse Museum** with its extensive collection of light station artifacts and U.S. Coast Guard memorabilia. **Main Street** is chockablock with restaurants, bars, boutiques, and art galleries. In nearby **Camden Hills State Park**, snatch a panoramic view of Maine's central coast and Penobscot Bay from the top of **Mount Battie**. Or take a **windjammer cruise** from the Camden waterfront. U.S. 1 continues across the radically modern **Penobscot River Bridge**, which features an observation deck at the top of one of its 420-foot-high (128 m) towers. From there it's just a 30-mile (48.3 km) drive to **Mount Desert Island**.

The island shelters two of Maine's iconic destinations: the old seaside resort **Bar Harbor** and neighboring **Acadia National Park**. Bar Harbor is a beehive of activity during the summer. Down along the waterfront, outfitters offer whale-watching, kayaking, sailing, lobster catching, wildlife-watching, and other aquatic adventures. The town also sports interesting hikes like the **Shore Path** and the sandy land bridge to **Bar Island**.

The first national park east of the Mississippi, Acadia has mountains, woodlands, lakeshores, and rocky seacoast that can be explored on foot, bike, horse, or car along a dense network of trails, old carriage routes, and the 27-mile (43.5 km) **Park Loop Road**. Several routes lead to the summit of 1,530-foot (466.3 m) **Cadillac Mountain**, one of the first places in the nation to catch the sunrise each morning. Visitors can learn more about Acadia's natural and human history at the island's **Hulls Cove Visitor Center, George B. Dorr Museum of Natural History, Abbe Museum**, and **Sieur de Monts Nature Center**.

The final stretch of the road trip traces Highway 1 along the wild and scenic **Bold Coast** of northern Maine to **Lubec**. Red-and-white striped **West Quoddy Head Lighthouse** (built in 1858) crowns the easternmost point on the U.S. mainland. Those with a passport can cross the bridge to **Roosevelt Campobello International Park** in Canada, which preserves the woodsy seaside retreat where FDR whiled away many a summer day before and during his White House years. ■

# Wandering the Adirondacks

## New York

Dotted with more than 3,000 lakes, rustic-chic camps, historic burgs, and the largest chunk of wilderness in the Northeast outside of Maine, the Adirondacks make for a fascinating road trip in upstate New York. The journey is especially alluring during the spring when the crowds are down and the fall when foliage colors are vibrant.

**THE BIG PICTURE**

**Distance:** ca 425 miles (684 km) round-trip from Albany

**Drive time:** 7 days

**Best overnights:** Saranac Lake, Lake Placid, Lake George, Warrensburg

**Best seasons:** Spring, summer, or fall

**Highlights:** Great camps, Adirondack Experience, Wild Center, Saranac Lake, Lake Placid, Lake Champlain, Lake George.

Fearful that New York City's water supply was being sullied by deforestation, New York State created Adirondack Park in 1894 with a declaration that the upstate highlands would be "forever kept as wild forest lands."

The "Blue Line" that legislators drew on their Adirondacks map continues to frame the largest state park in the lower 48 states. Roughly half the land is still privately owned, a public-private partnership that has nurtured the region from environmental devastation into one of the nation's top nature reserves.

With an estimated 10 million visitors annually, the Adirondacks often experience bumper-to-bumper traffic on both roads and trails during the busy summer. Otherwise, the highlands are refreshingly empty.

For many folks, Albany is the main gateway into the Adirondacks, a quick drive up the scenic **Northway** (I-87) via the historical, health, and sporting attractions of **Saratoga Springs**. Hopping off the interstate at **Warrensburg**, State Route 28 meanders up the **Hudson River** past **Gore Mountain** (outdoor recreation on offer in summer and winter) to the deep **Hudson Gorge Wilderness.** Rafting companies based at **Indian Lake** offer float trips down the gorge, 12 miles (19 km) of whitewater with rapids ranging up to class III.

A major crossroads in the southern Adirondacks, **Blue Mountain Lake** offers an excellent orientation to the area: the **Adirondack Experience**. Local culture, nature, and history unfold inside the museum's 23 buildings, many of them historic structures relocated from elsewhere in the mountains. The interactive **Life in the Adirondacks** gallery is a visitor favorite, but the coolest exhibit is **Boats and Boating** with its unique collection of vintage

Champion Sonja Henie's skates are displayed at the Winter Olympic Museum.

Saranac Lake offers historical sites, museums, and a lively downtown in addition to water activities and hiking.

wooden speedboats and handmade sailing craft.

West of Blue Mountain, Highway 20 leads along a chain of waterways to **Raquette Lake.** Wealthy families who spent the summer in the region during the early 20th century used a network of trains and steamboats to transit the lakes to posh waterfront compounds called "great camps."

Sightseeing or dinner cruises on Raquette Lake aboard the steamboat *W. W. Durant* are a reminder of those heady days. The boat is named after William West Durant, the architect and developer who created nearby **Great Camp Sagamore**. The one-time Vanderbilt summer home is now open to the public for guided tours and overnight stays during music and plein air art workshops, wood carving and writing weekends, and other special events.

Retracing your route back to Blue Mountain, State Route 30 heads north to the hamlet of **Long Lake**, perched beside a skinny 14-mile (22 km) eponymous body of water ideal for boating, fishing, or swimming off the sandy beach in the middle of town. **Helms Aero Services** offers scenic flights over the middle lakes region and the nearby **High Peak Wilderness** where 42 peaks rise to more than 4,000 feet (1,219 m). **Mount Marcy** and **Mount Algonquin**, the two highest peaks, are among the easiest to climb.

## EN ROUTE EATS

• **Campfire Adirondack Grill:** Meat, fish, and produce sourced in and around the Adirondacks is the signature of this spiffy new restaurant found on the ground floor of the Hotel Saranac; be sure to grab a drink in the Great Hall Bar before or after dinner; 100 Main St., Saranac Lake. hotelsaranac.com/dine/campfire

• **The Shamrock:** Great burgers, Adirondack beer, and loads of local color highlight this popular hangout off Route 86 between Paul Smiths and Saranac Lake; 83 County Route 55, Gabriels. shamrocksaranaclakeny.com

• **Well Dressed Food:** Hybrid deli, coffee shop, and gourmet food outlet on the main drag in Tupper Lake; 87 Park St., Tupper Lake. welldressedfood.com

• **Bistro LeRoux:** Truffled pomme frites, Cabernet-braised short ribs, and cognac bisque suffuse the menu at this family-run, French-American eatery; 668 Route 149, Lake George. bistroleroux.com

The Adirondack Wildlife Refuge cares for gray wolves and other local species.

Farther north along Highway 30 is **Tupper Lake**, where the awesome **Wild Center** renders a broad overview of Adirondacks nature and local Native American culture. Among its outstanding features are the **Wild Walk** elevated wooden trail, the musical **iForest**, and **Otter Falls** with its fish and mammals. **Adirondack Public Observatory** offers stargazing and dark-sky programs.

Highway 30 continues through the lake country to **Paul Smiths**, named after the fellow who founded one of the first resort hotels in the Adirondacks (opened in 1859). Eco-oriented **Paul Smith's College** offers a native species **Butterfly House** as well as 14 miles (22 km) of **interpretive and backcountry trails** that are groomed for **cross-country skiing**

and snowshoeing. Nearby **White Pine Camp** served as the summer White House for Calvin Coolidge in 1916 and offers public guided tours June to September.

Turning east, State Route 86 makes the run down to Saranac Lake with a possible detour along the way to the **Six Nations Indian Museum** in Onchiota, with a collection of more than 3,000 artifacts related to the Iroquois Confederation.

**Saranac Lake** was renowned between the 1880s and 1950s for its research and treatment of tuberculosis, a riveting story that unfolds at the **Saranac Laboratory Museum** and the surrounding **Church Street Historic District**. Famous TB victims are remembered at the **Robert Louis Stevenson Memorial Cottage** and **Béla Bartók Cabin**.

While it was revolutionizing health care, Saranac Lake was also evolving into an all-around holiday destination that now features the **Adirondack Carousel**, the **Adirondack Center for Loon Conservation**, paddling boats on the lake, the view from **Mount Baker**, and the annual **Winter Carnival**.

**Lake Placid** is just 15 minutes down Route 86. Host of the Winter Olympics in 1932 and 1980, the town is perhaps most famed for the 1980 "Miracle on Ice" when the Americans upset the highly favored Soviet ice hockey team at **Herb Brooks Arena**. That storied game and other moments are enshrined at the arena's **Lake Placid Olympic Museum**.

There are numerous ways to experience the world-class sports facilities, from extreme tubing at the **Olympic Jumping Complex** and the **Lake Placid Bobsled Experience** to downhill skiing and snowboarding at **Whiteface Mountain** and cross-

## LAY YOUR HEAD

• **Great Camp Sagamore:** Rough it like a Vanderbilt at this rustic Gilded Age retreat near Raquette Lake; all-inclusive; library, bowling, tennis, boating, hiking; from $398 per weekend. greatcampsagamore.org

• **White Pine Camp:** Large cottages on Osgood Pond, where President Coolidge decamped in the summer of 1926; hiking, fishing, boating, guided nature walks, bowling, billiards; from $165 (summer). whitepinecamp.com

• **Hotel Saranac:** This historic 1920s property towers over downtown Saranac; restaurant, bar, full-service spa, hair salon, fitness center, gift shop; from $110. hotel saranac.com

• **Posh Primitive:** Glamping Adirondack style, at a permanent tented camp near Lake George; all-inclusive; hiking, fishing, boating; from $198. poshprimitive.com

• **The Fern Lodge:** Romantic rustic honeymoon haven on the shore of Friends Lake; boating, hot tub, sauna, wine and beer bar, mini movie theater; from $395. thefern lodge.com

country skiing at **Mount Van Hoevenberg**. The **Barkeater Trails Alliance** maintains an extensive network of long-distance biking and ski touring trails around the area.

Threading a path between the **McKenzie Mountains** and the **Sentinel Range**, Highway 86 shoots northeast through **High Falls Gorge** with its rocky cascades and the town of Wilmington, where the **Adirondack Wildlife Refuge** rescues and rehabilitates wolves, bears, bobcats, birds of prey, and many other species currently or formerly found in upstate New York.

Farther down the Ausable River Valley is **Ausable Chasm,** where visitors can explore the "Grand Canyon of the Adirondacks" via rafting, tubing, rock climbing, rappeling, or hiking elevated walkways and cable bridges.

The Ausable River empties into **Lake Champlain**, which forms most of Adirondack Park's eastern boundary. Road trippers have several choices at this point. Head north along the shore to **Plattsburgh** with its **War of 1812 Museum** and various **lake boating** opportunities. Hop the one-hour ferry (summer and fall only) from **Port Kent** or **Essex** to the **Vermont** side. Or meander down the lake's southern shore through a part of the park flush with American history.

The last way—using the Northway and State Route 9—leads to **Westport**, where the **Depot Theatre** stages summer stock in the old train station. Farther south is a state historic park that preserves the remains of **Fort Crown Point,** which featured in the French and Indian War

and American Revolution. Beneath the fort, the **Lake Champlain Visitor Center** occupies the historic **Toll Collector's House** beside the **Lake Champlain Bridge** crossing to Vermont.

Even more of America's wartime heritage is on display at **Fort Ticonderoga**, where living history programs, restored structures, craft demonstrations, and a 90-minute lake cruise illuminate military life on the 18th-century frontier between the 13 colonies and Canada.

Just over the hill from Ticonderoga, long **Lake George** offers boating, fishing, swimming beaches, trails to the summit of **Tongue Mountain**, and living history at restored **Fort William Henry**. From the lake's south end, it's just an hour down the Northway to Albany. ■

Fort Ticonderoga sits on 2,000 acres (809.4 ha) of historic land, preserving the largest collection of Revolutionary War earthworks.

# Lower Hudson Loop
## New York

This 300-mile (482.8 km) loop between New York City and Albany covers both sides of the Lower Hudson Valley, a journey for all seasons and many reasons, from fine art and quirky history, to outdoor adventure and cutting-edge architecture.

Named for English mariner Henry Hudson, who sailed up the river as far as present-day Albany in 1609, New York's Hudson Valley presents a rich quilt of Americana. In addition to spawning an entire genre of landscape painting, the 150-mile-long (214.4 km) valley is renowned for its invaluable contributions to American architecture, gardening, transportation, politics, and outdoor recreation.

Overall, the riverside corridor between New York City and Albany harbors around 100 heritage sites, more than 3,000 miles (4,828 km) of hiking, biking, and walking trails, and an immeasurable wealth of American culture.

Exiting the Big Apple is never easy, especially for first-timers. But the least complicated way is probably via the **George Washington Bridge** and **Palisades Interstate Parkway** along the west bank of the Hudson.

Forty miles (64.4 km) up the road,

See the "Three Legged Buddha" and other sculptures at the Storm King Art Center.

**THE BIG PICTURE**

**Distance:** ca 300 miles (482.8 km) round-trip from New York City

**Drive time:** 4-6 days

**Best overnights:** Newburgh, New Paltz, Kingston, Albany, Hudson, Poughkeepsie, Fishkill

**Best seasons:** Anytime

**Highlights:** Bear Mountain, West Point, Storm King, Catskills, Albany, Vanderbilt Mansion, Hyde Park, Kykuit

**Bear Mountain State Park** is a great place to stretch your legs, especially on summit trails and turnouts along **Perkins Drive** overlooking the river and majestic **Bear Mountain Bridge** (the world's longest suspension bridge when it was completed in 1924).

At nearby **West Point**, road trippers can tour the **U.S. Military Academy** campus or visit Revolutionary War strongholds like **Fort Clinton** and **Fort Putnam**. Yet not everything dates from the 18th century. **Storm King Art Center** presents the nation's largest array of contemporary outdoor sculpture— 500 acres (202.3 hectares) sprinkled with works by Alexander Calder, Henry Moore, Richard Serra, and other modern masters.

Back along the river, **Newburgh** is flush with history of both the human and natural kind. Among its many landmarks are **George Washington's Headquarters**, a handsome **Dutch Reformed Church**, and **Hudson Highlands Nature Museum**.

Farther up the west bank are the **Gomez Mill House**—North America's oldest surviving Jewish homestead—and **Kingston**. Tracing its roots to 1614, Kingston was the first capital of New York after the Revolution. Today it's home to the **Hudson River Maritime Museum**, one of the main ports for **Hudson River cruises**,

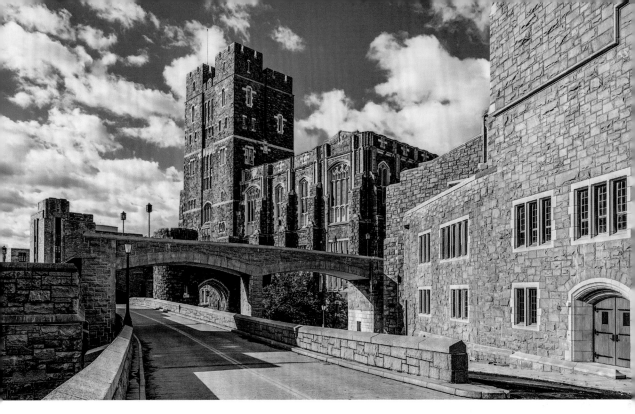

Tour numerous historic sites open to the public at the United States Military Academy at West Point.

as well as a gateway to hiking and camping in nearby **Catskill Park**.

For insight into the Hudson River school of 19th-century painting, pop into the **Thomas Cole House** in Catskill town. And then continue on Highway 9 to **Albany**, where the **State Capitol**, **New York State Museum**, and futuristic **Empire State Plaza** count among the main sights before crossing the Hudson.

U.S. Highway 9E runs down the eastern side of the valley, with possible stops along the way at **Martin Van Buren's Home** near Kinderhook, Frederic Church's plush Persian-style **Olana Estate**, or perhaps a concert, dance performance, or play at Bard College's excellent **Fisher Center for Performing Arts**.

On the outskirts of Rhinebeck, **Poets' Walk** affords a chance to stroll the same path that inspired Washington Irving to pen *Rip Van Winkle*. The **Old Rhinebeck Aerodrome** offers pre-1935 flying machines and biplane rides over the Hudson Valley.

The west bank between Rhinebeck and Poughkeepsie is famous for homes of the rich and famous, including the Joseph Tiffany–decorated **Wilderstein** manse, the stately 50-room **Vanderbilt Mansion**, and the **FDR Home, Library, and Museum** at Hyde Park.

Stretch your legs again on the **Walkway Over the Hudson** pedestrian bridge and **Loeb Art Center** at Vassar College in **Poughkeepsie**, before a home stretch back into New York City that features artist-inventor Samuel Morse's pseudo-Tuscan **Locust Grove** home, the **Hudson Valley Shakespeare Festival** at Boscobel, living history at **Van Cortlandt Manor**, and the Rockefellers' art-filled **Kykuit estate** in Tarrytown. ■

### ART AVENUES

- **Best Art:** The early 19th-century landscapes of Thomas Cole, Frederic E. Church, Jasper F. Cropsey, and other Hudson River school painters

- **Best Books:** *The Spy* by James Fenimore Cooper; *The Legend of Sleepy Hollow and Other Stories* by Washington Irving; *The Hudson River Valley Reader* edited by Edward Goodman

- **Best Movies:** *Hyde Park on Hudson* (2012) ; *A Quiet Place* (2018)

- **Best Music:** "My Dirty Stream (The Hudson River Song)" by Pete Seeger; *Hudson River Suite* by Ferde Grofé

- **Best TV:** *Sleepy Hollow* (2013-17); season 3 of *Turn: Washington's Spies* (2016)

# Berkshires Ramble
## Massachusetts

Rising to more than 2,800 feet (853.4 m), the rambling Berkshires of western Massachusetts offer a matchless American mosaic of art and music, woodlands and rivers, bucolic villages and reborn mill towns—a region that has long lured eastern urbanites seeking fresh air, autumn colors, and creative inspiration.

**THE BIG PICTURE**

**Distance:** 160 miles (257.5 km) round-trip from Springfield

**Drive time:** 5-6 days

**Best overnights:** Lennox, North Adams, Northampton

**Best seasons:** Anytime

**Highlights:** Stockbridge, Pittsfield, MASS MoCA, Mohawk Trail, Charlemont, Historic Deerfield, Northampton

An outlier of the northern Appalachians, the Berkshires are more like hills than mountains. But even a little bit more elevation sets them apart from surrounding flatlands. No matter what the season, the drive through these gorgeous highlands is a classic New England adventure.

You can approach the Berkshires from a dozen directions, but this drive starts from Springfield and a cruise along the Massachusetts Turnpike (Interstate 90) to **Stockbridge**. Norman Rockwell lived and painted here during the last 25 years of his life, and the town's **Norman Rockwell Museum** contains the largest collection of his works. **Chesterwood**, sculptor Daniel Chester French's summer home and studio, is also open to the public.

In nearby Lenox, fans of Edith Wharton can visit the **Mount**, the Gilded Age author's country home, or listen to summertime concerts by the Boston Symphony, Boston Pops, or local resident James Taylor at the legendary Tanglewood music venue. Farther north along Highway 7 is the **Arrowhead** home where Herman Melville wrote *Moby-Dick.*

Highway 7 soon rolls into **Pittsfield**, a one-time mill town that's morphed into the "Brooklyn of the Berkshires," a reborn city with a lively arts scene that includes the **Barrington Stage Company** and **Berkshire Museum**. Founded in 1783, **Hancock Shaker Village** is a throwback to old New England, while the **Ashuwillticook Rail Trail** offers a 12-mile (19.3 km) hiking, biking, and cross-country skiing route through the **Hoosic River Valley**. Between May and October, you can also ride the **Berkshire Scenic Railway** between Adams and North Adams.

North Adams boasts the incomparable **Mass Museum of Contemporary Art (MASS MoCA)**. Housed in more than two dozen 19th-century textile factory buildings, the museum is renowned for both its supersize art and year-round slate of concerts, comedy, and other performances.

Just up the road, **Williamstown** is another thriving arts village—home to the **Williams College Museum of Art**, the renowned Impressionist collection at the **Clark Art Institute**,

A malachite butterfly perches on a visitor to the Magic Wings Butterfly Conservatory.

Norman Rockwell's studio, at the Norman Rockwell Museum in Stockbridge, Berkshire County, Massachusetts

and the summer **Williamstown Theatre Festival**.

Following the path of an old Native American trade route between the Atlantic and Hudson Valley, the **Mohawk Trail** (State Route 2) wanders 59 miles (95 km) through the northern Berkshires between North Adams and Deerfield. The highway runs right through **Mohawk Trail State Forest** with its riverside camping and log cabins, and woodland hiking trails.

Downstream from the state forest, **Charlemont** is the region's adrenaline sports hub: whitewater rafting and kayaking, forest canopy tours, zip lines, a miniature roller-coaster, and the **Berkshire East Mountain Resort**, which doubles as a mountain bike park in the summer and ski and snowboard resort in the winter.

The Mohawk Trail dips into the **Connecticut River Valley** and

another time-trip—**Historic Deerfield**—an assemblage of 18th- and 19th-century houses and the **Flynt Center of Early New England Life**. The nearby **Magic Wings Butterfly Conservatory** hosts 4,000 fluttery creatures from around the world.

From Deerfield, Interstate 91

shoots down to **Northampton**, a hip college town with a lively main street that features the excellent **Smith College Museum of Art** and the **Calvin Coolidge Presidential Library and Museum**. Completing the Berkshire loop, Springfield is just half an hour farther down. ■

## LAY YOUR HEAD

• **The Porches Inn at MASS MoCA:** A 47-room boutique in restored Victorian row houses opposite the famed museum; bar, spa services, fitness center, swimming pool, from $159. porches.com

• **Wheatleigh:** A 19th-century Italianate mansion and 22 acres (8.9 ha) of parkland designed by Frederick Law Olmsted set the tone for this posh retreat in Lenox; restaurants, bar, swimming pool, tennis; from $595. wheatleigh.com

• **Hampton Terrace Inn:** Flamboyant Gilded Age decor and sumptuous breakfast mark this Victorian-era B&B in Lenox; swimming pool, fireplaces; from $189. hampton terrace.com

• **Hotel Northampton:** Five U.S. presidents, the Dalai Lama, and numerous music and movie stars have stayed at this historic 1920s colonial revival hotel; restaurant, bar, fitness center; from $160. hotelnorthampton.com

# Green & White Delights

## Vermont & New Hampshire

Flush with human and natural history, spectacular terrain, and outdoor recreation opportunities, the Green Mountains of Vermont and White Mountains of New Hampshire set the tone for a diverse figure-eight drive through northern New England.

Despite their legendary penchant for ingenuity, New Englanders showed an amazing lack of creativity when it came to naming their most prominent geographical features. Rather than grandiose appellations, they dubbed the snowcapped peaks of New Hampshire the White Mountains and the lush, forest-covered highlands of Vermont nothing more than Green Mountains. "Enough said" seemed to be their motto.

Barely two decades after the Pilgrims stepped ashore at Plymouth Rock (1620), people were scaling the highest peaks in these ranges; early adventurers, without even knowing it, were paving the way for the millions who have explored the

Whites and Greens since then. It's not just lofty summits that lure. The uplands of Vermont and New Hampshire also offer lakes and rivers, valleys and notches through the mountains, historic cities and handsome villages that reflect quintessential New England.

**Burlington**, Vermont, is far and away the region's largest population center and a great place to kick off the drive. Arrayed along the eastern shore of **Lake Champlain**, the city is both a college town and thriving business center. The **Island Line Trail** along an old railroad route runs 14 miles (22.5 km) down the lakeshore, connecting the **ECHO Leahy Center** aquarium, science, and nature museum with the historic **Moran Plant** and a string of waterfront parks.

Away from the water, Burlington revolves around **Church Street Marketplace**, a four-block, pedestrian-only precinct anchored by **Burlington City Arts** center and **Flynn Center for the Performing Arts** at one end, and the red-brick **First Unitarian Church** (erected in 1816) at the other.

Heading south from Burlington, U.S. Highway 7 soon reaches

**THE BIG PICTURE**

**Distance:** ca 425 miles (684 km) round-trip from Burlington, VT

**Drive time:** 7-10 days

**Best overnights:** Woodstock, Plymouth, Franconia, Conway, Squam Lakes, Waterbury/Stowe

**Best seasons:** Spring, summer, or fall

**Highlights:** Lake Champlain, Green Mountains, Woodstock, Franconia Notch, Mount Washington, Crawford Notch, Squam Lakes, St. Johnsbury

Snowboarders prepare to hit the slopes at Killington Mountain Ski Resort.

In autumn, visit Franconia Notch State Park, located in the heart of the White Mountain National Forest.

Shelburne, home to the **Vermont Teddy Bear Company** (30-minute factory tours) and the thoroughly diverse **Shelburne Museum**, a massive collection of Americana spread across 39 buildings and 20 gardens on a 45-acre waterfront estate. Twenty miles (32 km) farther south, the **Lake Champlain Maritime Museum** in Vergennes harbors a replica armada that includes the 1776 gunboat *Philadelphia* and **1862 canal schooner** *Lois McClure*.

Highway 7 continues its southward tack to Pittsford and its historic **covered wooden bridges** and Rutland, where the restored **Paramount Theatre** (opened 1914) presents a wide array of stage performances, music, dance, and movies. Then it's up into the **Green Mountains** on U.S. Highway 4, with several places where you can stop to hike, including the 3.6-mile (5.8 km) **Bucklin Trail** to the top of Killington Peak.

The highway wraps around the mountain to **Killington Resort**, renowned for winter sports and summer adventure offerings that include hiking and mountain biking trails, an 18-hole golf course, all-terrain vehicle tours, rock climbing, and an adventure park with a zip line and ropes course. President Calvin Coolidge was born in nearby **Plymouth Notch**, which preserves his birthplace in the back of a general store, as well as the family homestead and cheese factory.

Sliding down into the Connecticut River Valley, U.S. 4 glides into **Woodstock**, one of the oldest towns in Vermont (chartered 1761) and named the "prettiest small town in America" by *Ladies Home Journal*. In addition to a picture-perfect village green surrounded by historic

## ART AVENUES

- **Best Movies:** *Our Town* (1940); *On Golden Pond* (1981); *Dead Poets Society* (1989); *To Die For* (1995); *What Lies Beneath* (2000)

- **Best TV Shows:** *Peyton Place* (1964-69); *Newhart* (1982-1990); *North Woods Law* (2012-present)

- **Best Books:** *Affliction* by Russell Banks; *Walking to Vermont* by Christopher S. Wren; *Robert Frost's Poems* by Robert Frost; *Benedict Arnold's Navy* by James L. Nelson; *White Mountain Guide* by the Appalachian Mountain Club

- **Best Art:** The sculptures of New Hampshire's Augustus Saint-Gaudens and Daniel Chester French, and the Vermont scenes of Norman Rockwell

There's plenty to do on Lake Champlain, including boating, paddling, swimming, and fishing.

buildings, Woodstock features the **Marsh-Billings-Rockefeller National Historical Park**, where trails and carriage roads lead through an experimental forest and farm established in 1869.

The road trip continues along the scenic Ottauquechee River and 165-foot-deep (50 m) **Quechee Gorge**, one of Vermont's most impressive natural wonders. Visitors can hike to the bottom or look down at the gorge from the Highway 4 bridge. The adjacent **Vermont Institute of Natural Science** offers live raptor and reptile encounters at a rehab center that strives to introduce injured animals back into the wild.

Highway 4 crosses into New Hampshire at **White River Junction** and onward to the **Enfield Shaker Museum** on the shore of Mascoma Lake. The museum is tucked inside the Great Stone House and a cow barn that dates back to 1854. A zigzag ride along State Highways 118

and 25 takes the road trip to Plymouth, where the **Flying Monkey** arts center offers a year-round slate of often-offbeat music, comedy, movies, and more. The town's **Museum of the White Mountains** offers a great orientation to what lies just ahead.

Interstate 93 (aka Franconia Notch Parkway) leads due north along the Pemigewasset River into the heart of the **White Mountains**,

home to the highest peaks in the Northeast. Scaled down to just one lane in each direction, I-93 threads narrow **Franconia Notch**, a gorge flanked by 2,000-foot-high (609.6 m) granite walls.

The fabled Old Man of the Mountain— a rock formation that resembled a craggy human face— kept watch over the notch until 2003 when it suddenly crumbled

---

### OFF ROAD

• **Above Reality:** Hot-air balloon rides along the lakeshore and Green Mountain foothills near Burlington, Vermont. balloonvermont.com

• **Whistling Man Schooner Tours:** Two-hour daytime and sunset cruises on Lake Champlain from Burlington. whistlingman.com

• **Umiak Outdoor Outfitters:** Guided kayak trips on Vermont's Winooski and Lamoille Rivers, plus

kayak, canoe, and paddleboard rentals. umiak.com

• **Lakes Region Seaplane Services:** Half-hour scenic flights over New Hampshire's lake district from Paugus Bay in Laconia. seaplanetours.net

• **Squam Lakes Boat Tours:** Ninety-minute naturalist cruises hosted by Squam Lakes Natural Science Center between May and October. nhnature.org

to the gorge floor. The **Old Man of the Mountain Memorial** features seven steel profiles that help visitors imagine what the mountain looked like before the Old Man fell. Even without him, Franconia Notch offers plenty to see and do: hiking and biking trails, the **New England Ski Museum**, **Cannon Mountain Aerial Tramway**, a wooden walkway leading to a waterfall-splashed granite gorge called the **Flume**, and swimming, fishing, and boating on **Echo Lake**.

The route curls around the northern end of the White Mountains to **Bretton Woods**, one of the winter and summer outdoor sports and adventure hubs, as well as the base station for the **Mount Washington Cog Railway** to the top of the second highest peak east of the Mississippi. You can also hike to the top via various trails or drive on the historic **Mount Washington Auto Road**, accessed from U.S. 2 on the eastern side of the range.

From Bretton Woods, U.S. Highway 302 dives through another of the great mountain passes—**Crawford Notch**, home to 10 waterfalls and the **Appalachian Mountain Club Highland Center**, with its guided hikes, backpack camping trips, and outdoor skills classes. The highway follows the Saco River downstream into **Conway**, a cluster of villages with the largest concentration of hotels, restaurants, shops, and man-made tourist attractions in the White Mountains.

If peace and quiet are more your thing, continue along state routes 16 and 113 to the **Squam Lakes** region, where the movie *On Golden Pond* was famously filmed in the 1980s. Holderness lies astride the isthmus that separates the two lakes. The short hike to the crest of

---

## LAY YOUR HEAD

- **Made INN Vermont:** Designer-chic B&B tucked inside a restored Victorian manse in Burlington; gourmet breakfast, library, music and games parlor; from $249. madeinnvermont.com

- **The Shire:** This riverside hotel in Woodstock, VT, lies within walking distance of the town green and national historical park; four-poster beds, riverside lawn; from $139. shirewoodstock .com

- **Cottage Place on Squam Lake:** Cute cabins along the Squam lakeshore; kitchens, private beach, boat dock, barbecues, kayak rental, playground; from $129. cottageplaceon squam.com

- **Mount Washington Resort:** Historic lodging in Bretton Woods; restaurants, bars, spa, swimming pool, fitness room, golf course, tennis, winter and summer adventure sports; from $189. omnihotels.com

---

**Rattlesnake Mountain** affords great views of the lakes region, while the **Squam Lakes Natural Science Center** offers close-up views of animals like black bears and mountain lions that have traditionally inhabited the area.

Seeing as it was so spectacular the first time through, the drive offers a second chance to cruise through Franconia Notch. Only this time, drivers stay on I-93 all the way to **St. Johnsbury**, Vermont. The town's wealth of Victorian architecture includes the **St. Johnsbury Athenaeum Art Gallery** (opened 1871) and the **Fairbanks Museum and Planetarium** (opened 1890).

Climbing back into the Green Mountains, the final leg of the road trip, U.S. Highway 2 descends into **Montpelier**, with its golden-domed **Vermont State House**, and then onward to Burlington on Interstate 89—but not before a short stop in Waterbury, where **Ben and Jerry's** rounds out the drive in yummy fashion with a factory tour and flagship ice cream shop. ∎

Stop for ice cream and a factory tour at Ben and Jerry's in Vermont.

# Star-Spangled Banner Trail

## Maryland & Washington, D.C.

The War of 1812 is the focus of this national historical trail from the birthplace of the national anthem in Baltimore Harbor and the redcoat-sacked Washington, D.C., to the coast where the ragtag brawled with the British Royal Navy.

**THE BIG PICTURE**

**Distance:** 104 miles (167.4 km) from Baltimore, MD, to Solomons, MD

**Drive time:** 4 days

**Best overnights:** Hanover; Washington, D.C.; Prince Frederick; Solomons

**Best seasons:** Spring, summer, or fall

**Highlights:** Fort McHenry, U.S.S. *Constellation,* White House, National Museum of American History, Solomons

Perhaps we should blame Napoleon for the War of 1812. If it wasn't for his struggle to dominate Europe, the British would never have blockaded American shipping or shanghaied Yankee seamen into the Royal Navy—key issues that sparked the second Anglo-American war.

Much of the conflict played out on and around the **Chesapeake Bay**, including the celebrated night (September 12-13, 1814) when a young American attorney, Francis Scott Key, watched the British bombardment of Baltimore's Fort McHenry while aboard a ship anchored in the Patapsco River. Key was inspired to write a poem called "Defence of Fort M'Henry," which was later set to music as "The Star-Spangled Banner."

The modern **Star-Spangled Banner National Historic Trail** aptly starts at Baltimore Harbor at **Fort McHenry National Monument**. Historical exhibits are scattered throughout restored buildings inside the star-shaped citadel. There are two flag ceremonies each day, as well as ranger talks on the Battle of Baltimore and War on the Chesapeake.

Downtown Baltimore offers a number of other wartime sights, including the **Star-Spangled Banner Flag House** (where Mary Pickersgill created the flag that flew over Fort McHenry during the Battle of Baltimore) and the **U.S.S. Constellation**, a reproduction of a U.S. Navy ship that fought in the War of 1812.

Fighting also raged across Baltimore's east side on the star-spangled-banner night, clashes now marked by **North Point State Battlefield Park, Battle Acre Park, Todd's Inheritance Historic Site**, and **Fort Howard** at the end of the peninsula.

Instead of taking the busy interstate, cruise the leafy **Baltimore-Washington Parkway** down to **Bladensburg, Maryland**, where a riverside monument recalls an August 1814 battle during which the redcoats soundly defeated U.S. forces. Called "the greatest disgrace ever dealt to American arms," the victory allowed the British to invade nearby Washington, D.C. (your next stop).

The British promptly sacked and

A reproduction of the U.S.S. *Constellation* is docked in Baltimore's harbor.

WHAT SO PROUDLY WE HAIL'D AT THE TWILIGHT'S LAST GLEAMING,
WHOSE BROAD STRIPES AND BRIGHT STARS THROUGH THE PERILOUS FIGHT
O'ER THE RAMPARTS WE WATCH'D WERE SO GALLANTLY STREAMING?
AND THE ROCKETS' RED GLARE, THE BOMBS BURSTING IN AIR,
GAVE PROOF THROUGH THE NIGHT THAT OUR FLAG WAS STILL THERE;
O! SAY, DOES THAT STAR-SPANGLED BANNER YET WAVE,
O'ER THE LAND OF THE FREE, AND THE HOME OF THE BRAVE?

The 200-year-old flag that inspired "The Star-Spangled Banner" is on display at the National Museum of American History.

torched the **White House**, rebuilt in 1818 in its present form and open for public tours (reservations mandatory). The adjacent **White House Visitor Center** is open daily (no reservations needed). Delve deeper into the War of 1812 at the **National Society United States Daughters of 1812 Museum** on Rhode Island Avenue and the **National Museum of American History**, where the original star-spangled banner flag is on display.

As it exits the District of Columbia, **Pennsylvania Avenue** morphs into Maryland Route 4 and makes its way to Upper Marlboro, where old **Trinity Church, Darnall's Chance House Museum**, and the **tomb of Dr. William Beanes** commemorate the town's role in the War of 1812.

Route 4 continues down a narrow peninsula flanked by **Patuxent River** and the Chesapeake Bay to **Prince Frederick** (burned by the Brits) and **Jefferson Patterson Park and Museum**, which preserves relics from the Battles of St. Leonard's Creek, two 1814 skirmishes between the Chesapeake Bay Flotilla and Royal Navy that took place offshore from the modern museum.

The drive ends in **Solomons Island**, Maryland, where Commodore Joshua Barney formed his patchwork armada of gunboats, barges, and a floating artillery battery in 1812. Modern-day Solomons offers the eclectic **Calvert Marine Museum** featuring a maritime history gallery, the 1883 **Drum Point Lighthouse**, the **Estuarine Biology Gallery** with live otters and rays, and a historic boat collection. ◼

## OFF ROAD

• The Star-Spangled Banner National Historical Trail can also be done by private boat along a round-trip route from Elkton, MD, at the northern end of the Chesapeake Bay. After a detour up the Patapsco River to Baltimore, the water trail continues down the Chesapeake to Tangier Island before swinging up the Potomac River to Washington, D.C. In addition to historical **Tangier**, which the British used as a base for attacking Washington and Baltimore, the water route allows for visits to other local sites including the **U.S. Naval Academy** and the historic district in **Annapolis, Concord Point Lighthouse, Point Lookout State Park**, and the spot where the Battle of the Ice Mound, the last combat of the War of 1812, took place on **Taylor Island**.

# Yankee Passage
## NY, CT, RI & MA

Why drive the traffic-clogged interstate between New York City and Boston when you can follow back roads through salty old seaports, beguiling beaches, villages with historic ships, and presidential hometowns along the coastline that spawned Yankee ingenuity?

### THE BIG PICTURE

**Distance:** ca 520 miles (836.9 km) from New York City to Boston

**Drive time:** 10-14 days

**Best overnights:** Montauk, Mystic, Newport, Cape Cod, Plymouth

**Best seasons:** Spring, summer, or fall

**Highlights:** Montauk Point, U.S.S. *Nautilus,* Mystic Seaport, Newport mansions, New Bedford whaling, Cape Cod NS, Provincetown, Adams and Kennedy presidential sights

The word *Yankee* has a long and colorful lineage. It was born as a derogatory term that the Dutch of New Amsterdam applied to English settlers and that the British called the rebellious American patriots.

Americans later adopted the phrase as a badge of honor. Better to be damn a Yankee than a bloody redcoat. And thus the word evolved into a term of pride—and a famous baseball team.

This drive along America's northeastern coast starts in the hometown of the New York Yankees—or, more specifically, at JFK International Airport, which marks the eastern end of the Sunrise Highway (State Route 27) on Long Island.

For a quick fix of sea and sand, cross one of the causeways leading to the barrier islands that harbor popular **Jones Beach**, **Robert Moses State Park**, and **Fire Island National Seashore**. Farther along are the **Hamptons**, a celebrity-infused enclave that's worth a cruise down **Main Street** in East Hampton just for the people-watching.

Perched at the far end of Long Island, **Montauk Point State Park** offers 1,300 acres (526 ha) of forest, wetlands, beaches, sea cliffs, and rocky shoreline. In addition to hiking, biking, and horseback riding, visitors can climb 110-foot-high (33.5 m) **Montauk Lighthouse** (built in 1796) or join a ranger-led "seal hike" to observe Montauk's resident colony. The point is renowned for great surf fishing—and the breeding ground for great white sharks that lies just offshore.

Located on an old Army base, adjacent **Camp Hero State Park** hosted the Montauk Project, a supersecret government experiment that allegedly involved everything from mind control and time travel to teleportation and communicating with extraterrestrials. The project inspired the *Stranger Things* Netflix series.

Next stop: Connecticut. But "driving" there means hopping the **Cross Sound Ferry** from Orient Point to **New London**, about a 90-minute trip.

Set on either side of the Thames River, New London and twin city **Groton** have harbored American naval operations since the Revolution and display that heritage through the **U.S. Coast Guard Museum** and tours of the U.S.S. *Nautilus,* the nation's first nuclear-powered sub-

Uno, a 15-year-old beluga whale, greets visitors at Connecticut's Mystic Aquarium.

At the northern tip of Cape Cod, Massachusetts, seaside Provincetown is built on the site of the *Mayflower*'s 1620 landing.

marine, at the **U.S. Submarine Force Museum**. Among New London's other landmarks are 19th-century **Fort Trumbull** and **Monte Cristo Cottage**, the boyhood home of playwright Eugene O'Neill.

U.S. Highway 1 takes the road trip east along the Connecticut coast to **Mystic Seaport**. This replica of a 19th-century New England coastal village offers historic sailing ships and living history programs, as well as beluga whales, penguins, and the other denizens of the **Mystic Aquarium and Sea Research Foundation**.

After crossing the state line into Rhode Island, follow Route 138 across Narragansett Bay to well-heeled **Newport**. A seaside getaway for the rich and famous of the Gilded Age, Newport offers guided tours of the **Breakers, Rosecliff, Marble House**, and other old waterfront estates. Among the city's other treasures are **Touro Synagogue** (the nation's oldest, built in 1763), 19th-century **Fort Adams**, and **Bowen's Wharf**.

Newport also offers action on land

and by sea. Visitors can reach "game, set, match" playing on the grass courts of the **International Tennis Hall of Fame,** hike the **Cliff Walk National Recreation Trail**, or explore **Narragansett Bay** on America's Cup yachts or vintage schooners.

Just a half hour north of Newport, **Fall River**, Massachusetts, offers a totally different take on the Yankee coast that ranges from the infamous **Lizzie Borden House** (where one of

the most scandalous murders of the 1890s occurred) to the world's largest collection of World War II warships at **Battleship Cove** (including the U.S.S. *Massachusetts*).

The drive continues along U.S. Highway 6 to **New Bedford**, once the epicenter of the nation's whaling industry. The city's maritime heritage is on full display at the **New Bedford Whaling Museum**, the whaling-era **Rotch-Jones-Duff**

## PIT STOPS

• **Newport Jazz Festival:** Launched in 1954, the world-renowned music fest invades Fort Adams every year in late July or early August. newportjazz.org

• **Sailfest:** This annual July bash along New London's waterfront mixes music, food, fireworks, and tall ships. sailfest.org

• **Holy Ghost Festival:** Fall River's Portuguese American community celebrates this Azorean tradition with

traditional music, food, and a grand religious procession every August. fallriverma.org

• **Hamptons International Film Festival:** Emerging filmmakers from around the world take the spotlight at this October celebration on Long Island. hamptonsfilmfest.org

• **Fantasia Fair:** Provincetown provides the venue for the nation's longest running transgender event, first staged in 1975; October. fanfair.info

**House**, and **Seamen's Bethel** church, which inspired the "Whalemen's Chapel" of *Moby-Dick*.

Heading due east from New Bedford, Highway 6 runs alongside the Cape Cod Canal and across big **Sagamore Bridge** (opened in 1935) to fabled Cape Cod. Several towns along Nantucket Sound are worth exploring, including Hyannis, where the **John F. Kennedy Hyannis Museum** features exhibits, photos, and a Walter Cronkite–narrated video on JFK's lifelong relationship with the Cape. Farther along is **Chatham** with its photogenic waterfront, seafood eateries, and the **U.S. Coast Guard Lifeboat Station** that coordinated the rescue of 32 seamen from the S.S. *Pendleton* in 1952.

Beyond Orleans, the highway passes through **Cape Cod National Seashore** with its rolling dunes, coastal wetlands, and 40 miles (64.4 km) of continuous beach. **Salt Pond Visitor Center** offers a great introduction to one of the nation's best oceanfront parks, as well as trails around a nearby marsh and down to the shore. From guided kayaking trips and cycling the 22-mile (35.4 km) **Cape Cod Rail Trail** to 4x4 tours of the artistic **Dune Shacks** or stage plays at the **Payomet Performing Arts Center**, there are myriad ways to discover the national seashore.

Perched at the tip of the peninsula is storied **Provincetown**, where the Pilgrims lingered (and penned the Mayflower Compact) before moving across the bay to Plymouth. Today the salty seaside town is renowned for its alternative lifestyles and a waterfront area jam-packed with restaurants, galleries, and aquatic outfitters. Visitors can snatch bird's-eye views

The New Bedford Whaling Museum highlights human history with whales.

---

### ART AVENUES

- **Best Movies:** *The Russians Are Coming, the Russians Are Coming* (1966); *The Summer of '42* (1971); *Jaws* (1975); *JFK* (1991); *Amistad* (1997)

- **Best Books:** *Moby-Dick* by Herman Melville; *Cape Cod* by Henry David Thoreau; *The Great Gatsby* by F. Scott Fitzgerald; *An Unfinished Life: JFK 1917-1963* by Robert Dallek

- **Best TV Shows:** *John Adams* miniseries (2008); *Turn: Washington's Spies* (2014-17); *Wings* (1990-97); *Royal Pains* (2009-2016); *The Affair* (2014-19)

- **Best Play:** *Anna Christie* by New London native and Cape Cod resident Eugene O'Neill

- **Best Music:** Sea chanties by the U.S. Coast Guard Academy Idlers; "Old Cape Cod" by Patti Page; and anything by Long Island native Billy Joel

---

from the summit of the 252-foot-high (76.8 m) **Pilgrim Monument**, learn more about local history at the **Provincetown Museum**, or see how different artists have interpreted the Cape-scape at the **Provincetown Art Association and Museum**.

Unfortunately, there's no vehicle ferry from Provincetown to "main-land" Massachusetts. To reach Boston, road trippers have to backtrack along U.S. 6 and recross the Sagamore Bridge. If you're in a rush, hop on Interstate 495 for an hour-long drive to Boston. Otherwise, merge onto the Pilgrims Highway (State Route 3) and a saunter up the west side of **Cape Cod Bay**.

Although best known for its legendary rock, **Plymouth** offers numerous Pilgrim-centric sights. Foremost among these is **Plimoth Plantation**, a reproduction of the 17th-century settlement that offers living history from the perspective of both the English colonists and the Wampanoag people who welcomed them to the New World in 1620.

Route 3 continues into **Quincy**, hometown to five generations of the Adams family and two American presidents. **Adams National Historical Park** includes a downtown visitor center, as well as the homes where both John Adams and his son John Quincy Adams were born and raised.

From Quincy, you can take the interstate into **Boston** or detour via Quincy Shore Drive and Morrissey Boulevard to Columbia Point and the **John F. Kennedy Presidential Library**. From there it's a short drive into downtown Boston. ∎

---

### OFF ROAD

- **Block Island:** Year-round vehicle/passenger ferries from Port Judith, RI; seasonal summer passenger ferries from New London, CT; Fall River, MA; Newport, RI; and Montauk, NY. blockislandinfo.com

- **Martha's Vineyard:** Year-round vehicle/passenger ferries from Woods Hole, MA; seasonal summer passenger ferries from Hyannis, Falmouth, and New Bedford, MA;

Quonset Point, RI; and New York City. mvol.com/ferries

- **Nantucket:** Year-round vehicle/passenger ferries from Hyannis, MA; seasonal summer passenger ferries from New Bedford and Harwich Port, MA. nantucketferries.com

- **Fishers Island:** Year-round vehicle/passenger ferries from New London, CT. fiferry.com

# Susquehanna Trail

## D.C., MD, PA & NY

Called a "Road of Never-Ending Delight" and a "Ribbon of Concrete Through the American Beautyland" when it was created in the 1920s, the Susquehanna Trail was one of the early "auto trails" to stimulate motorcar vacations.

A lthough the name disappeared from road maps long ago, the Susquehanna Trail still delivers an intriguing and entertaining drive following the eponymous river between the nation's capital and Niagara Falls in New York.

From the starting point in **Washington, D.C.**, it's an easy cruise up I-95 to **Baltimore, Maryland**. Check out **Fort McHenry** and the **National Aquarium**—and catch a ball game at **Camden Yards** if the Orioles are playing at home—before heading north on I-83 into south-central Pennsylvania.

Reaching York, you can take a side trip to the **Gettysburg Battlefield** or the **Amish country** around Lancaster, or continue dead ahead to **Harrisburg**. Dedicated in 1906, the **Pennsylvania State Capitol** looms above the riverside city. Harrisburg also offers narrated cruises on the *Pride of the Susquehanna* sternwheeler and a chance to indulge your sweet tooth at nearby **Hershey's Chocolate World**.

## THE BIG PICTURE

**Distance:** ca 425 miles (684 km) from Washington, D.C., to Niagara Falls, NY

**Drive time:** 7-8 days

**Best overnights:** Baltimore, Harrisburg, Williamsport, Corning, Buffalo

**Best seasons:** Spring, summer, or fall

**Highlights:** Fort McHenry, Amish country, Hershey's Chocolate World, Pine Creek Gorge, Corning glass, Niagara Falls

The trail jumps onto U.S. Highway 15 for the next stretch along the river, one of the most gorgeous sections of the entire drive. Time-trip into the past on the little **Millersburg Ferry**, a staple on the Susquehanna since 1817. See works by Picasso, Rembrandt, Whistler, and Warhol in the **Samek Art Museum** at Bucknell University. And cozy up to chameleons and Komodo dragons at **Clyde Peeling's Reptiland** before rolling into **Williamsport** and its **Little League Baseball** sights.

Highway 15 carries on to the **Allegheny Plateau** and the **Pennsylvania Wilds**, named for its rugged nature and numerous parks. Hop off the highway at Mansfield and hike or bike a portion of the **Pine Creek Rail Trail**, a 65-mile (104.6 km) route that runs through the bottom of 800-foot-deep (243.8 m) **Pine Creek Gorge**— "the Grand Canyon of Pennsylvania."

Crossing the border into New York, the highway morphs into I-99 for a quick sprint up to **Corning**. The "Crystal City" is renowned worldwide for the **Corning Museum of Glass**, a collection that spans antiquity to modern times. Among the city's other offerings are the Smithsonian-affiliated **Norman Rockwell Museum**

The Corning Museum of Glass displays both ancient and contemporary works.

Middle Falls is the biggest of three must-see cascades on the Genesee River inside Letchworth State Park, New York.

(Native American and Western art) and the historic **Gaffer District** with its assortment of galleries, studios, and eateries.

Interstates 86 and 390 convey the trail along the western edge of the **Finger Lakes** region and its numerous wineries. Floating at the south end of **Keuka Lake**, Hammondsport offers vintage aeroplanes at the **Glenn H. Curtiss Museum** and antique watercraft at the **Finger Lakes Boating Museum**.

The home stretch of this road trip starts in Mount Morris, where **Letchworth State Park** offers a gorgeous 17-mile (27.4 km) stretch of the **Genesee River** with waterfalls spilling from 600-foot (182.9 m) cliffs. From there it's about an hour to **East Aurora**, where the **Millard Fillmore Home** shines the light on the 13th president, and lakeside Buffalo.

Finally coming into its own as a tourism destination after decades as a rust belt backwater town, Buffalo's eclectic attractions include the historic ships of the **Buffalo and Erie County Naval Park**, the cutting-edge art and events of the **Albright-Knox Art Gallery**, and the **Explore and More Children's Museum**.

Another 20 miles (32.2 km) up the interstate, **Niagara Falls** punctuates the Susquehanna Trail with one of the world's great natural wonders. ■

## PIT STOPS

• **Artsfest:** Two hundred fifty artists and performers from around North America strut their stuff in Harrisburg's Riverfront Park during this Memorial Day jamboree. artsfesthbg.com

• **Corning Glassfest:** Four days in May of glassmaking by skilled "gaffers" and quaffing beverages from glass receptacles in New York's Crystal City. gafferdistrict.com/glassfest

• **Night Nation Run Buffalo:** This after-dark running music festival takes over Buffalo's Outer Harbor district during a run- and fun-filled weekend in June. nightnationrun.com/buffalo

• **Yorkfest:** The Poetry Tent, colorful Chalk Walk, and Historic Codorus Creek Boat Parade are part of the happenings at this summer fine arts festival weekend in York; August. yorkcity.org/yorkfest

• **Little League World Series:** Fans, players, coaches, and media from around the world descend on Williamsport for an August baseball classic that started in 1947. littleleague.org

# Along the Delaware
## Delaware, Pennsylvania & New Jersey

Suffused with history, nature, and recreational opportunities, this meandering route along the Delaware River traces a waterway used for hundreds of years by Native Americans, European settlers, legendary generals, and captains of industry.

Although seldom mentioned in the same breath as other great rivers, the Delaware was key to the European settlement of the eastern seaboard and the nation that arose from the American Revolution. Dutch, Swedish, and English colonies rose along its banks, George Washington famously crossed the river to launch a surprise attack against the redcoats, and it helped fuel the U.S. industrial revolution by expediting the delivery of timber and coal.

Perched near the spot where the river flows into the broad Delaware Bay, **New Castle, Delaware**, is an apt place to kick off this road trip. Founded by Peter Stuyvesant and his Dutch West India Company in 1651, the settlement passed from Holland to Sweden to England during colonial days.

A throwback to 200 years ago, the town's common and quaint cobblestone streets are flanked by historic structures like **Jessop's Tavern** (erected in 1674), **Immanuel Episcopal Church** (1703), **New Castle Court House** (1732)—which later served as Delaware's first state capitol building—and even a 17th-century **Dutch dwelling**.

Follow Delaware Highway 9 a short way north to **Wilmington**. The Delaware metropolis owes a huge debt to French Huguenot immigrant Éleuthère Irénée du Pont de Nemours, who helped transform the riverside city into a 19th-century industrial powerhouse.

The du Pont family bequeathed many of the Wilmington area's cultural institutions, from the **Delaware Museum of Natural History** and **Winterthur Museum, Garden and Library** to the **Hagley Museum and Library** with its antique vehicle collection, sprawling French-style **Nemours Mansion and Gardens**, and DuPont Environmental Education Center at the unique **Russell Peterson Urban Wildlife Refuge**. Busy Interstate 95 takes the drive

Visit the iconic Liberty Bell outside Independence Hall in Philadelphia.

The former home of Alfred I. du Pont, Nemours Mansion and Gardens French-style estate is worth a tour when in Wilmington.

into Philadelphia. Among the must-see sights in the City of Brotherly Love are **Independence Hall** and the **Liberty Bell**, the **Philadelphia Museum of Art** (and its famous "Rocky Steps"), and the lofty observation deck on the 57th floor of the **One Liberty** skyscraper. Before you leave, hop down to **South Philly** and order one of those famous cheesesteaks.

Leaving Philly behind, I-95 heads for Levittown and **Pennsbury Manor** in Morrisville, Pennsylvania, the 17th-century riverside estate of colonial mastermind William Penn. Nearby **Summerseat** house in Morrisville was Washington's headquarters before his legendary Delaware crossing in 1776.

Pennsylvania Route 32 hugs the river's west bank for the next 40 miles (64.4 km), with stops along the way at **Washington Crossing** (where George and company launched their midnight raid), the vintage **New Hope and Ivyland**

**Railroad**, and the 300-foot (91.4 m) **Nockamixon Cliffs**.

Continuing northward on State Route 611, the river road rolls into **Easton, Pennsylvania**, and its downtown historic district, where the **Crayola Experience** features interactive adventures like Scribble Square. The **Signal Museum** highlights the region's colonial and pre-European heritage, while the restored **State Theatre** (opened 1925) stages live events. Easton also boasts the **National Canal Museum** and a lovely portion of the **Delaware and Lehigh National Heritage Trail**.

Thirty-five miles (56.3 km) farther upstream (via Route 611), the river cuts a 1,000-foot (304.8 m) gash in the **Delaware Water Gap**, used for around 10,000 years as a passage between the upper and lower river valleys. Arrayed along both the Pennsylvania and New Jersey shores, **Delaware Water Gap National Recreation Area** stretches 40 miles (64.4 km)

along the river, a wild and scenic segment with places to paddle, bike, and hike—including 28 miles (45.1 km) of the renowned **Appalachian Trail**. ∎

## SCENIC DETOURS

• **Delaware Route One** runs 90 miles (144.8 km) south from Wilmington to historic Dover, Bombay Hook National Wildlife Refuge, and Cape Henlopen State Park at the mouth of Delaware Bay.

• **New Jersey Route 29** covers 32 miles (51.5 km) of the New Jersey shore between Trenton and Frenchtown.

• **Lehigh Valley Thruway (U.S. 22)** heads west from Easton to industrial revolution attractions in Bethlehem and Allentown.

• **U.S. Highway 209** runs the length of Delaware Water Gap National Recreation Area and onward to Kingston, New York, on the Hudson River.

# Revolution Road

## MA, VT, NY, NJ, PA, MD & VA

From the cradle of rebellion and the "shot heard 'round the world" in Massachusetts to the birthplace of an American hero and the ignominious British surrender in Virginia, this road trip down the eastern seaboard traces the Revolutionary War from start to finish.

**THE BIG PICTURE**

**Distance:** ca 800 miles (1,287.5 km) from Boston, MA, to Yorktown, VA

**Drive time:** 10 days

**Best overnights:** Saratoga Springs, Princeton, Philadelphia, Annapolis, Fredericksburg

**Best seasons:** Spring, summer, or fall

**Highlights:** Freedom Trail, Concord, Saratoga, Morristown, Philadelphia, Valley Forge, Annapolis, Mount Vernon, Yorktown

Massachusetts ignited the first sparks of revolution in 1665 when the Sons of Liberty was formed in Boston. The flames were further stoked by the 1770 Boston Massacre and the 1773 Boston Tea Party, precursors to the outbreak of warfare at Lexington and Concord.

This means there's no better place to start a Revolutionary War road trip than the city where it all began. **Boston** makes its history easy via the **Freedom Trail** of 16 sites—marked by red bricks—connected to the birth of the United States.

Starting from **Boston Common**, which the redcoats used as a troop encampment, the trail leads to the **Old South Meeting House**, where the Tea Party was organized; the site of the **Boston Massacre**; **Paul Revere's House** in the North End; across the Charles River to the **U.S.S. Constitution**; and up **Bunker Hill**, where the patriots proved what a formidable force they would be.

On the western outskirts of Boston, the **Battle Green** in **Lexington** is where the first shots of the Revolution were fired on April 19, 1775. The alarm raised by the arrival of Paul Revere and William Dawes, the local militia confronted a much larger British force. Seven patriots died in that first skirmish—historians still debate who fired the first shot—and the redcoats marched on to nearby **Concord.**

**Minute Man National Historical Park** reveals the rest of what happened that fateful day through a **"Road to Revolution"** multimedia show at the visitor center, ranger programs at **North Bridge** (Concord) and **Hartwell Tavern** (Lexington), and a **Battle Road** hiking and biking trail along the route where the action played out in 1775.

From Concord, Massachusetts, Route 2 leads east to the **Connecticut River Valley**, where a short drive on Interstate 91 and Vermont Route 9 heads into the **Green Mountains.** The short-lived Vermont Republic declared its independence from everyone in 1777 but joined American forces in defeating the British at the Battle of Bennington that same year. The 306-foot-tall (93.3 m)

The 1773 Tea Party began at Boston's Old South Meeting House.

During a reenactment of the Battle of Lexington, redcoat actors take a stand on the Lexington Common.

**Bennington Battle Monument** (the tallest structure in Vermont) commemorates the clash. But the battle actually took place across the border in New York at **Bennington Battlefield State Historic Site**.

Bennington was a prelude to a much larger and far more important showdown called the Battles of Saratoga in New York. Historians consider **Saratoga** one of the turning points of world history, a resounding American victory that kept the British from splitting the colonies in two and convinced France to join the war effort on the side of the patriots—two developments that eventually ensured U.S. independence. **Saratoga National Historical Park** preserves much of the battlefield on dramatic bluffs overlooking the **Hudson River**.

Interstate 87/287 runs south through the Hudson Valley to **Washington's Headquarters State Historic** site near the **U.S. Military Academy** at West Point and **Morristown National Historic Park** in northern New Jersey, where General Washington and his Continental Army survived the frigid winter of 1779-80. A combination of I-287 and U.S. Highway 1 runs across the middle of New Jersey to **Trenton**, where **Washington Crossing State Park** marks the spot where the future president and his troops famously crossed the Delaware River on Christmas Day 1776 to stage a

## PIT STOPS

• **Washington's Birthday:** Mount Vernon celebrates the February event with military demonstrations, fife-and-drum music, and actors reenacting Washington's 18th-century battles and receiving birthday wishes as him. mountvernon.org

• **Patriots' Day:** Reenactments, ceremonies, and parades mark the April anniversary of Concord and Lexington at Minute Man National Historical Park. nps.gov/mima/patriots-day.htm

• **Fourth of July:** Philadelphia observes the birth of a nation with a Celebration of Freedom Ceremony and Independence Day parade that starts outside Independence Hall. nps.gov/inde

• **Saratoga Anniversary History Walks:** Rangers lead historic battlefield walking tours—one to two miles (1.6–3.2 km) on the Battles of Saratoga dates (September 19 and October 7). nps.gov/sara

Valley Forge preserves Revolutionary War history with monuments, meadows, and relics from the Continental Army encampment.

sneak attack on Britain's Hessian mercenaries.

From there, it's just a short drive into **Philadelphia** and its rich Revolutionary heritage. **Independence National Historic Park** harbors a number of American icons, including **Independence Hall** (birthplace of the Declaration of Independence and the U.S. Constitution), the glass-encased **Liberty Bell Center**, Ben Franklin's grave in **Christ Church Burial Ground**, and many more. Downtown Philly is also home to the new **Museum of the American Revolution** and the **Betsy Ross House**, where the stars and stripes may or may not have been born.

On the outskirts of Philadelphia is another place immortalized by the Revolution: **Valley Forge.** The Pennsylvania national historical park enshrines the place where Washington and 12,000 troops barely made it through the winter of 1777-78. The trials and tribulations of that crucial winter are told via guided trolley tours and history hikes, living history encampments, storytelling benches, and artillery demonstrations.

U.S. Highway 202 leads a half hour south to **Brandywine Battlefield Park**, where American and British forces fought the single largest (and longest) battle of the Revolutionary War in September 1777. With roughly 15,000 troops on both sides, the battle resulted in a British

---

## LAY YOUR HEAD

- **Brinckerhoff Inn:** Across the Hudson River from Washington's headquarters at Newburgh, this B&B in Fishkill, New York, hosted Washington, the Marquis de Lafayette, Benedict Arnold, and numerous other Revolutionary War notables; from $299. brinckerhoffinn.com

- **Historic Inns of Annapolis:** Washington may have stayed at one of these 18th-century lodges when he went to Annapolis to resign his commission in 1783; from $93. historicinnsofannapolis.com

- **Travelers Rest Farm:** Near the route between Washington's birthplace and Yorktown, it's said to be the place where the general rested during travels between Mount Vernon and Williamsburg, VA; from $150. travelersrestfarm.com

- **Smithfield Inn:** Located on the other side of Newport News, VA, from Yorktown, this 1750s B&B apparently hosted Washington during his presidential tours of 1789-1791; from $135. smithfield inn.com

victory and the redcoat occupation of Philadelphia.

From Pennsylvania, I-95 makes a beeline for **Baltimore, Maryland,** and **Fort McHenry**, constructed in 1776 to defend the city from redcoat attacks yet much better known for its role in the War of 1812. Charm City also boasts the **Casimir Pulaski Monument** (honoring a Polish general who fought alongside the Americans and created the U.S. Cavalry) and **Westminster Hall**, where many Revolutionary War veterans (and Edgar Allen Poe) are buried.

Thirty miles (48.3 km) south of Baltimore via I-97, **Annapolis** staged its own "tea party" by burning a British cargo ship on the **Chesapeake Bay** in 1774. The Maryland city served as capital of the U.S. government during the last two years of the war and first six years of independence (1781-89). The **Maryland State House**, topped by a lightning rod designed by Ben Franklin, is where George Washington resigned his commission in 1783. Maritime hero **John Paul Jones** is buried in the chapel crypt at the **U.S. Naval Academy**.

Washington, D.C., wasn't created until the late 1790s, so the Revolutionary road trip bypasses the national capital (via the beltway) to northern Virginia, where the **George Washington Memorial Parkway** winds along the Potomac River to **Mount Vernon**. Spread across 500 acres (202.3 ha), the estate features the Palladian-style mansion of George and Martha Washington and more than 30 outbuildings. In addition to two museums, the grounds harbor a working farm, 18th-century craft demonstrations, and **Washington's Tomb**.

The father of our country was born farther down the Potomac, on

the tobacco plantation of his grandfather near Wakefield Corner. Reached via I-95 and Virginia Route 3 (the "Historyland Highway"), **George Washington Birthplace National Monument** features a reproduction of the house where Mary Ball Washington gave birth to George on February 22, 1732, as well as a working farm with 18th-century plants and livestock.

Reaching the last stop on the road trip—and the end of the actual Revolution—requires a drive down U.S. Highway 17 and bridge crossings of both the **Rappahannock** and **York** Rivers.

Spread along the south bank of the latter river, **Yorktown Battlefield** is where Lord Cornwallis surrendered to the Franco-American forces of George Washington and the Comte de Rochambeau on October 19, 1781. Part of **Colonial National Historical Park,** the battlefield driving tour features redoubts, gun batteries, encampments, and cemeteries, as well as an excellent **Yorktown Visitor Center**, and the state-run **American Revolution Museum at Yorktown**. ■

See a Revolutionary War–era defense position on a visit to Yorktown, Virginia.

# Lakes-to-Sea Highway
## New Jersey & Pennsylvania

With sandy beaches, waterfront walks, and carnival attractions at both ends, this 450-mile (724.2 km) romp across New Jersey and Pennsylvania links Atlantic City on the seacoast with Erie's Great Lake shore.

**THE BIG PICTURE**

**Distance:** ca 450 miles (724.2 km) from Atlantic City, NJ, to Erie, PA

**Drive time:** 7 days

**Best overnights:** Philadelphia, Hershey/Harrisburg, State College, Dubois, Meadville

**Best seasons:** Summer or early fall

**Highlights:** Atlantic City, Pine Barrens, Philadelphia, Valley Forge, Hershey, Penn State, Cook Forest, Erie

This 21st-century take on the old Lakes-to-Sea auto trail linking the Atlantic and the Great Lakes offers a family-friendly escape that includes indoor fun and outdoor adventure starting from the oceanfront in **Atlantic City, New Jersey**.

Amble down the famous **Boardwalk**, take a spin on the **Wheel at Steel Pier**, wiggle your toes in the sand, and take a dip in the ocean before heading out of town on the Atlantic City Expressway.

Much of the drive across the Garden State is through the **Pine Barrens**, a heavily forested area renowned as the home turf of the mythical Jersey Devil and the largest tract of wilderness left along the Atlantic seaboard between Maine and southern Virginia.

For a taste of the New Jersey pinelands, slide off the expressway at exit 17 to visit **Batsto Village**, a historic bog iron and glassmaking settlement inside hiker- and biker-friendly **Wharton State Forest**.

The expressway leaps across the Delaware River into **Philadelphia**. From oldies-but-goodies like the **Liberty Bell** and **Independence Hall** to modern-day favorites like Philly cheesesteak sandwiches at Reading Terminal Market, climbing the cinematic **"Rocky steps,"** at the Philadelphia Museum of Art, and creepy tours of **Eastern State Penitentiary**, there are plenty of sidetracks in the City of Brotherly Love (and the beloved NFL Eagles).

Take the interstate to **Valley Forge National Historical Park**, where George Washington and his troops weathered the winter of 1777-78, and then cruise the Pennsylvania Turnpike through the scenic **Pennsylvania Dutch country**.

Just off the pike are the **Wolf Sanctuary of PA** and the **Mount Hope Estate**, which is home to a winery, dinner theater, and summer events like the **Celtic Fling and Highland Games** in June and **Pennsylvania Renaissance Faire** in August.

Half an hour farther west is **Hersheypark**, which includes 16 water rides, 14 coasters, **ZooAmerica North American Wildlife Park**, and yummy **Hershey's Chocolate World**.

In addition to the impressive

Festivalgoers dress up for the Pennsylvania Renaissance Faire.

A must-stroll on any visit to Atlantic City, the historic boardwalk offers restaurants, shops, and shore views.

Pennsylvania State Capitol, nearby Harrisburg offers the **National Civil War Museum** and scenic river cruises aboard the *Pride of the Susquehanna*.

U.S. Highway 322 carries the route into the land of the Nittany Lions—State College and **Penn State University**. Buy some swag at the college bookstore, peer into the jaws of **Beaver Stadium**, or catch a performance at the restored **State Theatre** (opened 1938) before moving on down the road.

The odyssey continues on Highway 322 as it climbs into the **Allegheny Mountains** through the Pennsylvania Wilds region. You can pop down to **Punxsutawney** to visit the **Weather Discovery Center** and the burrow where that famous groundhog lives. Or sidestep to **Cook Forest State Park** to walk among 350-year-old hemlocks and white pines in the **Forest Cathedral** or float down the easy-going **Clarion River**.

At Meadville in western Pennsylvania—home of the wacky **PennDOT Road Sign Sculpture Garden**—the Lakes-to-Sea route hangs a right onto U.S. Highway 19 for the rest of the drive to Lake Erie.

Between **Splash Lagoon** indoor water park, the old-fashioned **Waldameer and Water World amusement park** (opened 1896), and the great little **Erie Zoo**, there's plenty to keep the kids occupied in **Erie** city. But be sure to end the road trip with a walk along the beach and a lake swim at **Presque Isle State Park** on the other side of the bay from downtown Erie. ∎

### PIT STOPS

• **Groundhog Day:** Thousands gather on February 2 to watch Punxsutawney Phil predict an early spring or six more weeks of winter. groundhog.org

• **Wild Rib Cook Off and Music Festival:** Erie ushers in the summer with four days of food and tunes in Perry Square Park; June. erieribfest.com

• **Central Pennsylvania Festival of Arts:** Five days of sidewalk sales, street painting, sand sculpture, foot races, and kids' activities highlight this July event in State College. arts-festival.com

• **Philadelphia Fringe Festival:** More than 150 artists perform music, drama, dance, comedy, magic, and more at this 17-day September event. fringearts.com

# Midwest
# Road Trips

Explore natural sea caves on Lake Superior near Pictured Rocks National Lakeshore.

# Lake Michigan Circle Tour

## IL, WI, MI & IN

The only one of the Great Lakes completely within the United States, Lake Michigan lends itself to an awesome drive that traces the lakeshore through five states, two great American cities, and several national parks.

### THE BIG PICTURE

**Distance:** ca 900 miles (1,448.4 km) round-trip from Chicago

**Drive time:** 10-14 days

**Best overnights:** Milwaukee, Door Peninsula/Green Bay, St. Ignace/Mackinaw, Traverse City, Holland, New Buffalo/Michigan City

**Best seasons:** Spring, summer, or fall

**Highlights:** Chicago lakeshore, Milwaukee, Door Peninsula, Hiawatha National Forest, Mackinac Straits, Traverse City, Indiana Dunes

Just over 300 miles (483 km) from north to south and around 120 miles (193 km) across, Lake Michigan is the world's largest lake (by surface area) completely within one country and the ideal focus of a road trip starting in **Chicago.**

The Windy City's legendary boulevards—**Lake Shore Drive** and **Michigan Avenue**—enjoy an intimate relationship with the lake. And when residents want a breath of fresh air, they often find it on the beaches, bike paths, and boat basins

of Lake Michigan. Chicago's trio of great green spaces—**Grant Park, Lincoln Park**, and **Jackson Park**—perch along the shore. And from the **Field Museum** of natural history and **Adler Planetarium** to **Navy Pier**, many of its top attractions enjoy a lakefront location.

Starting out from Chicago, road trippers can circle the lake in either direction. This route runs clockwise, starting with a northward drive from the Windy City that can be accomplished quickly on Interstate 95 or

lazily along **Sheridan Drive**, an extension of Lake Shore Drive that reaches all the way from the north side of Chicago to Racine, Wisconsin.

Among the possible stops along the way are the **Block Museum of Art** on the campus of Northwestern University in Evanston, the **Frank Lloyd Wright** homes around Highland Park, **Illinois Beach State Park**, and **Kenosha's** artsy harbor area. From Racine, it's just a 25-mile (40.2 km) jaunt on **32nd Division Memorial Highway** (Route 32) to the second largest city on Lake Michigan.

Settled in the 19th century by a large number of German immigrants, **Milwaukee** retains something of a European air through local culinary treats like beer and pretzels, and architectural landmarks like **Turner Hall**, the **Pabst Mansion** and **Pabst Theatre** (built by the man who created Blue Ribbon beer), and the domed **Basilica of St. Josaphat**.

Milwaukee has long cherished its strategic location at the place where three rivers flow into Lake Michigan—which may be why its name supposedly means "Gathering Place of Waters" in the Potawatomi language. **Milwaukee RiverWalk** mean-

The Harley-Davidson Museum in Milwaukee showcases the history of motorcycles.

Beach, bluffs, forest, and spectacular views of Lake Michigan await at Sleeping Bear Dunes National Lakeshore Michigan.

ders three miles (4.8 km) along the waterways through restaurant- and brewpub-filled neighborhoods like the **Historic Third Ward** and **Beerline B**. Among other riverside attractions are the heavy metal **Harley-Davidson Museum** and the futuristic domes of **Mitchell Park Horticultural Conservatory**.

Beyond Milwaukee, Interstate 43 runs right along the lakeshore to **Kohler-Andrae State Park** near Sheboygan and **Green Bay**, where the **Green Bay Packers Hall of Fame** at legendary Lambeau Field pays homage to one of the nation's oldest and most successful NFL franchises.

Green Bay is also the gateway to the **Door Peninsula**, one of the most beautiful spots in the Midwest. Renowned for its cherry and apple orchards, adorable villages, forest walks, and sunset views across the bay, the peninsula emerged as a holiday destination more than a century ago. In addition to a number of lakeshore parks, including historic **Peninsula State Park**, the Door is

blessed with a 48-mile (77.2 km) hiking, biking, and winter sports route, the **Ahnapee State Trail**, along a former railroad right-of-way.

North of Green Bay, the lakeshore gets progressively wilder and more remote, a route best covered on U.S. Highway 41 to Marinette, where **Seguin's House of Cheese** provides a last chance to savor the state's dairy delights. Reaching **Rapid River** in Michigan's Upper Peninsula, the road trip makes a sharp turn to the east for a drive along U.S. Highway 2 through **Hiawatha National Forest** and its multiple opportunities for lakeside camping, fishing, and hiking.

The park's **Stonington Peninsula** is renowned for its migratory birds and fall monarch butterfly migration as well as little **Peninsula Point Lighthouse** (opened in 1865). The peninsula's **Maywood History Trail** takes hikers through a 200-year-old hemlock forest. On the other side of Big Bay De Noc, **Fayette Historic State Park** preserves a 19th-century

iron-ore smelting town through restored buildings and living history programs.

### SCENIC DETOURS

• **Interstate 41:** This alternative to the lakeshore route runs inland from Milwaukee to Lake Winnebago, Oshkosh, and onward to Green Bay.

• **U.S. Highway 2** runs west from Escanaba to Apostle Islands National Lakeshore and the Superior/Duluth metropolitan area on Lake Superior.

• **U.S. Highway 41:** From Rapid River, U.S. 41 cuts across Michigan's Upper Peninsula to Pictured Rocks National Lakeshore and Porcupine Mountains Wilderness State Park on Lake Superior.

• **U.S. Highway 23** hugs the western shore of Lake Huron between Mackinaw City and Detroit.

• **Interstate 75** links St. Ignace and the twin cities of Sault Ste. Marie (United States and Canada) on the Trans-Canada Highway.

As it hugs the lake's northern edge, Highway 2 offers several other intriguing stops like the **Top of the Lake Snowmobile Museum** in Naubinway, which features bizarre machines including the 1936 Westendorf and 1971 Phantom that look like something from a cheesy sci-fi movie. Then there's **GarLyn Zoo Wildlife Park**, where visitors can get up close to bears, badgers, bison, wolves, and other indigenous wildlife. And there has to be stop at **Mystery Spot**, a family-friendly theme park that includes a zip line, maze, and miniature golf.

The highway eventually glides into **St. Ignace** beside the fabled **Straits of Mackinac**, which separates Lake Michigan and Lake Huron, as well as Michigan's Upper and Lower Peninsulas. The road trip leaps the main strait on the **Mackinac Bridge**, one of the world's longest suspension spans at 26,372 feet (8,038.2 m).

On the far side is **Mackinaw City**, founded in 1715 when the French built **Fort Michilimackinac** to safeguard their claim to the Great Lakes region. Today the rebuilt bastion is a state park where historical reenactors make the past come alive through musket firing, hearth cooking, and other demonstrations. Nearby **Headlands International Dark Sky Park** offers stargazing and northern lights programs, while the *Icebreaker Mackinaw* floating museum provides a glimpse of Great Lakes maritime history.

Ferries from both St. Ignace and Mackinaw City ply the strait to **Mackinac Island**, where much of the region's history played out as British, French, and American troops fought

Find colorful meadows and Dutch windmills on Windmill Island in Holland, Michigan.

for control of the region during three different wars. The well-preserved **Victorian-era village** boasts numerous historical buildings, while the state park that covers around 80 percent of the island preserves **Fort Mackinac** (built in 1782) and other historic gems. Given that motor vehicles are banned, the island can only be explored by foot, bike, or horse.

South of the Straits, U.S. Highway 31 cuts across the Lower Peninsula to **Petoskey**, where author Ernest Hemingway spent many of his childhood summers, and onward to **Traverse City**, holiday hub of the lake's eastern shore.

Traverse revolves around **Front Street** and the **Boardman River Boardwalk**, where many of the city's restaurants, bars, and shops are located. From flyboarding and fishing charters to day sails on the tall ship *Manitou*, Traverse City also offers a wide variety of water activities. Just west of town lies **Sleeping Bear Dunes National Lakeshore**, a 35-mile (56.3 km) stretch with a medley of beaches, bays, islands, lakes, towering bluffs, coastal vil-

lages, and some of the best wreck diving in the Great Lakes.

Highway 31 runs another 180 miles (289.7 km) down the Michigan lakeshore to **Holland**. Founded by Dutch settlers in 1847, the town channels its heritage through the **Nelis's Dutch Village** historical theme park, **Veldheer Tulip Gardens**, and **Windmill Island**. From Holland, drivers can take the interstate all the way down to the Indiana border via a series of waterfront resort towns like **Saugatuck, South Haven, St. Joseph**, and **New Buffalo**.

Looming just across the border are the **Indiana Dunes**, 20 miles (32.2 km) of lakeshore on ether side of the Port of Indiana steel mills protected within the confines of a large state park and the nation's newest national park, declared in 2019. Besides some fine beaches, the parks boast hiking trails through a variety of habitats (dunes, wetlands, forest, prairie) and the 9.5-mile (15.3 km) **Calumet Bike Trail**. From the dunes, it's less than an hour back to downtown Chicago and the close of your loop around Lake Michigan. ∎

## EN ROUTE EATS

- **Shore Club Chicago:** Brunch, dinner, or cocktails on North Avenue Beach, with a choice of indoor or open-air seating right on the sand. 1603 N. Lake Shore Dr., Chicago, IL shoreclubchi.com

- **Harbor House:** Cioppino, seviche, calamari, and scallops flavor this elegant waterfront eatery in Milwaukee's Museum Center Park. 550 North Harbor Dr., Milwaukee, WI bartolottas.com/harbor-house

- **Fred and Fuzzy's:** Fresh seafood dishes and live music complement this sunset-sensational bar and grill on the Door Peninsula. 10620 Little Sister Rd., Sister Bay, WI. fredand fuzzys.com

- **Apache Trout Grill:** Lake Superior whitefish and walleye, and barbecued ribs count among the favorites of this Michigan lakeside eatery. 13671 Southwest Bay Shore Dr., Traverse City, MI. apachetroutgrill.com

- **Notos at the Bilmar:** Great Lakes meets Sicily in dishes like walleye nocciole and Michigan perch with an olive remoulade at this new Italian restaurant right on the beach in Grand Haven. 1223 South Harbor Dr., Grand Haven, MI. notosoldworld .com

# Land of Lincoln

## Kentucky, Indiana & Illinois

Tracing the life of Abraham Lincoln from cradle to grave, this rustic route through the American Midwest reflects the places that infused the 16th president with everything he stood for and the forces that helped shaped an entire nation.

Abraham Lincoln spent his formative years on the edge of the wild and rugged American frontier, a place where log cabin living was the norm rather than the exception. The date was February 12, 1809; the place was Sinking Spring Farm near **Hodgenville**, Kentucky. The home where he was born is long gone, but the **Abraham Lincoln Birthplace National Historical Park** marks the spot with a visitor center museum that contains relics like the original Lincoln family Bible and a symbolic birth cabin built 30 years after his death.

A dispute over property ownership forced the Lincolns to move two years after his birth to a log cabin beside **Knob Hill Creek** on the other side of Hodgenville. Young Abe spent the next five years (1811-16) there. That home was also demolished—the timber used to build a stable—but the nearby **Gollaher Cabin** dates from the same era and is lovingly preserved by the Park Service.

From nearby Elizabethtown, a combination of the Western Kentucky Parkway and the William Natchez Parkway leads to **Owensboro** and a leap across the Ohio River to **Lincoln State Park** and the adjacent **Lincoln Boyhood National Memorial** in southern Indiana.

The twin parks revolve around **Little Pigeon Creek**, a tiny pioneer settlement where Abe lived between the ages of seven and 21 (1816-30). "The very spot where grew the bread that formed my bones," Lincoln later wrote about Pigeon Creek.

The **National Memorial Visitor Center** offers exhibits and artifacts and five sculptured panels depicting significant moments from Lincoln's life. Scattered around the ground are a bronze outline of the Lincoln cabin, a replica 1820s homestead, a **Living Historical Farm** with crops that would have been grown in Abe's era, and the grave of his mother, Nancy Hanks Lincoln, who passed away in 1818.

Just across the road, the state park features a replica of the **Little Pigeon Baptist Church** that Abe and his father helped construct, the **Abraham Lincoln Bicentennial Plaza** with its

Visit Lincoln's childhood home in Lincoln Boyhood National Memorial.

The president and his wife, and three of their four sons, are laid to rest at the Lincoln Tomb State Historic Site in Springfield, Illinois.

tales of the future president's Indiana years, and the modern **Lincoln Amphitheater**, which stages a Lincoln drama each summer as well as concerts and movies.

In 1830, 21-year-old Lincoln split from his family and struck out for central Illinois on his own. And the Lincoln road trip does the same with a four-hour drive via several state and federal highways to **Springfield**, a city indelibly linked to the 16th American president.

The outstanding **Abraham Lincoln Presidential Library and Museum** in downtown Springfield traces the man's life through actual size dioramas and priceless artifacts like his handwritten draft of the Gettysburg Address and an autographed copy of the Emancipation Proclamation. Within walking distance are the **Lincoln-Herndon Law Offices** and

the **Lincoln Home National Historic Site**, his primary residence from 1844 until moving into the White House in 1861.

Elsewhere in Springfield, visit the **Lincoln Memorial Garden and Nature Center**, which nurtures native plants from the three home states, and the **Lincoln Tomb** in Oak Ridge Cemetery. Twenty miles (32.2 km) north of town, **Lincoln's New Salem State Park** re-creates the frontier settlement where Abe lived during his first six years in Illinois. ∎

## LAY YOUR HEAD

• **Country Girl at Heart Farm:** Cozy B&B on a working sustainable family farm where guests can pitch in; 24 miles (38.6 km) from Lincoln birthplace; from $119. bedandbreakfast kentucky.net

• **Falls of Rough Resort:** Live like Lincoln in a modern log cabin or in high style in a Green Farm Mansion suite at this rural getaway on the Rough River between Elizabethtown and Owensboro; from $129. fallsofroughresort.com

• **Harvest Moon:** A Queen Anne–style mansion morphed into a quaint B&B in Ferdinand, Indiana; 13 miles (20.9 km) from Lincoln State Park and Boyhood Memorial; from $85. harvestmoonbedandbreakfast.com

• **President Abraham Lincoln Hotel:** Downtown hotel in Springfield within walking distance of the Honest Abe attractions throughout the city; restaurant, bar, fitness center, indoor pool; from $129. doubletree3.hilton.com

# Great River Road
## Minnesota to Tennessee

Old Man River has always been a force to reckon with, and so is the Great River Road, a route along the Mississippi River from its source in the north woods of Minnesota through America's heartland and down into the South.

From Native American traders and French voyageurs to dapper riverboat gamblers, people have long used the Mississippi for transportation. But it wasn't until 1938 that the Great River Road came about—a 2,340-mile (3,765.9 km) network of national and state highways that motorists could follow along the Big Muddy.

Marked by green-and-white signs emblazoned with a paddle steamer and ship wheel, the highway passes through iconic countryside, great urban areas, and a surprising amount of parkland given the historic hustle and bustle along the Mississippi. This particular route covers the north and central sections of the Great River Road between Lake Itasca and Memphis. (Find the southern section—the Delta Blues Highway—on page 208.)

The Mississippi and the Great River Road start their long journey to the sea at **Lake Itasca**, about 200 miles (321.9 km) northwest of Minneapolis, Minnesota. Itasca is a mash-up of *veritas* and *caput*—the Latin term for "true head," in this case, the indisputable start of the river. Visitors can literally walk across the infant Mississippi on a string of stepping-stones as it pours forth from the lake.

Following the river, it's about 300 miles (482.8 km) from Itasca to Minnesota's Twin Cities. Stretching 72 miles (115.9 km) through the metropolitan area between **Dayton** and **Hastings**, the **Mississippi National River and Recreation Area** provides plenty of scope for hiking, biking, fishing, boating, bird-watching, and geocaching.

**Minneapolis** has a number of river-centric attractions, from **St. Anthony Falls** (the highest cascade along the entire length of the Mississippi) to the **Mill District** and **Northeast River neighborhood** with their food and entertainment. Farther downriver are historic **Fort Snelling** (where Dred Scott and his wife were once enslaved) and the **St. Paul waterfront**, where the **Science Museum of Minnesota** features the extensive Mississippi River Gallery.

South of Hastings, the Great River Road splits into two branches, one along the Minnesota bank, the other

**THE BIG PICTURE**

**Distance:** ca 1,400 miles (2,253.1 km) from Lake Itasca, MN, to Memphis, TN

**Drive time:** 7-10 days

**Best overnights:** Twin Cities, Dubuque/Galena, Quad Cities, Hannibal, St. Louis

**Best seasons:** Late spring, summer, or early fall

**Highlights:** Lake Itasca, Twin Cities, Galena, Hannibal, St. Louis, Memphis

Visit the headwaters of the Mississippi: Lake Itasca, a short drive from Minneapolis.

The *American Eagle,* the largest steamboat ever built, offers Mark Twain history river cruises.

across the water in Wisconsin. Two of the best stops along this stretch of the route are the **National Eagle Center** in Wabasha and the small but excellent **Minnesota Marine Art Museum** in Winona.

Looming beside the river in Iowa is **Effigy Mounds National Monument**, a cluster of more than 200 animal-shaped earthen mounds created by Native American groups in prehistoric times. During the summer, ranger-led interpretive programs explain how and why the mounds were built.

From bald eagles and alligators to snapping turtles, otters, and sturgeon, the **National Mississippi River Museum and Aquarium** in Dubuque showcases wildlife denizens of the Big Muddy, as well as its human heritage. Allegedly the world's steepest and shortest railroad line, **Fenelon Place Elevator** is a

19th-century funicular that climbs a hill overlooking the city and river.

On the Illinois side is bygone boomtown **Galena** and a historic district that includes more than 800 structures, such as the **DeSoto House Hotel** (opened 1855) and the **Ulysses S. Grant Home**.

State Highway 84 takes the trip along the Illinois riverside to Rock Island, where the **Mississippi River Visitor Center** features guided tours and videos of its namesake waterway. Right across the river, Davenport offers a second glimpse of Iowa—sights like the **Figge Art Museum** (housed in a glimmering glass structure), plays and concerts at the restored 1926 **Adler Theatre**, and the **German-American Heritage Center and Museum**—before continuing along the Illinois shore.

Two hours south of Rock Island, **Nauvoo** is a historic home of the

## OFF ROAD

- **American Cruise Lines** offers steamboat trips along the river's entire length including an eight-day Upper Mississippi River itinerary between St. Louis and St. Paul. americancruiselines.com

- **Great River Houseboats** in Alma, Wisconsin, rents modern houseboats that sleep two to 10 people for cruising Pool #4 on the Mississippi between Wisconsin and Minnesota. almamarina.net

- **CW Outfitting** in Clearwater, Minnesota, facilitates "wild and scenic" canoe, kayak, and paddleboard journeys on the Mississippi ranging from a few hours to multiple days. cwoutfitting.com

- **Big Muddy Adventures** in St. Louis offers guided canoe and kayak trips, full moon floats, and multiday kayaking and camping along the river between Missouri and Illinois. 2muddy.com

Church of the Latter-Day Saints and home to a number of its landmarks, including the rebuilt **Nauvoo Temple**, **Joseph Smith Historic Site**, and **Brigham Young Home**.

Flowing into Missouri, the river enters its most storied segments—the stretch around **Hannibal** that inspired the adventures of Tom Sawyer, Huck Finn, and other works by native son Samuel Clemens (aka Mark Twain). Hannibal has transformed the author's heritage into a cottage industry that includes the **Mark Twain Boyhood Home, Mark Twain Caverns, Tom Sawyer's Fence**, and **Becky Thatcher's House**, as well as an African-American museum, **Jim's Journey: The Huck Finn Freedom Center**. There are also **riverboat cruises**, evening **ghost tours**, and plenty of restaurants, bars, and souvenir shops along historic **Main Street**.

Drivers can continue south on either side of the river, flitting back and forth on intermittent bridges or the vehicular **Golden Eagle Ferry** (eight dollars per car) between Winneberger, Illinois, and Kampville, Missouri.

Just around the next big bend is the iconic confluence of the Mississippi and Missouri Rivers. **Columbia Bottom Conservation Area** on the southwest side in Missouri offers hiking and biking trails, viewing plat-

Take in iconic St. Louis sights, including the Old Courthouse and Gateway Arch.

forms, picnic areas, and boat launch ramps beside the confluence.

**St. Louis** looms next, with the **Gateway Arch** towering 630 feet (192 m) above the waterfront as the anchor of a national park that includes the **Old Courthouse** (where Dred and Harriet Scott unsuccessfully petitioned for their freedom); a must-see movie, *Monument to the Dream*; the revamped **Museum of Western Expansion**; **riverfront sightseeing cruises**; and a leafy **riverside promenade**.

**Laclede's Landing** along the St. Louis waterfront is a 19th-century warehouse district converted into a modern eating and entertainment area with a brewpub, wax museum, casino, and carriage rides. Stretch your legs with a stroll across steel-arch **Eads Bridge**, opened in 1874, or the **St. Louis Riverfront Trail**, a 12-mile (19.3 km) path between the Gateway Arch and **Old Chain of Rocks Bridge**.

The **Cahokia Mounds** near East St. Louis are the remnants of the largest known Native American city. Between A.D. 1000 and 1200, the Cahokia boasted as many as 40,000 people—that's a larger population than medieval London. The site safeguards more than 120 mounds,

The "I Am a Man" exhibit is a highlight at Memphis's National Civil Rights Museum.

the largest archaeological park north of Mexico City.

The Great River Road continues south via Illinois Route 3 with stops along the way at **Fort de Chartres** and **Fort Kaskaskia** (18th-century French bastions) and wilderness hiking in the **Trail of Tears State Forest**. Route 3 comes to an abrupt end in **Cairo**, where the Ohio River flows into the Big Muddy beside Civil War–era **Fort Defiance State Park**.

The **Cairo Ohio River Bridge** carries the Great River Road into

Kentucky and **Columbus Belmont State Park**. Dubbed the "Gibraltar of the West" during the Civil War, the riverside defenses featured siege guns and a giant iron chain across the Mississippi that prevented Union forces from steaming downriver—until Grant captured the heights in 1861.

Drivers can cross back into Missouri on the **Dorena-Hickman Ferry** ($14 per car) and continue into Arkansas. Or take U.S. Highway 51 through western Tennessee, where **Meeman-Shelby Forest State Park** harbors more than 12,000 acres (more than 4,856.2 ha) of hardwood bottomland beside the Mississippi, including cypress and tupelo swamp.

Home of the blues, birthplace of rock-and-roll, and holy grail of barbecued pork, **Memphis** is just a half hour away. Musical landmarks like **Graceland**, **Sun Studio**, **Beale Street**, and the **Rock 'n' Soul Museum** dominate the Memphis landscape, Bluff City also offers the **National Civil Rights Museum** in the Lorraine Motel where Martin Luther King, Jr., was assassinated in 1968. ∎

---

### LAY YOUR HEAD

- **Nicollet Island Inn:** A 19th-century door factory transformed into a romantic Mississippi island boutique hotel in Minneapolis; restaurant, piano bar, spa services; from $179. nicolletislandinn.com

- **Goldmoor Inn:** This castle-like lodge in Galena, Illinois, features suites, cottages, and cabins; restaurant, spa treatments, Mississippi River views; from $305. goldmoor.com

- **Rockcliffe Mansion:** This Hannibal, Missouri, historic B&B is a Georgian Revival beauty set on a limestone outcrop overlooking Mark Twain's hometown; from $159. rockcliffemansion.com

- **Hyatt Regency St. Louis:** You can almost reach out and touch the Gateway Arch from riverside rooms in this modern luxury hotel; restaurant, bar, fitness center, pet friendly; from $109. hyatt.com

# Ohio River Route

## PA, WV, OH, KY, IN & IL

One of the nation's most fabled rivers is the focus of this road trip between the Alleghenies and the Mississippi, a journey through six states, some of the great cities of the Midwest, and several centuries of American history.

**THE BIG PICTURE**

**Distance:** ca 850 miles (1,368 km) from Pittsburgh, PA, to Cairo, IL

**Drive time:** 5-7 days

**Best overnights:** St. Clairsville/ Wheeling, Huntington, Cincinnati, Louisville, Evansville, Paducah

**Best seasons:** Spring, summer, or fall

**Highlights:** Point State Park, Fort Steuben, Cincinnati, Louisville, Lincoln Boyhood Home, Angel Mounds, Audubon State Park, Cairo's confluence

The Ohio River Valley has been a vital waterway since prehistoric times: the cradle of advanced Native American civilizations, fought over by the French and British, and a major pathway for American exploration and settlement of the West.

The significance of this 980-mile-long (1,577.2 km) waterway can be gauged by the fact that Ohio means "great river" in the language of the Seneca people, who once lived along its banks.

Downtown **Pittsburgh, Pennsylvania,** is the starting point for the journey, at **Point State Park** and the remains of **Fort Duquesne**, where the Allegheny and Monongahela Rivers rendezvous into the mighty Ohio.

The bowstring **Fort Pitt Bridge** leaps the river to Pennsylvania Route 51, which meanders downriver to **Beaver** with its extensive historic district and a big bend that carries the river across the state line and the start of the **Ohio River National Scenic Byway**.

This first stretch of the byway (Route 7) includes several stops in Ohio to gather an informative introduction to the river trip like the **Steubenville Visitor Center** and reconstructed 18th-century **Fort Steuben**, and the **Ohio River Museum** in Marietta.

Across from **Huntington**, **West Virginia**, the byway segues into U.S. Highway 52 for a 160-mile (257.5 km) run down to Cincinnati that affords opportunities to hike the wilderness trails of **Wayne National Forest, Shawnee State Forest**, or the **Edge of Appalachia Nature Preserve** on the Ohio side.

Nicknamed the "Queen City" in riverboat days, **Cincinnati** offers plenty of waterfront attractions, from **Reds** (baseball) and **Bengals** (football) games at two riverside stadiums to the **Newport Aquarium**, the **National Underground Railroad Freedom Center**, and the **Purple People Bridge**.

Downstream from the Queen

It's hard to miss the Louisville Slugger Museum and Factory on your drive.

Baseball fans should make a stop at the Great American Ball Park stadium, home to the Cincinnati Reds.

City it's no more than 100 miles (160.9 km) along Interstate 71 to **Louisville, Kentucky**, where you can swing a bat at the **Louisville Slugger Factory**, learn more about "The Greatest" at the **Muhammad Ali Center**, and take a tour of **Churchill Downs** before moving on.

Crossing the river into Indiana, Interstate 64 carries the road trip to Carefree and a junction with State Road 66, which snakes along the river around 100 miles (160.9 km) to **Evansville**. A lot of this stretch is through **Hoosier National Forest** and another wild part of the Ohio Valley. And just north of Rockport is **Abraham Lincoln's Boyhood Home**.

On the eastern outskirts of Evansville, **Angel Mounds State Historic Site** preserves the remains of a fortified Native American town and religious center occupied between A.D. 1000 and 1450. In the archaeological park are 12 earthen mounds surrounding two central plazas, including a huge **Central Mound** where the paramount chief may have lived.

On the Kentucky side, **John James Audubon State Park** in Henderson offers a museum, nature center, and forest trails dedicated to the famed painter and ornithologist who lived nearby in the early 1800s.

From Henderson, U.S. Highway 60 offers a quick run along the river's south side to **Paducah**, where the **National Quilt Museum** and **Floodwall Murals** offer an artistic contrast to the city's popular **distilleries**.

Continue down Highway 60 to **Wickliffe, Ohio**, and the confluence of the Ohio and Mississippi Rivers. A long cantilever bridge jumps to the Illinois side, where **Cairo's Historic District** and the site of Civil War–era **Fort Defiance** round out the Ohio River drive. ■

---

### ART AVENUES

- **Best Music:** "Banks of the Ohio" by Joan Baez; the *Bonnie "Prince" Billy Sings Greatest Palace Music* album by Louisville-born Will Oldham; and the Cincinnati jazz of Bix Beiderbecke and the Wolverines

- **Best Art:** The wildlife paintings of John James Audubon, who honed his craft as a young man living along the Ohio River in northern Kentucky

- **Best Books:** *Uncle Tom's Cabin* by Cincinnati's Harriet Beecher Stowe; The Hollows series of fantasy mysteries by Kim Harrison; *Snapper* by Evansville's Brian Kimberling

- **Best Movies:** *Flashdance* (1983); *Striking Distance* (1993); *Secretariat* (2010)

# Northwoods Wander

## Minnesota, Wisconsin & Michigan

Woods, water, and wildlife make up this adventurous 800-mile (1,287.5 km) drive through the boreal forest of the Boundary Waters region and scenic south shore of Lake Superior—a road trip that can be undertaken in every season and just about any weather.

Isolated by water and severe winter weather, the Northwoods of Minnesota, Wisconsin, and Michigan harbor vast tracts of wilderness preserved within a great variety of national and state parks.

Named for the 18th-century French trappers who blazed the watery trails through this region, **Voyageurs National Park** in northern Minnesota kicks off this road trip with a warren of lakes, rivers, and islands best explored by kayak, canoe, and motorboat—or ski and snowmobile if it happens to be winter.

**Rainy Lake Visitor Center** provides all the information you need for exploring the park, as well as a free public boat launch in summer and access for vehicles to drive the **Rainy Lake Ice Road** in winter. Visitors can also join ranger-led canoe trips, rent a houseboat, or take a scenic cruise on the *Voyageur.*

Farther east along the watery U.S.-Canada frontier, the park's **Kabetogoma Lake** and **Ash River** areas offer more aquatic adventures, as well as some pretty good hikes—like the 28-mile (45.1 km), multiday **Kab-Ash Trail** through the heart of the Voyageurs wilderness.

U.S. Highway 53 runs due south from Kabetogoma, with a turnoff at Angora onto Minnesota Highway 1 and the amazing **Boundary Waters Canoe Area**. Fifteen major hiking trails and 1,200 miles (1,931.2 km) of canoe route afford access to the vast wilderness.

Even if you're not into hard-core paddling, historic **Ely** provides a glimpse of local wildlife at the **International Wolf Center** and **North American Bear Center**. If you've got time, pop into the **Dorothy Molter Museum** and learn about a tough-as-nails woman who lived for 56 years alone in the Boundary Waters.

Backtracking to Highway 53, you can undertake a side trip to Hibbing and its **historic iron mines**, as well as **Bob Dylan's Boyhood Home** and **Hibbing High School**, where he played in several bands before becoming an American music legend. Gape into the colossal trench created by the

A black bear stops for a bite in Ely, Minnesota.

More than 40 percent water, Voyageurs National Park is a unique maze of interconnected water highways.

**Hull-Rust-Mahoning Open Pit Iron Mine**, the world's largest operating iron ore quarry, and visit the town's **Greyhound Bus Museum** (the transport company was founded in Hibbing in 1914).

Just down the road is the waterfront city of **Duluth**, arrayed along the western end of Lake Superior. From the **Lake Superior Maritime Visitor Center** and **Great Lakes Aquarium** to the **Aerial Lift Bridge** and revitalized **Canal Park neighborhood**, most of the city's major attractions perch along the lake. During the warmer months, the **North Shore Scenic Railroad** offers narrated journeys through downtown Duluth, along the lakeshore, and into the Northwoods before returning to **Historic Union Station**.

Leaping across the St. Louis River, our road trip rolls into **Superior**, the biggest city in northern Wisconsin. Visit **Fairlawn Mansion** (built in

1890); the floating **S.S. *Meteor* Whaleback Ship Museum**; and a collection dedicated to World War II fighter ace and local hero **Richard I. Bong**, who holds the record for the most enemy planes shot down (40) by an American pilot in any war.

Wisconsin Highway 13 carries the route to the pristine **Apostle Islands National Lakeshore**. Renowned for their blend of temperate and boreal forest, half-sunken caves, and historic lighthouses, the 22 islands offer a glimpse of the Northwoods before humans arrived.

**Bayfield** is the hub for scenic cruises, water taxis, sailing charters, and guided kayak trips into the national lakeshore, as well as the vehicle ferry to bucolic **Madeline Island**—the only one of the Apostles you can drive around.

From the easternmost Apostle islands, you can see the **Porcupine Mountains**, the focus of Michigan's

largest state park. Driving there entails a two-hour journey along the lakeshore, much of it on U.S. Highway 2.

The state park protects 60,000 acres (24,281.1 ha) of old-growth maple, hemlock, and birch forest that provides a home for black bears, wolves, moose, and lynx. Spreading out from the **Porcupine Mountain Wilderness Visitor Center** at Union Bay, trails lead along the lakeshore and remote waterfalls. The nearby **Porkies Ski Area** boasts everything from bunny runs to black diamond pistes.

From the Porcupines, you can take a side trip to **Houghton** on the **Keweenaw Peninsula** that juts out into Lake Superior. There, you can catch a passenger-only ferry or floatplane across the lake to remote **Isle Royale National Park**.

Called *Minong* ("Good Place") by the Ojibwa people who once lived there, Isle Royale is made up of rocky shoreline and old-growth woods and is home to wolves and moose. There's plenty to do, hiking, kayaking, fishing, and wreck diving among the possibilities. The ferry here takes six hours—and operates only between April and October—so plan on staying over-

For epic views, climb to the top of Grand Portal Point in Pictured Rocks National Lakeshore.

night if that's your mode of transport.

Move on to State Highway 28, a long meander across Michigan's Upper Peninsula to **Pictured Rocks National Lakeshore**.

Stretching 40 miles (64.4 km) along the south coast of Lake Superior, the national lakeshore is celebrated for its chromatic sandstone cliffs (the "pictured rocks" of the name), 300-foot-high (91.4 m) dunes, and wild beaches. The **Interagency Visitor Center** in Munising and the nearby **Munising Falls Interpretive Center** offer a great introduction before exploring.

The namesake Pictured Rocks beyond **Miners Castle** and the

towering **Grand Sable Dunes** may draw the most attention, but some of the park's coolest features are found on trails less traveled: historic **Au Sable Lighthouse** (opened in 1874), the wildlife-rich **Beaver Basin Wilderness**, and the middle stretch of **Twelvemile Beach**.

It's another two hours on Highway 28 to **Sault Ste. Marie** and its Canadian twin city on the St. Marys River. The city's main attraction is **Soo Locks** (the world's busiest shipping canal). The **Tower of History** renders a bird's-eye view of the waterway, while the **Museum Ship** *Valley Camp* provides a great orientation to the maritime heritage of the Great Lakes. ∎

# Northern Plains Heritage Route

## North Dakota, Montana & South Dakota

Wide-open spaces, larger-than-life figures, and momentous events in American history highlight this ramble across the northern Great Plains, a journey from Bismarck to Billings and the fabled Black Hills.

From Mount Rushmore and Little Bighorn to close encounters at Devils Tower, there's an amazing array of American icons along this frontier road trip.

Founded as a railroad way station in the 1870s—and named after Otto von Bismarck in the hope that German immigrants would flock to the prairie—**Bismarck, North Dakota**, straddles the Missouri River at a point where Lewis and Clark once crossed.

Those early days are recalled at the city's **Camp Hancock State Historic Site**, which revolves around a 1909 Northern Pacific locomotive, North Dakota's oldest church, and a clapboard building used as officers'

**THE BIG PICTURE**

**Distance:** ca 940 miles (1,512.8 km) from Bismarck, ND, to Rapid City, SD

**Drive time:** 7-10 days

**Best overnights:** Medora, Billings, Sheridan, Deadwood, Sturgis, Rapid City

**Best seasons:** Spring, summer, or fall

**Highlights:** Theodore Roosevelt NP, Yellowstone Art Museum, Little Bighorn Battlefield, Devils Tower, Black Hills, Wind Cave, Mount Rushmore, Deadwood

quarters for the U.S. Army garrison protecting the railroad workers.

Love it or hate it, the **North Dakota State Capitol** remains Bismarck's most distinctive structure. A 19-story skyscraper rather than a traditional domed state house, it was erected in the 1930s after the original capitol burned down. Some call it a cement monstrosity, others an art deco masterpiece. The neighboring **North Dakota Heritage Center and State Museum** spotlights the state's history from prehistoric through modern times.

Across the river in Mandan, **Fort Abraham Lincoln State Park** illuminates local history via a reconstructed Mandan Indian village and the U.S. Army post where Custer and the Seventh Cavalry were based when they set off for the Little Bighorn. Guides in period costume give tours of the Victorian home where Custer lived with his family and beloved dogs.

Interstate 94 runs due west across the plains to **Theodore Roosevelt National Park** on the Little Missouri River. The park preserves the area where the future 26th president hunted buffalo and briefly ranched while recovering from the heartbreak of the back-to-back deaths of his mother and first wife in 1884.

You may spot grazing buffalo on your way though the Badlands.

Theodore Roosevelt National Park protects 70,447 acres (28,509 ha) and a dense population of bison, elk, and wild horses.

Among the park's T.R. relics are the **Maltese Cross Cabin** behind the **Medora Visitor Center** and the ruins of his **Elkhorn Ranch** house. The 36-mile (58 km) **Scenic Loop Drive** meanders through grasslands, verdant valleys, and badlands populated by prairie dogs, bison, and wild horses. Gateway to the national park, the town of **Medora** offers pioneer-era buildings and the summertime *Medora Musical* at the Burning Hills Amphitheater.

Crossing the state line into Montana, I-94 follows the Yellowstone River upstream to **Billings**. Named for a president of the Northern Pacific, the "Magic City" was also founded as a railroad town.

Home to numerous theater companies and the **Billings Symphony Orchestra**, the city has emerged as Montana's cultural capital. Chief among its cornerstones is the **Yellowstone Art Museum**, which specializes in the cutting-edge contemporary art of the Northern Plains and Rockies. The people of the Northern Plains—both Native Americans and European settlers—are the focus of the Smithsonian-affiliated **Western Heritage Center**.

Making an abrupt about-face, the drive swings around to the southeast, a cruise along I-90 that takes road trippers into the lands of the Crow Nation and **Little Bighorn Battlefield National Monument**.

The battle took place in June

## EN ROUTE EATS

• **Theodore's Dining Room:** Braised bison with horseradish creme fraiche, Thai pasta in coconut curry sauce, and pork osso bucco at the Rough Riders Hotel; Teddy never had it so good. 301 Third Ave., Medora, ND. medora.com

• **Vertex Sky Bar:** Artisan cheese trays, drunken clams, quinoa bowls, beef tenderloin, and craft cocktails on the roof of the Hotel Alex Johnson. 523 Sixth St., Rapid City, SD. vertexskybar.com

• **Peacock Alley:** North Dakota's oldest restaurant serves breakfast, lunch, and dinner—and an amazing array of two-for-one martinis on Tini Tuesday. 422 East Main Ave., Bismarck, ND. peacock-alley.com

• **Custer Battlefield Trading Post Cafe:** This Crow Nation eatery near Little Bighorn Battlefield National Monument offers buffalo and Angus beef steaks and burgers, as well as Native American treats like fry bread and Indian tacos. U.S. Highway 212, Crow Agency, MT. laststand.com

• **Ten:** Posh meets prairie at this upscale eatery in Montana's Northern Hotel; meat, fish, and pasta served with a wide selection of wines. 19 N. Broadway, Billings, MT. nhten.com

1876 as Custer and his Seventh Cavalry clashed with Sitting Bull, Crazy Horse, and their Lakota and Cheyenne warriors. Roads and trails lead to places where action took place, including **Last Stand Hill**. Get there when the park first opens to experience the battlefield in total silence. **Custer Battlefield Trading Post** on the Crow Reservation offers books and posters, as well as Native American art and accessories.

An hour south along I-90, Sheridan is named for the Civil War general who later fought in the Indian Wars and lobbied to get Yellowstone declared the first national park. The city offers several historical gems, including **Trail End mansion** (built between 1908 and 1913), the **Don King Museum** of saddles and other cowboy paraphernalia, and the reconstructed **Fort Phil Kearney**.

Continuing east on I-90 through Wyoming's wide-open spaces, slide off the freeway at Moorcroft and take U.S. Highway 14 toward that dark monolith looming on the horizon. Rising nearly 1,300 feet (396.2 m) above the prairie and forest, **Devils Tower National Monument** is one of the nation's unique landmarks.

Exhibits at the **Devils Tower Visitor Center**, constructed with Ponderosa pine logs in the 1930s, show how the huge volcanic plug was formed between 50 and 60 million years ago by the same geological forces that uplifted the Rocky Mountains and Black Hills.

Called *Mato Tipila* (Bear's Lodge in the Lakota language), **Devils Tower** has long been sacred to the region's Native American inhabitants. Teddy Roosevelt declared it the

Mount Rushmore features Presidents Washington, Jefferson, Roosevelt, and Lincoln.

---

---

nation's first national monument in 1906, and it achieved lasting cinematic fame as the alien landing site in *Close Encounters of the Third Kind*.

Highway 14 takes the road trip back to I-90 and the legendary **Black Hills** of South Dakota. A giant island of trees and rocky mounts in the middle of the Northern Plains, the hills rise to 7,244 feet (2,208 m) at **Black Elk (Harney) Peak**, the nation's highest point east of the Rockies.

Nearly all of the Black Hills area is protected within the confines of some sort of federal or state park. **Black Hills National Forest**—with its myriad hiking, biking, fishing, climbing, and camping options—sprawls across much of the range. The Forest Service's **Pactola Visitor Center** provides information on all of these activities and interpretive programs.

**Custer State Park** is renowned for its large bison herd—best viewed and

---

photographed along the park's 18-mile (29 km) **Wildlife Loop Road**—and summer stock theater of the **Black Hills Playhouse**. The state park is also the jumping-off point for hikes to the summit of **Black Elk Peak**. At the opposite extreme, you can hike *beneath* the Black Hills through 130 miles (209.2 km) of passages at **Wind Cave National Park** and 180 miles (289.7 km) of caverns at **Jewel Cave National Monument**.

Of course, the area is best known for **Mount Rushmore**, that granite tribute to four presidents sculpted by artist Gutzon Borglum and his son between 1927 and 1941. Among the activities available at **Mount Rushmore National Memorial** are a 20-minute film about the making of the monument at **Lincoln Borglum Visitor Center** and ranger talks at the **Sculptor's Studio**.

The Black Hills' other colossus is the **Crazy Horse Memorial**, an equestrian statue of the famed Lakota chief by the late Polish American sculptor Korczak Ziolkowski. Towering 563 feet (171.6 m) above Echo Valley, the memorial was started in 1948 but is a work in progress.

**Deadwood** is the range's most celebrated (and infamous) Wild West town. Tucked between the various gambling halls are the graves of Wild Bill Hickok and Calamity Jane in **Mount Moriah Cemetery**. On the outskirts of town, **Tatanka: Story of the Bison** offers a Native American perspective on Northern Plains history, culture, and wildlife.

This road trip ends in **Rapid City** on the eastern side of the Black Hills, although you can easily extend the drive to **Badlands National Park** an hour east or make your way back to Bismarck (300 miles/482.8 km) via the **Cheyenne River** and **Standing Rock** reservations. ∎

# Santa Fe Trail
## MO, KS, OK, CO & NM

Legendary gunslingers, frontier forts, and literary inspiration are the main attractions on this 840-mile (1,351.9 km) drive through the Great Plains between Missouri and New Mexico, a road trip that shadows the original route of the historic Santa Fe Trail.

**THE BIG PICTURE**

**Distance:** ca 840 miles (1,352 km) from Kansas City, MO, to Santa Fe, NM

**Drive time:** 3 days

**Best overnights:** Dodge City, Trinidad, Las Vegas

**Best seasons:** Spring, summer, or fall

**Highlights:** Kansas City, Dodge City, Trinidad, Las Vegas, Santa Fe

Initially used as a trade route between northern Mexico and the young United States, the Santa Fe Trail evolved into one of the main migration routes for American settlers heading to New Mexico, Arizona, and California.

The Santa Fe Trail started from several points around the confluence of the Missouri and Kansas Rivers, including the **Kansas City, Missouri,** riverfront, where the *Arabia Steamboat Museum* preserves the remains of a side-wheeler that

transported settlers and soldiers to the trailhead in the 1850s.

Main Street cuts south across the city center to **Old Westport**, where **Pioneer Square** and **Kelly's Westport Inn** (est. 1850) recall those early days on the trail. At nearby **Shawnee Indian Mission** in Kansas, Methodist missionaries opened a school for Native American children in 1839.

Starting with Shawnee Mission Parkway, U.S. Highway 56 traces the old Santa Fe Trail route across

Kansas through a Great Plains landscape that inspired Laura Ingalls Wilder to pen *Little House on the Prairie* and Dorothy to utter those immortal words, "There's no place like home."

Another popular stop on the trail, **Council Grove** offers a wooden **Pioneer Jail**, **Last Chance Store** (1857), and **Madonna of the Trail** monument, as well as Native American history at **Kaw Mission** and **Allegawaho Heritage Memorial Park**. Twenty minutes south of town, **Tallgrass Prairie National Preserve** offers a glimpse of natural landscape from the Santa Fe Trail days.

West of Council Grove, wagon trains and other travelers sought supplies and shelter at U.S. Army outposts like the well-preserved **Fort Larned National Historic Site.** Farther down the trail, **Dodge City** came to epitomize the wilder side of the Wild West, a heritage that lives on in the **Boot Hill Museum, Gunfighters Wax Museum**, and the **Trail of Fame** through the downtown historic district.

Beyond Dodge City, the Santa Fe Trail split into the shorter "Cimarron Route" across the Oklahoma Panhandle and the longer but better-watered "Mountain Route" through Colorado's southeast corner. Our road trip

A sculpture of American frontiersman Wyatt Earp is part of Dodge City's Trail of Fame.

Bent's Old Fort National Historic Site includes a reconstructed 1840s fur trading post.

traces the latter, a drive along U.S. Highway 50 via **Holcomb**, Kansas—where the real-life crime that inspired Truman Capote's *In Cold Blood* took place in 1959.

A fur trading post, **Bent's Old Fort National Historic Site**, was a major stop on the trail's Colorado segment. The reconstructed adobe bastion offers guided tours and living history events like Santa Fe Trail Day in June.

Reaching **La Junta**, the route switches to U.S. 350 for an 80-mile (128.8 km) run down to **Trinidad**. Hop aboard the **Trinidad Trolley** for a free guided tour of the town's historic district, and visit the **Mitchell Museum of Western Art** for a blend of Native American, Hispanic, and Western art and collectibles, including paintings by hometown hero A. R. Mitchell.

Interstate 25 takes drivers over **Raton Pass** and into New Mexico. The ghostly ruins of **Fort Union** are all that's left of a U.S. Army post that protected this leg of the Santa Fe Trail for 40 years (1851-91). Nearby **Las Vegas** was another wild town along the route, renowned for Teddy Roosevelt's Rough Riders and desperadoes like Billy the Kid and Jesse James.

The Santa Fe Trail traverses the **Sangre de Cristo** mountains—and **Pecos National Historic Park** with its historic adobe and Civil War battlefield—before reaching the bright lights of **Santa Fe**. ■

## ART AVENUES

• **Best Book:** *In Cold Blood* by Truman Capote, *Little House on the Prairie* by Laura Ingalls Wilder, and *Singing Cowboy* by Margaret Larkin

• **Best Movies:** *Santa Fe Trail* (1940) and *Wyatt Earp* (1994)

• **Best TV Shows:** *Gunsmoke* (1955-1975) and *Smallville* (2001-2011)

• **Best Music:** "Home on the Range" (Kansas state song); the country tunes of Kansas-born Martina McBride

• **Best Art:** The vivid Depression-era Regionalist paintings of John Steuart Curry; the colorful cowboy images of Trinidad's Arthur Roy Mitchell

• **Best Poetry:** Just about anything by New Mexico cowboy bard S. Omar Barker

# Silos & Smokestacks

## Iowa

Nothing else typifies the heartland like Iowa, a patchwork of farms, towns, and factories. A road trip between Des Moines and the Mississippi River reflects the rich heritage of American agriculture as well as what often seems like a drive through *The Music Man* sets.

### THE BIG PICTURE

**Distance:** 418 miles (672.7 km) round-trip from Des Moines

**Drive time:** 4 days

**Best overnights:** Mason City, Waterloo, Cedar City, Iowa City

**Best seasons:** Spring, summer, or fall

**Highlights:** Prairie School architecture, John Deere factories, Grant Wood, Herbert Hoover, Amana Colonies

Created in 1996, the Silos and Smokestacks National Heritage Area encompasses 90 communities and a number of public and private sites that reflect the legacy of American agriculture between pioneer days and today.

Des Moines is the obvious place to launch the drive, starting with a quick run up Interstate 35 to **Ames**. The Iowa State University campus harbors the recently revamped **Brunnier Art Museum** and the 17-acre **Reiman Gardens** with its butterfly pavilion, tropical conservatory, and the world's largest concrete garden gnome.

Continue north along I-35 to **Mason City**, where *Music Man* composer Meredith Willson was born and raised. The town's melodious repertoire includes the **North Iowa Symphony Orchestra** and **Music Man Square** with its 1912 replica streetscape and Willson's boyhood home. Mason City is also renowned for its **Prairie School architecture**, including structures designed by Frank Lloyd Wright and Walter Burley Griffin.

The Cedar River (and U.S. Highway 218) flows southward to **Waterloo**, which rose to prominence in the early 20th century as a meatpacking and tractor manufacturing hub. Tours of Waterloo's three **John Deere factories** and the **John Deere Tractor and Engine Museum** are among the city's top attractions. **Grout Museum District** in downtown Waterloo tenders the **Sullivan Brothers Iowa Veterans Museum**, the **Bluedorn Science Imaginarium**, and several historic house museums. If you've got the kids along, there's also **Lost Island Water Park**.

Another hour down the interstate is **Cedar Rapids**. Founded in 1838, the city made its name on corn and cattle. Today it offers a broad array of artistic venues from the studio where **Grant Wood** painted "American Gothic" and the early 20th-century American collection at the **Cedar Rapids Museum of Art** to live music and stage at the 1928 **Paramount Theatre** and the historic **Czech Village/New Bohemia District**.

The House Chamber at the University of Iowa's Old Capitol Museum

Cut through soybean fields and picturesque farmsteads on your way to Des Moines, Iowa.

Thirty-four miles (54.7 km) farther south is another thriving college town—**Iowa City**. The Greek Revival–style **Old Capitol Building** (1842) is where Iowa's state government first met, as well as the place where the University of Iowa began in the 1850s. The campus also offers the university **museums of art and natural history**.

In addition to a good selection of student bars and eateries, downtown Iowa City features the **Iowa Street Literary Walk**, a series of bronze panels that celebrates 49 writers with ties to the Hawkeye State, including Kurt Vonnegut, Tennessee Williams, Jane Smiley, and Bill Bryson.

On the outskirts of Iowa City, **Herbert Hoover National Historic Site** in West Branch is dedicated to Iowa's only president. The site harbors the Hoover Presidential Library and Museum, the last resting place of Hoover and his wife, and the house where the 31st president was born.

Rather than rush back to Des Moines on Interstate 80, take a slow drive along U.S. Highway 6 through the Iowa countryside. The route passes through the **Amana Colonies**, seven communal villages founded in the 1850s by German immigrants. Scattered among the villages are the **Amana Heritage Society Museums**, arts and craft shops, a winery and microbrewery, as well as drama, musicals, comedies, and children's shows at the **Old Creamery Theatre Company**. ■

## PIT STOPS

- **Amana Winterfest:** Log sawing, ice sculpting, ham chucking, and cookie decorating are just a few of the activities at this late January bash in the colonies. festivalsin amana.com

- **North Iowa Band Festival**: Founded in 1936, this annual gathering of marching bands from around the Midwest brings music to the streets of Mason City over Memorial Day Weekend. nibandfest.com

- **Sturgis Falls Festival:** Iowa's largest free urban celebration unfolds each June in parks across the city, a mash-up that includes a parade, carnival rides, arts and crafts fair, colossal pool party, and plenty of food and live entertainment. sturgisfalls.org

- **Iowa Irish Festival:** Waterloo hosts a three-day August shindig that includes Highland Games, whiskey tasting, Irish food and beer, and Celtic dance and song. iowairishfest.com

# American Motor History
## Michigan & Indiana

The early days of automobiles and motor sports come alive during this cruise through the cities of Michigan and Indiana where the horseless carriage morphed into vehicles that could be driven by ordinary people and raced by professional drivers.

**THE BIG PICTURE**

**Distance:** 460 miles (740.3 km) from Detroit, MI, to Indianapolis, IN

**Drive time:** 2-3 days

**Best overnights:** Lansing, Auburn, South Bend

**Best seasons:** Spring, summer, or fall

**Highlights:** Henry Ford Museum, Auburn Cord Duesenberg Museum, Indianapolis Motor Speedway

German Karl Benz may have created the first motorcar in 1886, but it was a cluster of American inventors, engineers, industrialists, and daredevils who made cars available to the motoring masses and pioneered auto racing in the early 20th century. Most of their efforts took place in Detroit, Indianapolis, and smaller cities in between—a region where American motoring was born and became a global phenomenon.

Although he didn't invent the automobile or the assembly line, Henry Ford is hailed as the father of the modern motorcar industry. The spot where the Model T was created, **Ford's Piquette Avenue Plant** near downtown Detroit, boasts more than 40 historic vehicles and re-creations of Henry Ford's office and auto-design workshop.

Ford's lavish **Fair Lane estate**, influenced by the designs of Frank Lloyd Wright, is 20 minutes west via Interstate 94. The grounds are open to the public; the interior has been under renovation and is scheduled to reopen by late 2020. The nearby **Henry Ford Museum and Greenfield Village** complex features Ford's childhood home and a behind-the-scenes factory tour, as well as the Lincoln Continental convertible that John F. Kennedy was riding in when he was killed, the bus that Rosa Parks rode and became a civil rights icon, the first Mustang, and an original Oscar Mayer Wienermobile.

It was actually Ransom Eli Olds, another Michigan native, who devised the first mass-produced car and auto assembly line. Ninety miles (144.8 km) west of Detroit, the **R. E. Olds Transportation Museum** in Lansing offers 60 historic vehicles including an 1886 Oldsmobile Steam Carriage.

It's a straight shot down I-69 to northern Indiana, where the city of Auburn gave its name to another early automobile. More than 120 classics made by Indiana carmakers are on display at the **Auburn Cord Duesenberg Automobile Museum**, housed in the original art deco–style Auburn Automobile Company headquarters building. Among its many chrome-and-steel treasures are

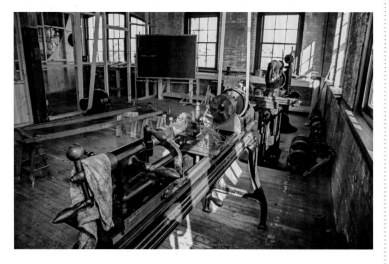

See the secret experimental room at the Henry Ford Piquette Avenue Plant.

Henry Ford Museum visitors cruise through Greenfield Village in a vintage Ford.

gangster John Dillinger's 1933 Essex Terraplane getaway car and a 1927 Duesenberg racer.

Just around the corner, Auburn's **National Auto and Truck Museum** offers an even wider selection of vintage vehicles, from a rare 1953 General Motors Futurliner bus to a pristine pedal car.

**Mae West's 1931 Chevrolet Housecar**—a gift from Paramount Studios when its executives were trying to lure the legendary entertainer from vaudeville to movies—takes the spotlight at the **RV Hall of Fame, Museum and Library** in Elkhart. Located 80 miles (128.8 km) from Auburn via Interstates 69 and 80, the museum also displays a 1954 Spartan Imperial Mansion built with surplus aircraft aluminum and a travel trailer custom-built for aviator Charles Lindbergh.

Half an hour farther west, the **Studebaker National Museum** includes motorcars, horse-drawn wagons, and military vehicles made by the South Bend automaker between 1852 and 1967, as well as a collection of presidential carriages.

U.S. Highway 31 makes a beeline from South Bend to the Indiana state capital and the legendary **Indianapolis Motor Speedway**. Even if you're not there for a big event like the iconic Indy 500, the racetrack offers a **museum**, a narrated **lap around the track**, various grounds tours, a speaker series, and a chance to play the **Brickyard Crossing Golf Course**. ■

## PIT STOPS

• **Indianapolis 500:** First staged in 1911, America's most famous auto race roars around the speedway every year on Memorial Day Weekend. indianapolismotorspeedway.com

• **Detroit Grand Prix:** The Indy Car race and motor sports festival on Belle Isle in the Detroit River takes place the weekend after the Indy 500. detroitgp.com

• **Old Car Festival:** The nation's longest running antique car show rolls into Greenfield Village at the Henry Ford Museum in early September. thehenryford.org

• **24 Hours of Lemons:** This fun-filled endurance race for vehicles costing less than $500 is staged mid-October at GingerMan Raceway in South Haven, Michigan. 24hoursoflemons.com

# Reinventing Ohio's 3-C Highway
## Ohio

Inspired by one of the early 20th-century auto roads, the 3-C route runs across the heart of Ohio, a drive from Cleveland to Columbus to Cincinnati that features many of the sights (and sounds) that make the Buckeye State so special.

Created in 1923 to encourage driving those newfangled motorcars and expedite transit between the state's three largest cities, the 3-C Highway (aka State Route 3) was one of the nation's first long-distance road trip routes.

Our updated version starts exactly where bygone 3-C began—in **Public Square** in downtown Cleveland. Several of the city's landmarks are arrayed around the square, including the **Old Stone Church** (built in 1855) and **Higbee's Department Store,** which costarred in the 1983 film *A Christmas Story*.

Exiting the square on the south side, the route follows Ontario

**THE BIG PICTURE**

**Distance:** ca 310 miles (498.9 km) from Cleveland to Cincinnati

**Drive time:** 7 days

**Best overnights:** Akron, Canton, Berlin, Columbus, Dayton

**Best seasons:** Anytime

**Highlights:** Cuyahoga Valley, Stan Hywet Hall, Pro Football Hall of Fame, Amish country, Columbus neighborhoods, Dayton

Avenue and Interstate 77 to **Cuyahoga Valley National Park**. Arrayed along the path of the Ohio and Erie Canal and the old Baltimore and Ohio Railroad, the valley is a tribute to Ohio's industrial revolution.

In addition to hiking, biking, horseback riding, and paddling, Cuyahoga Valley offers an array of winter sports, the **Canal Exploration Center**, and rides on the vintage **Cuyahoga Valley Scenic Railroad** between Rockside and Akron.

The **Ohio and Erie Canalway National Scenic Byway** runs all the way through the park and southward to **Stan Hywet Hall and Gardens**. Built in 1915 by the man who founded Goodyear Tire and Rubber, the estate offers guided tours of the 65-room Tudor Revival manor house and 70 acres (28.3 ha) of landscaped grounds.

The byway ambles into **Akron**, once renowned as the world's "Rubber Capital" but now better known as the hometown of LBJ (LeBron James, not the 36th president). Check for live music and other events at the wonderfully restored **Akron Civic Theatre** (opened in 1919) or **Lock 3 Park** beside the Ohio and Erie Canal.

Back on I-77, the drive continues to **Canton**, home of the **Pro Football Hall of Fame** and **McKinley Presidential Library**, as well as a **Down-**

Make way for horse-drawn buggies on the road through Ohio's Amish country.

The 65-foot (19.8 m) Brandywine Falls can be seen from a boardwalk in the Cuyahoga Valley National Park.

town **Arts District** with more than 30 galleries and studios, plus eateries and live music venues.

U.S. Highway 62 heads southeast into Ohio's **Amish Country**. Home to more than 50,000 Amish—the nation's second highest concentration after Lancaster, Pennsylvania—the bucolic countryside offers stops like the **Amish and Mennonite Heritage Center** and comedy variety shows at the **Amish Country Theater** in Berlin, plus the tasty **Guggisberg Cheese Factory** in nearby Millersburg.

**Columbus** lies another 80 miles (128.8 km) down U.S. 62. **Ohio State University** may be the big man on campus, but the state capital also offers free guided tours of the **Ohio Statehouse**, the boyhood home of writer and cartoonist **James Thurber**, and funky neighborhoods like the **Short North Arts District, German Village**, and downtown **Arena District**.

From Columbus, it's a straight shot down I-71 to Cincinnati. Or you can detour to the west on a drive along I-70 to **Dayton** to explore the genesis of human flight. **Dayton Aviation Heritage National Historical Park** preserves the legacy of the Wright Brothers, while the **National Museum of the U.S. Air Force** at Wright-Patterson Air Force Base offers more than 350 historic aircraft and missiles.

Interstate 75 provides the home stretch down to **Cincinnati** and a spin around the traffic circle beside the **"Sing the Queen City"** sign and the **Ohio River**. ■

## PIT STOPS

• **Lyceum Distinguished Speakers:** Cuyahoga Valley Institute hosts in-depth discussions of history, nature, and adventure at venues in the national park between January and May. conservancyforcvnp.org

• **Cincinnati Music Festival:** "A" list jazz, blues, soul, and hip-hop artists flavor this melodious July event at Paul Brown Stadium. cincymusic festival.com

• **Dayton Celtic Festival:** This three-day feast of everything Irish takes place in July at RiverScape Metro Park on the Miami River. daytonceltic festival.com

• **Ohio State Fair:** Nearly a million people flood the Expo Center in the Columbus fairgrounds in late July and early August for one of the nation's oldest and largest state fairs. ohiostatefair.com

• **Berlin Harvest Festival:** The Amish country's big September bash features live country tunes, a rib cook-off, and an old fashioned, small-town parade. berlinharvest festival.com

# Southern
## Road Trips

Clouds hover in the peaks of Great Smoky Mountains National Park at sunrise.

# Natchez Trace
## Tennessee, Alabama & Mississippi

One of the many road and recreation projects born of the Great Depression, the Natchez Trace Parkway traces the route of a bygone path between Tennessee and the Lower Mississippi now strung with nature areas, historic sites, and antebellum towns.

**THE BIG PICTURE**

**Distance:** 444 miles (714.6 km) from Nashville, TN, to Natchez, MS

**Drive time:** 3-5 days

**Best overnights:** Franklin, Florence, Tupelo, Jackson, Vicksburg, Natchez

**Best seasons:** Anytime

**Highlights:** Highland Rim, Shiloh, Tishomingo, Tupelo, Vicksburg, Port Gibson, Emerald Mound, Natchez

Originally blazed by Native Americans as an overland trade route, the Natchez Trace evolved into a pathway for American settlers, soldiers, and slaves after the Louisiana Purchase.

The trace starts just south of **Nashville, Tennessee,** with its medley of music sights, not far from **Franklin** and its five historic districts. The first 100 miles (160.9 km) of the parkway meander across Tennessee's Western Highland Rim, with places like **Jackson Falls,** **Devil's Backbone,** and **Fall Hollow** begging you to stretch your legs.

Farther along is **Grinder's Stand,** a replica of the roadside inn where famed explorer **Meriwether Lewis** mysteriously died during an 1809 journey along the trace. A turnoff at mile 370 leads to **David Crockett State Park,** where the legendary frontiersman built mills and a distillery in 1817.

The Natchez Trace makes quick work of Alabama, a 33-mile (53.1 km) stretch that features the **Rock Spring Nature Trail** and historic Colbert Ferry on either side of the **Tennessee River**. Just downstream is **Shiloh National Military Park,** where one of the bloodiest battles of the Civil War waged in 1862.

Crossing the state line into Mississippi, the trace runs beside **Tishomingo State Park,** a rambling wild area in the southern foothills of the **Appalachians**. Trails lead along sandstone cliffs and boulder-strewn creeks like paddle-friendly **Bear Creek**.

Slip on your blue suede shoes, because up ahead is **Tupelo,** where Elvis Aaron Presley was born in 1935. In addition to the **Elvis Birthplace** home and the king of rock-and-roll's childhood church, the city also hosts the official **Natchez Trace Parkway Visitor Center,** where exhibits, a short film, and bookstore shed light on the historic pathway.

There's history too: **Tupelo National Battlefield,** the place where Spanish explorer **Hernando de Soto** and his men bivouacked in the winter of 1540-41; the 2,000-year-old **Bynum burial mounds**; and reminders of both the Choctaw people and the extinct passenger pigeon at **Pigeon Roost**.

Going down to Jackson, the trace offers a wooden boardwalk trail

Pay homage to the King at Elvis Presley's birthplace in Tupelo, Mississippi.

Stretch your legs on the Cypress Swamp Trail to marvel at the tupelo and bald cypress trees.

through **Cypress Swamp** and eight miles (12.9 km) of shoreline along **Barnett Reservoir**. Take a peak at the "new" **State Capitol** building (opened in 1901) and the underrated **Museum of Mississippi History** before heading on down the line.

Around 40 miles (64.4 km) south of Jackson, an old cotton-farming settlement, **Rocky Springs**, is now a ghost town. It never recovered from the Civil War and the siege that doomed nearby **Vicksburg** in 1863. The antebellum core of **Port Gibson** survived because Union General Grant allegedly found it "too beautiful to burn." On the outskirts of town, **Sunken Trace** affords a chance to hike an original stretch of the trail.

The last stretch of the Natchez Trace features two of its best known landmarks. Founded in 1780, **Mount Locust** is the last of the original "stands," or roadside inns, that served early travelers along the route. Grass-covered **Emerald Mound** was the hub of a Native American ceremonial center that flourished between the 13th and 18th centuries.

While the modern parkway ends on the edge of **Natchez** town, the spiritual end of the Natchez Trace lies farther west—a journey down Liberty Road and Franklin Street to Bluff Park overlooking the Mississippi River. ■

## EN ROUTE EATS

• **Junkyard Dog Steakhouse:** Just off the trace in Tennessee, the "Dog" offers steak, seafood, and local favorites like gumbo, fried okra and pickles, and honey-glazed pork; 18 North Maple St., Hohenwald, TN. junkyarddogsteakhouse.com

• **Blue Canoe:** Nightly live music, craft beer, and tasty burgers are the lure at a joint that Elvis would have loved; 2006 North Gloster St., Tupelo, MS. bluecanoebar.com

• **Walker's Drive-In:** With dishes like Wagyu short ribs, miso-marinated sea bass, portobello fries, and gourmet shrimp and grits, this is definitely not your typical drive-in; 3016 North State St., Jackson, MS. walkersdrivein.com

• **Old Country Store:** Travel back in time at this roadside restaurant near Port Gibson renowned for pork chops and fried chicken; 18801 Hwy. 61, Lorman, MS. 601-437-3661

# Skyline & Blue Ridge
## Virginia & North Carolina

Stretching nearly 600 miles (965.6 km) down the wooded ridges that divide lowland Virginia and North Carolina from the Appalachians, Skyline Drive and the Blue Ridge Parkway provide absorbing insight into the natural and human history of one of the nation's most storied regions.

### THE BIG PICTURE

**Distance:** 574 miles (923.8 km) from Front Royal, VA, to Cherokee, NC

**Drive time:** 6 days

**Best overnights:** Shenandoah NP, Waynesboro, Roanoke, Asheville, Mount Pisgah/Brevard, Cherokee

**Best seasons:** Spring, summer, or fall

**Highlights:** Shenandoah NP, Mabry Mill, Blue Ridge Music Center, Flat Top Manor, Mount Mitchell, Biltmore Estate, Pisgah National Forest

The mountains were already there—the vaunted Blue Ridge range that flanks the eastern side of the Appalachians highlands—but the roads were not. Like so many other park projects, they were children of the Great Depression, a means to lessen the burden of unemployment and give something back to the nation. That's how Skyline Drive and the Blue Ridge Parkway were born.

Originally called the Appalachian Scenic Highway, the Blue Ridge route came along first, with construction starting in 1935. Stretching 469 miles (754.8 km) from end to end, it's America's longest linear park, the entire route managed by the National Park System.

Work on Skyline Drive kicked off in 1939. While the route through Shenandoah may look totally natural, landscape architects carefully planned every bend and overlook along Skyline to take full advantage of the lofty views.

**Skyline Drive** starts near **Front Royal, Virginia.** Outfitters like **Downriver Canoe Company** and **Front Royal Canoe** make it easy to paddle the nearby Shenandoah River. **Shenandoah National Park**'s north gate is just five minutes from downtown Front Royal. And not far beyond is **Dickey Ridge Visitor Center** with its information desk, small museum, and swag shop.

The stretch of Skyline between the visitor center and **Thornton Gap** provides some of the best views across the lush Shenandoah Valley and the higher, hazy Appalachian Mountains to the west.

The road continues to climb to **Skyland**, the highest point along the drive at 3,680 feet (1,121.7 m), where the historic lodge provides food, drink, horseback riding, and overnight stays for both drivers and backpackers on the 100-mile (160.9 km) segment of the **Appalachian Trail** that runs through the park. Skyland also offers less challenging hikes, like the 1.6-mile (2.6-km) circuit to the top of **Stony Man Summit** and the ADA-accessible **Limberlost Trail.**

**Big Meadows** boasts the park's other (larger) visitor center and museum, as well as another historic

Mabry Mill, a gristmill constructed in 1910, sits at milepost 176.1.

Asheville's Biltmore Estate—"America's Largest Home"—offers guided tours of the house, gardens, and winery.

lodge, campground, and the park's only gas station. In addition to easy hikes through the surrounding woods and across large, grassy open spaces, Big Meadows offers trails to **three waterfalls** (Dark Hollow, Rose River, and Lewis) and **Rapidan Camp**—Herbert Hoover's Summer White House from 1929 to 1933. **Brown House**, the presidential cabin, has been restored to its 1929 appearance, and rangers offer walking tours of the camp from spring through fall.

South of Big Meadows, Skyline Drive runs through the wildest part of Shenandoah, 50 miles (80.5 km) of overlooks and trailheads with only a few visitor services along the way. **Lewis Mountain** campground and picnic area was the park's "Negro Area" from 1939 to the 1950s, when the park was finally desegregated.

Twisting down from the higher elevations, Skyline ends at **Rockfish Gap**—but this road trip continues. On the other side of Interstate 64 is

the northern end of the **Blue Ridge Parkway**. The parkway's **Humpback Rocks Visitor Center** is just 10 minutes farther south. Humpback hosts free **Mountain Music Concerts** on Sunday afternoons between May and September, and nearby is **Mountain Farm Outdoor Museum**, a collection of vintage buildings.

Where you linger along the Blue Ridge Parkway largely depends on what you like to see or do. **Raven's Roost** (mile 10) is popular with rock climbers and hang gliders. **James River Visitor Center** (mile 63) offers restored locks and exhibits along the old Kanawha Canal. The **Peaks of Otter** area (miles 84-87) features routes to the top of three mountaintops, as well as a campground and visitor center.

The parkway curves around the east side of **Roanoke**, with a chance to drive a one-way loop to the top of **Roanoke Mountain** (mile 120) or side trip to nearby **Booker T. Washington National Monument**.

### SCENIC DETOURS

• **Stonewall Jackson Memorial Highway:** U.S. Highway 340 runs the length of the Shenandoah Valley west of the national park, with various Civil War sites along the way.

• **U.S. Highway 58:** Runs west from Meadows of Dan through the country music heartland of western Virginia and eastern Kentucky.

• **U.S. Highway 250/I-64:** Starting from Rockfish Gap, a drive through American history that includes Thomas Jefferson's Monticello and Civil War sites near Richmond.

• **New River Valley Byway:** A 35-mile (56.3 km) drive through the North Carolina backcountry from Booneville to Laurel Springs.

• **Newfound Gap Road (U.S. 441):** From Cherokee, the road runs up and over the Appalachians through the heart of Great Smoky Mountains National Park.

Farther south is **Mabry Mill** (mile 176), which offers summertime skills demonstrations at its historic grist-mill, sawmill, and blacksmith shop.

Virginia's stretch of the parkway ends in awesome fashion with the **Blue Ridge Music Center** near Galax (mile 213), which includes the **Roots of American Music Exhibition** and performances of old-time music from May through October.

Crossing into North Carolina at **Cumberland Knob** (mile 217), the parkway runs down to **Stone Mountain State Park** and **Brinegar Cabin** (mile 238), a farm where a home-stead family lived between the 1880s and 1935. There's more heritage at **Northwest Trading Post** (mile 258), where rural North Carolina arts and crafts are offered for sale. **Daniel Boone's Trace**, blazed by the legendary frontiersman in 1775, crosses the parkway at mile 285.

Reaching **Pisgah National Forest,** the parkway runs through the 3,500-acre **Moses Cone estate** (miles 292-95) with its forest trails, fishing lakes, and **Flat Top Manor**, a sprawling Gilded Age mansion that's now the home of the **Southern Highland**

It's a 1.4-mile (2.2 km) out-and-back hike to Dark Hollow Falls in Shenandoah National Park.

---

---

**Craft Guild** and its locally produced folk art treasures.

A little farther along is **Julian Price Memorial Park** (miles 295-98) and the spectacular **Tanawha Trail** (13.5 miles/21.7 km) to the top of **Grandfather Mountain**, at 5,946 feet (1,812.3 m) the highest peak on the eastern escarpment of the entire Blue Ridge. **Linville Falls** (mile 316) is one of the more spectacular cascades along the drive, while **Mount Mitchell State Park** (mile 355) is the highest point east of the Mississippi—6,684 feet (2,037.3 m). There's a strenuous, six-mile (9.7 km) trail to the summit.

Descending into the Asheville metropolitan area, the road calls on the **Folk Art Center**, where the Southern Highlands Craft Guild showcases Appalachian crafts, as well as a bookshop and live demonstrations. Just up the road is the main **Blue Ridge Parkway Visitor Center**, the extraordinary **Biltmore Estate** (the nation's largest privately owned home), and the leafy **North Carolina Arboretum**.

The home stretch snakes through the southern section of Pisgah National Forest to lofty **Mount Pisgah** with its campground and hiking trails, across **Waterrock Knob** with its bird's-eye view of the nearby Smoky Mountains, and finally through the **Cherokee Indian Reservation** and the east entrance to **Great Smoky Mountains National Park**. ∎

---

# Trail of Tears
## North Carolina to Oklahoma

This 1,000-mile (1,609.3 km) odyssey through seven states traces the infamous Trail of Tears, the forced expulsion of the Cherokee and other Native American peoples from their homeland in the Southeast to Oklahoma—what was then the Far West.

In 1830, President Andrew Jackson signed the Indian Removal Act to relocate Native Americans from southern lands coveted by white settlers to a newly created Indian Territory.

More than 12,000 Cherokee were forced to leave North Carolina and Georgia during the winter of 1838-39. Thousands perished along the way; their memory is preserved by the Trail of Tears National Historic Trail.

A handful of Native Americans managed to remain in the East, like those who founded **Cherokee**, North Carolina. In addition to nearby **Great Smoky Mountains National Park**, the town offers the **Museum of the Cherokee Indian**, **Oconaluftee Indian Village**, and a summer outdoor drama about the Cherokee Nation, ***Unto These Hills***.

U.S. Highway 74 carries the route through the **Blue Ridge Mountains** to Murphy and the **Cherokee County Historical Museum**, an interpretive center for the national historic trail.

The same highway jumps across the state line to Cleveland in the

### THE BIG PICTURE

**Distance:** ca 975 miles (1,569 km) from Cherokee, NC, to Tahlequah, OK

**Drive time:** 6 days

**Best overnights:** Cleveland, Nashville, Paducah, Cape Girardeau, Springfield

**Best seasons:** Anytime

**Highlights:** Cherokee (NC), Cherokee Removal Memorial, Trail of Tears Commemorative Park, Mantle Rock, Trail of Tears State Park, Ozarks, Tahlequah

Tennessee River Valley and a drive along State Route 60 to **Cherokee Removal Memorial Park** at historic Blythe Ferry where 9,000 Cherokee crossed the river at the start of the notorious trek. In addition to Native American music and interpretive programs, the park features a library where visitors can trace their Cherokee ancestry or examine Trail of Tear documentation.

From the western side of the **Tennessee River**, a string of highways (27, 111, 70S) traces the original Trail of Tears to Interstate 24 in Murfreesboro and a straight shot to **Nashville**. By 1837, Andrew Jackson had retired to his **Hermitage** home and no doubt witnessed some of the misery he caused by backing the Cherokee removal.

Interstate 24 continues into Kentucky, with stops along the way at **Port Royal State Park** (where visitors can hike an original section of the trail) and the **Trail of Tears Commemorative Park** in Hopkinsville. The last resting place of two Cherokee chiefs, Whitepath and Fly Smith, who perished along the trek, the park hosts a **Trail of Tears Pow Wow** every Labor Day.

Reaching Eddyville, you can take

Watch live demonstrations in the Oconaluftee Indian Village.

A traditional Cherokee winter house, made from wattle and daub, can be viewed at the Cherokee Heritage Center in Tahlequah.

a side trip to **Mantle Rock Nature Preserve**, where thousands of Cherokee took shelter from winter storms before crossing the ice-choked Ohio River. Otherwise, cruise I-24 into southern Illinois and head west along State Route 146 to **Anna** (three more original sections of the route) and the **Trail of Tears State Forest** (hiking, fishing, camping).

When you reach the banks of the Mississippi, you can see **Trail of Tears State Park** in southern Missouri across the water. Driving there requires a 28-mile (45.1 km) detour through Cape Girardeau. In addition to exhibits, the state park visitor center offers a 23-minute film on the Trail of Tears produced by the National Park Service.

Still facing harsh winter conditions, the Cherokee were marched through the rugged **Ozarks**, a route our road trip follows on State Route 72 through **Mark Twain National Forest** to Rolla, and then I-44 down **to Springfield**. The crossroads city offers an original portion of the trail along **Old Wire Road**, as well as Native American galleries at the new **History Museum on the Square**.

You'll need GPS or a good road map for the final stretch of the trail, a zigzag drive across southwestern Missouri and northwestern Arkansas. The trip runs past the **Pea Ridge National Military Park** where a fierce Civil War battle was waged, and through **Bentonville** and **Fayetteville** before crossing into Oklahoma.

**Tahlequah** marks the end of the original Trail of Tears and this commemorative drive. Founded in 1839 as the capital of the Cherokee Nation, the city's population remains 30 percent Native American.

The great trek is recalled at the **Cherokee Heritage Center** with its reproduction 18th-century village and numerous living history and cultural programs, the **Cherokee National Prison Museum**, and the self-guided **Tahlequah History Trail**, as well as **Hunter's Home**, an antebellum Cherokee plantation house. ∎

### ART AVENUES

• **Best Books:** *Trail of Tears* by John Ehle; *The Earth Is Weeping* by Peter Cozzens; *The Heart of Everything That Is* by Bob Drury and Tom Clavin; *Bury My Heart at Wounded Knee* by Dee Brown; *Only the Names Remain* by Alex W. Bealer and Kristina Rodanas

• **Best Art:** Featured paintings and sculptures from the annual Trail of Tears Art Show at the Cherokee Heritage Center, which began in 1972 and is the longest running Native American art show in Oklahoma

# Outer Banks Scenic Byway

## North Carolina

Linking national seashores, state parks, wildlife refuges, quaint coastal villages, and several spots significant in American history, this casual drive along North Carolina's barrier islands offers beautiful beaches, outdoor recreation, plenty of fresh air, and two short ferry rides.

There's no more fitting place to start a drive along the North Carolina coast than the place where America *almost* began—**Roanoke Island**, where settlers established the first English colony in North America in 1585. **Fort Raleigh National Historic Site** relates the story of the doomed settlement through a reconstructed earthwork fort, Elizabethan Gardens, and a music drama, *The Lost Colony*, performed in a waterfront amphitheater each summer.

The **North Carolina Aquarium** and **Roanoke Maritime Museum** also beg a visit before leaping Roanoke Sound to **Bodie Island** and its own slice of the American pie: the place where Wilbur and Orville Wright first took to the air. **Wright Brothers National Memorial** in Kill Devil Hills preserves the spot where their iconic first flight took place on December 17, 1903. You can experience an inkling of what the brothers must have felt at nearby **Jockey's Ridge State Park**, where hang gliders take off from the tallest natural

### THE BIG PICTURE

**Distance:** 174 miles (280 km) from Roanoke Island to Atlantic Beach

**Drive time:** 5 days

**Best overnights:** Nags Head, Buxton, Ocracoke, Beaufort, Atlantic Beach

**Best seasons:** Spring or fall

**Highlights:** Fort Raleigh, Wright Bros. Memorial, Cape Hatteras, Ocracoke Island, Beaufort

sand dunes on the eastern seaboard (60 feet/18 m high).

**Cape Hatteras National Seashore** starts just south of Whalebone Junction. The National Park Service's **Bodie Island Visitor Center** offers information, maps, and off-road vehicle (ORV) permits for driving on the park's Atlantic beaches.

The byway (Route 12) leaps Oregon Inlet to **Pea Island National Wildlife Refuge** and long, thin **Hatteras Island**, framed by spectacular beaches on one side and the paddle-friendly waters of **Pamlico Sound** on the other. Services are clustered at **Cape Point** with its campground, visitor center, **Museum of the Sea**, and 210-foot-high (64 m) **Cape Hatteras Lighthouse**. The island is home to half a dozen villages, including romantic **Rodanthe** of film and literary (*Nights in Rodanthe*) fame.

The little **Hatteras-Ocracoke Ferry** takes passengers and vehicles across Hatteras Inlet, a 45-minute journey to **Ocracoke Island**. The national seashore occupies the entire isle other than fabled **Ocracoke Village**, where a unique American subculture survives through music, folk art, and "High Tider" dialect.

Another relic of Ocracoke's bygone days is the **Pony Pen,** which shelters the last of the "Bankers"—wild horses that once roamed the Outer Banks.

The Wright Brothers National Monument in Kill Devil Hills, North Carolina.

The Ocracoke Lighthouse, built in 1923, stands 75 feet (22.9 m) tall next to the Light Station's Double Keepers' Quarters.

Among the island's other sights are the 1823 **Ocracoke Lighthouse**, the **Ocracoke Preservation Society**, the **Working Watermen's** museum, and the **Teach's Hole Blackbeard Exhibit** about the famous pirate who died at Ocracoke in 1718 during a skirmish with the Virginia militia.

Using the **Ocracoke-Cedar Point Ferry** (2.5 hours), the byway jumps to the North Carolina mainland. **Cedar Island National Wildlife Refuge** is best known for fishing and bird-watching, but the reserve also renders hiking trails and canoe-kayak routes through forest and wetlands.

South of Cedar Point, the byway continues as U.S. Highway 70 to **Davis** and **Harkers Island**, both of which offer ferries across the sound to secluded **Cape Lookout National Seashore**.

Beyond the North River is **Beaufort**, founded in 1703 and the third oldest town in North Carolina. The town's **North Carolina Maritime Museum** covers the region's seafaring heritage, while **boat tours** embarking from the Beaufort waterfront visit the **Rachel Carson Reserve** and other sights along the sound.

The road trip ends at **Atlantic Beach** on **Bogues Bank** island, where old **Fort Mason** (opened in 1834) and several **nature trails** offer an alternative to sun, sand, and sea. ∎

## PIT STOPS

• **Ocracoke Festival:** Three days of traditional folk music, storytelling, artwork, and coastal cuisine flavor this June fest in the historic village. ocracokealive.org

• **Wings Over Water:** This wildlife festival on Hatteras Island features more than 90 birding, paddling, natural history, art, and photography programs for outdoor enthusiasts from October to December. wingsoverwater.org

• **North Carolina Seafood Festival:** Morehead City hosts three days of great food, live music, and craft beer near Beaufort and Atlantic Beach; October or November. ncseafoodfestival.org

• **First Flight Anniversary:** The Park Service and First Flight Society celebrate the Wright Brothers' first heavier-than-air, controlled, powered flight every December 17 at Kitty Hawk. firstflight.org

# Delta Blues Highway

## Tennessee, Mississippi & Louisiana

This 480-mile (772.5 km) journey along the western edge of the Mississippi River between Memphis and New Orleans cruises through a region where several distinct forms of American music—blues, jazz, soul, rhythm and blues, and rock-and-roll—were born and raised.

**THE BIG PICTURE**

**Distance:** ca 468 miles (753.2 km) from Memphis, TN, to New Orleans, LA

**Drive time:** 4-5 days

**Best overnights:** Clarksdale, Vicksburg, Natchez, Baton Rouge

**Best seasons:** Anytime

**Highlights:** Graceland, Beale Street, Clarksdale, Grammy Museum, Dockery Farm, B.B. King Museum, New Orleans jazz

The music that was born along the lower stretch of the Mississippi traces its roots to several sources, from the work songs and spiritual melodies of African Americans to the folk tunes of the French, Italian, Spanish, and Anglo-Irish groups that settled the region, and even the rousing marches of American composer and conductor John Philip Sousa.

From Reconstruction through World War II, this musical cauldron was largely stirred by the region's African-American population, who honed their melodious skills on the farms of Mississippi and Louisiana, in towns along the river, and in big cities like Memphis, Tennessee, and New Orleans, Louisiana. By the 1950s, white musicians were also strumming along, in particular a young man from northern Mississippi by the name of Elvis Aaron Presley.

"The King" will forever be associated with **Memphis**, the city that rocketed him to global fame and where he eventually passed away in 1977. **Graceland** is the holy grail of every Elvis fan, not just the mansion with its green shag-carpeted Jungle Room and other eccentricities, but his grave in the Meditation Garden and the museums that house his legendary pink Cadillac and private jets.

The city's other iconic Elvis site is **Sun Studio** on Union Avenue, where he cut his first record in 1953. Considered the birthplace of rock-and-roll, the studio offers tours of a musical melting pot where Johnny Cash, Roy Orbison, B.B. King, and Jerry Lee Lewis, among many others, also recorded. Nearby **Beale Street** is flanked by live music venues like **B.B. King's Blues Club** and **Jerry Lee Lewis' Honky Tonk**, as well as musical museums and monuments.

From downtown Memphis, U.S. Highway 61 quickly crosses the state line into Mississippi. Fifteen miles (24.1 km) south of the border, **Gate-**

Elvis Presley made his first record at the famous Sun Studio in Memphis, Tennessee.

Memphis's 1.8-mile (2.9 km) historic Beale Street is dubbed "Home of the Blues" and is a mecca for live music.

way to the Blues Visitor Center and Museum—tucked into Tunica's 1895 railroad station—offers an introduction to the musical history that lies ahead. You can continue south along the freeway or cruise Old Highway 61, the original route of the Blues Highway, just to the west of the modern thoroughfare.

Both the old and new roads continue down to Clarksdale, where blues legend Robert Johnson allegedly sold his soul to the devil in the early 1930s in exchange for playing the guitar better than anyone else on earth. If you're a nonbeliever, visit the Devil's Crossroads monument at the intersection of State Street and DeSoto Avenue.

Clarksdale is flush with other musical landmarks: the Delta Blues Museum in the old train depot; the cabin where Muddy Waters was raised; the historic Hopson Planta-

tion Commissary and its "cotton pickin' blues"; and live concert venues at spots like the Cat Head music store and the Ground Zero Blues Club (owned by Clarksdale native Morgan Freeman).

Putting Clarksdale in the rearview mirror, cruise Highway 61 to Cleveland, where the Grammy Museum Mississippi on the campus of Delta State University features interactive exhibits on music,

---

### ART AVENUES

- **Best Music (Old Time):** *The Complete Recordings* by Robert Johnson; *Father of the Delta Blues* by Son House; *Rabbit Foot Minstrels, 1923-1928* by Madam Gertrude "Ma" Rainey; *Best of Delta Blues* by Charley Patton; *Mississippi Delta and South Tennessee Blues* by James "Son" Thomas

- **Best Music (Modern):** Elvis Presley's self-titled 1956 debut album; *Highway 61 Revisited* by Bob Dylan; *The One & Only Sam Cooke*; *Live at the Regal* by BB King; *The Ultimate Collection* by John Lee Hooker; *The Anthology* by Muddy Waters

- **Best Books:** *Escaping the Delta: Robert Johnson and the Invention of the Blues* by Elijah Wald; *Blues Traveling: The Holy Sites of Delta Blues* by Steve Cheseborough; *Eat Drink Delta* by Susan Puckett

- **Best Movies:** *New Orleans* (1947), *King Creole* (1958), *Crossroads* (1986), *Great Balls of Fire* (1989), *O Brother, Where Art Thou?* (2000)

- **Best Play:** *Cat on a Hot Tin Roof* by Clarksdale's own Tennessee Williams

A trumpet player from the Free Spirit brass band performs on Jackson Square in the French Quarter in New Orleans.

dance, stage fashion, and musical instruments. Not surprising, Mississippi claims more Grammy winners per capita than any other state.

Ten minutes east of Cleveland, along State Route 8, is fabled **Dockery Farms**. Founded in 1895, the cotton plantation evolved into a place where musically inclined sharecroppers gathered on their day off for informal jam sessions.

"Father of the Delta Blues" Charley Patton was the first of them; he was later joined by Robert Johnson, Son House, Howlin' Wolf Burnett, Honeyboy Edwards, and other pioneers of the delta sound. Listed on the National Register of Historic

Places, Dockery is open daily for self-guided and guided tours of the grounds, cotton gin, and other vintage buildings. The farm also hosts live blues, jazz, and country music.

Highway 61 continues south to **Leland**, the home of gravedigger-turned-blues master James "Son" Thomas and the boyhood hangout of blues-rock guitarists Johnny and Edgar Winter. It's also where the man behind Kermit the Frog and other Muppets was born, a story told at the town's **Jim Henson Museum**. In addition, there's a **Highway 61 Blues Museum** in the old Montgomery Hotel.

Twenty minutes east of Leland

via U.S. Highway 82, the **B.B. King Museum and Delta Interpretive Center** in Indianola spins tales of the blues and one of its all-time greats. Born in nearby Itta Bena, King worked at a cotton gin in Indianola and perfected his distinctive voice and guitar sound at local churches, juke joints, and radio stations.

Slicing across the cotton country of west-central Mississippi, Highway 61 continues through a string of largely forgotten towns like Panther Burn, Nitta Yuma, and Anguilla, noteworthy more for their names than anything else. But then you reach **Vicksburg**, the riverside town renowned for its crucial Civil War battle.

## PIT STOPS

• **New Orleans Jazz and Heritage Festival:** One of the nation's premier music events stretches across two April and May weekends at Fairgrounds Race Course. nojazzfest.com

• **Juke Joint Festival:** This four-day April bash in Clarksdale celebrates delta blues and small-town Mississippi. jukejointfestival.com

• **Natchez Festival of Music:** Stretching across nearly all of May, this eclectic event features everything from blues, rock-and-roll, and country to opera, Hollywood show tunes, and Liberace. natchezfestivalofmusic.com

• **Memphis in May International Festival:** This month-long urban event combines the Beale Street Music Festival, World Championship BBQ Contest, and Great American River Run. memphisinmay.org

• **Mississippi Delta Blues and Heritage Festival:** The world's oldest continuously run blues fest takes over riverside Greenville in September. deltabluesms.org

While **Vicksburg National Military Park** dominates the cityscape, some of the more offbeat attractions are civilian in nature, like the **Biedenharn Coca-Cola Museum** in the red-brick building where the drink was first bottled in 1894. There's also the **Jesse Brent Lower Mississippi River Museum**, with its interactive exhibits and historic Army Corps of Engineers watercraft. Catch the blues and other live tunes at **Cottonwood Public House** on historic Washington Street.

Half an hour south of Vicksburg, **Port Gibson** was the site of another epic Civil War battle as well as home base of the **Rabbit Foot Minstrels**, an all-black vaudeville company that helped spread blues across the South and is honored by a historical market in the city. Port Gibson's architectural gems include the grandiose **Claiborne County Courthouse** and the 1892 **Gemiluth Chassed** synagogue, a Moorish Revival style structure that's the state's oldest place of Jewish worship.

From Port Gibson, road trippers can continue south on Highway 61 or the adjacent **Natchez Trace Parkway**; the two come together again in riverside **Natchez** with its abundant antebellum mansions. The flamboyant homes offer stark contrast to the city's **Forks of the Road Monument** on the site of a former slave market and the **Rhythm Night Club Memorial Museum** at the place where the popular blues and jazz dance hall burned to the ground in 1940 at the cost of more than 200 lives.

Around 40 miles (64.4 km) south of Natchez, Highway 61 rolls into Louisiana on a stretch that includes historic plantations like the **Myrtles, Rosedown**, and **Oakley**, all now impressive home and garden museums. **Baton Rouge** boasts two strikingly different state capitol buildings and the sprawling campus of **Louisiana State University**. Yet by this point in the road trip, you're really yearning for the Big Easy, another 80 miles (128.8 km) down the road.

Those in a rush can hop onto Interstate 10. But anyone humming delta blues as they cruise will want to stick to Highway 61 all the way into **New Orleans**. The city's music scene still swirls around the **French Quarter**, with legendary spots like **Preservation Hall** presenting live Dixieland jazz in a venue that seems little changed since the 19th century.

Learn more about the local music scene—and catch some live tunes—at the **New Orleans Jazz Museum** in the Old U.S. Mint building. Or cruise the music clubs along nearby **Frenchmen Street**, places like the **Spotted Cat, Blue Nile**, and **Snug Harbor** that keep the notes flowing until well after midnight. ■

See cultural memorabilia at the Biedenharn Coca-Cola Museum in Vicksburg, MS.

# Marching Across Georgia

## Tennessee & Georgia

Tracing Sherman's route from the Appalachians to the Atlantic Ocean, this journey through southern history features Civil War battlefields, antebellum towns, and various aspects of modern Georgia—from a presidential peanut farmer to telegenic zombies.

In 1864, Union major general William Tecumseh Sherman devised a bold plan to cleave the Confederate States of America by marching across Georgia to the sea. The first half of his march—from Chattanooga to Atlanta—was called the Atlanta campaign. The second half, from Georgia's capital city to Savannah, has been immortalized as Sherman's March to the Sea. His brutal scorched-earth policies are still detested by many southerners.

One of the linchpins of the Civil War, Chattanooga in southwestern Tennessee is surrounded by famous battlefields, including Lookout Mountain and Chickamauga, both of them now part of the **Chicka-mauga and Chattanooga National Military Park**. Although neither battle involved Sherman, they set the stage for his invasion of Georgia.

Interstate 75 runs southeast from

### THE BIG PICTURE

**Distance:** 500 miles (804.7 km) from Chattanooga, TN, to Savannah, GA

**Drive time:** 5 days

**Best overnights:** Atlanta, Warm Springs, Americus

**Best seasons:** Anytime

**Highlights:** Chickamauga, Kennesaw Mountain National Battlefield Park, Atlanta, FDR's Warm Springs, Andersonville Prison

Chattanooga into the heart of the southernmost Appalachians. Dalton makes a great starting point for those who want to explore the highlands on the short **George Disney Trail** (2.4 miles/3.9 km) or more challenging walks along the 25 miles (40.2 km) of hiking, biking, and horseback trails in **Fort Mountain State Park**.

Battlefields, cemeteries, monuments, and other Civil War sites are scattered along the interstate in northwestern Georgia, including **Kennesaw Mountain National Battlefield Park** and its excellent visitor center museum. The battlefield hovers above **Marietta**, where the *Gone with the Wind* **Movie Museum** displays original costumes and scripts in antebellum Brumby Hall mansion.

Sherman famously burned **Atlanta** to the ground. But the city rebounded into the metropolis of the New South, now a vibrant city of more than five million souls, with a thriving economy and an energetic social scene. Among its many high points are the **Martin Luther King Jr. National Historic Park**; the excellent **Georgia Aquarium** and its 120,000 aquatic creatures; the **Atlanta History Center** with its three museums and 22 acres (8.9 ha) of gardens and trails; history and hiking at **Stone Mountain Park**; and the **Margaret Mitchell House**,

Visit FDR's Little White House, where he retreated for solace from his polio.

The Georgia Aquarium in Atlanta houses more than 100,000 animals, including whale sharks, beluga whales, and sea lions.

where the author penned her classic *Gone with the Wind*.

State Route 85 runs due south from Atlanta into the heart of *Walking Dead* country, home base for the long-running zombie TV show. The cute little town of **Senoia** (Se-noy) is home to Riverwood Studios and show spin-offs like the **Woodbury Shoppe**.

Another 40 minutes down the road is **Warm Springs**, where Franklin D. Roosevelt sought solace and treatment for his polio from 1924 until his death in 1945. **Roosevelt's Little White House** is preserved as a state historic site.

There's more presidential history near **Americus**, where the **Jimmy Carter National Historic Site** in Plains features his boyhood home and artifact-packed former high school. Over on the east side of Americus, **Andersonville National Historic Site** revolves around the Civil War's more notorious prisoner-of-war camp and the **National Prisoner of War Museum**.

Turning right out of Andersonville, State Route 26 makes its way into **Warner Robins**, where the **U.S. Air Force Museum of Aviation** displays more than 70 military aircraft ranging from bombers and fighters to helicopters and the legendary SR-71A Blackbird spy plane.

From there, I-16 makes it easy to reach Savannah, 160 miles (257.5 km) to the east. Sherman's troops marched a little north of where the modern interstate runs. Hop off the freeway at Statesboro to visit the **Garden of the Coastal Plain** and **Center for Wildlife Education** at Georgia Southern University. One more hour of driving and you're arriving at historic **Savannah** with its celebrated dining and nightlife scene. ■

### ART AVENUES

- **Best Books:** *Sherman's March* by Burke Davis; *A Full Life* by Jimmy Carter; *Midnight in the Garden of Good and Evil* by John Berendt

- **Best Movies:** *Gone with the Wind* (1939); *Andersonville* (1996); *Warm Springs* (2005)

- **Best TV Shows:** *The Walking Dead*; *Dukes of Hazzard*; *Atlanta*

- **Best Music:** *Ray Charles Greatest Hits* (1962 edition); *The Bluegrass Album* by Alan Jackson; and anything by the B-52's

# Country Music Roads

## Virginia & Kentucky

American country music was born and bred along the Crooked Road in western Virginia and U.S. Highway 23 in eastern Kentucky, a route that crosses the Appalachians and features harmonious history, melodious festivals, and live music.

### THE BIG PICTURE

**Distance:** 430 miles (692 km) from Roanoke, VA, to Ashland, KY

**Drive time:** 5-6 days

**Best overnights:** Galax, Abingdon, Bristol, Pikeville, Ashland

**Best seasons:** Spring, summer, or fall

**Highlights:** Blue Ridge Institute, Floyd Country Store, Rex Theater, Carter Family Fold, Ralph Stanley Museum, Butcher Hollow, Paramount Theater

Nashville may be "Music City, U.S.A." but the origins of American country, bluegrass, folk, and mountain music are firmly rooted in the Appalachians. Virginia and Kentucky honor that legacy with musical routes through the mountains.

Meandering through 19 counties and more than 50 towns, Virginia's **Crooked Road** kicks off in Roanoke with a half-hour run down U.S. Highway 220 to Rocky Mount and the new **Harvester Performance Center**, with its year-round slate of country and folk artists.

Just up the road (Highway 40) is Ferrum, where the **Blue Ridge Institute and Museum** spotlights the folk heritage of the Blue Ridge region through exhibits, concerts, and a working farm.

Continue along the Crooked Road to Floyd, where the legendary **Country Store** presents the Friday Night Jamboree of old-time music, cloggers, and flatfoot dancers. Around the corner on Main Street, the **County Sales record shop** boasts the world's largest selection of bluegrass and regional folk tunes.

U.S. 221 takes the route to Galax and two live music venues: the **Blue Ridge Music Center and Museum** (run by the National Park Service as part of the Blue Ridge Parkway) and the **Historic Rex Theater**, which stages a live radio show with bluegrass and old-time music every Friday night.

Cruise the interstate or Highway 58 to Abingdon to the **Birthplace of Country Music Museum** and **Ernie Ford House** in Bristol on the Virginia-Tennessee state line. The Crooked Road continues to Hiltons, where the **Carter Family Fold** features a rustic performance venue and log cabin where family patriarch A. P. Carter was born in 1891.

A sharp right at Duffield takes the route into U.S. Highway 23 for the rest of the run-up to the Ohio River. The last stop in Virginia is Clintwood, where the **Ralph Stanley Museum and Traditional Mountain Music Center** looks back at the life and music of the legendary bluegrass picker.

Crossing the state line at Pound Gap, U.S. 23 morphs into Kentucky's **Country Music Highway** as

Stop by Loretta Lynn's Homeplace in Butcher Hollow, Kentucky.

See live performances at the Floyd Country Store on your way through Virginia's Blue Ridge Mountains.

it meanders through the old coal country to Pikeville. Although best known for the Hatfield and McCoy feud—visit the **Big Sandy Heritage Center Museum** and **Dils Cemetery** to learn more about that—Pikeville also presents A-list country music stars at the 7,000-seat **Eastern Kentucky Expo Center**.

Farther up U.S. 23 are **Betsy Layne** (Dwight Yoakum's hometown) and **Loretta Lynn's Homeplace at Butcher Hollow**, where the Queen of Country Music was born in 1932. The **Country Music Highway Museum** in nearby Paintsville presents Front Porch Pickin' bluegrass and dancing every Thursday evening.

Thirty miles (48.3 km) north of Paintsville, the oddball **Kentucky Paveillon at Falls Creek** does triple duty as a gas station, ice cream parlor, and roadside country music museum.

The highway reaches the Ohio River near **Ashland**, one of the oldest towns on the western side of the Appalachians and a longtime country music lodestone. Catch lives acts at the historic **Paramount Theater** and browse exhibits about the Judds, Billy Ray Cyrus, and other locally born stars at the **Highlands Museum and Discovery Center**. ∎

## PIT STOPS

- **Old Fiddlers Convention:** Started in 1935, the world's oldest and largest fiddlers' event takes over Galax, Virginia, the second week of August. oldfiddlersconvention.com

- **Blue Ridge Folklife Festival:** Mules, horses, tractors, moonshiners, crafts, and 21 hours of music on three stages are part of this October fest in Ferrum, Virginia. ferrum.edu/blue-ridge-folklife-festival

- **Roots of American Music Concert Series:** Blue Ridge Music Center in Galax, Virginia, hosts major bluegrass, country, and old-time music acts every Saturday night between Memorial and Labor Days. blueridgemusiccenter.org

- **Kentucky Apple Festival:** Loretta Lynn's apple turnovers, Wynonna Judd's applesauce cake, and Dolly Parton's apple stack cake are just three of the treats at this August get-together in Paintsville, Kentucky. kyapplefest.org

- **Poage Landing Days:** The Ed Haley Fiddle Fest is just one part of this September tribute to the family that founded Ashland, Kentucky, in 1786. poagelandingdays.com

# The Forgotten Coast

## Florida

The Sunshine State boasts a lot of terrific coastal areas. Yet one of Florida's most alluring shores flies beneath the radar—the Forgotten Coast between Tallahassee and Panama City—a journey through the swamps, sand dunes, and seaports of Florida's Big Bend region.

**THE BIG PICTURE**

**Distance:** 135 miles (217.3 km) from Tallahassee to Panama City

**Drive time:** 1-2 days

**Best overnights:** Apalachicola, Port St. Joe, Mexico Beach

**Best seasons:** Fall or winter

**Highlights:** Wakulla Springs, St. Marks, St. George Island, Apalachicola, St. Joseph Peninsula

Residents of Florida's Big Bend region call their home the Forgotten Coast because it always seems to take a backseat to the state's more popular beach areas. And that's fine by them. It will be for you too, because it's the quiet beaches, pristine wetlands, old-time seafood eateries, and lack of mega-resorts that make this drive such a refreshing escape.

Florida's **Old State Capitol** (erected in 1845) and the **Museum of Florida History** are worth a look in downtown Tallahassee before heading south on Monroe Street (Highway 373) into the wilds that still cover so much of the panhandle. Half an hour south of the capital, **Wakulla Springs State Park** is your close encounter of the nature kind where you can swim, hike, or hop a scenic boat cruise through cypress wetlands inhabited by gators, numerous bird species, and even manatees.

More nature awaits at nearby **St. Marks National Wildlife Refuge**, where 150 miles (241.4 km) of roads, levees, and trails lead to remote wetlands areas and the historic **St. Mark's Lighthouse** (1842) overlooking the Gulf of Mexico. Inquire about interpretive activities at the refuge visitor center. **Palmetto Expeditions** offers guided paddle tours on the Wakulla, St. Marks, and other local rivers.

From St. Marks, head west on U.S. Highway 98—aka the **Big Bend Scenic Byway**—and another rendezvous with the Gulf shore near **Bald Point State Park** and its 18 miles (29 km) of hiking and biking trails, canoeing, kayaking, and shore fishing. The adjacent **Alligator Point** peninsula is a hub for deep-sea fishing or catamaran cruises on the Gulf with **Allegro Sailing**.

The scenic byway continues along the coast to **Carrabelle**—home of the **World's Smallest Police Station**—and onward to **Eastpoint** and the **Apalachicola National Estuarine Research Reserve Nature Center**, where aquariums house Gulf, bay, and river habitats with local flora and fauna.

Across Apalachicola Bay, St. George is the largest of the region's barrier islands with 28 miles (45.1 km) of white-sand beaches often

Wakulla Springs State Park protects 6,000 acres (2,428.1 ha) of wildlife.

Pelicans and shorebirds gather on a sandy peninsula in Bald Point State Park on the Ochlockonee Bay.

ranked among the nation's best. Loggerhead turtles lay their eggs on the isle between May and October. **St. George Island State Park** offers birding, biking, boat ramps, and beachside camping.

**John Gorrie Memorial Bridge** leaps from Eastpoint to **Apalachicola**, the unofficial capital of the Forgotten Coast. Founded as an early19th-century British trading post, Apalachicola grew into a thriving fishing port and commercial center, as well as the home of air-conditioning pioneer and ice machine inventor John Gorrie.

With more than **900 historic structures** and shrimp boats docked along the downtown waterfront, Apalachicola offers a sense of old Florida. Among its many landmarks are **Trinity Episcopal Church** and historic **Orman House** (both built in 1838) as well as the **Apalachicola Maritime Museum** and the **Dixie**

**Theater** (1913) with its year-round slate of theater, music, and movies.

The Forgotten Coast bottoms out at **Cape San Blas** and the **St. Joseph Peninsula**, where visitors have a chance to wander among coastal dunes, talcum-powder-fine beaches,

and wetlands with copious bird species and marine life. Slowly curving to the northwest, Highway 98 runs through **Port St. Joe**—with its multiple options for fishing and water-sport activities—and **Mexico Beach** before breezing into **Panama City**. ■

---

## PIT STOPS

• **Forgotten Coast en Plein Air:** Among the world's top landscape painting festivals, this 10-day May event features exhibitions, demonstrations, guest speakers, and renowned landscape artists from around the world in Port St. Joe and Apalachicola. forgottencoastcultural coalition.wildapricot.org

• **Running for the Bay Marathon:** This October event takes runners across John Gorrie Memorial Bridge on a long-distance course that spans Apalachicola and Eastpoint. The race includes full, half, and ultra

marathons, plus 5K and 10K options. runningforthebay.com

• **St. Marks Stone Crab and Monarch Butterfly Festivals:** The town throws a seafood fest while the wildlife refuge showcases its migrating monarchs on the same October weekend. stmarksstonecrabfest .com; fws.gov/refuge/st_marks

• **Florida Seafood Festival:** Live music, carnival rides, arts and crafts, and fresh seafood are the main attractions of this November tradition in Apalachicola. floridaseafood festival.com

# Sea Island Shuffle

## South Carolina, Georgia & Florida

Remote islands, secluded sands, and fabled seaports provide the stepping-stones for a journey along the South Carolina and Georgia coast to places that often seem like something from long ago rather than 21st-century America.

In antebellum times, the islands and coastal lowlands of Georgia and South Carolina were dominated by rice, indigo, and long-staple cotton plantations, home to wealthy landowners and thousands of slaves.

When many of the plantation owners failed to return after the Civil War, their newly freed slaves claimed the abandoned land. For more than a century, they lived in isolation, developing a unique subculture that blends African and European tradi-

tions. Called Gullah in South Carolina and Geechee in Georgia, their hybrid heritage endures.

The Sea Islands blend aspects of these diverse traditions: the Old South that continues to thrive in Charleston and Savannah and the unique African-American culture that endures on the more isolated islands.

Sprawling across a thumb-shaped peninsula in the Low Country of South Carolina, old and venerable **Charleston** anchors the northern end

of this road trip. Founded in 1670 by the British, the city offers colonial and antebellum relics, legendary Civil War sites, and a panache that makes Charleston one of the belles of southern culture past and present.

Charleston's past is reflected in various ways, including the **Historic Charleston City Market** where 300 vendors offer traditional Low Country arts and crafts. Historic homes like the **Calhoun Mansion** (built in 1876), **Aiken-Rhett House** (1818), and **Russell House** (1808) are open for guided tours, while the eclectic **Charleston Museum** offers everything from ancient Egyptian artifacts to colonial and early American relics.

The city's most iconic attraction lies in the middle of the harbor—**Fort Sumter National Monument,** where the first shots of the Civil War were fired in 1860. The only way to reach the island is by ferry from the park's visitor center on **Aquarium Pier.** Arriving on the heavily fortified island, join a ranger-led tour.

U.S. Highway 17 bids adieu to Charleston on the old **Ashley River Drawbridge** (opened 1926). On the other side, **Charles Towne Landing State Historic Site** preserves the spot where English settlers founded the city. The eclectic park features every-

Find traditional sweet grass baskets for sale in Charleston's Old City Market.

A cannon sits at Fort Frederica, built by James Oglethorpe and used to defend against the Spanish from 1736 to 1748.

thing from archaeological exhibits and a replica 17th-century sailing ship to an 1840s plantation house and an **Animal Forest** with bison, black bears, mountain lions, and other creatures that would have roamed colonial Carolina.

Continuing into the wetlands that characterize much of the Carolina coast, Highway 17 runs across the **ACE Basin**—a combined watershed of Ashepoo, Combahee, and Edisto Rivers that harbors one of the largest undeveloped estuaries along the eastern seaboard. Bone up on basin flora and fauna at the **Caw Caw Interpretive Center** in Ravenel before visiting the **Hollings ACE Basin National Wildlife Refuge** and the seaside **Botany Bay Plantation Heritage Preserve** on **Edisto Island**.

Several outfitters offer watercraft adventures in the ACE Basin, including **Coastal Expeditions** (guided kayaking tours), **Botany Bay Eco-tours** (dolphin encounters and remote island excursions), and **Edisto Saltwater Tours** (wildlife cruises).

The south side of the ACE Basin is framed by St. Helena Sound and **Port Royal Island**, named by a 1562 expedition that established the first French settlement on American soil. The waterfront of **Beaufort**, the island's largest town, is laced with restaurants, art galleries, and mansions.

Adjacent **St. Helena Island** nurtures Gullah culture through the **Penn Center** museum, the old **Brick Church** (built 1855), and the tiny **Coffin Point Praise House**. Sea Island Parkway runs across the island to the pristine beach and historic

---

## LAY YOUR HEAD

• **HarbourView Inn:** Waterfront rooms and a cool roof terrace are two of the charms of this boutique hotel in Charleston's historic district; bar, bikes, nightly special events; from $234. harbourviewcharleston.com

• **Cuthbert House Inn:** This historic riverside B&B once served as headquarters for the Yankee general who captured Beaufort during the Civil War; garden, loaner bikes, southern-style breakfast; from $205. cuthbert houseinn.com

• **Mansion on Forsyth Park:** Swank digs in a red-brick Romanesque "castle" in Savannah's historic district; restaurant, bar, cooking school, spa, fitness center, outdoor pool; from $179. marriott.com

• **Greyfield Inn:** Romance on remote Cumberland Island in a turn-of-the-20th-century mansion still run by heirs of the Carnegie family; dining room, bar, naturalist hikes, fishing, boating, bikes, and beach equipment; from $525. greyfieldinn.com

lighthouse of **Hunting Island State Park**. South of Beaufort, civilians can visit the **U.S. Marine Corps Museum** on Parris Island.

Thirty miles (48.3 km) farther south (along Routes 170 and 278), **Hilton Head Island** renders a completely different take on southern comfort. This well-heeled retreat revolves around golf courses, tennis courts, and resort hotels scattered along 12 miles (19.3 km) of white-sand beach. After dark, the island's **Arts Center of Coastal Carolina** offers concerts, plays, and other special events.

Crossing into Georgia, the road trip cruises into charming, cultivated, and mysterious **Savannah**. Founded in 1733 as the capital of Britain's Georgia colony, the city harbors America's largest **National Historic Landmark District**, featuring more than 100 city blocks of mansions, monuments, museums, and a seemingly endless selection of places to eat, drink, and be merry.

It's best to park your car and explore the city center on foot, lingering in the lovely squares or benches arrayed along **River Walk**. Many old mansions are open to the public, including the **Owens-Thomas House** with its preserved slave quarters and the **Mercer-Williams House** of *Midnight in the Garden of Good and Evil* fame. After dark, catch a concert or play at the **Historic Savannah Theatre** or take a ghost tour of old **Bonaventure Cemetery**.

An hour south of Savannah on I-95, a turnoff for State Route 99 leads to the visitor center for **Sapelo Island**, one of the last authentic Geechee settlements along the Georgia coast. Guided tours of the island, which start with a 20-minute ferry

Tour the Mercer-Williams House (1868) and museum in Savannah, Georgia.

ride across Doboy Sound, include the village of **Hog Hammock**, the 1890s **First African Baptist Church** at Raccoon Bluff, and the ruins of the 18th-century **Chocolate Plantation**, the walls of which are constructed with Sea Island "tabby"—a mixture of sand, lime, shells, and broken pottery.

Highway 17 makes its way back to the coast for the drive down to **Brunswick**. In addition to a historic district filled with landmark buildings, the city is renowned for shrimp, clams, and other seafood delights.

The beaches, golf courses, and seaside resorts of **Jekyll** and **St. Simons Islands** lie just across the sound from Brunswick. And there's plenty of history in the wetlands that surround the city. **Hofwyl-Broadfield State Historic Site** revolves around an antebellum rice plantation founded in 1806, while **Fort Frederica National Monument** preserves the ruins of an early 18th-century British stronghold that helped repel a Spanish invasion of Georgia.

The vertiginous Sydney Lanier Bridge takes the route back to I-95 and a 40-mile (64.4-km) drive to **St. Marys**, which does double duty as a

submarine base and gateway to Georgia's largest and wildest insular possession. **Cumberland Island National Seashore** safeguards maritime forest, wetlands, rolling dunes, and a 16-mile-long (25.8 km) beach. From sea turtles, horseshoe crabs, and alligators to bobcats, armadillos, and feral horses, the island also shelters a range of creatures great and small.

If you don't have your own boat, the only way to reach Cumberland is the ferry from the park's visitor center in **St. Marys**. Those who don't stay overnight on the island can join a ranger-led **Lands and Legacies** tour or explore the island on foot or bikes.

Although nature is the island's main attraction, Cumberland also boasts man-made landmarks like the 19th-century **First African Baptist Church** where John F. Kennedy, Jr., and Carolyn Bessette were married, the ruins of **Dungeness Mansion**, and a Carnegie vacation home, **Plum Orchard**, restored to its Edwardian-era elegance.

Back on the Georgia mainland, it's less than an hour's drive down I-95 to **Jacksonville, Florida**, and the end of the Sea Islands road trip. ∎

## EN ROUTE EATS

- **Circa 1886:** African peanut soup, grilled cheese with ham and caviar, and Huguenot torte soufflé count among the inventive dishes at this elegant Low Country eatery. 149 Wentworth St., Charleston, SC. circa1886.com

- **Saltus River Grill:** A patio overlooking the water complements the raw bar, sushi menu, and fresh fish at this hip seafood grill. 802 Bay St., Beaufort, SC. saltusrivergrill.com

- **Gullah Grub:** She-crab soup, fried shark strips, shrimp gumbo, and sweet potato pie are favorites at this

renowned restaurant on St. Helena Island. 877 Sea Island Pkwy., Frogmore, SC. gullahgrub.com

- **Signe's Heaven Bound Bakery:** Locals swear by the deep-dish French toast, Swedish butter buns, shrimp and grits, and other all-day breakfast treats. 93 Arrow Rd., Hilton Head, SC. signesbakery.com

- **Georgia Sea Grill:** Crab-stuffed hushpuppies, cornmeal-dusted oysters, and shrimp corndogs take seafood to a whole new level at this island eatery. 407 Mallery St., St. Simons, GA. georgiaseagrill.com

# Piedmont Passage

## North Carolina, South Carolina & Georgia

The rambling foothills of the Carolinas and northeastern Georgia are the focus of a road trip through the fabled Piedmont region, an area rich in military history, outdoor adventure, and stunning views.

**THE BIG PICTURE**

**Distance:** ca 330 miles (531.1 km) from Charlotte, NC, to Atlanta, GA

**Drive time:** 7 days

**Best overnights:** Spartanburg, Brevard, Sapphire, Clayton, Gainesville

**Best seasons:** Spring, summer, or fall

**Highlights:** Kings Mountain, Cowpens, Spartanburg, Caesars Head, Brevard, Gorges SP, Chattooga River, Tallulah Falls

Wedged between the Appalachians and the Atlantic coastal plain, the Piedmont Plateau is a celebrated slice of the Southeast. Originally the heart of the Cherokee Nation, the region's rich soil and thick woods attracted European settlers who would help the 13 colonies win their independence.

**Charlotte, North Carolina,** is the starting point for this passage across the Piedmont. Interstate 85 heads west to **Crowders Mountain State Park** with its rugged terrain, rock climbing, backcountry camping, and diverse hiking trails.

Along the same ridgeline, **Kings Mountain National Military Park** in South Carolina is where one of the pivotal battles of the American Revolution played out in 1780.

Sixteen miles (25.8 km) farther down I-85 is the turnoff for another Revolutionary War site—**Cowpens National Battlefield**—where the Americans won another decisive victory over the redcoats.

Founded in 1785 and named after one of the patriot regiments that fought at Cowpens, nearby **Spartanburg** preserves its past in the historic buildings of **Morgan Square** and **Hampton Heights**, as well as the **Walnut Grove Plantation** and the **Hub City Railroad Museum**.

Climbing even higher into the Piedmont, a drive along I-26 and the **Cherokee Foothills National Scenic Highway** (Route 11) takes road-trippers to **Mountain Bridge Wilderness Area**. Set along the rocky, wooded peaks of the Blue Ridge Escarpment, the 13,000-acre (5,260.9 ha) reserve harbors two popular state parks: **Caesars Head** and **Jones Gap**. South Carolina's largest network of trails takes hikers to waterfalls, lakes, and lofty granite outcrops with panoramic views.

Make your way through the Devils Kitchen in Caesars Head park, South Carolina.

Visit Tallulah Gorge State Park and its 1,000-foot (304.8 m) chasm and stunning eponymous waterfall.

Coming down from Caesars Head, U.S. Highway 276 takes the route back into North Carolina and the funky little town of **Brevard**, renowned for road and mountain biking and the varied outdoor pursuits of neighboring **Pisgah National Forest**.

Beyond Brevard, Highway 64 leads to **Gorges State Park**. Established in 1999, this new park offers a mosaic of peaks and valleys explored along 10 major trails, plus a new state-of-the-art **Visitor Center** with exhibits and ranger programs on wildlife.

The road trip continues on NC 281 to **Whitewater Falls** and a turnoff for SC 107, which meanders back down to South Carolina. Stop at **Oconee State Park** and the town of **Mountain Rest** for guided rafting trips on the **Chattooga National Wild and Scenic River**.

Follow Chattooga Ridge Road to U.S. Highway 76 and leap across the river into northeastern Georgia. Take a left onto U.S. 23 in Clayton and cruise down to **Tallulah Gorge State Park**. The 1,000-foot-deep (304.8 m) "Grand Canyon of the South"—where some of the key scenes from the movie *Deliverance* were filmed—features five waterfalls and a spectacular gorge trail with a pedestrian suspension bridge.

From Tallulah Gorge, it's a straight shot to **Atlanta** on Highway 23 and Interstate 985 that takes around two hours to drive. ∎

## SCENIC DETOURS

• **Overmountain Victory National Historic Trail:** Starting from Kings Mountain and Cowpens, this commemorative motor route links Revolutionary War sites across Virginia, South and North Carolina, and Tennessee.

• **Forest Heritage National Scenic Byway:** This 76-mile (122.3 km) loop through Pisgah National Forest kicks off from Brevard, NC.

• **Waterfalls Scenic Byway:** More than 100 cascades tumble beside U.S. Highway 64 as it makes its way across the Appalachians between Gorges State Park and Murphy, NC.

• **Savannah River National Scenic Byway:** A hundred miles (106.9 km) of farms, forests, lakes, and small towns highlight this route between Seneca, SC, and Augusta, GA.

• **Russell-Brasstown National Scenic Byway:** Set in Chattahoochee-Oconee National Forest to the west of Tallulah Gorge, this 40-mile (64.4 km) loop offers two places where you can hike the Appalachian Trail.

# African American Heritage Trail
## Washington, D.C., to Louisiana

This nearly 1,200-mile (1,931 km) drive through African-American history features landmarks in five states between Washington, D.C., and New Orleans that highlight the black experience in America over the course of more than 300 years.

V arious cities, states, and regions boast African-American heritage drives or routes, and the National Park Service devotes an entire section of its website to a patchwork of historic sites and national monuments significant to black history and culture. Still, there isn't a national heritage trail that unites these pivotal places in a single trip. That doesn't mean there can't be. We've mapped the route for you.

Unveiled in 2016, the **National Museum of African American History and Culture** in the nation's capital offers a natural starting point for the journey with its 37,000 historical artifacts, documents, sounds, and images. Among its many relics are items owned by Harriet Tubman

and Nat Turner, a slave cabin, a segregated railcar, a guard tower from Angola Prison in Louisiana, and a Tuskegee Airmen biplane.

Washington, D.C., is flush with other African-American tributes, including the stately **Cedar Hill** House where Frederick Douglass lived, the **African American Civil War Museum**, and **Bethune Council House**, where educator and stateswoman Mary McLeod Bethune advanced the causes of African-American women.

The **Lincoln Memorial** is pivotal not just as a monument to the president who signed the Emancipation Proclamation, but also the place where Dr. Martin Luther King, Jr., delivered his immortal "I Have a Dream" speech in 1968. King's own **memorial statue** sits nearby on the banks of the Tidal Basin. And 19 different neighborhoods, including Georgetown and Dupont Circle, in the District offer their own African-American heritage trails.

Roughly 120 miles (193 km) southwest of Washington, D.C., lies Thomas Jefferson's **Monticello** plantation. Completed just before the American Revolution, the Virginia estate encompassed both commercial

A Tuskegee Airman plane in Washington, D.C.'s African-American history museum

The Martin Luther King Jr. Memorial was opened in 2011 in West Potomac Park next to the National Mall.

tobacco fields and the future president's experimental crop gardens— worked by around 400 slaves. Today Monticello offers exhibits and guided tours on slavery at the plantation and on Sally Hemings, a Monticello slave who was most likely Jefferson's longtime companion.

**Booker T. Washington National Monument** lies another two hours to the south, near Roanoke in the Appalachian foothills. Ranger-led guided tours and living history demonstrations headline an old tobacco farm where the famed orator and author was born into slavery in 1856.

U.S. Highway 220 crosses the state line into North Carolina and the city of **Greensboro**, which became a focal point of the civil rights movement. The **International Civil Rights Center and Museum** preserves the Woolworth's department store whites-only lunch counter where four African-American students staged a 1960

sit-in to spark desegregation in the southern city. On the eastern outskirts of Greensboro, the **Charlotte Hawkins Brown Museum** in Sedalia recalls the life of the groundbreaking African-American educator who founded a school on the site in 1902.

From Greensboro, it's only 90

minutes along I-85 to **Charlotte** and the **Harvey B. Gantt Center for African-American Arts + Culture**. Through art, lectures, workshops, films, and live performances, the center showcases the contributions of both Africans and African Americans to American culture. The building is an artwork all on its own, a modern

---

### ART AVENUES

• **Nonfiction:** *Narrative of the Life of Frederick Douglass, an American Slave* by Frederick Douglass; *Up from Slavery* by Booker T. Washington; *The Autobiography of Martin Luther King, Jr.* by Martin Luther King, Jr., and Clayborne Carson

• **Fiction:** *The Color Purple* by Alice Walker; *Roots: The Saga of an American Family* by Alex Haley; *The Help* by Kathryn Stockett; *The Autobiography of Miss Jane Pittman* by

Ernest J. Gaines; *To Kill a Mockingbird* by Harper Lee

• **Movies:** *In the Heat of the Night* (1967); *Mississippi Burning* (1988); *Malcolm X* (1992); *Ghosts of Mississippi* (1996); *12 Years a Slave* (2013); *Selma* (2014), *BlacKkKlansman* (2018)

• **Documentaries:** *Eyes on the Prize* (1987-90); *Scottsboro: An American Tragedy* (2001); *February One* (2003); *Breaking the Huddle: The Integration of College Football* (2008); *The Loving Story* (2011)

Dr. King preached at the Dexter Avenue Memorial Baptist Church in Montgomery.

steel-and-glass masterpiece opened in 2009.

Interstate 85 continues down to **Greenville**, where 13 African-American cultural sites are marked by information signs. These range from several historic Baptist and Methodist churches to the **Bruton-town** neighborhood and the spot where the last lynching in South Carolina took place in 1947.

Another two and a half hours down the interstate lies **Atlanta**, the city at the heart of the civil rights movement. **Dr. Martin Luther King Jr. National Historic Site** features the house where he was born, the **Ebenezer Baptist Church** where he preached, and the tombs of Dr. King and his wife.

In downtown Atlanta, the innovative **Center for Civil and Human Rights** links the African-American experience to struggles happening around the world. Exhibits run a broad gamut from Dr. King's papers and letters to a rogues' gallery of global dictators. For a complete change of pace, the nearby **College**

**Football Hall of Fame** honors the contributions of Jim Brown, Her-

---

### PIT STOPS

• **New Orleans Jazz and Heritage Festival:** This world-class musical extravaganza also features a Louisiana Folklife Village, Food Heritage Stage, and Congo Square African Marketplace; April-May. nojazzfest.com

• **Juneteenth Atlanta Parade and Music Festival:** Three days of music, food, fireworks, and a black history parade celebrate emancipation and African-American accomplishments. juneteenthatl.com

• **National Black Theater Festival:** Winston-Salem, North Carolina, hosts this annual ode to black stage classics and rising African-American playwrights; July-August. ncblackrep.org

• **African American Cultural Festival:** Raleigh and surrounding Wake County in North Carolina offer this Labor Day smorgasbord of art, music, food, and family activities. aacfestival.org

---

schel Walker, Bo Jackson, and other great black athletes.

Leaving Atlanta behind, I-85 slides across the state line into Alabama and two iconic African-American institutions in **Tuskegee**. Founded in 1881 by a former slave, the **Tuskegee Institute** evolved from a teacher-training school into a world-renowned university and scientific research center. The entire campus, designed by the first African-American graduate of MIT, is a national historic site that includes the **Oaks** (home of institute co-founder Booker T. Washington) and the **George Washington Carver Museum**. On the outskirts of town, **Tuskegee Airmen National Historic Site** revolves around two hangar museums beside the field where the legendary black aviators trained for World War II combat missions.

Forty miles (64 km) farther west lies **Montgomery**, which became a focal point of the civil rights movement in 1955 when Rosa Parks refused to give up her bus seat to a white man and Martin Luther King, Jr., helped organize the Montgomery Bus Boycott. Both are the focus of local landmarks: **Rosa Parks Library** and **Rosa Parks Museum** (which includes an actual size replica of that famous bus) and the **Dexter Parsonage Museum** in the home where King lived during his six-year stay in the city.

Alabama's capital city offers many related sights. Among them are the **Freedom Rides Museum** and the **Legacy Museum** at the National Memorial for Peace and Justice; the **Dexter Avenue King Memorial Baptist Church** where King preached; and the nearby **Civil Rights Memorial Center**, which chronicles the history of the civil rights movement.

**Selma to Montgomery National Historic Trail** traces the 54-mile (87 km) route of the 1965 voting rights protest marches. Spread along U.S. Highway 80, interpretive panels tell the story of those fateful events all the way down to the **Edmund Pettus Bridge** in Selma, where Bloody Sunday played out on March 7 of that year. Among Selma's many shrines to the struggle are the trail's **Selma Interpretive Center** and the **National Voting Rights Museum**.

The road trip wraps up in **New Orleans**, one of the nation's oldest cities and one that reflects the incredible diversity of the African-American experience. Owing to the many free people of color who lived there prior to the Civil War, the riverside city offered a striking contrast to the African-American circumstances elsewhere in the nation. Meshed with French and Spanish colonial culture, the local black population of the city has had a profound impact on everything

from food and music to Mardi Gras.

Louisiana's excellent **African American Heritage Trail** includes a number of New Orleans stops such as the **Le Musée de f.p.c.** (Free People of Color Museum), the old slave gathering spot at **Congo Square**, the **McKenna Museum of African-American Art**, and the "high rise" **St. Louis Cemeteries No. 1 and 2**, where many of the city's prominent African Americans are buried, including "Voodoo Queen" Marie Laveau and New Orleans mayor Ernest "Dutch" Morial.

A great way to round off the trip is by listening to traditional New Orleans jazz—largely pioneered by black musicians like Louis Armstrong, Jelly Roll Morton, and King Oliver—at **Preservation Hall** or the **New Orleans Jazz Museum**. ∎

Powerful civil rights history exhibits are offered at the Rosa Parks Library and Museum in Montgomery, Alabama.

# Razorback Run

## Arkansas

This zigzag journey across Arkansas takes in many landmarks, from the wild Ouachita Mountains and storied Ozark Plateau to historic bathhouses, bass-fishing hot spots, melodious mountain towns, and the mines that give the Diamond State its nickname.

Legend holds that Spanish explorer Hernando de Soto brought the first hogs to Arkansas on his 16th-century journey across the South. Some went wild, transformed into vicious beasts that American pioneers dubbed razorbacks on account of their attitude and bristly coat.

Even if you don't come across feral pigs on this 340-mile (547.2 km) meander across Arkansas, you're bound to meet fans of the university football team that adopted the wild hog moniker in 1910.

Start your razorback run from **Texarkana** with a journey along Interstate 30 to **Hope**, birthplace of Bill Clinton and Mike Huckabee. **President Clinton's boyhood home** is the town's top attraction.

Nearby Washington was a popu-

## THE BIG PICTURE

**Distance:** 340 miles (547.2 km) from Texarkana to Mountain View

**Drive time:** 4-5 days

**Best overnights:** Mount Ida, Russellville, Jasper, Mountain View

**Best seasons:** Spring, summer, or fall

**Highlights:** Historic Washington, Crater of Diamonds, Lake Ouachita, Buffalo National River, Ozark Folk Center

lar stopover on the 19th-century Southwest Trail to Texas and the Arkansas state capital during the Civil War. **Historic Washington State Park** preserves a number of buildings and relics from that era, including the majestic **County Courthouse** and 1832 **Williams Tavern**.

A combination of U.S. Highway 278 and State Route 27 leads to **Murfreesboro** and **Crater of Diamonds State Park**—the world's only public diamond mine. Visitors have discovered more than 33,000 of the glittery gems (which they are free to take home) since the park opened in 1972 on the site of an ancient volcano.

Route 27 carries the road into the rugged **Ouachita Mountains** of central Arkansas, where the town of **Mount Ida** offers **rock-hound shops, crystal mines,** and the **Front Porch Stage** with its free folk music concerts between May and October.

Nearby **Lake Ouachita** ("Striped Bass Capital of the World") is a haven for all kinds of outdoor sports, from hiking and biking its shoreline trails to **fishing, power boating, paddling,** and **snorkeling** or **scuba diving** its incredibly clear waters.

From Mount Ida, Route 27

A woman demonstrates basket weaving to visitors at Ozark Folk Center State Park.

Mount Magazine State Park offers a hiking trail that leads to sprawling views of the Ozarks at its summit.

snakes its way north through the Ouachitas to **Danville** and a turnoff to **Mount Magazine State Park**, the highest point in Arkansas at 2,753 feet (839.1 m). The route dips down into the **Arkansas River Valley**, with possible stops at **Mount Nebo State Park** and **Holla Bend National Wildlife Refuge** with its copious bird life.

Perched on the river's north bank, **Russellville** offers the **Arkansas River Visitor Center** beside the **Dardanelle Lock and Dam**, the historic **Potts Inn** stagecoach station, and the **Horseshoe Canyon Ranch zip line** for those who need a quick adrenaline rush.

State Route 7 climbs into **Ozark National Forest** with its lofty viewpoints, hiking trails, and old-time **Hankins Country Store** (opened in 1930). Numerous switchbacks take the highway down to **Jasper** and **Buffalo National River**. One of the

last undammed rivers in the lower 48 states, the Buffalo offers 135 miles (217.3 km) of Ozark wilderness with multiple campsites, hiking trails, and canoe trips.

The razorback road trip ends with a two-hour drive to **Mountain View**, cultural hub of the Ozarks and the self-proclaimed

Folk Music Capital of the World. In addition to annual events like the Arkansas Folk Festival, Bluegrass Festival, Iris Festival, and Great Outhouse Race, the town's **Ozark Folk Center State Park** offers an almost year-round slate of live music, craft demonstrations, and folk art classes. ■

---

## SCENIC DETOURS

- **US Highway 270** leads 36 miles (57.9 km) east from Mount Ida to Hot Springs with its historic Bathhouse Row, 47 naturally heated springs, and soothing thermal spa treatments.

- **Sylamore Scenic Byway** (26 miles/41.8 km) runs north from Mountain View into a superscenic portion of the Ozarks that includes Blanchard Springs Caverns in the Ozark–St. Francis National Forest and Calico Rock on the White River.

- **Talimena National Scenic Byway** follows Arkansas Route 88 and Oklahoma Route 1 across the crest of the Ouachita Range, a grand total of 101 miles (162.5 km) if you're driving all the way from Mount Ida, AR, to Talihina, OK.

- **Pig Trail Scenic Byway** starts its vertiginous run in the Arkansas River Valley just upstream from Russellville, a 28-mile (45.1 km) route between Ozark and Brashears deemed one of the nation's best motorcycle rides.

# Red River Road Trip

## TX, OK, AR & LA

Although its significance has waned in modern times, the Red River of the South remains a mighty watercourse. And a road trip along the river from the Texas Panhandle to the Louisiana bayous unlocks human stories and natural wonders unknown to most Americans.

Named for the ruddy soil along much of its course, the Red River is rarely listed among America's great waterways. But once it was one of the nation's most important rivers—a watery boundary between the United States and Mexico prior to the Texas Revolution that Thomas Jefferson deemed a "most interesting water."

The Red River begins as several tributaries flowing across the bleak Llano Estacado plains near **Amarillo** in the Texas Panhandle, including the oddly named Prairie Dog Town Fork that tumbles off an escarpment and down through **Palo Duro Canyon**.

The nation's second largest canyon after that big one in Arizona, Palo Duro stretches 120 miles (193.1 km) from east to west. Once a Comanche hideout and cattle spread owned by legendary rancher Charles Goodnight, the canyon is now an outdoor

**THE BIG PICTURE**

**Distance:** 720 miles (1,158.7 km) from Amarillo, TX, to Natchitoches, LA

**Drive time:** 6-7 days

**Best overnights:** Wichita Falls, Paris, Texarkana

**Best seasons:** Spring or fall

**Highlights:** Palo Duro Canyon, River Bend Nature Center, Showmen's Rest, Shreveport's Red River District, Cane River Creole NHP

playground for **hiking, biking**, and **horseback riding**. It's also the alfresco setting for *Texas*, a musical tribute to Lone Star history staged in the park's Pioneer Amphitheater on summer evenings.

From Amarillo, U.S. Highway 287 runs across the endless West Texas plains to **Vernon**, where the **Red River Valley Museum** illuminates local art and history from the Comanche and Kiowa tribes through the great cattle drives and the music of Roy Orbison, who was born in Vernon.

Another 50 miles (80.5 km) down Highway 287 is **Wichita Falls** and close encounters with living plants and animals that inhabit the Red River Valley at the excellent **River Bend Nature Center**, housed in a giant glasshouse. Wichita Falls is also home to the **Pro Wrestling Hall of Fame and Museum** and the 1908 **Wichita Theater**, a restored art deco gem with a year-round slate of music, drama, dance, and comedy.

Highway 82 tracks the river's south bank to **Lake Texoma**—a great place to swim, fish, or boat—and the town of **Paris**, where a miniature version of the **Eiffel Tower** is topped with a giant red cowboy hat. Drivers can hop across the river to

The Cane River Creole National Park in Natchitoches Parish, Louisiana

Swap car tires for bike tires for a ride on red-dirt trails inside Palo Duro Canyon State Park in Texas.

Hugo, Oklahoma, and **Showmen's Rest**, a cemetery reserved for former circus performers, before continuing on U.S. 82.

Straddling the Texas-Arkansas border, **Texarkana** tenders its own oddball landmarks, including a 1933 beaux arts **post office and courthouse** split by the state line and the **Ace of Clubs House**—allegedly shaped like the playing card symbol because the owner earned the money to build the 1885 Italianate Victorian mansion in a poker game.

Interstate 49 takes the road trip down to **Shreveport**, Louisiana, the last Confederate command to surrender at the end of the Civil War, as well as a hotbed of early African-American jazz and blues. Catch live tunes or local Cajun and Creole cooking at the city's restored **Red River District**. Among other local highlights are narrated **riverboat cruises**; the **Swamp Dragons**, a minor league baseball team; the **American Rose Center** gardens; and **Barksdale Global Power Museum** in neighboring **Bossier City**.

Farther south along the Red River is **Natchitoches**, the oldest town in Louisiana (founded 1714). The city's French, antebellum, and African-American roots are enshrined in the downtown **Historic District** and **Cane River Creole National Historical Park**. Arrayed along a tributary of the Red River, the latter includes the **Magnolia and Oakland plantations** and their gardens.

**Melrose Plantation** near Natchitoches also begs a visit, as do the city's **National Fish Hatchery and Aquarium**, reconstructed **Fort St. Jean Baptiste State Historic Site**, and **Kaffie-Frederick General Mercantile Store** (oldest in Louisiana, established in 1863). ■

### ART AVENUES

• **Best Music:** The *Orbisongs* album by Roy Orbison; *The Midnight Special and Other Southern Prison Songs* by Shreveport's Lead Belly; the ragtime of Texarkana's Scott Joplin

• **Best Movie:** Natchitoches-filmed *Steel Magnolias* (1989)

• **Best Books:** *Lone Star Literature: From the Red River to the Rio Grande* edited by Don Graham, with a foreword by Larry McMurtry; the Louisiana-based novels and short stories of Kate Chopin

• **Best Art:** The vivid Palo Duro paintings of Georgia O'Keeffe

# Wilderness Road

## Virginia, Tennessee & Kentucky

Daniel's Boone's trail-blazing route through the Cumberland Gap makes for an intriguing road trip across three states and through Appalachian hills, dales, and rural towns that time has largely forgotten.

Native Americans traded, raided, and migrated via the Cumberland Gap thousands of years prior to the arrival of the first Europeans. But it was pioneer Daniel Boone and his axmen who immortalized the route when they blazed the Wilderness Road along old Indian tracks in 1775 to advance the colonization of Kentucky.

The modern iteration follows a series of federal and state highways across the Appalachians starting from **Bristol**, a twin city that straddles the Virginia-Tennessee border. Renowned for both its country music and motor racing heritage, Bristol is divided by historic **State Street**, which runs right along the border and kick-starts the Wilderness Road trip.

**Gate City Highway** (U.S. 58/421) takes the route westward up the North Fork of the Holston River

**THE BIG PICTURE**

**Distance:** ca 244 miles (392.7 km) from Bristol, VA, to Lexington, KY

**Drive time:** 2-3 days

**Best overnights:** Kingsport, Middlesboro, London

**Best seasons:** Spring, summer, or fall

**Highlights:** Moccasin Gap, Natural Tunnel, Wilderness Road SP, Cumberland Gap NHP, Levi Jackson SP

and into the Appalachian foothills to **Moccasin Gap** in Virginia, where **Homeplace Mountain Farm and Museum** provides a glimpse into early 19th-century life along the trail through living history programs and original structures from that era. Nearby **Anderson Blockhouse** is a faithful reconstruction of a small log fort that anchored the road's eastern end in pioneer times.

Past **Gate City**, the route leaps watersheds into the Clinch River Valley and **Natural Tunnel State Park**, a massive limestone gap with a railroad line down the middle. Daniel Boone was allegedly the first European to walk the tunnel, a huge tourist attraction in the 1800s. In addition to the thrill of watching a coal train pass through the tunnel, the park features a **Wilderness Road State Park**, visitor center with **exhibits**, **cave tours**, **canoe trips**, and seven **hiking trails** ranging from easy to difficult.

In nearby **Duffield**, hikers can follow an original section of the Wilderness Road through **Kane Gap** along the Daniel Boone section of the **Virginia Bird and Wildlife Trail**.

An hour farther west along U.S. 58 is **Wilderness Road State Park**, which revolves around a reconstruction of **Martin's Station**, a 1769

Scan the skies for the Blackburnian warbler on the Virginia Birding and Wildlife Trail.

Cumberland Gap National Historical Park sits on the borders of Kentucky, Tennessee, and Virginia.

homestead that predates Boone's trailblazing. The park **visitor center** offers exhibits on local human and natural history, as well as interpretive and living history activities. Hikers, bikers, and horseback riders can explore an 8.5-mile (13.7 km) stretch of the **Wilderness Road Trail**, with links to another 50 miles (80.5 km) of the trail outside the park.

A few of those trails and the highway lead to **Cumberland Gap National Historical Park**, which harbors the famous pass and a 20-mile (32.2 km) stretch of mountains astride the Virginia-Tennessee-Kentucky border. In addition to a museum, bookshop, and interpretive movies, **Daniel Boone Visitor Center** gives information on various park activities, among them hiking and backpack camping along 80 miles (128.8 km) of trail, Civil War forts, and ranger tours of **Gap Cave**.

After threading the gap, the **Wilderness Road Heritage Highway** takes the road trip through eastern Kentucky via U.S. Highway 25 and State Route 229. **Levi Jackson Wilderness Road State Park** offers hiking trails along the road's original path, a pioneer cemetery, a reproduction watermill,

and the **Mountain Life Museum** pioneer settlement.

Along its final stretch, the road trip runs across a portion of the **Daniel Boone National Forest**, through the country music–heavy Renfro Valley, and past Berea, a Certified Kentucky Creative District, before ending in Lexington. ■

## SCENIC DETOURS

• **Great Wagon Road:** Interstate 81 and U.S. 11 trace the path of an 18th-century migration route between Winchester and Roanoke, Virginia, via the Shenandoah Valley between the Blue Ridge and Allegheny.

• **Fincastle Turnpike:** Virginia State Routes 42 and 61 (also known as the Fincastle and Blue Ridge Turnpike Company) follow an early 19th-century toll road through the Allegheny foothills between Fincastle

and the Wilderness Road near Moccasin Gap.

• **Carolina Road:** This southern extension of the Great Wagon Road (U.S. 220) links Roanoke, Virginia, and Greensboro, North Carolina, via Maggoty Gap, Rocky Mount, and Martinsville.

• **Logan Trace:** U.S. 150 traces the western branch of the Wilderness Trail between Mount Vernon, Virginia, and Louisville, Kentucky.

# Cruising Cajun Country
## Louisiana

This drive across the wetlands of southern Louisiana accentuates a unique American subculture, a Cajun nation with its own food, festivals, folklore, and music spread across the bayou country west of New Orleans.

Created in the late 18th century when the British forced thousands of French settlers to relocate from Canada to the Mississippi Delta, the Acadiana region of Louisiana continues to adhere to the motto *laissez les*

Dive into fresh crawfish on your way through Louisiana.

**THE BIG PICTURE**

**Distance:** ca 700 miles (1,126.5 km) round-trip from New Orleans

**Drive time:** 5-6 days

**Best overnights:** Grand Isle, Houma, Lafayette, Lake Charles

**Best seasons:** Anytime

**Highlights:** Barataria Preserve, Grand Isle, Avery Island, Lafayette, Vermilionville, Lake Martin, Lake Charles, Eunice

*bon temps rouler* ("let the good times roll").

And that's exactly what this road trip does, starting with a drive across Crescent City Bridge to **Barataria Preserve** on the south side of the metropolitan area. Part of **Jean Lafitte National Historical Park**, the preserve safeguards 23,000 acres (9,307.8 ha) of bayou where visitors can watch birds, gators, and other critters along trails and wooden boardwalks.

A combination of U.S. 90 and State Highway 1 takes the Cajun trail down to **Grand Isle** on the Gulf Coast. Jean Lafitte's old hangout is renowned for its fishing charters, waterfront cantinas, and seven miles (11.3 km) of sandy shore punctuated by **Grand Isle State Park**.

Backtracking along Highway 1, the next stop is **Thibodaux** and the **Wetlands Acadian Cultural Center**, which spotlights Cajun culture through folk art, films, food demonstrations, and **Monday Music** sessions featuring blues, jazz, and zydeco swamp rock. Another unit of Jean Lafitte National Historical Park, the center also offers walking tours of Thibodaux's historic district, *Cercle Francophone* sessions where French speakers (and listeners) help preserve the region's unique dialect, and guided boat tours on **Bayou Lafourche**.

Back on U.S. 90, the drive

Kayak through sunken tupelo and cypress forests as you look for waterfowl and gators in Lake Martin.

continues through the bayou country to **Avery Island**, where Tabasco sauce was born in 1868. Still owned and operated by the McIlhenny family, the island features factory tours and **Jungle Gardens** with its native flora and fauna.

Half an hour up the road is **Lafayette**, the largest city and unofficial capital of Acadiana. With its own world-class **art museum, symphony, ballet**, and other artistic entities, Lafayette gives New Orleans a run for its money when it comes to high culture.

But the city on Bayou Vermilion doesn't forsake its Cajun roots. The **Acadian Cultural Center** presents an array of local music, dance, storytelling, and culinary events. Down on the bayou, the **Vermilionville Living History and Folklife Park** offers more live performances, traditional Acadiana crafts, historic buildings, and ranger-led boat tours.

Just east of Lafayette, **Lake Martin** harbors one of the nation's largest waterfowl nesting areas and a pretty good gator population, as well as a

sunken tupelo and cypress forest that can be explored via **Cajun Country Swamp Tours** and other outfitters. Nearby **Longfellow-Evangeline State Historic Site** on Bayou Teche highlights the region's unique human heritage, a mix of Cajuns and Creoles, African Americans and Native Americans, Spanish and French.

Slake your appetite for Cajun cuisine in **Breaux Bridge**, the world's "Crawfish Capital," before heading west on Interstate 10 to **Lake Charles** and the unique **Mardi Gras Museum of the Imperial Calcasieu**.

If you've got time, cruise down Highway 27 to the **"Cajun Riviera"** on the Gulf Coast for the sandy strands or bird-watching at **Sabine National Wildlife Refuge**.

If it's Saturday, head back to New Orleans on U.S. Highway 190 rather than the interstate and stop in **Eunice** for the *Rendez-vous des Cajuns* music show at the historic **Liberty Theatre** and *The Cajun Way* music and dance performance at the neighboring **Prairie Acadian Cultural Center**. You'll be humming those tunes all the way back to the Big Easy. ■

## PIT STOPS

• **Lafayette Mardi Gras:** Louisiana's second biggest carnival includes six parades organized by the city's 20 carnival krewes, plus a Mardi Gras grand ball. gomardigras.com

• **World Championship Crawfish Étouffée Cook-Off:** One of Louisiana's iconic eats is the focus of a March food fest in Eunice that also features Cajun music, arts, and crafts. etouffeecookoff.org

• **Louisiana Pirate Festival:** Lake Charles goes rogue during this week-long invasion of music, food, fireworks, costume contests, and cannon demonstrations in May. louisianapiratefestival.com

• **Festivals Acadiens et Créoles:** Lafayette's other big annual bash is an October shindig that features a craft fair, culinary demonstrations, six stages of live music, and a symposium on Cajun culture. festivalsacadiens.com

# Tropical
# Road Trips

Palm trees frame Biscayne Bay in Biscayne National Park, Florida.

# Overseas Highway

## Florida

**THE BIG PICTURE**

**Distance:** 166 miles (267.2 km) from Miami to Key West

**Drive time:** 1-3 days

**Best overnights:** Key Largo, Key West, Bahia Honda

**Best season:** Winter

**Highlights:** Key West, Biscayne Bay NP, John Pennekamp Coral Reef

One of the great feats of American highway engineering, the incredible Overseas Highway links the Florida mainland south of Miami with cool, colorful Key West on the cusp of the Atlantic Ocean and the Gulf of Mexico. The route's 42 bridges connect a string of islands blessed with white-sand beaches, coral reefs, tropical resorts, and loads of quirky history.

A train made the first leap across the Florida Keys—Henry Flagler's Florida Overseas Railroad. People hailed it as both "Flagler's Folly" and the "Eighth Wonder of the World" when the island-hopping iron horse debuted in 1912. It lasted barely two decades before it was destroyed by the Labor Day Hurricane of 1935.

The wreck was a huge loss for train passengers but a huge gain for motorists: The government purchased Flagler's right-of-way and transformed it into an elevated roadway: the Overseas Highway. Completed in 1938, it connects Florida's mainland with Key Largo, Key West, and dozens of other islands along the way.

While it's tempting (for historical reasons) to begin the journey on U.S. Highway 1 in downtown Miami, a much faster way to flee the traffic-clogged central city is by driving the

Don Shula Expressway and Ronald Reagan Turnpike to the start of the Overseas Highway in **Homestead**.

Home to Miami's **NASCAR speedway**, Homestead boasts vintage Florida tourist attractions like the **Everglades Alligator Farm**, an architectural curiosity called the **Coral Castle**, and the aromatic **Fruit and Spice Park** with its tasty tropical café. It's also the gateway to **Biscayne National Park**, which embraces the top end of the 190-mile-long (305.7 km) Keys archipelago. The park's **Dante Fascell Visitor Center** is the main hub for water sports on the bay, including guided snorkel, kayak and sailing trips; equipment rentals; ranger talks; and evening programs like stargazing and sea chantey sing-alongs.

After crossing the Southern Glades on an arrow-straight road with a cement divider down the middle, Highway 1 hops across the water to **Key Largo** and the official start of the Overseas Highway. The longest and largest of the Florida Keys, Largo was immortalized by the 1948 movie of the same name in which Humphrey Bogart and Lauren Bacall survive a hurricane and mobsters.

Boutique beach resorts and water-front restaurants dominate Largo's urban landscape. The island's leeward side is ideal for **kayaking**—with a chance to spot the rare American

View coral and marine life from a glass-bottom boat in John Pennekamp State Park.

Kayak among mangroves in Biscayne National Park, which is home to 10,000 years of human history, including shipwrecks.

crocodile (only around 2,000 left in the wild). Much of the island's east coast is framed by **John Pennekamp Coral Reef State Park**, established in the 1950s as the nation's first underwater nature reserve. The park truly is stunning in both the number of coral and tropical fish species and their pristine state after nearly 70 years of preservation. There are several ways to experience the reef, including guided **scuba, snorkel**, and **glass-bottom boat excursions** as well as **kayak, paddleboard**, and **powerboat rentals**.

Twenty minutes farther down the Overseas Highway, the town of **Islamorada** on Upper Matecumbe Key is the jumping-off point for a number of natural and man-made attractions. Renowned for both its fishing and scuba diving, Islamorada was the long-time home of Boston Red Sox legend Ted Williams, who took up angling after he retired from baseball. The town also offers the **History of Diving Museum**, as well

as the **Florida Keys History and Discovery Center**, which illuminates the archipelago's rich human and natural legacy.

Islamorada is flanked by several small but very interesting island parks: **Windley Key Fossil Reef Geological State Park** preserves an old limestone quarry that provided

building blocks for the Overseas Railroad. The 8-foot (2.4 m) quarry walls are encrusted with fossilized brain coral and other ancient sea creatures. Tiny **Indian Key State Historic Park**, on an island that comprises just 11 acres (.04 sq km), safeguards the remains of an early 19th-century American settlement

### LAY YOUR HEAD

• **Kona Kai:** A small private beach, lush gardens, and cute cottages make this the perfect place to stay in Key Largo; swimming pool, art gallery, spa treatments, tennis, kayaks, paddleboards; from $219. konakairesort.com

• **Rio Honda State Park:** Beachfront campsites ($36 per night) and cabins ($120-$160 per night) are on offer inside the park. floridastateparks.org/parks-and-trails/bahia-honda-state-park#

• **Little Palm Island:** This posh private island resort near Little Torch

Key is a favorite for weddings, honeymoons, and Sunday brunch; restaurant, bars, private beach, swimming pool, marina, dive shop, Zen garden, spa and fitness center, library; from c. $540 per person, all-inclusive. littlepalmisland.com

• **The Gardens:** Party-hearty Duval Street is just a block away from this chic boutique on the grounds of a 19th-century Victorian home, which offers peace and quiet amid the big trees and orchids; swimming pool, bar, bike rental, pet friendly; from $219. gardenshotel.com

that survived on fishing, turtle hunting, and shipwreck salvaging. Lush **Lignumvitae Key Botanical State Park** preserves a pristine tropical hardwood "hammock" (a slightly elevated forested area) flush with holywood lignum-vitae, gumbo limbo, strangler figs, and other native trees.

West of Islamorada, a series of long bridges connects the middle part of the archipelago and attractions like the **Dolphin Research Center** on Grassy Key, the hands-on **Florida Keys Aquarium Encounters** in Marathon (where visitors can snorkel or swim with various sea creatures), and **Crane Point Hammock**, a nonprofit museum, nature center, and nature trail that strives to educate humans and rescue orphaned or injured wildlife.

Erected in 1982, **Seven Mile Bridge** replaced a 1930s span that now carries part of the **Florida Keys Overseas Heritage Trail**, a 106-mile (170.6 km) hiking-biking route between Key Largo and Key West. The longest bridge on the Overseas Highway, Seven Mile is four times longer than the Golden Gate Bridge. Pull-offs provide parking for short walks across the vintage bridge. Anchoring the bridge's west end is **Bahia Honda**, another popular state park, renowned for its waterfront camping, water sports, and the hulking skeleton of an immense Flagler rail bridge with its middle spans missing.

Nearby **Big Pine Key** is the best place in the islands to spot the endangered key deer, a diminutive species found nowhere else on the planet. Pushed to the brink of extinction in the 1950s, the population has recovered from a low of just 25 animals to more than 700 thanks to efforts by

The Seven Mile Bridge connects Knight's Key to Little Duck Key.

---

## ART AVENUES

• **Best Music:** *A Pirate's Treasure* greatest hits by Jimmy Buffett

• **Best Movies:** *Key Largo* (1948); *License to Kill* (1989); *Out of Time* (2003)

• **Best Television Show:** *Bloodline* (2015-17)

• **Best Books:** *Hoot, Razor Girl,* and *Bad Monkey* by Carl Hiaasen

• **Best Art:** *Birds of the Florida Keys* by John James Audubon

---

local residents and the U.S. Fish and Wildlife Service.

The homestretch of the Overseas Highway down to Key West is dominated by marinas and waterfront residential developments. But the offshore waters are still pristine, protected within the confines of the **Florida Keys National Marine Sanctuary**, one of the nation's largest and most diverse underwater reserves. Any seawater below the mean high-tide mark is part of a sanctuary that is best explored by boat—either your own, a rental, or part of a guided tour. **Key West Eco Tours** on Geiger Key offers several ways to explore the mangroves and inshore waters via kayak, sailboat, paddleboard, or powerboat.

Discovered by Spanish explorer

Ponce de Leon in 1521 and originally dubbed Cayo Hueso ("Bone Island")—allegedly because the Native American inhabitants used the island as a communal graveyard—**Key West** dominates the island chain in many ways. It attracts the most tourists (around three million each year), boasts the largest population (27,000), and hosts the county government and an important U.S. Navy base.

Key West offers a variety of ways to while away a tropical island vacation, from the good-natured, rowdy ambience of the countless bars along **Duval Street** and the street performers who hijack **Mallory Square** at dusk, to just about any water sport in existence and many historical gems.

Among the island's more celebrated attractions are the **Ernest Hemingway Home** (and its famed six-toed cats), the free-flying winged creatures of the **Butterfly and Nature Conservatory**, the shipwreck relics of **Mel Fisher Maritime Museum**, and the **Audubon House**, an elegant Victorian manse that recalls the 1830s sojourn in Key West by the noted naturalist and painter.

The Overseas Highway (U.S. 1) cuts straight across the island via Roosevelt Boulevard and Truman Avenue, finally petering out at the intersection of Whitehead and Fleming Streets, where **Mile Marker Zero** provides a popular spot for selfies. ∎

---

## OFF THE ROAD

• While the Overseas Highway ends in Key West, the Florida Keys definitely do not. The chain extends another 70 miles (112.7 km) into the Gulf of Mexico and a spectacular termination in the **Dry Tortugas**. All seven of these islands fall within a supersecluded national park reached by private boat, the high-speed catamaran *Yankee Freedom III,* or the floatplanes of **Key West Seaplane Adventures**. In addition to pristine coral reefs, the park includes **Fort Jefferson**, a massive Civil War–era citadel that's also the largest brick masonry structure in the Americas.

# The Big Island's Belt Road

## Hawaii

Hawaii's largest island offers plenty of space for a multiday drive that covers the coffee-growing Kona Coast, the volcanic landscapes of the east side, and the lush cowboy country of the Kohala Peninsula.

**THE BIG PICTURE**

**Distance:** ca 260 miles (418.4 km) round-trip from Kona Airport

**Drive time:** 5-8 days

**Best overnights:** Kona, Volcano, Hilo, Waimea,

**Best seasons:** Anytime

**Highlights:** Kona Coast, Kealakekua Bay, Hawai'i Volcanoes NP, Hilo, Waimea cowboy country, Kohala Peninsula

Making up around two-thirds of the state's entire landmass, the Island of Hawaii is a road tripper's paradise of scenic coastal roads, twisting mountain routes, and even a few urban thoroughfares.

From Kona Airport, our recommended route goes counterclockwise, starting with a leisurely drive on Highway 11 along the **Kona Coast**. Right off the bat there's something to see: **Kaloko-Honokōhau National Historical Park**, where an ancient Hawaiian village and fish ponds are preserved amid an immense lava flow.

Farther south, the deeply indented Kona Coast offers plenty of places to take a dip or observe dolphins, whales, sea turtles, and tropical fish that frequent local waters. **Keauhou Bay** is renowned for the manta rays that gather there each night to feed on plankton and do underwater somersaults in front of divers and snorkelers.

Twenty minutes away, **Kealakekua Bay** is where Captain James Cook was slain in a battle against native Hawaiians in 1779. Framed by 500-foot (152.4 m) cliffs, the bay is also a marine sanctuary for spinner dolphins, coral reefs, thousands of yellow tang, and other marine life. Nearby **Pu'uhonua o Hōnaunau National Historical Park** (City of Refuge) preserves the remains of a sanctuary where Hawaiians who broke *kapu* (the ancient code of conduct laws and taboos) fled to escape execution.

Highway 11 continues around the south side of Hawaii, through the coffee and macadamia plantations of the lush **Ka'u District**.

Just before Wai'ōhinu is the turnoff to **South Point**, a 12-mile (19.3 km) side trip along a rough and narrow road to the southernmost point in both Hawaii and the United States. On the other side of Wai'ōhinu, **Punalu'u Black Sand Beach** has extraordinarily dark, obsidian-colored sand framed by tide pools and coconut palms. Look for nēnē geese grazing on the golf course.

Swinging to the island's east coast, Highway 11 makes a beeline for rainforest-enveloped **Volcano Village** and **Hawai'i Volcanoes National Park**, which harbors two of the world's most noteworthy volcanoes.

Mauna Kea, at 14,000 feet (4,267.2 m), is a prime stargazing spot.

Waipi'o Valley's wilderness and taro fields meet the ocean with stunning black-sand beaches.

**Mauna Loa**, which dominates the park's remote western half, is a massive shield volcano that last erupted in 1984 and the planet's single largest mountain, comprising an estimated 19,999 cubic miles (83,359.5 cubic km) of earth. Rising around 56,000 feet (17,068.8 m) above the sea floor, Mauna Loa is also one of the world's highest mountains from top to bottom—more than 27,000 feet (8,229.6 m) higher than Mount Everest if you count everything that lies beneath the ocean's surface.

Reaching the summit requires a 27-mile (43.5 km) drive along a one-lane road to **Mauna Loa Lookout**, and then a 19-mile (30.6 km) hike to the 13,677-foot (4,168.8 m) summit and a view down into **Moku'āweoweo Caldera**.

Low-rise **Kīlauea**, in the park's eastern sector, may look mild by comparison, but its fury is unmatched. The volcano erupted continuously between 1983 and 2018, causing considerable damage throughout the park.

**Kīlauea Visitor Center** and the historic **Volcano House** hotel (opened in 1877) are located near the park's main entrance. The western end of **Crater Rim Road**, the **Jaggar Museum**, and **Thurston Lava Tube** are closed indefinitely due to recent seismic and volcanic activity. However, it's still possible to hike three sections of the **Crater Rim Trail** and the **Kīlauea Iki Crater**.

**Chain of Craters Road** meanders across old lava flows to the park's rugged shoreline, with plenty of places to park and take off on a walk. Near the end of the road are the **Pu'u Loa Petroglyphs, Hōlei Sea Arch**, and the start of a coastal trail that leads more than 20 miles (32.2 km) to remote backcountry campsites.

From Volcano village, Highway

11 makes a long downhill run into **Keaau**, where a turnoff on Highway 130 enables a detour to the lava fields caused by the 1990 and 2018 Kīlauea eruptions, including a brand-new black-sand beach at **Kaimū Park.**

From Keaau, it's less than 10 miles (16.1 km) into central **Hilo**. In addition to a downtown spangled with **art deco architecture**, the island's largest city features the small but excellent **Panaʻewa Rainforest Zoo and Gardens**, the **Lyman Museum and Mission House**, and the daily **Hilo Farmers Market**.

Along the waterfront, the **Pacific Tsunami Museum** elucidates the 1946 and 1960 tidal waves that hit Hilo. Across the road in **Kaipalaoa Landing Park** is a white tower that shows the wave height during both of those deadly disasters. **Mokupāpapa Discovery Center** reveals the natural history of Hawaii's remote northwest islands, including Midway Atoll.

The road trip continues on Highway 19 along the northeast shore. After around 20 minutes on the road, you'll find a turnoff to the old sugarcane town of **Honomū** and 442-foot (134.7 m) **ʻAkaka Falls**, the state's highest single-drop waterfall.

Veering away from the coast, the

Lava spills into the ocean from Kīlauea Volcano

highway ascends to **Waimea** town, hub of the island's ranch country and *paniolo* cowboy culture. The legendary **Parker Ranch** opens two of its historic houses to self-guided tours, and several local spreads offer guided horseback riding tours of the lush, green highlands. With its **Keck Observatory** visitor center, Waimea is also a jumping-off spot for drives up the side of 13,803-foot (4,207.2 m) **Mauna Kea**, celebrated for its sunset views and evening stargazing.

From Waimea, scenic **Kohala Mountain Road** (Highway 250) climbs up and over a lofty ridge with views of **Haleakalā** volcano on distant Maui before descending to **Hāwī**. The one-time sugarcane town is renowned as the birthplace of Kamehameha I, the king who united Hawaii in 1810.

Local cane fields were once irrigated by the 14.5-mile (23.3 km) **Kohala Ditch**, constructed by Japanese laborers in 1905-06. Visitors can now take guided kayak tours on a portion of the ditch.

On the western side of the peninsula are the ruins of an old fishing village at **Lapakahi State Historical Park**, the placid waters of **Spencer Beach Park**, and adjacent **Puʻukoholā Heiau National Historic Site**, which showcases a huge fortified temple compound erected by Kamehameha I in the 1790s. ∎

# Hana Highway
## Hawaii

With more than 600 curves, dozens of narrow bridges, and sheer drops along much of the route, Maui's celebrated Hana Highway offers a meandering journey through paradise and a hand-sweating test of a driver's skill.

**THE BIG PICTURE**

**Distance:** 52 miles (83.7 km) from Kahului to Hana

**Drive time:** 1 day

**Best overnights:** Pāʻia, Hana

**Best seasons:** Anytime

**Highlights:** Pāʻia town, Jaws surf break, Garden of Eden, Hana Lava Tube, Waiʻānapanapa black-sand beach

This vertiginous route across Maui's north shore was the brainchild of 16th-century King Piʻilani. Originally paved with volcanic stones—and swinging vines rather than bridges across the numerous streams and gulches—the modern 52-mile (83.7 km) highway wasn't completed until the 1960s.

Get an early start if you plan on driving all the way to Hana and back on the same day. The western end starts beside **Maui Mall** in Kahului, a divided highway that slices through sugarcane fields on its way to the north shore. Dead ahead is **Pāʻia**, a former sugarcane company town now renowned for its world-class surfing and bygone main street lined with restaurants, bars, and art galleries. Pāʻia is the last best place to stop for breakfast or lunch or to load up on snacks if you haven't yet, because there are not a lot of options on the road ahead until you reach Hana.

Just up the coast, **Hoʻokipa Beach Park** is one of the world's most celebrated surf spots, a hot spot for board sports since the 1930s and annual host to a number of professional competitions. There's a lofty lookout point for those who want to watch rather than hang ten.

Ten minutes farther up the highway is the turnoff for an even more famous surf spot—the mighty **Peʻahi "Jaws" break** at the ocean end of Hahana Road, where daredevil big wave surfing was pioneered on waves that often reach 60 feet (18.3 m) between December and March.

Jaws marks the start of the serious stretch of the Hana Highway, the hairpin turns, narrow spans, and vertiginous cliffs. One of first roadside attractions is the **Garden of Eden Arboretum**, a 25-acre (10.1 ha) tropical oasis with native plants from Hawaii and around the Pacific—and a chance to plunge down the park's 130-foot-high (39.6 m) Puohokamoa Falls with adventure company **Rappel Maui**. Nearby **Kaumahina State Wayside** offers a tranquil place to pull off and take in the coastal panorama.

The highway zigzags down to sea level at Keʻanae, a fertile volcanic peninsula that Hawaiians have cultivated since ancient times. **Keʻanae Arboretum** showcases taro, bananas, yams, and other tropical food plants. Near the tip of the peninsula, **Aunt Sandy's Banana Bread** stand is a local eating institution.

See otherworldly rainbow eucalyptus trees in the Keʻanae Arboretum.

Watch as surfers take on big waves, including Jaws (Pe'ahi) off Maui's coast.

The road climbing back into the rainforest leads to **Pua'a Ka'a State Wayside**, the best place along the Hana Highway for a freshwater plunge. There's a swimming hole beneath a small waterfall and short jungle trails that make a great break from the winding road.

The copious curves finally peter out on the homestretch into Hana, but not the roadside attractions. **Hana Lava Tube** is one of Hawaii's largest and most accessible basalt caverns. A 40-minute, self-guided tour takes in odd underground sights like frozen lava waterfalls, lava balls, and tube slime. It's privately owned, and there's an admission charge to enter.

Nearby is another amazing volcanic relic: the beautiful black-sand strand of **Wai'ānapanapa State Park**.

The water is a bit too rough for swimming, but shore fishing is allowed. The three-mile (4.8 km) **Ke Ala Loa O Maui/Piilani Trail** traces the route of the 16th-century King's Highway along the shore to a sea arch, blowholes, ancient burial ground, and pu hala (screwpine) forest. **Hana town** is just 10 minutes up the road from here. ∎

### SCENIC DETOURS

• **Piilani Highway:** Another way to reach Maui's eastern shore is a 38-mile (61.2 km) rugged rural route that wraps around the bottom of Haleakalā Volcano between Ulupalakua Ranch and 'Ohe'o Gulch. Along the way are the historic Kaupo General Store and Charles Lindbergh's grave beside Palapala Ho'omau Church.

• **Kahekili Highway:** A single lane for much of its length, this back way between Kapalua and Kahului meanders 30 miles (48.3 km) along Maui's remote and sometimes rugged northwest shore. Worthwhile stops include Nakalele Blowhole, the Olivine tide pools, and 2.5-mile (4 km) Waihee Ridge Trail.

• **Haleakalā Highway:** This 37-mile (59.6 km) route between sea-level Kahului and the 10,000-foot (3,048 m) summit of Haleakalā features lush farmland, multiple switchbacks, and some of the best views in the entire Pacific.

# Hopping Across St. John

## U.S. Virgin Islands

Talcum-powder-fine beaches and historic sugar plantations sprinkle this circular drive around St. John, a road trip that also includes jungle hiking trails, underwater snorkeling adventures, and other wild sides of the U.S. Virgin Islands.

St. John has endured a lot of change since Columbus arrived in 1493 and christened the tropical archipelago after St. Ursula and her 11,000 holy virgins. Oddly, it was the Danes who colonized the island nearly 200 years later, transforming its land into Scandinavian-style sugar plantations.

Intent on forging a larger naval presence in the Caribbean, the U.S. government purchased the Virgin Islands from Denmark in 1917. But instead of a Navy base, St. John morphed into a playground for the rich and famous. Among them was Laurence Rockefeller, who in 1956 donated his land, now protected within the confines of Virgin Islands National Park.

It takes only a day to drive around St. John, but there's plenty to see and do along the route. Most of the island's rental car and jeep agencies are located along King Street in **Cruz Bay**, all of them within walking distance of the main ferry pier. From there, it's a short drive along North Shore Road to the **Cruz Bay Visitor Center**, where drivers can pick up national park maps and information on ranger-guided hikes and snorkel excursions.

As the name suggests, **North Shore Road** hugs the island's north coast, a gorgeous drive that combines pristine beaches like **Hawksnest Bay** and **Trunk Bay** with historical sites like the **Peace Hill Windmill** and the moody ruins of **Dennis Bay Great House**, both constructed in the early 19th century when the island was part of the Danish West Indies. In addition to some fine sand, Trunk is also renowned for its **Snorkeling Trail**, a 650-foot (198.1 m) path with underwater plaques that describe the bay's flora and fauna.

Farther along the shore, **Cinnamon Bay**'s aquatic center offers **kayak, paddleboard, catamaran,** and **windsurfer rentals**, as well as sailing, scuba diving, and snorkeling excursions. A self-guided **nature trail** includes the ruins of a sugar plantation, while the **Cinnamon Bay Heritage Center and Archeology Lab** renders insights into the island's history.

Beyond America Point are **Maho Bay** with its resident turtle popula-

**THE BIG PICTURE**

**Distance:** ca 32 miles (51.5 km) round-trip from Cruz Bay

**Drive time:** 1 day

**Best overnights:** Cruz Bay, Cinnamon Bay

**Best seasons:** Anytime

**Highlights:** Trunk Bay Snorkeling Trail, Cinnamon Bay water sports, Maho Bay sea turtles, East End, Ram Head, Centerline Road

Snorkel and swim among green sea turtles in Maho Bay.

Follow a self-guided underwater snorkeling trail past beautiful coral reefs and sea life in Trunk Bay.

tion and **Annaberg Historic District**, which revolves around the ruins of a sugar, molasses, and rum plantation developed in the early 1700s by the Danish governor.

Reaching the far end of North Shore Road, hang a left (beside the smoothie stand) onto Centerline Road and coast downhill into **Coral Bay**, where **the old Emmaus Moravian Church and Manse** (badly damaged by Hurricane Irma in 2017) was founded by slaves who worked the Danish sugar plantations. Highway 10 continues to secluded **East End**, where **North Haulover Beach** provides views across Sir Francis Drake Channel to the British Virgins.

Retracing your steps to Coral Bay, head down St. John's east coast to **Mandal**, where the short **Saltpond Bay, Drunk Bay**, and **Ram**

**Head trails** lead through dry tropical forest to remote points along the national park shore.

Backtracking one last time to Coral Bay, take a left onto **Bordeaux Mountain Road** (108) or **Centerline Road** and the start of a westward journey across the island's rugged spine. The drive to Cruz Bay

takes less than half an hour if you motor straight through. But there are several intriguing stops along the way. **Reef Bay Trail** leads 2.2 miles (3.5 km) downhill to ancient Taino petroglyphs and the ruins of a waterfront plantation. Farther along are the ruins of the 18th-century **Catherineberg Sugar Mill**. ■

# Circling Puerto Rico

## Puerto Rico

A circular road trip around the big Caribbean island yields all kinds of surprises, from an observatory where NASA tracked aliens and the only jungle in the National Forest system to incredible beaches, bioluminescent bays, and historic bluff-top lighthouses.

### THE BIG PICTURE

**Distance:** ca 300 miles (482.8 km) round-trip from San Juan

**Drive time:** 7-10 days

**Best overnights:** Isabela, Mayagüez, Ponce, Fajardo

**Best seasons:** Anytime

**Highlights:** Arecibo Observatory, Isabela beaches, Cabo Rojo, Ponce's Cultural District, Fajardo, El Yunque

A U.S. territory since the Spanish-American War, Puerto Rico offers an intriguing blend of Hispanic culture and tropical island landscapes arrayed along a modern road network that radiates out from the capital. While driving the narrow, cobblestone lanes of Old San Juan is an acquired skill, navigating a week-long road trip around the island is a breeze.

Leaving the traffic of San Juan far behind, start your circumnavigation with a cruise along **Expreso 22**, a four-lane toll road on the island's north shore. About an hour out is Arecibo, where the **Plaza de Recreo** is flanked by Spanish colonial buildings like **San Felipe Apostol**.

Balanced on a mountaintop behind the city is one of the strangest sights in the Caribbean: the **Arecibo Observatory**. Constructed in the early 1960s, the massive radio telescope (the second largest on the planet) is used for astronomy and atmospheric science. But it's best known for SETI—the Search for Extraterrestrial Intelligence—used by the U.S. government to determine whether we share the universe with other intelligent life forms. Visitors can watch a **20-minute film** about the observatory, take a **self-guided tour**, or join a **VIP behind-the-scenes tour.**

The mountains near Arecibo are also renowned for their limestone caves. Peer into the gaping holes in the earth like **Cueva Ventana** (Window Cave), where the 45-minute guided tour revolves around flora and fauna found in and around the cavern as well as the Taino Indians who once lived along this coast.

Beyond Arecibo, the expressway segues into Highway 2 and a gentle bend around the island's northwest coast and Puerto Rico's "surfing safari" region. With some of the best waves in the Caribbean, beaches near **Isabela** town like **Playa Jobos** and **Playa Middles** lure surfers from the around the world. Arrayed along the shore are surf shops, beach bars, and plenty of places to stay. If hanging ten isn't your thing, the area also offers golfing at the spectacular cliff-top **Royal Isabela Golf Course**, jungle hikes in **Guajataca State Forest**, and history at a ruined 18th-century

Cuevo Ventana ("window cave") looks out over the Arecibo.

The Arecibo Observatory radio telescope operates 24 hours a day and is used to study asteroids that fly close to the Earth.

Spanish church, the **Ermita San Antonio De Padua De La Tuna.**

**Mayagüez** anchors the island's west coast, another old Spanish colonial city with a charming old town and lively cultural scene. Even if you don't speak Spanish, try to catch music or dance at **Teatro Yagüez**, an eclectic 1921 structure on the National Register of Historic Places. Performances are also offered at the nearby **Museo Casa Pilar Defillo**, dedicated to the life and times of celebrated cellist and composer Pablo Casals, whose mother was born in the house.

Route 100 continues along the coast to **Cabo Rojo** (Red Cape), where the historic **Faro Los Morrillos** lighthouse (built in 1882) crowns a peninsula flanked by beaches, bays, and ruddy cliffs. Much of the area falls within **Cabo Rojo National Wildlife Refuge**, where hiking, biking, and bird-watching are the main activities. The **Caribbean Islands** and **Salt Flats** visitor centers render information and exhibits on the refuge.

From Cabo Rojo, the road trip meanders along the island's arid south coast with several intriguing stops along the way. The second oldest city in Puerto Rico, **San Germán** (founded 1511), offers a treasure of colonial architecture, including the small but exquisite **Convento de Porta Coeli** (Gateway to Heaven) church.

Back on the coast, **Guánica State Forest** and **United Nations Biosphere Reserve** shelter the Caribbean's largest remaining patch of

## LAY YOUR HEAD

• **Royal Isabela:** This sprawling cliff-top resort near the island's west end boasts luxury casitas with spectacular ocean views; 18-hole golf course, restaurant, bar, tropical gardens, beach access; from $350. royalisabela.com

• **Posada Hotel Colonial:** Tucked inside a restored convent, this modest boutique lies near Plaza Colón in the heart of the Mayagüez historic district; parking, Wi-Fi; from $69. hotelcolonial.com

• **Hilton Ponce:** Beach and bay access are the coolest things about this south coast resort; restaurants, bars, pools, golf, tennis, fitness room, water sports; from $174. hilton.com

• **Wyndham Grand Rio Mar:** This posh resort near Fajardo has everything you need for a great beach vacation; restaurants, bars, golf, tennis, pools, spa, casino, salsa lessons, iguana feeding; from $231. wyndhamriomar.com

tropical dry forest. Thirty-six miles (57.9 km) of hiking and biking trails lead to hilltop viewpoints and the ruins of an old Spanish fort. The park's shoreline offers secluded beaches like **Playa Tamarindo** and **Playa Ballena,** as well as boat trips to **Cayo Aurora** (aka Gilligan's Island) for snorkeling, swimming, or exploring the mangroves.

Dead ahead is **Ponce**, the queen of the south coast and Puerto Rico's second largest city. The meticulously preserved **Cultural District** revolves around **Plaza Degetau** with its whitewashed **Cathedral of Our Lady of Guadalupe** and the oddball **Parque de Bombas** fire station museum. The surrounding streets are flush with **Ponce Creole–style mansions** converted into restaurants, shops, and entertainment venues.

The city's pride and joy is the **Museo de Arte de Ponce**, considered one of the finest in all of Latin America. The collection, which includes more than 4,500 pieces, revolves around the three cultures that have shaped modern Puerto Rico: Europe, Africa, and the Americas. Its most iconic pieces are "Flaming June" by Frederic Leighton and "The Last Sleep of Arthur in Avalon" by Edward Burne-Jones. The museum also boasts works by Rubens, Murillo, Delacroix, and Lichtenstein.

Down along the shore is **La Guancha de Ponce**, a waterfront boardwalk with restaurants, bars, and boats offering day trips to **Isle de Caja de Muertos** (Coffin Island). Located eight miles (12.9 km) offshore, the island is now a nature reserve with beaches and hiking trails. Various theories attribute the odd name to long-ago pirates or the fact that it

Faro Los Morrillos de Cabo Rojo (built 1882) watches over the Caribbean Sea.

resembles a reclining corpse when viewed from mainland Puerto Rico.

East of Ponce, road trippers have a choice to speed along the four-lane toll road (Expreso 52) or enjoy a slow mosey through the coastal villages scattered along Highway 1. At **Salinas**, the expressway veers off to the north and a quick return to San Juan for drivers who prefer a shorter version of the circumnavigation.

The coast route continues along Highway 3 and a big bend around the remote southeast coast. Among the landmarks (and photo ops) along this stretch are the old Spanish lighthouse at **Punta Tuna** (1892) and the **Bosque de Pterocarpus** near Palmas

## PIT STOPS

• **Liga de Béisbol:** Between November and January, winter league baseball—featuring many Major League stars—plays out on fields around Puerto Rico like Estadio Isidoro García in Mayagüez. ligapr.com

• **Carnaval de Ponce:** More than 100,000 people pour into the streets of Ponce before Lent for a week of parades, music, flamboyant *vejigante* (a folkloric character) costumes, and the climactic Entierro de La Sardina (Burial of the Sardine).

• **Los Reyes Magos de Juana Díaz:** First celebrated in 1884, this south coast yuletide festival honors the Three Kings, an event that culminates with a grand parade through the streets of Juana Díaz on the Epiphany (January 6). reyesde juanadiaz.com

• **Fiestas Tradicionales de Santiago Apóstol:** Puerto Rico's African heritage and culture is the focus of this carnival-like celebration that takes over Loíza on the feast day of St. James the Apostle at the end of July.

del Mar, one of the island's last remaining swamp forests. Farther north, **Humacao** is a prime spot for scuba diving and sea kayaking, as well as a good place to hop onto Puerto Rico's east side toll road (Route 53).

Just half an hour farther up the coast is **Fajardo**, one of the island's main vacation areas and the main gateway for day trips to the islands east of Puerto Rico—**Culebra, Vieques, Arrecifes de Cordillera**, and the other bits and bobs that make up the Spanish Virgins. Scuba and snorkel trips, scenic cruises, guided kayak excursions, fishing charters, and passenger ferries depart from marinas and piers along the **Bahia de Fajardo**.

Puerto Rico's northeast corner is crowned by a rugged headland, **La Cabezas de San Juan** and a whitewashed lighthouse of the same name that's been illuminating this coast since the 1880s. The surrounding nature preserve features hiking trails, remote beaches, and the bioluminescent **Laguna Grande Norte** for night kayak tours to view the incredible neon-blue marine organisms.

Looming in the mist-shrouded mountains that rise behind Fajado is **El Yunque National Forest**, the only tropical rainforest in the U.S. national forest system. Home to many endemic plant and animal species (including 16 species of coquí frogs), El Yunque was badly damaged by Hurricanes Irma and Maria in 2017, but many of the roads and trails have been reopened.

From Fajardo, road trippers can cruise the expressway all the way back to San Juan (36 miles/57.9 km) or take Route 187 through the popular beach areas that spangle the coast to the east of the capital city: **Loíza, La Pocita, Piñones, Isla Verde**, and high-rise **Condado** with its Miami Beach vibe. ∎

# Tamiami Trail
## Florida

Stretching from the Atlantic to the Gulf of Mexico and flanked by the Everglades and Big Cypress Swamp, this casual cruise through southern Florida features incredible beaches, sleepy seaside towns, and close encounters of the critter kind.

**THE BIG PICTURE**

**Distance:** 270 miles (434.5 km) from Miami to Tampa

**Drive time:** 5 days

**Best overnights:** Naples, Fort Myers, Sarasota

**Best seasons:** Winter, spring, or fall

**Highlights:** Everglades, Big Cypress, Naples, Fort Myers, Sarasota

When road crews began building this cross-peninsula route in 1915, Floridians suggested catchy nicknames for U.S. Highway 41. The name that finally stuck was a mash-up of "Tampa to Miami"—the burgeoning urban areas at either end of the Tamiami Trail.

Born amid the skyscrapers of downtown Miami, the highway heads due west through **Little Havana**, with its fabulous Latin eateries. Make a quick stop at the legendary **Versailles Cuban Bakery** to pick up some snacks for the road before heading into the swamps.

Starting in 2013, the state began elevating long stretches of the Tamiami Trail through the Everglades to expedite water flow through the nation's largest tropical wetlands and reverse more than a century of ecological damage, so don't be surprised to encounter construction along this portion of the route.

**Everglades National Park** stretches along the highway's south side, with a turnoff at **Shark Valley** for a visitor center that offers hiking, biking, and guided tram tours along a 15-mile (24.1 km) loop trail through the "river of grass" with plenty of birds, turtles, and gators along the way.

Farther along is **Big Cypress National Preserve**, another huge wetlands and primary range of the Florida panther, the official state animal. **Oasis Visitor Center** and the **Big Cypress Swamp Welcome Center** have the lowdown on park activities like hiking, biking, camping, paddling, airboat tours, and ATV trails.

Just west of the welcome center is the turnoff to **Everglades City** and the far western sector of the national park. **Gulf Coast Visitor Center** offers guided boat tours to the remote **Thousand Islands** as well as the jumping-off spot for the **Wilderness Waterway**, a 99-mile (159.3 km) canoe or kayak camping route through the warren of mangroves and sawgrass.

The highway hits the Gulf in **Naples**, founded in the 1880s by real estate developers who claimed the mild climate was just as sublime as its Italian namesake. Naples is now renowned for its **fishing charters,** talcum-powder-fine **beaches,** abundant **art galleries**, and **hiking trails** through the nearby **Corkscrew Swamp Sanctuary** and **Bird Rookery Swamp**.

Route 41 makes a sharp right in downtown Naples and follows the Gulf Coast in a northerly direction

See the experiment laboratory in the Thomas Edison and Henry Ford Winter estates.

The Long Pine Key Trail runs seven miles (11 km) between Long Pine Key campground and Pine Glades Lake.

to **Fort Myers**. Like several other South Florida cities, Fort Myers was once a wintertime bastion of the rich and famous. The former vacation estates of Thomas Edison (**Seminole**) and Henry Ford (**Mangoes**) offer guided tours. The restored **Arcade Theatre**, where Edison screened movies for his illustrious friends, is now home to the **Florida Repertory**.

After curving around **Gasparilla Sound** and **Charlotte Harbor**, the Tamiami Trail reaches the Gulf again at **South Venice**, where visitors can hop the little **Beach Ferry** to secluded shores on a slender barrier isle.

Another 40 minutes north is **Sarasota**, the undisputed queen of Florida's Gulf Coast and a city long renowned for art, architecture and entertainment. More than 70 structures are on the National Register of Historic Places, including **Ca' d'Zan**, the fabulous Mediterranean Revival estate of circus mogul John Ringling, and the **John and Mable Ringling Museum of Art** with its European Old Masters. Among the city's other cultural cornerstones are the **Sarasota Opera**, the **Marie Selby Botanical Gardens**, and the **Circus Arts Conservatory**.

The Tamiami Trail continues for another 50 miles (80.5 km)—via **Bradenton** and its vibrant **Village of the Arts** neighborhood—to the Selmon Expressway on the east side of **Tampa**. ■

---

### SCENIC DETOURS

• **State Road 29** cuts straight across Big Cypress Swamp to the Florida Panther National Wildlife Refuge—for close encounters of the wildlife kind—and Seminole Casino in Immokalee.

• **State Road 865** leads to fabulous beaches between Naples and Fort Myers on Estero, Sanibel, and Captiva Islands.

• **Gulf of Mexico Drive (Route 789)** leaps across the Ringing Causeway in downtown Sarasota to the Mote Aquarium and beaches along Longboat Key and Anna Maria Island.

• **U.S. Highway 19** is an alternate route around Tampa Bay that runs across the long Sunshine Skyway Bridge to St. Petersburg, Clearwater, and Tarpon Springs.

# Cruising "Main Street"
## Florida

Stretching 400 miles (643.7 km) along the Atlantic coast between Miami and Jacksonville—with much of the route on barrier islands—State Highway A1A offers plenty of sun, sea, and sand along a roadway that's splashed with 500 years of Florida history.

## THE BIG PICTURE

**Distance:** ca 400 miles (643.7 km) from Miami Beach to Amelia Island

**Drive time:** 7 days

**Best overnights:** Fort Lauderdale, Palm Beach, Titusville, Daytona Beach, St. Augustine, Jacksonville Beach

**Best seasons:** Anytime

**Highlights:** Miami Beach, Fort Lauderdale, Palm Beach, Kennedy Space Center, Canaveral National Seashore, Daytona International Speedway, St. Augustine, Timucuan

In a 1974 album, *Highway A1A,* Jimmy Buffett describes the coastal road as Florida's "Main Street." And that's exactly what the route is in real life—the main drag through a string of coastal towns with names that conjure visions of palm-shaded paradise.

**South Beach** anchors the southern end of this sun-splashed route with its Collins Avenue strip that flaunts rowdy beach bars, landmark **art deco architecture**, high-rise hotels, and loads of people who just want to be seen.

After passing through **Hollywood**, where you can stretch your legs on the long **Beach Boardwalk**, the highway curls around the **Port Everglades** cruise terminal before resuming its run along the shore. In addition to 23 miles (37 km) of beach, **Fort Lauderdale** is home to the **International Swimming Hall of Fame** and plantation-style **Bonnet House Museum and Gardens**.

Forty miles (64.4 km) farther north, there's more poshness: **Palm Beach**, one of the nation's wealthiest communities, is home to tycoon **Henry Flagler**'s 73-room mansion, the high-end boutiques of **Worth Avenue**, and the edgy **Norton Museum of Art**.

A1A continues from **Vero Beach** and **Cocoa Beach** to **Cape Canaveral** and the **Kennedy Space Center Visitor Complex**. From the **Astronaut Hall of Fame** and guided tours of the launch pads to a virtual **Space Shuttle Experience** and an **IMAX** show, the complex offers an array of space-race activities.

Just north of the cape, **Canaveral National Seashore** is a great place to view rocket launches, kayak a wilderness lagoon, watch nesting sea turtles, or relish that rarest of Florida creatures—a totally undeveloped beach.

A much different engine roar is heard up the shore at **Daytona Beach**—stocks cars racing around **Daytona International Speedway**. In addition to the annual Daytona 500, the raceway offers a chance to drive NASCAR vehicles or ride along with professional drivers at the **Richard Petty Racing Experience**.

Visitors can see the *Atlantis* space shuttle at the Kennedy Space Center.

Founded in 1565, St. Augustine claims to be the oldest European town in the United Sates, known for Spanish colonial architecture.

You can also drive your own car on designated areas of hard-packed sand along Daytona Beach or sample the grub and carnival attractions along **Atlantic Avenue** (A1A).

The next stretch of A1A is a journey back into time to Spanish Florida and the birth of tourism along the First Coast. Perched on one of the barrier islands, **Fort Matanzas National Monument** preserves the ruins of an 18th-century Spanish bastion and the surrounding salt marsh.

The main Spanish settlement is a few miles farther north, in **St. Augustine**. Founded in 1565, it's the nation's oldest continuously occupied European town and the cradle of Florida tourism. Among its many throwbacks are 17th-century **Castillo de San Marcos**, the **Lightner Museum** in the old Hotel Alcazar, and the bevy of historic structures along **St. George Street**.

North of Jacksonville Beach, the **St. Johns River Ferry** carries Highway A1A across the water to **Timucuan Ecological and Historic Preserve**, a joint state-federal park that blends 6,000 years of human history with hiking, biking, boating, and camping. A final bridge takes the coast road over to **Amelia Island** and stops at **Fort Clinch State Park** and the resort town of **Fernandina Beach**. ■

## LAY YOUR HEAD

• **Fontainebleau:** Mafia dons and movie stars made this chic Miami Beach hotel the place to stay in the 1950s and 1960s; restaurants, bars, spa, pools, beach, marina; from $299. fontainebleau.com

• **The Breakers:** Famous names (think Rockefellers and Vanderbilts) have been vacationing at this palatial Palm Beach resort since the 1890s; restaurants, bars, pools, beach, golf, tennis, spa; from $795. thebreakers.com

• **La Quinta Inn Cocoa Beach/Port Canaveral:** The original seven Mercury astronauts owned a piece of this 1950s-style motel on Atlantic Avenue (A1A); restaurants, bar, pool, shuffleboard; from $115. laquinta cocoabeachportcanaveral.com

• **Casa Monica:** Moorish Revival meets Spanish Baroque at this historic hotel in St. Augustine, opened in 1888; restaurant, bar, spa; from $202. marriott.com

• **Amelia Schoolhouse Inn:** A vintage 1880s brick school transformed into a modern boutique in Fernandina Beach; pool, putting green, bar; from $165. ameliaschoolhouseinn.com

# Oahu Circle Island Drive

## Hawaii

Big city Honolulu, the laid-back North Shore, and cinematic history burnish this 100-mile (161 km) swing around the island of Oahu, a drive that showcases the incredible diversity of America's 50th state.

**THE BIG PICTURE**

**Distance:** ca 100 miles (161 km) round-trip from Daniel Inouye International Airport

**Drive time:** 3-5 days

**Best overnights:** Waikiki, Kailua, Kahuku, Kapolei

**Best seasons:** Anytime

**Highlights:** Waikiki, Diamond Head, Kāneʻohe Bay, Kualoa Ranch, Polynesian Cultural Center, Pearl Harbor

Daniel Inouye International Airport offers the ideal start for circumnavigating Oahu. The first stop—just four miles (6.4 km) east along Honolulu's busy H-1 Freeway—is the distinguished **Bishop Museum**, a treasure chest of Hawaiian natural and cultural history, including the royal regalia of the islands' kings and queens.

Farther along H-1 is the exit (20B) for **Chinatown** and **ʻIolani Palace**, home to Hawaii's last monarchs and the territorial/state capitol until 1969. Ala Moana Boulevard leads to **Waikiki Beach** with its chic shopping, celebrated surf break, and historic hotels like the **Moana Surfrider**, opened in 1901 as Waikiki's first hotel.

Looming behind the beach, **Diamond Head** volcano offers hiking trails across the crater floor and around the rim. State Highway 72 whisks drivers to Oahu's east end, past picture-perfect **Hanauma Bay**

**Nature Preserve** (where Elvis Presley shot two movies), **Hālona Beach Cove** (where the scandalous *From Here to Eternity* beach scene was shot), and **Makapuʻu Point Lighthouse Trail.**

Reaching **Kailua**, the road trip segues onto Highway 83 for a dramatic drive across the North Shore. The first stretch features **Hoʻomaluhia Botanical Garden** with its tropical plants from around the world, the Japanese-style **Byodo-In Temple**, and **Heʻeia State Park**, which overlooks pristine **Kāneʻohe Bay**. In addition to providing a scenic backdrop for *Gilligan's Island,* the bay is the only place in Hawaii with fringing, barrier, and patch reefs. Kayak, paddleboard, and snorkel rentals as well as catamaran tours are available at the state park.

Rising behind the bay are the towering cliffs of **Kualoa Ranch**, founded in 1850 as one of Hawaii's first cattle spreads. The 4,000-acre (1,618.7 ha) property is now a private nature reserve with myriad adventure activities—zip lines, mountain biking, horseback riding, and quad biking in primeval valleys where *Jurassic Park, 50 First Dates, Lost*, and *Kong: Skull Island*, among others, were filmed.

Twelve miles (19.3 km) farther

Saddle up for a ride through Kualoa Ranch's stunning wilderness.

Follow trails to the edge of 300,000-year-old dormant Diamond Head Volcano, which looms over Waikiki.

along the North Shore is the **Polynesian Cultural Center**, a South Pacific theme park with luaus, live shows, and cultural presentations in six villages, each representing a different Polynesian island group.

Crowning the top end of Oahu is **James Campbell National Wildlife Refuge**, which protects monk seals, pueo owls, 'alae 'ula birds, and other rare or endangered Hawaiian species. Wild things of a different kind— some of the world's best surfers— inhabit the big wave **Banzai Pipeline** a little farther along the shore.

**Waimea Valley** with its waterfall, botanic garden, and cultural events offers a last stop along the North Shore before the route turns inland with a drive along Highway 99 through the old pineapple country.

**Dole Plantation** features a 20-minute toy train tour through the pineapple fields, as well as a huge pineapple-shaped maze.

Highway 99 reaches the south coast near **Pearl Harbor**, where the **U.S.S. *Arizona* Memorial, Battle-** ship *Missouri*, and **U.S.S. *Bowfin* Submarine Museum** are among the many World War II historic sites along the waterfront. The Pearl Harbor visitor center is just a 10-minute drive from the airport and the end of the Oahu road trip. ■

## EN ROUTE EATS

• **Highway Inn:** Serving kālua pig, lau lau, lomi salmon, poi, and other authentic island dishes since 1947. 680 Ala Moana Blvd. #105, Honolulu. myhighwayinn.com

• **Haili's Hawaiian Foods:** Island-style brunch and lunch in a throwback café owned and operated by the same family since 1950. 760 Palani Ave., Honolulu. hailis hawaiianfood.com

• **Moke's Bread and Breakfast:** Popular breakfast, brunch, and lunch joint on the northeast coast—try the Loco Moco or farm-fresh omelets. 27 Hoolai St., Kailua. mokeshawaii.com

• **Kahuka Food Truck Market:** More than a dozen mobile eateries cluster at this North Shore eating institution, with shrimp and barbecue as the favorite bites. Highway 83 at Burroughs Rd., Kahuka

# Canada
# Road Trips

Between Jasper and Banff, stop at Sunwapta Falls on the Icefields Parkway

# Tracking Cabot & Marconi

## Nova Scotia

A modified figure-eight drive around Cape Breton Island blends local French and Gaelic culture and follows routes dedicated to two of the most influential people in Nova Scotia history: explorer John Cabot and inventor Guglielmo Marconi.

In 1497, John Cabot was likely the first European to cast eyes upon Nova Scotia. Four centuries later, Guglielmo Marconi transmitted the first radio message between North America and Europe from Nova Scotia. Both men are honored by namesake scenic drives on Cape Breton Island.

With its restaurants, pubs, and historic **Waterfront District**, the seaport city of **Sydney** is a natural start for this drive. Head north on Highway 4 to **Glace Bay** and **Marconi National Historic Site**, where the celebrated inventor staged his landmark broadcast in December 1902. The nearby **Cape Breton Miners Museum** traces 250 years of local coal mining history with

### THE BIG PICTURE

**Distance:** ca 320 miles (500 km) round-trip from Sydney

**Drive time:** 5-6 days

**Best overnights:** Sydney and North Sydney, Ingonish, Chéticamp, Baddeck

**Best seasons:** Anytime

**Highlights:** Sydney waterfront, Marconi NHS, Louisbourg Fortress, Cape Breton Highlands NP, Whale Interpretive Centre, Baddeck

exhibits and a guided underground mine tour.

Following routes 255 and 22, **Marconi Trail** hugs the shore all the way down to the **Fortress of Louisbourg**, a massive French colonial citadel later captured by the British during their conquest of Canada. Using living history to full effect, the national historic site re-creates the life and times of an 18th-century fortified town in New France.

Complete the first loop by driving the **Louisbourg Highway** (Route 22) back to Sydney, and then a portion of the **Trans-Canada Highway** (Route 105) to the start of the **Cabot Trail** near Englishtown. You can follow the trail either way, but opt for a run up the east coast on the start of a 185-mile (298 km) loop around the Cape Breton Highlands.

After crossing Jersey Cove on the **Englishtown Ferry**, the route continues north along the coast to **Cape Breton Highlands National Park** with its forested canyons, rocky heights, and stunning shorelines. **Ingonish Visitor Centre** offers information on park activities like golfing **Cape Breton Highlands Links** and hiking the spectacular **Middle Head Trail**.

Road trippers can take a dip in the sea at **Black Brook Cove** and

See a model of Marconi's Table Head Station at the Marconi National Historic Site.

Take in water views and autumn colors as you drive the winding roads of Cape Breton's Cabot Trail.

pop into the **North Highlands Community Museum** before the Cabot Trail turns inland for a scenic climb into the mountains. The highway hits the Gulf of St. Lawrence at **Pleasant Bay**, where the outstanding **Whale Interpretive Centre** sheds light on the 16 species of gentle giants found around Cape Breton Island.

A series of wicked switchbacks lifts the Cabot Trail into the **Fishing Cove River Valley**, where the **Bog Trail** boardwalk across a wetlands area offers a chance to spot moose and insect-eating plants. Just beyond **French Lake**, the **Skyline Trail** leads to a lofty headland with a view across the gulf. The **Chéticamp River Valley** affords one last chance to swim or hike before the highway exits the park into farmland around the old Acadian town of **Chéticamp.**

The next stretch of coast boasts several photogenic lighthouses and the **Mi-Carême Interpretive Centre** in Grand-Étang, which elucidates the region's Acadian culture and history via artifacts and a dinner theater.

Reaching Margaree Forks, the Cabot Trail makes a sharp turn to the east and a final run across the middle of the island to **Baddeck**, renowned as the gateway to boating and fishing on **Lake Bras d'Or** and the home of telephone inventor **Alexander Graham Bell** between 1885 and 1922. By now, you're back on the Trans-Canada for an easy return to Sydney. ∎

## PIT STOPS

- **Baddeck Gathering Ceilidhs:** Pronounced "Kay-lee," this feast of traditional Cape Breton music features more than 50 live performances in July and August. baddeckgathering.com

- **Festival Masque et Mer:** Grand-Étang recalls its Acadian roots with the revival of a carnival that features flamboyant costumes and masks; July. micareme.ca/en

- **Hike the Highlands Festival:** Ten days of walking activities in the national park culminates in the Cape Breton Highlands Three Peaks Challenge every September. hikethehighlandsfestival.com

- **Lumière Arts Festival:** Contemporary visual art, theater, dance, and music are the focus of the September fest in historic downtown Sydney. lumierecb.com

- **Celtic Colours International Festival:** Hundreds of events and activities—from concerts to craft shows—color this October event in towns along the Marconi Trail. celtic-colours.com

# Along the Alaska Highway

## British Columbia to Alaska

Grizzly bears and gnarly moose, rushing whitewater rivers, and snowcapped peaks are just a few of the things that helped transform this one-time military road between British Columbia and the Last Frontier into one of the world's most adventurous road trips.

**THE BIG PICTURE**

**Distance:** 1,365 miles (2,196 km) from Dawson Creek, BC, to Delta Junction, AK

**Drive time:** 7-10 days

**Best overnights:** Fort Nelson, Watson Lake, Whitehorse, Haines Junction

**Best seasons:** Late spring to early fall

**Highlights:** Northern Rockies, Muncho Lake, Watson Lake, Whitehorse, Haines Junction/ Kluane

The great irony of the Alaska (Alcan) Highway is the fact that Canada initially rejected its development over suspicions that the Americans would use it for military purposes. It then quickly rubber-stamped the project after both nations were drawn into World War II.

In one of the great feats of 20th-century engineering, construction was completed in less than eight months (March-October 1942), although the highway wasn't fully paved until 1992. Historic signs and interpretive panels are scattered along the entire route. For more than 70 years, the *Milepost* magazine (and later website) has provided information on road conditions, services, and sights along the route.

Homesteaded in the early 20th century, **Dawson Creek** slowly matured from a farming community into a railway hub and southern terminus of the highway. The whitewashed **Milepost Zero Monument** at the intersection of 10th Street and 102nd Avenue is a magnet for selfies, while the adjacent **Alaska Highway House** does double duty as an information center and museum that screens a documentary, *The Building of the Alaska Highway*.

On the way out of town, **Walter Wright Pioneer Village** offers a blast from the frontier past that includes a number of vintage buildings and vehicles relocated from elsewhere in the region.

With Dawson Creek in the rearview mirror, it's about a five-hour drive to Fort Nelson, with possible stops along the way at **Kiskatinaw Provincial Park** and its historic wooden bridge or **Trapper's Den Wildlife Emporium** with its eclectic selection of North Country clothing and accessories, from mukluks, wool long johns, and porcu-

Liard River Hot Springs is the second largest hot springs in Canada.

Kluane National Park and Reserve is home to the highest peak in Canada—Mount Logan—and its largest ice field.

pine quill earrings to birchbark baskets and snowshoes.

Tacking to the west, the highway meanders through the northernmost part of the **Canadian Rockies**, a stretch that includes the hiking trails and waterways of **Stone Mountain Provincial Park**, gorgeous **Muncho Lake**, and **Liard River Hot Springs Provincial Park** with its steamy pools amid the spruce forest.

The Alaska Highway traces the Laird River upstream into the Yukon Territory and the town of **Watson Lake**. With numerous lodging and eating options, this remote town is a great place to break the drive. But there's also the **Northern Lights Centre**, with interactive displays and an excellent video on the science and folklore of the aurora borealis. And then there's the town's

celebrated **Sign Post Forest**, populated with around 80,000 road, town, and other signs from around the world.

Three hours farther up the road is super-long **Teslin Lake**, which

stretches 75 miles (120 km) through the British Columbia/Yukon wilderness. In addition to **Nisutlin Bay Bridge,** the longest span along the highway's entire length, **Teslin** village offers the **George Johnston**

---

## PIT STOPS

• **24 Hours of Light:** The June midnight sun provides a backdrop for this two-day binge of mountain bikes and beverages in Whitehorse. 24hoursoflight.ca

• **Kluane Mountain Bluegrass Festival:** Three days of pickin' and singing at St. Elias Convention Centre and St. Christopher's Church in Haines Junction every June. yukonbluegrass.com

• **Adäka Cultural Festival:** The

traditional music, dance, storytelling, and art of the Yukon's First Nations peoples are the highlights of this yearly summer event at the Kwanlin Dün Cultural Centre in Whitehorse. adakafestival.ca

• **Dawson Creek Stampede:** This August rodeo and agricultural fair features five days of bucking broncos, chuckwagon races, mechanical bulls, barbecue, and live music. dawsoncreekfair.com

Visitors bring signposts from home to add to the Watson Lake Sign Post Forest.

**Museum**, dedicated to an early 20th-century Tlingit elder who was also a motoring pioneer and avid photographer.

Snaking its way through the lake country of south-central Yukon, the highway soon reaches **Whitehorse**, the territorial capital and one of the most colorful towns in Canadian history. A child of the Klondike gold rush, the city was founded in 1898 at the point on the Yukon River where prospectors had to portage around the White Horse Rapids. Completion of a narrow-gauge railway from Skagway, Alaska, in 1900 cemented the town's position as Canada's northern metropolis.

Prospector and pioneer days are recalled at the **MacBride Museum**, while the city's **Kwanlin Dün Cultural Centre** showcases the life and times of the First Nations people who called the area home for thousands of years before gold was discovered. The **Yukon Beringia Interpretive Centre** focuses on the region's prehistoric roots, including early humans and Ice Age animals

like the woolly mammoth, giant ground sloth, and Beringian lion that once roamed the northern plains and woods.

Much of gold-rush-era Whitehorse has disappeared. But here and there relics remain, like the **S.S. Klondike** stern-wheeler floating museum and the **Old Log Church** on Elliott Street (built in 1900).

The White Horse Rapids—named for the resemblance of the rushing water to the flowing mane of a galloping white horse—are also gone, drowned in 1958 by the rising waters of **Lake Schwatka** reservoir. At the **Whitehorse Fishladder and Hatchery** below the dam, visitors can view Chinook salmon runs through an underground window and on television monitors. Beyond the lake, the hiking trails of **Miles Canyon** provide a quick wilderness escape that includes an old suspension bridge over the Yukon River (built in 1922).

Just north of Whitehorse, the main road splits into the Klondike Highway (Route 2) and Dawson Creek and a continuation of the Alaska Highway that veers west along the Takhini River. Near the junction are two worthwhile stops: the soothing mineral pools of **Takhini Hot Springs** and the **Yukon Wildlife Preserve**, where visitors can observe musk oxen, wood bison, caribou, moose, and other Yukon creatures.

Around 100 miles (160 km) west of Whitehorse, the highway rolls into **Haines Junction**, founded in 1942.

## EN ROUTE EATS

• **Stuie's Diner:** Classic roadside eatery with burgers, fries, milkshakes, clam chowder, and the occasional Elvis impersonator. 10516 Eighth St., Dawson Creek, BC. Phone: (250) 782-3463

• **Gourmet Girl Cafe:** Freshly made soups, salads, sandwiches, wraps, and delicious just-baked scones found right off the Alaska Highway. 5415 51 Avenue West, Suite 107, Fort Nelson, BC. Phone: (250) 774-9362

• **Upper Liard Lodge:** A schnitzel bar, rack of lamb, and Greek appetizers flavor the menu at this restaurant overlooking the Liard River. Mile 642 Alaska Hwy., Watson Lake, YT. upperliardlodge.com

• **Antoinette's:** Canada meets the Caribbean at this restaurant that serves everything from coconut-carrot salad and mango spring rolls to "jahito" cocktails and lime-infused vanilla ice cream. 4121 4th Ave., Whitehorse, YT. antoinettesrestaurant.com

• **Mile 1016 Pub:** Get your fill of poutine, perogies, halibut and chips, deep-fried cherry rolls, and other local favorites at one of the last eateries before the U.S.-Canada border. 118 Marshall Creek Rd., Haines Junction, YT. Phone: (867) 634-2093

## SCENIC DETOURS

- **Liard Highway (BC 77):** The only road connection between British Columbia and the Northwest Territories spans a lonesome 308 miles (495 km) between Fort Nelson and Fort Simpson on the Mackenzie River.

- **Stewart–Cassiar Highway (BC 37):** Traversing British Columbia's most remote corner, the road runs 460 miles (740 km) between Watson Lake and Kitwanga, with an onward drive along Highway 16 to Prince Rupert on the Pacific coast.

- **South Klondike Highway (Route 2):** This 109-mile (176 km) route joining Whitehorse, Yukon, and Skagway, Alaska, follows the historic corridor the Klondike gold rushers used.

- **North Klondike Highway (Route 2):** Connects Whitehorse with Dawson City, the Yukon's other historic gold rush town, 330 miles (530 km) to the north.

- **Haines Road (Route 3):** Flows 108 miles (175 km) south from Haines Junction along the eastern edge of Kluane National Park to Haines, Alaska, on the Pacific coast.

The town would not have existed if not for construction of the wartime highway to Alaska. It is now a hub for outdoor adventure: backpacking, climbing, and scenic flights over nearby **Kluane National Park and Reserve**.

Canada's fifth largest national park harbors **Mount Logan**, the nation's highest peak (19,551 feet/5,959 m) and Canada's largest ice field, as well as an amazing array of wildlife scattered across habitats ranging from wetlands and boreal forest to tundra and glaciers. If you haven't prebooked activities, the **Kluane National Park Visitor Centre** in Haines Junction offers advice and information on exploring the vast (almost roadless) wilderness.

The Parks Canada desk is located inside the new **Da Kų Cultural Centre**, which reveals the culture and traditions of the Champagne and Aishihik First Nations people. Several areas along the eastern edge of Kluane National Park are accessible by car both north and south of Haines Junction, including pretty **Kathleen Lake** and the dramatic **Slim River** area, where the **Tachāl Dhāl Visitor Center** highlights the Dall sheep that inhabit nearby slopes.

North of the park, the Alaska Highway continues along the western shore of **Kluane Lake** to Bur-wash Landing, where the small but interesting **Kluane Museum of Natural History** offers displays on north country wildlife and the Southern Tutchone people. From there it's around a three-hour drive to the **Canada-U.S. border** at the twin towns of Beaver Creek, Yukon, and the appropriately named Alcan, Alaska. The highway continues another 200 miles (300 km) to **Delta Junction** (its official end) and an additional 95 miles (153 km) to **Fairbanks**, Alaska. ◼

Sparkling Kathleen Lake offers hiking, boating, and camping in Kluane.

# Glacier Alley

## Alberta

One of the world's most scenic drives, Alberta Highway 93 meanders through Jasper and Banff National Parks in the Canadian Rockies. The roadway is flanked by whitewater rivers and alpine lakes, dozens of snowcapped peaks, and more than 100 glaciers.

**THE BIG PICTURE**

**Distance:** 179 miles (288 km) from Banff to Jasper

**Drive time:** 2 days

**Best overnights:** Banff, Lake Louise, Jasper

**Best seasons:** Anytime

**Highlights:** Jasper, Athabasca Glacier, Glacial Skywalk, Lake Louise, Banff

The idea of blazing a tourist trail through the Canadian Rockies—via Lake Louise and the Sunwapta River Valley—was first broached in 1885 when the Canadian Pacific Railway reached Banff and the surrounding wilderness was declared the world's third national park. That early horse-and-carriage path endured until the 1930s, when a combination of the Banff-Windermere Parkway and Icefields Parkway made it possible to motor the route.

Set at the confluence of the Athabasca and Sunwapta Rivers, **Jasper Village** is the undisputed hub of its national park. The bygone fur trading post is now an adventure outpost that offers everything from summer **hiking, biking**, and **horseback riding** to winter **cross-country skiing** and **snowshoeing**.

Get the lowdown on park activities at **Jasper Park Information Centre** (behind the big totem pole) or learn more about the park's human and natural history at the **Jasper-Yellowhead Museum and Archives.**

The celebrated **Icefields Parkway** runs south from Jasper, snaking beside the turbulent **Sunwapta River** and its Class III rapids—the park's top spot for whitewater rafting and kayaking. The best photo ops along this part of the drive are the turnoffs for **Athabasca Falls** and **Sunwapta Falls**.

Looming dead ahead is **Columbia Icefield**, a massive cloak of snow and ice covering an area the size of Atlanta or Kansas City. In addition to interpretive exhibits, **Columbia Icefield Glacier Discovery Centre** offers guided snow-coach tours to **Athabasca Glacier** and a vertigo-inducing glass-floored **Glacier Skywalk** perched 984 feet (300 m) above the valley floor.

Heading downhill into **Banff National Park**, the parkway leaps across the **Saskatchewan River** at a place called the **Crossing** before heading up majestic **Mistaya Canyon**. The next summit is crowned by turquoise-colored **Peyto Lake** and lofty **Bow Pass**, the highest point along the drive at 6,791 feet (2,070 m).

Icefields Parkway ends at dazzling **Lake Louise**, with snowy peaks all around and the lovely **Chateau Lake Louise hotel** poised beside the water. A great place to pause the drive no matter what the season, Louise offers a variety of adventures and activities. Summer visitors can hike the **Plain of the Six Glaciers Trail** around the shore and up an alpine valley to **Lake**

Take in the Columbia Icefield from the glass-floored Glacier Skywalk.

Surrounded on three sides by mountains, Spirit Island, a small peninsula, juts out into Maligne Lake in Jasper National Park.

**Agnes Tea House.** During the cold months, there's ice skating on the lake and downhill skiing, snowboarding, and fresh-powder backcountry skiing at **Lake Louise Ski Resort**.

From Lake Louise, road trippers can either jump on the **Trans-Canada Highway** for a fast drive down to Banff or mosey down the **Bow Valley Parkway** (Highway 1A) with stops along the way at picture-perfect **Morant's Curve**, the **Castle Mountain Lookout Trail**, **Johnson Falls**, and **Backswamp Viewpoint** before cruising into the Banff Valley.

**Banff National Park Visitor Centre** in the heart of the village has the lowdown on everything there is to do. Indoor attractions include the **Banff Park Museum, Whyte Museum of the Canadian Rockies,** and **Cave and Basin Hot Springs**. And outdoor recreation ranges from the historic **Banff Springs Golf Club,** boating or scuba diving **Lake Minnewanka,** and adrenaline sports on **Mount Norquay** (skiing, snowboarding, biking, hiking) to fly-fishing and float trips on the **Bow River**. ∎

# Viking Trail
## Newfoundland

Norsemen set foot in North America roughly 500 years before Columbus, a brief but significant heritage reflected in the modern Viking Trail, a road trip down Newfoundland's rugged, windswept west coast.

**THE BIG PICTURE**

**Distance:** 314 miles (505 km) from L'Anse aux Meadows to Deer Lake

**Drive time:** 3 to 4 days

**Best overnights:** St. Anthony, Rocky Harbour, Norris Point, Deer Lake

**Best seasons:** Summer

**Highlights:** L'Anse aux Meadows, Burnt Cape, Port au Choix, Gros Morne

Until the 1960s, when archaeologists discovered the remains of timber and sod structures, scholars believed that stories about Norseman landing in the Americas were nothing more than myth and legend. **L'Anse aux Meadows**, which crowns the tip of the **Great Northern Peninsula**, proves them wrong. In addition to ruins dated to around A.D. 1000, the UNESCO World Heritage site and Parks Canada National Historic Site offers summertime guided tours, saga storytelling, a living history encampment, and the new **Test of Tykir** escape room experience.

There are more costumed interpreters at nearby **Norstead Viking Village**, which replicates a medieval Norse seaport via a living history demonstration in a replica workshop, church, chieftain's hall, and longboat. Visitors can also get their fortunes read with rune stones.

Farther down the peninsula, stretch your legs with a hike across the glacier-carved tundra terrain of **Pistolet Bay Provincial Park** or **Burnt Cape Ecological Reserve.** Pistolet also has opportunities for camping, canoeing, and fishing, while the limestone cliffs at Burnt Cape are an idea perch for sighting icebergs and whales in the **Strait of Belle Isle.** The parks also harbor around 30 species of rare subpolar plants.

Leaving the peninsula behind, Route 430 makes its way down Newfoundland's west coast to **Saint Barbe**, where you can hop the auto ferry over to **Labrador**, and **Port au Choix National Historic Site**, where a visitor center and archaeological sites shed light on the Maritime Archaic, Paleo-Eskimo, and other indigenous peoples who lived along the island's shoreline prior to European settlement.

At nearby Hawke's Bay, the **Torrent River Salmon Interpretation Centre** offers insight into how the nonprofit fosters local salmon spawning and restocking, as well as viewing windows where visitors can watch salmon swimming up the fishway.

**The Arches Provincial Park** near Portland Creek is another great place for a stroll, this time along the **Gulf of St. Lawrence.** The park takes its name from a cluster of dolomite arches carved by waves over hundreds of years.

The southern end of the Viking Trail is anchored by **Gros Morne National Park**, one of Maritime Canada's most alluring landscapes, The coastline, riven with bays, beaches, and colossal fjords, could easily be mistaken for the coast of Norway.

The Viking Trail glides into the

L'Anse aux Meadows is the only known Viking settlement in North America.

From a hike to the top of Gros Morne Mountain, you can stare down into Ten Mile Pond.

park at **Shallow Bay**, the best place along this entire coast for summer swimming. Farther along are the **Broom Point Fishing Exhibit** and **Lobster Cove Head Lighthouse**. As one of the park's visitor centers, the lighthouse offers outdoor fire circles (summer) and indoor storytelling and music (year-round).

There's another visitor center at Rocky Harbour, an old fishing village that also offers guided boat tours of fjord-like **Bonne Bay** and **Western Brooke Pond** as well as **cod jigging cruises** that blend fishing and local traditions.

Among the national park's primo hikes are the short (2.5 miles/4 km) but spectacular Tablelands Trail across a rocky moonscape, the climb up 2,644.4-foot (806 m) **Gros Morne Mountain**, and a 21.8-mile (35 km) trek called the **Long Range Traverse** through the backcountry.

The Viking Trail continues down to **Deer Lake**, where it intersects the Trans-Canada Highway for those who want to go east to **St. John's** (396 miles/637 km) or south to **Channel-Port aux Basques** (164.7 miles/265 km) and the vehicle ferry across the **Cabot Strait** to Nova Scotia. ■

## LAY YOUR HEAD

• **Grenfell Heritage Hotel:** The closest lodging to L'Anse aux Meadows, this 20-room lodge in St. Anthony offers rooms with kitchens and harbor views; gift shop, laundry, Wi-Fi; from C$139. www.grenfell heritagehotel.ca

• **Ocean View Hotel:** Live music, craft beer, pub grub, and a waterfront location make this Rocky Harbour motel the place to stay in Gros Morne National Park; restaurant,

bar, ATM, Wi-Fi; from C$129. the oceanview.ca

• **Neddies Harbour Inn:** Boutique hotel on Bonne Bay fjord in the heart of the national park; restaurant, fitness center, sauna; from C$165. theinn.ca

• **Bonne Bay Inn:** Cozy B&B at Woody Point, across the fjord from Norris Point; restaurant, bar, outdoor deck; from C$199. woodypoint magic.com

# Trans-Canada Highway
## Newfoundland to British Columbia

Stretching from St. John's, Newfoundland, on the Atlantic coast to Victoria, British Columbia, on the Pacific shore—and featuring two major ferry crossings—the Trans-Canada Highway provides an epic means to explore the world's second largest nation.

The world's longest national road rambles through 10 provinces as it spans Canada from sea to sea. But it's not just length that makes the Trans-Canada Highway (TCH) an all-time great road trip. The route also encompasses a wide variety of Canadian culture and geography.

Launched in 1962 along preexisting highways and finished in 1972, the TCH is actually "double tracked"—southern and northern routes marked by distinctive white-and-green maple leaf road signs. Our road trip combines aspects of both on a 4,500-mile (7,300 km) journey that kicks off in **St. John's, Newfoundland**.

**Mile Zero** of the TCH is marked by a large compass rose and route map between City Hall and the Mile One Centre sports arena. Right across the road is St. John's truly aged **old town**, which traces its roots to the 1630s when "North America's Oldest City" was founded by English settlers. But old doesn't mean decrepit: with its raucous pubs, **George Street** is the hub of the city's nightlife and the Jellybean Row Houses of **Kimberley Row** are the most colorful homes in all of Canada.

Learn more about Britain's first overseas colony at the **Rooms** provincial museum and adjacent **Fort Townsend National Historic Site** before hitting the road. The TCH runs roughly 560 miles (900 km) through the woodsy, glacier-carved heart of Newfoundland to **Channel-Port aux Basques** and a rendezvous with the **Marine Atlantic Ferry** across the Cabot Strait. The crossing takes around seven hours.

On the other side is **North Sydney** near the top end of Nova Scotia. It's easy to reach wild and wonderful **Cape Breton Highlands National Park** from here. But otherwise the TCH makes quick work of Nova Scotia, crossing over to mainland Canada

**THE BIG PICTURE**

**Distance:** 4,541 miles (7,308 km) from St. John's, Newfoundland, to Victoria, BC

**Drive time**: 14-21 days

**Best overnights:** Moncton, Quebec City, Montreal, Ottawa, Winnipeg, Regina, Calgary, Banff, Vancouver

**Best seasons:** Spring, summer, or fall

**Highlights:** Cape Breton, Quebec City, Montreal, Ottawa, Lake Superior, Canadian Prairies, Calgary, Banff NP, Vancouver, Vancouver Island

Find quaint cafés and charming eateries in downtown Montreal.

Ottawa's Parliament Hill buildings overlook the Ottawa River between Quebec and Ontario.

at **Port Hawkesbury** on a five-hour drive to **Moncton**, New Brunswick, with the possibility of side trips to **Prince Edward Island** and the turbulent **Bay of Fundy**.

Crossing into Quebec province, the highway follows the south bank of the mighty St. Lawrence River to **Quebec City**, where the old **walled city** (a UNESCO World Heritage site) presents a mosaic of Canadian history, culture, and cuisine. Sticking to the *rive droite*, the TCH continues to **Montreal** with its own cobblestoned old town and renovated port area, as well as lush **Mont-Royal Park** and islands in the St. Lawrence.

**Ottawa** is only two hours farther west along the TCH. Canada's national capital revolves around Parliament Hill with its Gothic Revival–style **Parliament Buildings**. Catch a live performance at the **National Arts Centre**, browse the city's numerous museums, and climb the **Peace Tower** before moving on.

West of Ottawa, the Trans-Canada ambles more than 1,200 miles (2,000 km) across the farmlands and forests of Ontario, the longest stretch through any province. There's a brief flirtation with **Lake Huron** before rolling into **Sault Ste. Marie** and a scenic drive along the northern shore of **Lake Superior** and onward to Manitoba.

As the undisputed "Gateway to the West," Winnipeg marks the

---

### ART AVENUES

- **Best Fiction Books:** *Anne of Green Gables* by L. M. Montgomery; *The Apprenticeship of Duddy Kravitz* by Mordecai Richler; *The Shipping News* by Annie Proulx; *Alias Grace* by Margaret Atwood

- **Best Nonfiction Books:** *Souvenir of Canada* by Douglas Coupland; *The Inconvenient Indian* by Thomas King; *99: Stories of the Game* by Wayne Gretzky; *The Vinyl Café Notebooks* by Stuart McLean; *Traveling the Trans-Canada* by William Howarth

- **Best Movies:** *Goin' Down the Road* (1970); *My American Cousin* (1985); *Jesus of Montreal* (1989); *Black Robe* (1991); *Les Boys* (1997), *Seducing Dr. Lewis* (2004); *My Winnipeg* (2007); *One Week* (2008)

- **Best TV Shows:** *Due South* (1994-99); *Slings and Arrows* (2003-2006); *Corner Gas* (2004-2009); *Heartland* (2007-present); *Murdoch Mysteries* (2008-present); *Bad Blood* (2017-present); *Kim's Convenience* (2017-present)

transition into the seemingly endless Canadian Prairies, a status celebrated at **Forks National Historic Site** and its 6,000 years of local history. Among the other must-see sites are **the Canadian Museum of Civil Rights**, the Francophone **St. Boniface** neighborhood, and the **Royal Canadian Mint**.

It's another long haul to Regina. But there are quirky stops along the way: the **World's Tallest Coca-Cola Can** in Portage la Prairie, the **Manitoba Antique Automobile Museum** in Elkhorn, and **Wolseley Swinging Bridge**.

Named for Queen Victoria, **Regina** has grown up around **Wascana Lake**, created just a year after the provincial capital was founded (1882). Most of the city's major attractions hug the lakeshore, including the **Royal Saskatchewan Museum, MacKenzie Art Gallery**, **Saskatchewan Science Centre**, and **Queen Elizabeth II Gardens**. Away from the water, the **Royal Canadian Mounted Police Heritage Centre** honors the red-suited Mounties who helped settle Canada's Wild West.

West of Regina, the monotony of the flatlands is broken by intriguing highland areas easily accessible from the TCH. North of the highway, the **Great Sandhills Ecological Reserve** protects shifting dunes. South of the highway, **Cypress Hills Interprovincial Park** floats like a giant island of trees amid a prairie sea.

Named for the unique eagle-feather headdress of a Blackfoot shaman, **Medicine Hat** anchors the eastern end of the TCH in Alberta. The innovative **Medalta** museum and arts center pays tribute to the ceramic masters who once labored in the city's **Clay Industries National Historic District**. Half an hour west is a turn-

The Royal Canadian Mounted Police run drills in Regina, Saskatchewan.

---

## SCENIC DETOURS

- **Great Northern Peninsula Highway:** Also called the Viking Trail, Route 430 heads from Deer Lake, Newfoundland, to Gros Morne National Park and the Norse settlement at L'Anse aux Meadows.

- **Quebec Route 138:** Hugs the north bank of the St. Lawrence River between Quebec City and Kegashka at the remote east end of the Côte-Nord.

- **Ontario Highway 11:** From North Bay, Route 11 provides access to big Algonquin Provincial Park and the Toronto metropolitan area.

- **Louis Riel Trail:** Saskatchewan Highway 11 connects Regina with Saskatoon and Prince Albert, a journey that gradually segues from prairie to aspen parkland and boreal forest.

- **Icefields Parkway:** One of the world's most attractive routes spans Banff and Jasper in the Canadian Rockies.

- **BC Highway 97:** Runs right down the middle of the wine-rich Okanagan Valley on a 180-mile (286 km) journey between Kamloops and Osoyoos on the British Columbia–Montana border.

---

off for the must-stop **Dinosaur Provincial Park**.

The Canadian Rockies loom in the distance, but not before a short sojourn in **Calgary**. In addition to the **Calgary Stampede** (July) Alberta's largest city offers other Wild West–centric attractions like **Heritage Park Historical Village** and old **Fort Calgary** (established 1875). But the city also boasts a modern side, personified by the 626-foot (190.8 m) **Calgary Tower** and the futuristic **Studio Bell National Music Center**.

Rising quickly into the **Rockies**,

the highway passes through **Banff National Park** and Kicking Horse Pass into **Yoho National Park** on the British Columbia side of the range. A zigzag route through British Columbia's coastal ranges takes the TCH through **Glacier National Park of Canada**, along the shore of **Shuswap Lake**, and down into historic **Kamloops**, a former gold mining boomtown and railway hub renowned for its homegrown wines.

As it traverses the **Fraser River Valley**, the Trans-Canada reaches the sea again in **Vancouver**, a melting pot of culture with a striking skyline. One of North America's great urban green spaces, **Stanley Park** offers a warren of hiking and biking trails, Shakespeare in the park, the **Vancouver Aquarium**, famous totem poles, and spectacular views of the **Lions Gate Bridge**. The old docks and warehouses of **Granville Island** have morphed into a modern eating and entertainment district, while the **Gastown** neighborhood harbors Victorian architecture and bars.

**Horseshoe Bay** in West Vancouver is where the TCH starts another water leg—a one-hour, 40-minute passage on **BC Ferries** to Nainamo on **Vancouver Island**. Nainamo's handsome waterfront is the jumping-off point for all sorts of outdoor adventures, from orca-watching cruises and day sails to fishing charters and flightseeing over the **Strait of Georgia** and the **Sunshine Coast**.

The highway's home stretch is a 90-minute drive down to **Victoria**. Navigating downtown via Douglas Street, the TCH glides past landmarks like the historic **Empress Hotel**, the **BC Royal Museum**, and the totem poles of **Thunderbird Park** before reaching Victoria's version of the **Mile Zero Monument** in seaside **Beacon Hill Park**. ∎

# Mackenzie Highway
## Alberta & Northwest Territories

Canada's real-life ice road is the Mackenzie Highway, a 700-mile (1,126.5 km) route from the prairies of northern Alberta to the boreal forest and tundra plains of the Northwest Territories, a drive that requires ferry crossings in summer and ice bridges in winter.

### THE BIG PICTURE

**Distance:** ca 1,040 miles (1,673 km) from Edmonton, AB, to Wrigley, NWT

**Drive time:** 5-7 days

**Best overnights:** Peace River, Hay River, Fort Simpson

**Best seasons:** Summer, fall, or winter

**Highlights:** Peace River, Great Slave Lake, Wood Buffalo NP, Fort Simpson, Mackenzie River

Started in the 1930s as a way to connect the remote settlements of the Northwest Territories with the rest of Canada, the Mackenzie Highway wasn't fully complete until the 1990s. Even today, it's one of North America's most remote and adventurous roads, a largely unpaved route that counts large wildlife, extreme weather, and utter wilderness among its numerous driving hazards.

Most Mackenzie road trips start from **Edmonton** with a five-hour drive across the northern Alberta prairie and not an awful lot to do along the way—other than pose for selfies beneath the **"world's largest bee"** in Falher.

Reaching **Peace River** comes as a huge relief to drivers itching for something to see. Founded in 1792 by highway namesake and intrepid Scottish explorer Alexander Mackenzie, the town offers plenty of roadside wonders, from the **Peace River Museum** and **St. Augustine Mission** to hiking or biking **Peace River Wildland Provincial Park** and guided **river trips.**

The highway's **Mile Zero Monument** is 20 minutes farther west in **Grimshaw**, where the visitor information center dispenses maps and tips on what lies ahead. After filling your gas tank and stocking up on road food, you are ready for the first leg: a 340-mile (550 km) drive into the Northwest Territories (NT) through a landscape that segues from grain fields to boreal forest.

The 60th parallel defines the boundary between Alberta and the NT, and smack dab on the latitude line is the **Sixtieth Parallel Territorial Park and Visitor Centre**. Open May to September, the center offers audiovisual presentations, First Nations arts and crafts, hot coffee, cold water, and a campground. Farther along are **Alexandra Falls** and the big road junction at **Enterprise**.

For those who aren't in a hurry, the **Hay River Highway** (Route 2) connects Enterprise with **Wood**

Nahanni National Park Reserve is a dedicated UNESCO World Heritage site.

The aurora borealis performs its nightly dance over Great Slave Lake in the Northwest Territories.

**Buffalo National Park** and **Hay River** town on the south shore of **Great Slave Lake**. The Mackenzie Highway (route 1) veers off to the northwest on a 240-mile (400 km) run through the remote Deh Cho region to Fort Simpson. The drives include a crossing of the **Liard River** by vehicle ferry (May to October) or ice bridge (November-April).

Established in 1803 as a fur trading post, **Fort Simpson** harbors relics like **McPherson House, Ehdaa National Historic Site**, and a brand-new **Heritage Center** museum. It's also the jumping-off spot for floatplane tours of **Nahanni National Park Reserve**. And visitors can play a round of nine at **Seven Spruce Golf Course**, one of the continent's most northerly links.

North of Fort Simpson is where it gets *real* wild. The last leg is a 140-mile (220 km) drive through the cold, boggy, uninhabited flats along the **Mackenzie River** to remote **Wrigley**.

Venturing farther down the thousand-mile-long (1,609.3 km) Mackenzie (Canada's longest river) entails a boat or floatplane in summer or snowmobiles or dogsleds in winter—on an ice road that forms over the frozen river. By water or ice, it's 200 miles (321 km) from Wrigley to **Normal Wells** above the Arctic Circle. ∎

## PIT STOPS

- **Carnaval de St.-Isidore:** The French Canadian hamlet near Peace River marks Lent with a February carnival featuring snow sculpting, log sawing, hayrides, bonfire, and beard contest. centreculturelstisidore.ca

- **Beavertail Jamboree:** Fort Simpson celebrates the end of winter with a week of snowmobiling, live music, cooking contests, and fireworks in early March. fort-simpson.com

- **Beaumont Blues and Roots Festival:** Canadian country, folk, blues, and rockabilly music is the focus of this June jamboree. bbrf.ca

- **Open Sky Festival:** Fiddling, traditional dance, soapstone carving, and birchbark crafts are just a few of the events that color this First Nations June or July fest at the confluence of the Liard and Mackenzie Rivers in Fort Simpson. openskycreative society.com

- **North Peace Stampede:** Come August, broncobusters, steer riders, and chuckwagon racers invade La Cardinal Sports Ground near Grimshaw during northern Alberta's biggest rodeo event. northpeace stampede.com

# Lake Huron's Eastern Shore
## Ontario

A rustic lakeshore, scenic ferry ride, and the largest island in the Great Lakes region are the highlights of this offbeat journey along Lake Huron's eastern shore through a part of Ontario that remains largely unknown to road trippers.

### THE BIG PICTURE

**Distance:** ca 280 miles (450 km) from Sarnia, ON, to McKerrow, ON

**Drive time:** 5-6 days

**Best overnights:** Kincardine, Sauble Beach, Tobermory, Little Current

**Best seasons:** Spring, summer, or fall

**Highlights:** Pinery Provincial Park, Bluewater Highway towns, Bruce Peninsula, Lake Huron ferry, Manitoulin Island

Lake Huron may be the second largest of the Great Lakes, but it's by far the least traveled today. There are no great cities, illustrious national parks, or world-renowned waterfalls along its shore. But you'll find plenty of peace and quiet, remarkably unspoiled landscapes, and throwbacks to the Canada of 100 years ago or more.

The twin cities of **Port Huron**, Michigan, and **Sarnia**, Ontario—located at the point where Lake Huron empties into the St. Clair River—anchor the southern end of this road trip with a number of lake-related sights including the **Huron Lightship Museum** and **Fort Gratiot Light Station** (second oldest lighthouse in the Great Lakes). The riverfront also boasts the **Thomas Edison Depot**, where inventor Edison sold newspapers and candy as a young man.

The immense Blue Water Bridge leaps the St. Clair River into Canada and the start of a drive along Lakeshore Road (Route 7) to **Pinery Provincial Park**. That's a definite misnomer, because the park protects the largest stand of oak savanna left in Ontario, as well as coastal dunes, pristine beaches, and an old stretch of the **Ausable River**. Hiking, biking, paddling, fishing, cross-country skiing, and camping are the main activities.

North of Pinery, the coastal road morphs into the **Bluewater Highway** (Route 21) and a pastoral coast settled by 19th-century Scottish immigrants. The meandering Maitland River flows through **Goderich** with its art galleries, nature trails, and **Huron Historic Gaol**. Farther up the shore, **Kincardine** offers splendid Victorian architecture, Scottish culture, and myriad outdoor sports (on land and water). Southampton tenders a **lakeshore boardwalk** and the excellent **Bruce County Museum** with exhibits on the region's natural and human history.

Routes 13 and 6 connect Southampton with the **Bruce Peninsula**, which separates Lake Huron and broad **Georgian Bay**. Farmland fades into forest and natural landmarks like **Sauble Falls, Lion's Head**, and gorgeous Grotto and Indian Head Cove on **Bruce Peninsula National Park.** The road ends in **Tobermory**, the

Fort Gratiot Lighthouse (1825) is the second oldest on the Great Lakes.

More than 20 historic shipwrecks can be seen from above and below the water at Fathom Five National Marine Park.

spot for diving the 22 wrecks of offshore **Fathom Five National Marine Park**, as well as the southern terminus of the ferry **MS Chi-Cheemaun**. The service runs early May through mid-October, a two-hour crossing to **South Baymouth** on Manitoulin Island.

**Manitoulin**, the planet's largest freshwater island, means "cave of the spirit" in the language of the indigenous people who have lived here for thousands of years. The name derives from the belief that the Great Spirit dwells in a local underwater cavern. First Nations people comprise around 40 percent of the current population, and Manitoulin boasts eight Anishinaabe Indian reserves.

The island offers two ways to continue the road trip. The quickest is Route 6 along the eastern shore, a distance of 50 miles (80.5 km) to **Little Current Swing Bridge** and mainland Ontario. A more in-depth drive (Routes 542 and 540) makes a huge loop through Manitoulin's middle and west end.

The latter route is longer (165 miles/265.5 km) but features a number of the island's top sights, including **Misery Bay Provincial Nature Reserve**, **Mississagi Lighthouse**, **Old Mill Heritage Center**, **Bridal Veil Falls**, and the **Ojibwe Cultural Foundation** museum and arts center. ■

## PIT STOPS

- **Huron Fringe Birding Festival:** This springtime feathered-friend fiesta takes place in the "Huron Fringe" along the west coast of the Bruce Peninsula. friendsofmacgregor.org

- **Scottish Pipe Band Parade:** Bagpipes take over Queen Street in downtown Kincardine on summer Saturday nights in a tribute to the region's tartan heritage. explorethe bruce.com

- **Manitoulin Country Fest:** More than 20,000 fans flock to Little Current each August as Canadian country music takes the stage at this three-day outdoor event. manitoulin countryfest.com

- **Celtic Roots Festival:** The music of Ireland, Scotland, and Wales and their North American derivatives are the focus of the annual August bash in Goderich. celticfestival.ca/festival

# Water & Woods

## Quebec

More like a drive through Europe than a North American road trip, this journey across Canada's Quebec province meanders through big cities and small towns, boreal forest and bucolic farmland on an excursion down the valley of the St. Lawrence River to the sea.

**THE BIG PICTURE**

**Distance:** ca 820 miles (1,320 km) from Montreal to Gaspé

**Drive time:** 10-14 days

**Best overnights:** Montreal, Mont-Tremblant, Saint-Donat, Trois-Rivières, Quebec City, Saguenay Fjords, Baie-Comeau, Gaspé

**Best seasons:** Anytime

**Highlights:** Montreal, Mont-Tremblant, Quebec City, Saguenay Fjords, St. Lawrence ferry, Gaspé Peninsula

Founded by explorer Jacques Cartier in 1534 and originally called Nouvelle-France, Quebec province cherished the tricolor and fleur-de-lis for more than 230 years before falling to Britain during the French and Indian War. The Quebecois stubbornly preserved their French language and other Gallic traditions, a legacy that continues into the 21st century and flavors this wide-range road trip across the province.

The place to start is **Old Montreal**, where Cartier stepped ashore on his second voyage. He was greeted by Iroquois people living in a fortified village at the foot of a mountain that Cartier dubbed Mont-Royal after the French king.

A cobblestoned plaza, **Place Jacques-Cartier**, honors his memory, although one wonders what the 16th-century explorer might have thought of the assorted fire-eaters, mimes, and acrobats who entertain in the square today. With exhibits and artifacts that illuminate more than 1,000 years of local history, the **Pointe-à-Callière** museum is the place to learn about Quebec Province's past before hitting the road.

Exit the old town on **Boulevard St. Laurent**, a heritage road originally laid out in the 17th century and a certified national historical site. Called "The Main" by locals because of its ongoing importance to the city, St. Laurent runs through neighborhoods like **Chinatown**, the old **Jewish Quarter, Little Portugal**, and **Little Italy** that reflect Montreal's melting pot and the fact it's much more than just a French Canadian city.

Just over five miles (8.3 km) from the river, follow the signs to Autoroute 40 Ouest and a quick transition onto Autoroute 15 Nord. Eventually you emerge from the seemingly endless suburbs that surround Montreal into the Quebec countryside, a mosaic of farmland and forest that renders a preview of what lies ahead along much of this drive.

Slide off the freeway at Saint-Faustin-Lac-Carré and follow the signs to Lac-Supérieur and **Mont-Tremblant National Park** in the Laurentian mountains. One of the largest, oldest, and most versatile parks in eastern Canada, it offers a

The "Fresque de Quebecois" wall mural highlights historical characters.

Historic Château Frontenac, now a luxury hotel, sits inside the walls of Old Quebec City.

wide array of outdoor activities in all seasons.

**La Diable** is the park's epicenter, a heavily wooded wilderness valley flanked by granite cliffs and dissected by a chain of lakes and the copper-colored **Rivière du Diable**. In addition to the activities one might expect (hiking, biking, canoeing), La Diable features offbeat adventures like a **via ferrata** rock climbing experience and ranger-guided paddles in *rabaska* **birch-bark canoes**.

A drive along the Chemin du Nord connects La Diable with the park's eastern **La Pimbina** sector and another huge expanse of wilderness ripe for outdoor adventures like hiking, paddling, and wildlife-watching. Nearby **Saint-Donat** village, flanked by lakes and downhill ski areas, does double duty as a winter sports hub and summer waterfront retreat.

The next leg of the drive traverses the gorgeous countryside between Mont-Tremblant and the St. Lawrence River, a sequence of lightly trafficked rural routes (125, 347, 348) past picture-perfect farms, sleepy villages, and the occasional tourist attraction. **Vignoble**

## LAY YOUR HEAD

• **William Gray:** Chic modern boutique inside an 18th-century mansion in Old Montreal, right off the Place Jacques-Cartier; restaurants, bar, spa, fitness center, library/lounge; from C$189. hotelwilliam gray.com

• **Le Germain:** Tucked inside a former bank building, this cozy retreat in Quebec City blends old-world charm and modern amenities; courtesy car, fitness room; from C$239. legermainhotels.com

• **Auberge la Fjordelaise:** Located in L'Anse-Saint-Jean on Saguenay Fjord, this French Canadian–style B&B boasts lake-view rooms; restaurant; from C$65. fjordelaise .com/english

• **Hôtel Le Manoir:** A luxury hotel with a modern take on the French colonial manor house overlooking the St. Lawrence Estuary in Baie-Comeau; restaurant, bar, spa; from C$128. manoirbc.com/en

• **Perce Au Pic de l'Aurore:** Cozy cliff-top chalets with fireplaces, kitchenettes, and living rooms near the tip of the Gaspé Peninsula; bar/lounge; from C$84. percechalet.com

**Saint-Gabriel** is a combination winery and tractor museum where visitors can indulge in charcuterie, cheese, and wine before moving on down the road.

Route 348 ends at the busy T-junction in Louisville. Hang a left and follow the signs through the rotary to Autoroute 40 Est. Twenty minutes ahead is **Trois-Rivières**, at the confluence of the Saint-Maurice and St. Lawrence Rivers. Quebec's second oldest city (founded 1634) offers architectural gems like the **Ursuline chapel and gardens** and **Our Lady of the Cape Shrine**. However, its main attraction is the **Musée POP**, which combines exhibits on contemporary Quebec culture with the thoroughly creepy **Old Prison** (constructed in 1822).

Another 80 miles (130 km) along the autoroute is **Quebec City**, the provincial capital and one of the

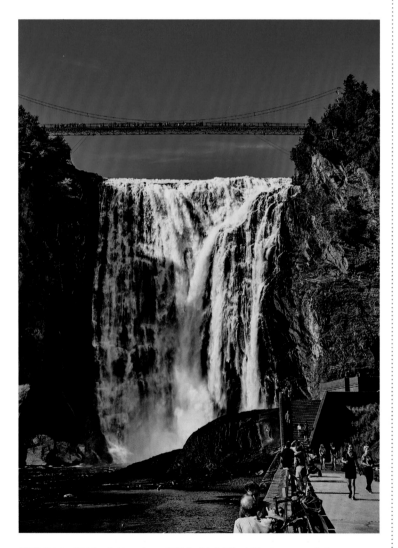

Walk the pedestrian bridge above 272-foot-tall (83 m) Montmorency Falls.

world's most distinctive urban areas. A blend of French and British architecture and influences, **Old Quebec** in the city center is the only walled town left in North America. Perched on commanding heights with the riverfront below, the warren of cobblestone streets, steep hills, and staircases is ready-made for walking. Park your car and strike out on foot.

Orient yourself to the cityscape with a stroll along **Dufferin Terrace** and the **Governors' Walkway**, part of the ramparts that once protected Quebec City from enemy attack. Along the way, pop into the **Château Frontenac** for a glance at Canada's most famous hotel (opened in

1893) and the adjacent **Musée du Fort**, where scale models of the old city and a 30-minute sound and light show spin tales of Quebec's colorful past.

The city offers plenty of ways to while away a day (or two or three). Visit the outdoor cafés along the **Grande Allée**, the historic **Plains of Abraham**, the architecturally impressive **Musée national des beaux-arts du Québec**, and the cobblestone **Place Royale** with its immense **"Fresque des Québécois"** mural depicting 400 years of local history and the exquisite **Notre-Dame-des-Victoires**, the continent's oldest stone church, built in 1688.

The road trip continues with thundering **Montmorency Falls** (and its vertiginous pedestrian bridge) on the northern outskirts of Quebec City. From there it's a 120-mile (200 km) drive up Route 138 to the majestic **Saguenay Fjord**.

One of Canada's most stunning natural attractions includes the land-based **Saguenay Fjord National Park** and the **Saguenay–St. Lawrence National Marine Conservation Area**, which safeguards beluga whales and other creatures that frequent local waters. Activities range from camping, hiking, and rock climbing to kayak whale-watching, scuba diving, and boat tours.

The passenger and vehicle ferry takes Route 138 (and road trippers) across the mouth of the fjord. On the north shore, **Tadoussac** village offers a range of hotels, restaurants, and adventure outfitters, as well as the **Marine Mammal Interpretation Centre** with its interactive exhibits, impressive skeleton collection, and whale song workshops.

The rustic shoreline north of Saguenay, the **Côte-Nord**, is a string of picturesque French Canadian

Saguenay Fjord National Park sits on the eastern end of the Saguenay River.

fishing villages strung along Route 138. **Baie-Comeau** is a timber industry and hydroelectric hub that is gradually transitioning into tourism with sights like the **Mont-Tibasse** ski area and **Jardin des Glaciers** museum of geology and glaciation.

You can end the road trip in Baie-Comeau or roll onto the **MV Apollo**, a passenger and vehicle ferry that crosses the St. Lawrence Estuary in two and a half hours. On the

far shore is **Matane** village, where seafood eateries, art galleries, and a historic red-and-white lighthouse line the waterfront.

Route 132 runs north along the shore to Sainte-Anne-des-Mont, gateway to the caribou herds and hiking trails of **Gaspésie National Park** and **Mont-Albert** in the highlands, and then onward to the spectacular sea cliffs of **Forillon National Park** and the town of **Gaspé** at the tip of the peninsula. ■

## PIT STOPS

- **Quebec Winter Carnaval:** This cold-weather version of pre-Lenten festivities features parades, masquerade balls, snow-sculpting contests, outdoor banquets, and an ice canoe race on the frozen St. Lawrence; February or March. carnaval.qc.ca/en

- **Just for Laughs:** The biggest international comedy fest lures A-list jokers from around the globe to four days of fun in July in Montreal. comedypro.hahaha.com

- **Festival de Musique du Bout du Monde:** A circus big top and the bluffs at Cap-Bon-Ami are just two of the venues for this August music fest in Gaspé town. musiqueduboutdumonde.com/en

- **International Poetry Festival:** Trois-Rivières celebrates the art form of verse with 10 October days of poetry readings, slams, workshops, and contests featuring around 80 poets from around the world. fiptr.com/en

# Discovery Coast
## British Columbia

Suffused with pristine beaches, bays, and islands, plus a wildlife-rich temperate rainforest, British Columbia's Pacific Coast offers an adventurous road trip into the realm of killer whales and grizzly bears.

**THE BIG PICTURE**

**Distance:** ca 470 miles (760 km) from Victoria to Bella Coola

**Drive time:** 7-10 days

**Best overnights:** Nanaimo, Port Campbell, Port Hardy, Bella Coola

**Best seasons:** Summer or early fall

**Highlights:** Victoria, Campbell River adventure, Telegraph Cove orcas, Discovery Route ferry, Great Bear Rainforest

From the middle of June to early September, BC Ferries makes it possible to "drive" the Discovery Coast—a wild and remote shoreline that lies astride the Inside Passage. The special passenger and vehicle ferry service docks at secluded towns and islands unreachable by road.

Perched at the southern end of Vancouver Island, **Victoria** makes a perfect starting point for this drive up Canada's west coast. True to its name, the provincial capital is awash in grand Victorian architecture, visible in majestic structures like the **Empress Hotel** (finished in 1908) and the neo-baroque **Legislature Building** (1897) arrayed around the busy **Inner Harbour**.

The natural and human history exhibits of the **Royal BC Museum**, as well as the First Nations totem poles in neighboring **Thunderbird Park**, offer a clue to what lies ahead on this road trip. But not before one last stop in Victoria: the glorious **Butchart Gardens** in Brentwood Bay, a flora fantasyland that blooms in an old cement quarry, lies half an hour out of the central city.

Hop the **Brentwood Bay Ferry** to Mill Bay (nine services each day) and make for the northbound Trans-Canada Highway. An hour up the road, **Nanaimo** is a former coal mining town now renowned as the place to catch the Vancouver ferry and a hub for **orca-watching cruises** in the Strait of Georgia. Stretch your legs walking the lovely **Harbourfront Walkway** between the historic **Port Theatre** and the Nanaimo Yacht Club before hitting the road again.

North of Nanaimo, the scenic **Inland Island Highway** (19) stretches along the Strait of Georgia and the narrow Johnstone Strait to the north end of Vancouver Island. Along the way, the town of **Campbell River** offers a wide array of outdoor adventure pursuits, from whale-watching boat tours and whitewater rafting to fishing charters and numerous

An orca breaches the surface of the Campbell River in British Columbia.

Take in the spectacular colors, flowers, and landscaping at the Butchart Gardens.

trails for hiking **Elk Falls Provincial Park**.

Farther north, the **Whale Interpretive Centre** in Telegraph Cove offers excellent insight into orcas and other marine mammals, while several outfitters in the town offer **guided kayaking excursions** to paddle alongside the beautiful black-and-white creatures.

**Port Hardy** is the place to board the **MV *Queen of Chilliwack*** ferry on a "Discovery Route" through scores of islands along the central coast. You've got two options: take the ferry all the way through to Bella Coola in one shot (10 hours) or break up the journey by spending a day or two on **Bella Bella** or **Denny Island** before catching an onward ferry to Bella Coola. However, accommodation on both islands is limited, and

onward ferries to Bella Coola run just once a week.

If you do break up the trip, both islands offer sailing, kayaking, wildlife tours, and halibut and salmon fishing. On Bella Bella, visit the **Heiltsuk Cultural Education Centre**.

Located at the end of a long fjord called the North Bentinck Arm, **Bella Coola** is the gateway to the wilderness of the legendary **Great Bear Rainforest**. Local outfitters like **Copper Sun Journeys** lead guided trips into the forest to see First Nations totem poles and petroglyphs, as well as hikes to **Odegaard Falls** and rafting trips on the **Bella Coola River**. More wilderness awaits in massive **Tweedsmuir South Provincial Park**, just 30 miles (48 km) east of town.

From Bella Coola, you can take

the BC Ferry back to Port Hardy and drive to Vancouver (620 miles/1,000 km) via central British Columbia. ■

---

### ART AVENUES

- **Best Art:** The cubism-influenced British Columbia landscapes of Victoria native Emily Carr; the frontier-era First Nations portraits of Irishman Paul Kane

- **Best Music:** The contemporary jazz of Nanaimo-born Diana Krall; the world beat pop of Victoria's Nelly Furtado

- **Best Books:** *The Adventures of John Jewitt* by John Rodgers Jewitt; *The Forest Lover* by Susan Vreeland; *A Recipe for Bees* by Gail Anderson-Dargatz

- **Best Movie:** The documentary *Cry Rock* (2010) by Bella Coola's Banchi Hanuse

# Canada's 1812 Trail

## Quebec to Ontario

Canada's pivotal role in the War of 1812 is the focus of a military history road trip between Montreal and Niagara Falls that revolves around stout fortifications and critical battlegrounds that kept the invading Americans at bay during the three-year conflict.

### THE BIG PICTURE

**Distance:** ca 475 miles (760 km) from Montreal, QC, to Niagara Falls, ON

**Drive time:** 5-6 days

**Best overnights:** Kingston, Toronto, Hamilton, Niagara Falls

**Best seasons:** Spring, summer, or fall

**Highlights:** Châteauguay, Crysler's Farm, Fort Henry, Toronto, Hamilton, Fort George, Queenston Heights, Lundy's Lane, Niagara Falls

With Britain mired in Europe's Napoleonic Wars, the Canadian provinces and colonies were largely left on their own to fight the War of 1812 against the United States. Canadians of all persuasions responded with a steadfast defense of their territory, a series of battles that played out along the upper St. Lawrence Valley and lower Great Lakes.

**Montreal** is the starting point for this drive through history. Both American attempts to capture the city were thwarted by the Canadians, including the 1813 skirmish along the **Châteauguay River** during which a ragtag band of local militia, volunteers, and indigenous allies defeated a much larger force of U.S. regulars.

Just an hour south of the city center via Route 138, the **Battle of the Châteauguay National Historic Site** offers a museum, guided tours, living history programs, and an eight-mile (14 km) **Battlefield Trail.**

After crossing the **St. Lawrence** via bucolic **Grande-Île,** Highway 401 leads along the river's north bank to **Crysler's Farm,** where the Canadians once again faced and defeated a much larger American force— a victory that permanently ended U.S. plans to capture the St. Lawrence Valley. Beside the battle monument is **Upper Canada Village,** where 40 historic structures and living history actors re-create life in 19th-century British Canada.

Highway 401 continues to historic **Fort Henry** at the confluence of the St. Lawrence and **Lake Ontario,** and onward to **Toronto,** where **Fort York National Historic Site** near the lakeshore harbors Canada's largest ensemble of original War of 1812 buildings. In spring 1813, Fort York was briefly captured by U.S. invaders arriving by ship across Lake Ontario.

Queen Elizabeth Way (Highway 403) carries you to **Hamilton Military Museum** at the lake's western extreme. Located atop a British gun battery built during the war, the museum overlooks the spot where the Battle of Stoney Creek took place in 1813. Queen Elizabeth Way continues along the lakeshore to the

The Six Nations and Native Allies Commemorative Memorial

In a memorial to the War of 1812, military reenactors take formation at Fort York National Historic Site in Toronto.

Canadian side of the **Niagara region** and its numerous 1812 sites.

**Fort George National Historic Site** near the mouth of the **Niagara River** recalls the war with guides in period costumes, musket demonstrations, fife-and-drum corps music, and a massive living history event in July that re-creates the 1813 Battle of Fort George. A fort for all seasons, George also offers a winter **ice-skating rink, whisky-tasting sessions, historical dinners**, and **ghost tours**.

Farther up the Niagara Gorge, **Queenston Heights Park** marks the site of the first major battle of the war: an October 1812 clash during which British General Isaac Brock died leading His Majesty's forces to victory. **Brock's Monument** marks his final resting place.

The **Niagara Falls History Museum** (near the famous cascades) offers a self-guided walking tour of the **Lundy's Lane Battlefield**, which includes the **Drummond Hill Cemetery** and the **Battle**

**Ground Hotel Museum**. South of the falls, **Chippewa Battlefield** preserves a riverside landscape that has been little changed since the American forces won a victory there in summer 1814. ∎

## SCENIC DETOURS

• **Quebec Route 223** (east of Montreal) links two important 1812 war sites along the Richelieu River, Fort Chambly and Fort Lennox on the Île aux Noix, where much of Britain's Lake Champlain fleet was constructed.

• **Autoroute 15 and Interstate 87** connect Montreal and Plattsburgh, New York, where the War of 1812 Museum spins tales of the war-ending Battle of Lake Champlain.

• **Ogdensburg-Prescott International Bridge** leaps the St. Lawrence from Ontario to upstate New York, where Fort de La Présentation Park recalls a British victory in the 1813 Battle of Ogdensburg.

• **Ontario Highways 403 and 401** run east from Hamilton to Thamesville, where the 1813 Battle of the Thames took the life of Tecumseh, the great Shawnee leader and British ally.

# Yellowhead Highway
## Manitoba to British Columbia

Canada's road-less-traveled to the Pacific Coast is the Yellowhead Highway (Route 16), an alternative to the Trans-Canada Highway that follows an old Hudson Bay Company trading route through the prairie provinces and mountains of British Columbia.

**THE BIG PICTURE**

**Distance:** 1,777 miles (2,859 km) from Winnipeg, MB, to Prince Rupert, BC

**Drive time:** 10-14 days

**Best overnights:** Saskatoon, Edmonton, Jasper, Prince George, Prince Rupert

**Best seasons:** Spring, summer, or fall

**Highlights:** Winnipeg, Riding Mountain NP, Saskatoon, Battleford, Edmonton, Jasper NP, Prince George, Prince Rupert

Shortly after World War I, Canadian motorcar enthusiasts launched a competition to prove it was possible to pilot a vehicle from Edmonton to the Pacific via Yellowhead Pass in the northern Rockies.

Making their way over the pass on an abandoned railroad grade, a Model-T Ford and Willys-Overland Model 4 arrived on the British Columbia coast at roughly the same time. Little did the drivers know that one day the route would stretch more than 1,700 miles (2,800 km) across two-thirds of Canada.

The Yellowhead Highway (National Route 16) begins at the corner of Main Street and Portage Avenue amid the skyscrapers of downtown **Winnipeg**.

Many of the city's major landmarks—from the **Manitoba Museum** and **Old Market Square** to the **Canadian Museum for**

**Human Rights** and the **Centennial Concert Hall**, home of Winnipeg's world-class symphony, ballet, and opera company—are within a 10-minute walk of Portage and Main.

Over the course of its first 62 miles (100 km), the Yellowhead shares tarmac with the Trans-Canada Highway. It's not until **Portage la Prairie** that it splits off from the mother road. Snap a selfie in front of the **World's Largest Coca-Cola Can** (formerly a water tower) and visit old **Fort Le Reine** (established 1938).

Minnedosa is the place to turn off for **Riding Mountain National Park**, where three Manitoba habitats merge—prairie, boreal forest, and deciduous woodland. The park's **Clear Lake** attracts swimmers, anglers, and boaters, while an extensive trail system expedites hiking and biking in the warmer months and a variety of snow sports come winter.

**Yorkton** is the first town of any size along the Yellowhead when you cross the provincial boundary. Indoor and outdoor exhibits at the Yorkton branch of the **Western Development Museum** celebrate more than a century of Saskatchewan history and the diverse ethnic groups that pioneered the Canadian Prairies.

Fireworks lighten the sky above the bridge and river in Winnipeg.

Travelers can take a tour bus fit for ice and snow through Athabasca Glacier and the Columbia Icefield.

Plunkett is the place to turn off for the **Manitou Beach**. For more than a century, folks have flocked to the resort for the therapeutic mineral waters and a chance to float on a lake with similar buoyancy to the Dead Sea.

Saskatoon beckons with bright lights and big buildings like the new **Remai Modern Art Gallery**; the Saskatoon branch of the **Western Development Museum**, with its early 20th-century innovation theme; and **Wanuskewin Heritage Park**, dedicated to the history and living culture of the indigenous peoples of the Northern Plains.

From hot-air ballooning to paddling on the **South Saskatchewan River**, the city also has its outdoor lures. The **Meewasin Valley Trail** system offers 37 miles (60 km) of waterfront routes for hiking, biking, and cross-country skiing. And although Saskatoon was founded in 1883 by the Temperance Colonization Society, the one-time dry town now offers half a dozen delectable **craft breweries**.

The Yellowhead moves on to **North Battleford**, where the **Royal Canadian Mounted Police** maintained a frontier outpost between 1876 and 1924 that's now a national historic park. Five of the original structures remain. Nearby **Blue Mountain Adventure Park** lives up to its name with zip lines, climbing walls, paintball, aerial and

## PIT STOPS

- **Winter Magic:** Hinton, Alberta, blows away the winter blues with two February weeks of snow sports, ice fishing, dinner theater, and a lantern festival along the lake. hinton.ca

- **Yorkton Film Festival:** Canada's first movie fest, which focuses on films with a Canadian connection, has been a prairie fixture since 1950; May. yorktonfilm.com

- **Shakespeare on the Saskatchewan:** July and August is the time for Saskatoon's midsummer night's dream of plays, banquets, and art exhibits in riverside tents. shakespearesask.com

- **Edmonton Folk Music Festival:** Joni Mitchell, David Byrne, Norah Jones, and k.d. lang are just a few of the big names who have performed at this four-day August bash in Gallagher Park. edmontonfolkfest.org

- **Kispiox Valley Rodeo:** Bull riding, broncobusting, and barrel riding are among the main events at this long-running First Nations June event near Hazelton. rodeobc.com

obstacle courses, and paddle sports.

The old Ukrainian settlement of **Vegreville** is your first stop in Alberta—for another selfie, this time with the **World's Largest Easter Egg**. The highway cuts across **Elk Island National Park** (with its bison, moose, elk, and other wildlife) before rolling into the third of the big cities along the route—**Edmonton**. Set along the banks of the North Saskatchewan River, the prairie metropolis is Alberta's political and cultural capital.

**Churchill Square** in the city center harbors many of Edmonton's more elegant institutions: musicals and serious drama at the **Citadel Theatre**, symphony and choral at the **Winspear Centre**, and eclectic creation at the **Art Gallery of Alberta**. Across the river, the historic **Old Strathcona** neighborhood revolves around funky cafés, indie boutiques, and live music venues. For something completely different, the colossal **Edmonton Mall**—North America's largest indoor retail and entertainment complex—offers carnival rides, a water park, an ice rink, and more than 800 shops and restaurants.

West of Edmonton, the highway transitions from the Canadian Prairies into the Rocky Mountains. **Hinton's** claim to fame is a two-mile (3 km) **Beaver Boardwalk** through wetlands that harbor beavers, bears, and moose.

The Yellowhead follows the Athabasca River into **Jasper National Park**, a great place to break for a day or two of hiking, biking, boating, horseback riding, or winter sports if you're there at the right time of year. Visitors can trek **Maligne Canyon**, ride the **SkyTram** to the top of Whistler Peak, or cruise down

Cycle the peaks at the Top of the World trail on Whistler Mountain.

---

## OFF ROAD

• **Canoe/Ski Discovery** offers a wide variety of guided paddling in and around Saskatoon, from one-day urban trips on the North Saskatchewan River to longer trips on the Churchill River or Prince Albert National Park. canoeski.com

• **Jasper Rafting Adventures** hosts whitewater trips on the Athabasca and Sunwapta Rivers in the national park. jasperrafting adventures.com

• **Northern Outback** near Prince George sets up fly-fish camping and heli-fishing trips in the remote Omineca range. northernoutback.wixsite.com/ northernoutback

• **Skeena Kayaking** in Prince Rupert focuses on multiday kayak camping tours through offshore islands and inlets or down the Skeena River. skeenakayaking.ca

• **Adventure Tours** launches marine mammal and grizzly-watching cruises in three boats based in Prince Rupert. adventure tours.net

---

the **Icefields Parkway** to the fabled **Columbia Icefield**.

Beyond Jasper, the highway rambles through **Yellowhead Pass**, named for Métis-Iroquois fur trapper Pierre Bostonais, whom people called Tête Jaune ("Yellow Head") because of his fair hair. At the crossing into British Columbia, the route flows past **Moose Lake** and through **Mount Robson Provincial Park** before descending into the broad **Fraser River Valley**.

The Yellowhead meanders beside the scenic Fraser River for 120 miles (190 km). You can whitewater-raft with local outfitters, dogsled in the winter at Cold Fire Creek, or walk

among the old-growth red cedars of the Ancient Forest/Chun T'oh Whudujut (British Columbia's newest provincial park), some of them more than 2,000 years old.

Perched at the confluence of the Fraser and Nechako Rivers, **Prince George** is an old railroad and sawmill town slowly evolving into an outdoor adventure hub. **Tabor Mountain** facilitates winter snowboarding or skiing and summertime hiking and mountain biking. South of town, **El Shaddai Ranch** offers trail rides in the lush Fraser Valley.

The Yellowhead follows the **Nechako River** into the Coastal Range, the slopes and valleys covered in temperate rainforest. This portion of the highway passes through the middle of the **Northern BC Lakes District**, which has more than 300 lakes and plenty of choices for boating, fishing, and camping, especially along the 18-mile (30 km) **Nanika-Kidprice Lakes Basin Canoe Route**.

The highway reaches its northernmost point at **Hazelton** on the Skeena River, where **'Ksan Historical Village** highlights the region's indigenous Gitxsan people through art, architecture, artifacts, and dance.

From there it's an easy drive down the **Skeena Valley** through the **Great Bear Rainforest** to the British Columbia coast. Named for a German nobleman who helped found the Hudson's Bay Company, **Prince Rupert** is Canada's wettest city, but also boasts the most rainbows.

There are plenty of ways to pass a day in and around Prince Rupert. Go to the **Khutzeymateen Grizzly Bear Sanctuary** to see the great rainforest bears. Snatch a bird's-eye view of whales, waterfalls, and glaciers with **Ocean Pacific Air**. Or dine on some of the freshest seafood you can imagine. ∎

# Trans-Labrador Highway
## Quebec and Labrador

Canada offers plenty of wilderness roads out west. But one of the nation's most rustic routes is a 1,000-mile (1,700 km) marathon journey through boreal forest between Baie-Comeau on the St. Lawrence River in Quebec Province and the chilly Labrador coast.

Until the completion of the Trans-Labrador Highway in 2000, the Labrador coast was completely cut off from the rest of Canada except by sea and air. Although it's a daunting drive—with perils like bad weather, infrequent gas stations, and the occasional angry moose—the wilderness route has opened up a whole new region to road trip aficionados.

Five hours north of Quebec City via the road along the north shore of the St. Lawrence, **Baie-Comeau** is an old time paper mill town that's slowly transitioning to tourism. Its main attraction is the summertime **Jardin des glaciers**, an interactive, educational theme park that revolves around three themes: the Ice Age, climate change, and Canada's First Nations people.

Daniel-Johnson Dam is the world's largest arch-and-buttress construction.

### THE BIG PICTURE

**Distance:** 1,063 miles (1,710 km) from Baie-Comeau, QC, to Blanc-Sablon, QC

**Drive time:** 4-5 days

**Best overnights:** Labrador City, Goose Bay, Forteau

**Best season:** Summer

**Highlights:** Daniel-Johnson Dam, Mont-Wright Mine, Battle Harbour, Red Bay

The long drive to Labrador starts on Quebec Route 389, which runs due north from Baie-Comeau through endless boreal forest to the gargantuan **Daniel-Johnson Dam**—the world's largest arch-and-buttress barrage. Looking more like something the ancient Romans might have built, the dam offers two-hour guided tours in summer.

Behind the dam is vast **Manicouagan Lake**, the world's fifth largest reservoir. Its even more of a geographical oddity because its water fills much of the **Manicouagan Impact Crater**, which was created by a meteor that hit the Earth more than 200 million years ago. The highway runs along the eastern rim of the crater, with boat rentals, fishing guides, and lakeside cabins available at **Relais Gabriel**.

It's around 150 miles (250 km) from the lake to the Quebec-Labrador border and the town of **Fermont**, where tours of the open-pit **Mont-Wright Iron Mine** include close encounters with Godzilla-size ore trucks, drills, shovels, and other extraction machinery.

Finally crossing the border, the highway makes a beeline for **Labrador City**, where the **Gateway Labrador Visitor Center** offers maps, brochures, and current road conditions. If you're spending the night, catch a concert, play, or comedy

Take in the Atlantic Ocean from inside the glass top of the Point Amour Lighthouse on Belle Isle.

show at the **Arts and Culture Centre–Labrador West.**

Beyond Labrador City the highway shoots east to **Churchill Falls,** a 245-foot (75 m) cascade on the Churchill River, before dropping down to the coast at **Happy Valley–Goose Bay.** Founded as a Royal Canadian Air Force base during World War II, the town's pride and joy is the **Labrador Military Museum** and its vintage warplane collection. It's also the starting point for passenger ferries traveling up the roadless north coast with **Nunatsiavut Marine.**

After cutting inland for nearly 300 miles (460 km), the Trans-Labrador meets the coast again at **Mary's Harbor** on the open Atlantic. **Cloud 9 Charters** offers summer sightseeing cruises to **Battle Harbour**—a historic 18th-century fishing village on an island off the coast—a journey that often includes whale and iceberg sightings.

Farther south is **Red Bay National Historic Site,** the remains of a 16th-century Basque fishing settlement. Costumed living history guides, a visitor center museum, and archaeological digs bring the site alive between June and September.

Hugging the coastline of the Strait of Belle Isle, the highway continues its southward drift to the **Labrador Straits Museum** in L'Anse au Loup and the **Point Amour Lighthouse** near Forteau. **Tour Labrador** in Forteau offers scenic cruises, lighthouse dinners, salmon fishing, and a five-day hike along the Labrador shore.

It's the end of the road at seaside **Blanc-Sablon** in northeastern Quebec. From there, you can hop vehicle ferries across the strait to Newfoundland and onward to mainland Canada. ∎

# Ambling Through Old Acadia

## New Brunswick & Nova Scotia

Although France lost control of Acadia in the 1760s—and many of the Gallic settlers fled to Louisiana—French influence remains strong along this 700-mile (1,126.5 km) drive around the energetic Bay of Fundy and bucolic south side of Nova Scotia.

Italian explorer Giovanni da Verrazzano christened a portion of the New World coast "Acadia" during a 16th-century voyage. He allegedly chose the name because he found the shore so idyllic. Arriving a century later, French settlers adopted the name.

Founded in 1630 by French settlers, **St. John, New Brunswick**, which owes its long history and location to the turbulent **Bay of Fundy**, offers a natural starting point for this road trip. Route 111 heads north along the coast to the **St. Martins Sea Caves** and the **Fundy Trail**

### THE BIG PICTURE

**Distance:** ca 680 miles (1,090 km) from St. John, NB, to Halifax, NS

**Drive time:** 5-6 days

**Best overnights:** Alma, Moncton, Wolfville, Annapolis Royal-Digby, Yarmouth

**Best seasons:** Spring, summer, or fall

**Highlights:** Bay of Fundy, Moncton, Grand-Pré, Nova Scotia wine country, Annapolis Royal, Yarmouth, Lunenburg

**Parkway**, a mixed-use hiking, biking, and motoring route with 20 overlooks and observation decks. Ranger-led talks and tours are offered at the trail's **Interpretive Centre**.

Another hour up the coast is **Fundy National Park**, where nature's fluvial dynamics reach fever pitch along a rugged coast with the world's highest tides (50 feet/15 m). Visitors can walk the beaches, watch for whales, kayak the extreme tides, or hike and bike inland trails leading to waterfalls in the lush Acadian forest.

Route 114 rambles northward to **Moncton**, the province's largest French-speaking city and a cornerstone of Acadian culture. Despite its Scottish name, the **Centre Culturel Aberdeen** offers a year-round slate of Francophone artistic, educational, and cultural programs. The **Musée Acadien de l'Université de Moncton** offers more than 42,000 Acadian artifacts and the eclectic *L'Aventure Acadienne* (Acadian Adventure).

The Trans-Canada Highway whisks drivers from Moncton across the **Isthmus of Chignecto** to the Nova Scotia town of **Truro**, where a right turn takes road trippers onto a route leading down the eastern side of the Bay of Fundy. The **Glooscap Trail** (Route 215)

Hike to Dickson Falls in Fundy National Park.

See a dory workshop at Le Village Historique Acadien de la Nouvelle-Ecosse, a re-creation of a 1900s Acadian village.

hugs the upper bay's shore, passing through pastoral countryside and several interesting villages. Get the inside scoop at the **Fundy Tidal Interpretive Centre** in South Maitland and learn more about the conflict between the British and French that led to the deportation of 10,000 Acadians at Fort Edward in Windsor.

Farther down the Fundy shore, the **Grand-Pré National Historic Site** showcases Acadian culture in theatrical productions, puppetry, song, and architectural preservation. Nova Scotia's small but tasty **wine country** unfolds along the **Harvest Highway** (Route 1) to **Annapolis Royal**, which served as both the French and British capital of Nova Scotia. **Fort Anne** and **Port-Royal** national historic sites offer museums and living history programs.

Nearby **Digby** offers ferry service on the *Fundy Rose* across the bay to St. John. Or drivers can continue down the Nova Scotia coast to **Yarmouth**. In addition to offering ferry service to Portland, Maine, Yarmouth is also known for its lobster catch and **Cape Forchu Lighthouse** (built in 1839). The area's maritime heritage comes to life on guided boat tours of the nearby **Tuck Islands** that include sea chanties, seafood chowder, heaps of local history, and even a little lobster fishing.

**Pubnico** punctuates the bottom end of Nova Scotia with **Le Village Historique Acadien de la Nouvelle-Ecosse**, a living history museum on the site of one of the province's oldest Acadian settlements. From there it's 163 miles (262 km) on the **Fishermen's Memorial Highway** (Route 103) to **Halifax** via Nova Scotia's southeastern coast and British-era sights like the **Black Loyalist Heritage Centre** in Birchtown and historic **Lunenburg** with its brightly painted Victorian homes. ∎

## ART AVENUES

- **Best Books:** *Pelagie: The Return to Acadie* by Antonine Maillet; *A Great and Noble Scheme: The Tragic Story of the Expulsion of the French Acadians from Their American Homeland* by John Mack Faragher

- **Best Poetry:** *Evangeline: A Tale of Acadie* by Henry Wadsworth Longfellow

- **Best Music:** The *Libre* album by Angèle Arsenault; *Désormais* by Moncton-born singer-songwriter Julie Doiron

- **Best Art:** The retro folk art paintings of Mario Doucette that reimagine Acadian history and myth

- **Best Movies:** The silent black-and-white classic *Evangeline* (1913), the first feature film made in Canada; the documentary *Tintamarre* (2004)

# ACKNOWLEDGMENTS

A special shout-out to my late parents—Henry and Marjorie Yogerst—for taking me on so many road trips as a kid. To my grandmother, Kate Alexander Purefoy, who made the first great family overland journey when she followed dusty roads and highways from Arkansas to Arizona after World War I. And to my Uncle Emile Luna and his collection of vintage American gas station road maps that so stoked my youthful imagination.

Julia Clerk, my wife of almost three decades and a talented writer in her own right, came along on many of the routes I drove for this book, including the Adirondacks, Quebec province, Florida's Overseas Highway, all of the Hawaiian islands, the ramble through the Berkshires, and the drive from Glacier to Yellowstone.

There were plenty of others who road shotgun or contributed local insights on other trips: my old friend Duncan Beniston in Georgia and the Carolinas; Steve Juarez on that lonely road across the middle of Nevada (which we drove in snowy January); Dave White and Bob Deter in Texas; Brooke Harwood Voss in the Land of Lincoln; Rebecca Morales in Puerto Rico and northern Florida; and Catherine Binette and Suzanne Labreque in Canada; as well as Jane Behrend and Hunter George for their priceless tips on the southeastern United States.

I've also got my team at National Geographic to thank, in particular Allyson Johnson, the project editor and an invaluable confederate from start to finish. And kudos to the rest of those who worked on *100 Drives*, including photo editor and designer Kay Hankins, art director Elisa Gibson, creative director Melissa Farris, director of photography Susan Blair, senior production editor Judith Klein, and managing editor Jennifer Thornton.

# ABOUT THE AUTHOR

During three decades as an editor, writer, and photographer, Joe Yogerst has lived and worked in Asia, Africa, Europe, and North America. His writing has appeared in *Condé Nast Traveler, CNN Travel, Islands* magazine, the *International New York Times* (Paris), the *Washington Post,* the *Los Angeles Times*, and *National Geographic Traveler*. He has written for 34 National Geographic books, including the best-selling *50 States, 5,000 Ideas* and the sequel, *100 Parks, 5,000 Ideas.* His first U.S. novel, a murder-mystery titled *Nemesis,* was published in 2018. Yogerst is the host of a National Geographic/Great Courses video series on America's state parks.

# ILLUSTRATIONS CREDITS

Front cover: (Main), Sean Ferguson/Getty Images; (UP LE), Michael Snell/Alamy Stock Photo; (UP RT), Thomas Barwick/Getty Images; (LO LE), mandritoiu/Shutterstock; (LO CTR), abrunk/Getty Images; (LO RT), 4FR/Getty Images. Back cover: Michael Urmann/Shutterstock. Spine: Daniel Kim Photography/Stocksy. Front matter: 2-3, Glenn W. Wheeler/Shutterstock; 4, Education Images/Universal Images Group via Getty Images; 6, doratoy/Shutterstock.

## WEST COAST

8-9, Sierralara/Shutterstock; 10, Hector Amezcua/Sacramento Bee/MCT via Getty Images; 11, Jorge Moro/Shutterstock; 12, crbellette/Shutterstock.com; 13, Michael Urmann/Shutterstock; 14, gnohz/Shutterstock.com; 15, Gagliardi Photography/Shutterstock.com; 16, travelview/Shutterstock.com; 17, Schroptschop/Getty Images; 18, Nickolay Stanev/Shutterstock; 19, IanintheWild/Shutterstock.com; 20, George Ostertag/Alamy Stock Photo; 21, Art Wittingen/Shutterstock; 22, ARTYOORAN/Shutterstock.com; 23, Dancestrokes/Shutterstock; 24, Dennis Frates/Alamy Stock Photo; 26, Arlene Waller/Shutterstock; 27, Purplexsu/Shutterstock.com; 28, Nagel Photography/Shutterstock.com; 29, Steve Heap/Shutterstock; 30, CSNafzger/Shutterstock; 31, Stephen Moehle/Shutterstock; 32, Brad Mitchell/Alamy Stock Photo; 33, Roman Khomlyak/Shutterstock; 34, explorehoodcanal.com; 35, Pierre Leclerc/Shutterstock; 36, Kenneth Rush/Shutterstock; 37, randy andy/Shutterstock; 38, Joshua Rainey Photography/Shutterstock.com; 39, Dene' Miles/Shutterstock; 40, Kris Wiktor/Shutterstock; 42, Melanie Faulstick/Shutterstock; 43, Nagel Photography/Shutterstock.com; 44, Johnny Adolphson/Shutterstock; 45, Dan Leeth/Alamy Stock Photo; 46, Tada Images/Shutterstock; 47, Tomasz Wozniak/Shutterstock; 48, Benny Marty/Shutterstock; 49, Mariusz S. Jurgielewicz/Shutterstock; 50, Clark James Mishler/Design Pics Inc/Alamy Stock Photo; 52, cpaulfell/Shutterstock; 53, MLouisphotography/Alamy Stock Photo.

## ROCKY MOUNTAIN

54-5, SNEHIT/Shutterstock; 56, EB Adventure Photography/Shutterstock; 57, Jeffrey T. Kreulen/Shutterstock; 58, Images By T.O.K./Alamy Stock Photo; 59, Lane V. Erickson/Shutterstock; 60, Margaret.W/Shutterstock; 62, Brian Chase/Shutterstock; 63, Elena Arrigo/Shutterstock; 64, Witold Skrypczak/Alamy Stock Photo; 65, William Silver/Shutterstock; 66, Nagel Photography/Shutterstock; 67, Richard Susanto/Shutterstock.com; 68, Andriy Blokhin/Shutterstock.com; 69, Pat Canova/Alamy Stock Photo; 70, M. Timothy O'Keefe/Alamy Stock Photo; 71, Sean Pavone/Shutterstock; 72, Inge Johnsson/Alamy Stock Photo; 74, Michael Gordon/Shutterstock.com; 75, corumov/Shutterstock; 76, Jon Kraft/Shutterstock.com; 77, AZCat/Shutterstock; 78, CrackerClips Stock Media/Shutterstock.com; 79, Purplexsu/Shutterstock.com; 80, Roman Khomlyak/Shutterstock.com; 81, superjoseph/Shutterstock; 82, Geir Olav Lyngfjell/Shutterstock; 84, FloridaStock/Shutterstock.com; 85, John Hoffman/Shutterstock; 86, Kent Ellington/Shutterstock; 87, West Coast Scapes/Shutterstock; 88, Nikolas_jkd/Shutterstock; 89, Zack Frank/Shutterstock.

## PAN-REGIONAL

90-1, CTD Photography/Shutterstock; 92, Michael Ventura/Alamy Stock Photo; 93, David Byron Keener/Shutterstock; 94, Alan Copson/Jon Arnold Images Ltd/Alamy Stock Photo; 95, Jeffrey Greenberg/Universal Images Group via Getty Images; 96, Della Huff/Alamy Stock Photo; 98, Traveller70/Shutterstock.com; 99, ESB Professional/Shutterstock; 100, Nagel Photography/Shutterstock; 101, Paul Brady Photography/Shutterstock.com; 102, BLM Photo/Alamy Stock Photo; 104, Rachel Goad/Shutterstock.com; 105, Jam Norasett/Shutterstock; 106, N8Allen/Shutterstock.com; 107, Steve Heap/Shutterstock; 108, Thomas Carr/Shutterstock.com; 109, Nagel Photography/Shutterstock; 110, Patricia Hofmeester/Shutterstock.com; 111, ciapix/Shutterstock.com; 112, Wolfgang Kaehler/LightRocket via Getty Images; 113, Zack Frank/Shutterstock; 114, Tony Campbell/Shutterstock; 115, Leslie Parrott/Cavan/Alamy Stock Photo; 116, Dennis MacDonald/Alamy Stock Photo; 117, Visual Mining/Alamy Stock Photo; 118, Sean Pavone/Shutterstock; 119, T photography/Shutterstock.com; 120, Igor Kovalenko/Shutterstock; 122, Sean Pavone/Shutterstock.com; 123, George Rose/Getty Images; 124, Richard Green/Alamy Stock Photo; 125, Clint Farlinger/Alamy Stock Photo; 126, Dennis K. Johnson/Alamy Stock Photo; 127, welcomia/Shutterstock; 128, Regine Poirier/Shutterstock.com; 129, SF photo/Shutterstock; 130, EQRoy/Shutterstock.com; 131, Dennis K. Johnson/Alamy Stock Photo.

## NORTHEAST

132-3, Anthony Heflin/Shutterstock; 134, Lori Epstein/National Geographic Image Collection; 135, Jumping Rocks/Universal Images Group/Alamy Stock Photo; 136, Pat & Chuck Blackley/Alamy Stock Photo; 138, Walter Bibikow/mauritius images GmbH/Alamy Stock Photo; 139, heipei/Shutterstock; 140, Bruce Hamms/Alamy Stock Photo; 141, Phil Degginger/Alamy Stock Photo; 142, Wendy Stone/Corbis via Getty Images; 143, John Greim/LightRocket via Getty

## MIDWEST

## SOUTHERN

## TROPICAL

## CANADA

# INDEX

# 100 DRIVES 5000 IDEAS

Since 1888, the National Geographic Society has funded more than 13,000 research, exploration, and preservation projects around the world. National Geographic Partners distributes a portion of the funds it receives from your purchase to National Geographic Society to support programs including the conservation of animals and their habitats.

National Geographic Partners
1145 17th Street NW
Washington, DC 20036-4688 USA

Get closer to National Geographic explorers and photographers, and connect with our global community. Join us today at nationalgeographic.com/join

For information about special discounts for bulk purchases, please contact National Geographic Books Special Sales: specialsales@natgeo.com

For rights or permissions inquiries, please contact National Geographic Books Subsidiary Rights: bookrights@natgeo.com

Library of Congress Cataloging-in-Publication Data

Names: Yogerst, Joseph R., author. | National Geographic Society (U.S.)
Title: 100 drives, 5,000 ideas : where to go, when to go, what to see, what to do / Joe Yogerst.
Other titles: One hundred drives, five thousand ideas
Description: Washington, D.C. : National Geographic, 2020. | Includes index.
Identifiers: LCCN 2019030818 | ISBN 9781426220906 (Trade Paperback)
Subjects: LCSH: Automobile travel--United States--Guidebooks. | Automobile travel--Canada--Guidebooks. | Roads--United States. | Roads--Canada. | United States--Description and travel. | United States--Guidebooks. | Canada--Description and travel. | Canada--Guidebooks.
Classification: LCC GV1024 .Y45 2020 | DDC 917.3--dc23

LC record available at https://lccn.loc.gov/2019030818

Printed in China

19/RRDS/1

The information in this book has been carefully checked and to the best of our knowledge is accurate. However, details are subject to change, and the publisher cannot be responsible for such changes, or for errors or omissions. Assessments of sites, hotels, and restaurants are based on the author's subjective opinions, which do not necessarily reflect the publisher's opinion.